Mothering

NEW FEMINIST PERSPECTIVES
Edited by Mary Vetterling-Braggin

BEYOND DOMINATION
New Perspectives on Women and Philosophy
Carol C. Gould, editor

WOMEN AND SPIRITUALITY
Carol Ochs

WOMEN, SEX, AND THE LAW
Rosemarie Tong

Mothering

ESSAYS IN FEMINIST THEORY

Edited by
Joyce Trebilcot

ROWMAN & ALLANHELD
PUBLISHERS

ROWMAN & ALLANHELD

Published in the United States of America in 1984
by Rowman & Allanheld, Publishers
(A division of Littlefield, Adams & Company)
81 Adams Drive, Totowa, New Jersey 07512

Library of Congress Cataloging in Publication Data
Main entry under title:

Mothering: essays in feminist theory.

   (New feminist perspectives)
   Includes biographical references.
   1. Motherhood—Addresses, essays, lectures.   2. Mothers
—Addresses, essays, lectures.   3. Feminism—Addresses,
essays, lectures.   4. Patriarchy—Addresses, essays,
lectures.   I. Trebilcot, Joyce.   II. Series.
HQ759.M88 1983   306.8'58   83-4517
ISBN 0-8476-7115-1
ISBN 0-8476-7235-2 (pbk.)

83 84 85/ 10 9 8 7 6 5 4 3 2 1
Printed in the United States of America

Contents

PART IV *PRONATALISM AND RESISTANCE*

Preface

When Mary Vetterling-Braggin, women's studies editor at Littlefield, Adams and Co., first invited me to edit a volume on mothering for this series of anthologies of feminist philosophy, my immediate reaction was to decline. The topic was wrong for me, I thought, because I am not a mother, never have been, and never have wanted to be. But Mary asked me to take some time to think about her proposal.

As I did so, I remembered myself as a child of perhaps nine or ten, sitting in a certain chair in my mother's living room and reading one of the women's magazines that came regularly to the house, probably *McCall's*. "Marriage or Career?" was the choice presented in the headline, and the article made it clear that one could not have both. I decided then that I would have a career rather than marriage and the children who went with it. So I have known since that afternoon in the 1940s that I would not be a mother.

But as I thought more about Mary's invitation, and about the meaning of my life as a woman and a feminist, it became clear that mothering is central for *every* woman in patriarchy, whether or not we bear or care for children, and that an understanding of mothering, both as it exists in patriarchy and as it might exist (if at all) in women-centered communities, is central to feminist theorizing. I realized that, whether or not one is a mother, mothering is a necessary focus for work in feminist theory.

So I called Mary and told her that I would accept the project, and thus began the process of this book. Although Mary and I have never met face to face, her consistent support, through frequent phone calls and letters between her home in New Jersey and mine in St. Louis, has been indispensable. I am deeply grateful for the many kinds of help she has given me and for the confidence she has unfailingly shown.

I am grateful also to the students of my women's studies ovular at Washington University in the spring semester of 1982. During that semester we read and discussed many of the materials that were contributed for the book, and those discussions, together with the papers the students wrote, contributed much to the shape of this volume. I am sorry that I was not able to use the class's favorite title for the book, *Crying Over Spilt Milk*. I hope they understand.

Finally, I want to express my appreciation to Anne Elizabeth Schulherr Waters, a feminist philosopher and loving friend, who inspired, sustained, and assisted me throughout this work.

Introduction

In many societies, women are under intense pressure to be mothers both in the sense of giving birth and in the sense of nurturing; women who do not have children are defined as defective, as are women who are not nurturant to men. In addition, women's experiences of being mothered are a major influence on who we turn out to be. Mothering, then, is central in women's lives, and this centrality is reflected in feminist theorizings.

The mothering typical of patriarchies helps to perpetuate hierarchical societal arrangements in a variety of ways: women are required to give birth only to children of their own race; mothers are required to make children conform to gender roles according to biological sex; mothers are expected to transmit the values of the dominant culture, whatever they may be, to their children, and more generally, to teach their children to be obedient participants in hierarchy; and women are expected not only to reproduce patriarchy in children but also to care for the men who create and maintain it. No wonder some women refuse to mother, and urge us all to withdraw from mothering!

At the same time, some women are concerned to reconceive mothering, to create new concepts of reproducing and nurturing that will better express their own values, including their commitments to the transmission of feminism from one generation to the next and to the production and reproduction of women's cultures. This book addresses both the meanings of mothering within patriarchy, and the possibilities of women-defined "mothering" outside of it.

Because the main purpose of this book is to explore the role of mothering in feminist theory, its organization is based on the nature and structure of that theory. To emphasize the connections between theory and issues in daily life, I have begun with a set of papers that focuses on the practical question of who is to take the day-to-day responsibility for looking after children. Should fathers have as much responsibility as mothers, as the essays by Virginia Held and Diane Ehrensaft suggest? Should members of a community who have decided *not* to be parents be expected to participate in childcare, as Lucia Valeska urges? Related issues include the question of why most men prefer not to care for children, discussed by Rivka Polatnick, and whether the term "parenting" is an "obfuscatory euphemism" that works against women's interests, as Susan Rae Peterson claims. Consideration of these and related questions establishes at the outset ties between ordinary experience and values, on the one hand, and theory, on the other; it sets the stage for the understanding that our common activities, thoughts, and feelings are formed by theory, and also give form to theory.

Following upon the introductory discussions of "shared parenting" in Part I, the essays in Part II address issues closer to the heart of feminist theory. I find it helpful to think of that theory as having three major parts:

1. Analyses of patriarchy
   a. *Interpretations* of patriarchy in the light of women's experiences and values, including critiques of patriarchal scholarship.
   b. *Explanations* of patriarchy, that is, accounts of the original and sustaining "causes" of patriarchy in society (of patriarchal institutions and practices) and in individuals (of patriarchal psyches).
2. Realizings of women-identified values
   a. *Creating* women-identified realities here and now; that is, creating women's cultures, including feminist theories.
   b. *Envisioning* the future.
3. Strategies. Plans for getting from the patriarchy analyzed in *1* to the realities envisioned in *2*. (Strictly speaking, category *3* does not exist, because feminist strategies are themselves realizations of women's values, so they belong to *2*.)

In this book, each of the three sections after the first has as its primary emphasis one of the three main categories of feminist theory. In the second part of the book, the focus is on *1*, the analysis of patriarchy and, in particular, on explanations (rather than interpretations) of patriarchy. The essays in this section might well be used in a classroom as occasion for the explication of major kinds of feminist theory. The first two (by Azizah al-Hibri and Eva Feder Kittay) concern male responses to the fact that women give birth; these essays may be understood as contributions to radical feminist theory, i.e., to theories which claim that the fundamental cause of women's oppression is sex difference itself and not capitalism or some other factor. The next two essays (by Iris Young and Pauline Bart) are discussions of recent work by Nancy Chodorow and others on the psychological consequences of mothering by women; this work is criticized by Young from a socialist feminist perspective and by Bart from a radical and lesbian feminist perspective. The last essay in this section (by Ann Ferguson) attempts to overcome weaknesses in socialist feminism, that is, in "dual systems theory," by creating a "multi-systems theory."

But the heart of feminist theory is not the analysis of patriarchy; it is, rather, the process of conceiving women-identified forms of life—what I have called "realizing women-identified values." The essays in the third part of this book belong to this category. They contribute to women-centered understandings of maternal instinct (Caroline Whitbeck), of parent-child relationships (Janet Farrell Smith), of maternal thinking and women's power to make peace (Sara Ruddick), of relationships among women (Eléanor Kuykendall), and of relationships among people and groups generally, including those among nations (Barbara Love and Elizabeth Shanklin). These essays articulate women's spaces, both the spaces women create for ourselves now in the interstices of patriarchy, and those we are preparing for the future.

The fourth section of the book is about pronatalism and resistance to motherhood. The first essay in this section, by Martha Gimenez, presents a Marxist analysis of pronatalism and claims that feminism itself has tended to be pronatalist; Gimenez holds that feminism ought to value the decision *not* to be a mother at least as much as it values motherhood. Jeffner Allen, in the final essay, opposes motherhood entirely; women, she argues, *ought not* to have children. These essays belong to that part of feminist theory concerned with strategies, insofar as they claim that refusing to engage in mothering is a means to women's liberation.

At this point the book turns back on itself. The last section, about strategy, clearly links theory and practice. Similarly, the first section about "shared parenting," which connects practice and theory, is also about strategy. Thus, the book may be seen as making a circle; the last and first sections could be construed as one. The two major strategies discussed in the book, then, are to restructure day-to-day childcare so that it is not the responsibility primarily of mothers, or of mothers and other female relatives, and to refuse to mother. This last notion—that it is reasonable, or even required, for women to withdraw from mothering—is one of the book's central messages.

One image I have of *Mothering* is of a collection of threads gathered together; each thread can be followed to reveal a rich and complex body of feminist thought. This image is appropriate partly because of the diversity of the authors. They are all currently living in the United States, most are academics, and most of those are trained in philosophy. Nevertheless, they represent a wide range of feminist orientations: some write in the spirit of lesbian feminism, others of radical, or socialist, or Marxist, or liberal feminism. One writer is an Arab, and another has a Latin American background; at least two are Jewish. Some identify as lesbians, others are heterosexuals. But despite this relative diversity, the volume of necessity presents only a small portion of women's insights and values about mothering.

One relevant topic not discussed here is the rapid current development of reproductive technology, which gives men even greater control than they already have over women's reproduction. This topic would require another volume. It deserves brief mention here, nevertheless, because the study of mothering needs to be carried out with consciousness of men's increasing capacity to control it. The discussions in this book—analyses of patriarchy, realizings of women-identified values, and strategies for change—are best read, as most of them were written, with awareness of this threat. All of the essayists, despite their differences, share the conviction that mothering must now be defined and controlled by women.

PART ONE

Who Is to Look After Children?

1

The Obligations of
Mothers and Fathers

VIRGINIA HELD

The continued existence of humanity may require that we cease to turn "mothering" into an activity filled only by mothers. If it is true that the human personality is formed very early in life, and if it is true that our social practice of making mothers but not fathers the primary caretakers of small children forms the male personality into one in which the inclination toward combat is overdeveloped and the capacity to feel for others is stunted, our survival may depend on a reorganization of parenting. Instead of forming girls into human beings with a weak sense of self and a diminished ability to assert their independence, and boys into human beings "whose nurturant capacities . . . have been systematically curtailed and repressed,"[1] we ought to transform the social institution of parenting into one performed equally by women and men.

The extent to which parenting is *not* tied to biology but is instead a social construction can be suggested by considering the entirely different meanings we give to the sentences "he fathered the child" and "she mothered the child." Mothers *need* not be the ones who "mother," and we may have urgent reasons to turn the parenting done by fathers and mothers into entirely similar activities. But I shall not consider these arguments in this article, nor shall I take up questions concerning the raising of children in households in which the adults are of the same sex.

Rather, I shall consider the arguments for a change in parenting practices based on principles of equality applied to parents. I shall discuss the rights of children to receive care, but not their rights to the formation of a healthy per-

An earlier version of this article appeared in *Having Children: Philosophical and Legal Reflections on Parenthood,* edited by Onora O'Neill and William Ruddick (N.Y.: Oxford University Press, 1979). Reprinted by permission of the author and publisher.

sonality, although on this latter ground, as well as on grounds of our concern for humanity in general, the argument for equal parenting may be decisive. If, as Nancy Chodorow writes, "the very fact of being mothered by a woman generates in men conflicts over masculinity, a psychology of male dominance, and a need to be superior to women,"[2] both girl and boy children may have rights to equal parenting. But my arguments will deal with a different issue: What does a commitment to considering female and male parents as persons of equal human worth require as applied to parenting?

Over and over, one encounters the argument that if a woman chooses to become a mother, she must accept a recognized set of responsibilities and obligations that are quite different from the responsibilities and obligations of being a father. Many people expect a father to contribute some of his income for the expenses his child makes necessary. A mother is expected to give up whatever other work may interfere with her availability to care for her child and to take full care of the child—cheerfully and contentedly, to whatever extent, and as long as the child needs it. And if it is thought that the child will develop problems due to early separations from a parent, it is the mother who is thought responsible for preventing them.

Recent and still-existing law, in its characteristically obtuse way in this domain, deals almost entirely with "support" of the child in the sense of paying the bills for the child's food, clothing, shelter, etc. This is thought to be the father's obligation; if he is unwilling or unable to fulfill it, it becomes the mother's. The mother, just by virtue of being a wife, has standardly been expected by law to "render services in the home," and these services include caring for any children who happen to be in it. As summarized in a recent legal textbook, "the husband is to provide the family with food, clothing, shelter, and as many of the amenities of life as he can manage. . . . The wife is to be mistress of the household, maintaining the home with the resources furnished by the husband, and caring for the children." And as the author says, in a judgment not yet outdated, "a reading of contemporary judicial opinions leaves the impression that these roles have not changed over the last two hundred years."[3]

A few states have made some changes to bring the law into line with state equal rights amendments. And if the federal Equal Rights Amendment is adopted, it may bring about significant changes in the law. But courts will continue to be dominated for a long time by conservative, middle-aged men; more important, the law seldom enters into the domestic picture until the breakdown of a marriage. While the marriage is intact, the law leaves husband and wife great latitude to work out their domestic arrangements; when the marriage falls apart, courts decide how to divide up possessions and obligations. The possibilities of dividing parental obligations equally, even at this point, are only beginning to be explored.[4]

In the attitudes of society, "motherhood" is often take to be an occupation (though unpaid) that women can perform the way men can be auto workers, bankers, or professors. A recent article by a social scientist states: "Once these successive needs—the physical, the social-affectional, and the equal esteem or dignity needs—are sufficiently gratified, humans are not even then content: they then begin to look for that kind of activity that is particularly suited to them as unique individuals. Whether their competence is to be a ditchdigger, a powershovel operator, a construction foreman, a civil engineer or a building contractor, an architect, a mother, a writer, or a politician—they must do these things when they have become rather sure in the gratification of their even more basic physical, social and esteem needs."[5]

At least the ranking in this list is favorable. In contrast, the skill level thought to be needed by a homemaker, childcare attendant, or nursery school teacher was rated in a recent U.S. Department of Labor publication at only 878 on a scale from 1, the highest skill level, to 887, the lowest (hotel clerks were at 368).

Just how ludicrous it is from the point of view of equality to see motherhood as an occupation can be seen if one substitutes "father" for "mother" in such lists. As we all know, and yet as even a rudimentary sense of equality must protest, women have routinely been asked to choose between parenthood and having an occupation (or another occupation, if one counts parenthood). Men have routinely been expected to be able to enjoy *both* parenthood *and* an occupation (or another occupation).

The common view that motherhood is one occupation among others, but virtually the only one open to mothers not driven to factory or farm labor in addition to motherhood, was shared, one regrets to note, by John Stuart Mill, despite his awareness, quite unusual among philosophers along with nearly everyone else, that women were entitled to equal rights.[7] It has sometimes been suggested that any different view of the occupational possibilities of women had to await the development of industrialization in the 19th century or the later development of birth-control techniques. But that this is a lame excuse for millennia of exploitation can be seen in the perfectly imaginable alternative view given by Plato in *The Republic*. Plato pointed out that whether one bears or begets children is not a relevant basis on which to determine whether one is fit to govern.[8] The same argument could be applied to the whole range of occupations. Instead, the link between giving birth and caring for children is still assumed to be necessary and inevitable.

That so few have been able to imagine, much less support, the notion of both mothers and fathers caring for children while they are engaged in other occupations is part of the problem of turning conceptions of equality into practice. But it is unclear, perhaps, what might be required by equality, or what parents who acknowledge each other to have equal obligations toward their children need to do to fulfill these requirements and obligations. It is this question that I shall now explore.

Equal Obligations

Must we suppose that equality requires both parents to do approximately the same tasks, taking approximately the same length of time, so that one parent might, for instance, be completely in charge of the children from 6 A.M. to 2 P.M., and the other parent completely in charge from 2 P.M. to 10 P.M., while both work at paid jobs in the hours they are not engaged in childcare, and both take turns at whatever getting up in the night is needed? Are staggered and perhaps shorter work shifts in industry and the professions an obvious objective?

Or should we consider the possibility that if the abilities of the two parents differ significantly, the child is entitled to care "from each according to his or her ability," rather than "from each the same kind of activity for the same length of time"? It has often been supposed that women have greater natural talents for and are more skillful at taking care of small children, and that men have greater natural talents for and are more skillful at obtaining the objects and/or money with which to provide material goods for the child. It seems highly probable that many such differences in skill levels would disappear if both parents had been brought up as equals from childhood, and if they, as parents, shared both kinds of activities. But if it should happen that some significant differences remained in particular cases, and that a given infant's mother, say, really did have much more talent than the infant's father for making the infant comfortable, happy, friendly, and eager for new experiences, while the infant's father really did have much more talent at earning the family's income, would the parents have an obligation to accept a traditional division of labor, she at home caring and he in the world earning, each working *equally hard* at contributing what they did best to the well-being of the child?

And what about preferences? If one parent greatly prefers to earn an income from outside work, rather than to take care of children, should this guide the parents' decisions on how to divide their obligations equally? Or if a child, especially at a given age, greatly prefers being taken care of by one parent rather than the other, should the parents accede to the child's wishes? Are such preferences largely the result of the habitual inequalities built into the traditional gender roles of men and women and the expectations of children raised in sexist societies, and should they on these grounds be discounted? Or can they be legitimate preferences which should be considered when parents try to work out cooperative arrangements?

It is inadequate to consider questions of parental obligation in isolation from the social situation. Societies ought to recognize their obligations to their children. Societies ought to provide adequate levels of part-time and full-time childcare, of support for parents who take care of children at home if they choose to, of medical care and education. But in the United States, measures to do so are, unfortunately, a long way off. In what follows, I shall deal with the equal obligations of parents in terms of *given* levels, however inadequate, of social support. I do not imply that current social arrangements are satisfactory, only that women and men may try to do the best they can to respect each other as equal persons within existing social structures. And the questions I shall consider are primarily moral ones. Whether or not law and social arrangements are changed to reflect moral requirements, morally concerned persons must deal with these issues and try to arrive at reasonable solutions of the problems involved. My question, then, is: if individual women and men recognize principles of equality, and if both really do respect each other as persons of equal worth, entitled to equal liberty and justice,⁹ with equal rights to choose how to live their lives, what are the implications of this for their obligations as mothers and fathers?

Much of what is said here may apply to housework apart from childcare, but I shall not discuss such applications. The difficulties of deciding how to divide housework equally are much less complex; a willingness to share equally goes far, if persons living together agree on what needs to be done. But the restrictions and demands of parenthood raise complications of a different order, since the rights and interests of other human beings are involved, and since small children require someone "on duty" continually. These new complications often disrupt the equitable arrangements that might be worked out apart from children, as when it is assumed that since the mother will be home with the children anyway, she might as well do most of the housework.

Many of the activities involved in caring for children are intrinsically pleasurable. Sometimes, to be with one's child may be much closer to leisure enjoyment than to work. To play with a child for a few hours in the evening after a day of work away from home, for instance, may be a reward, not a burden, of parenthood. But the burden of caring for children can become routine drudgery or emotional torment when it is done constantly, repeatedly, because of one's obligations, and when it consumes nearly all of one's energies and time, as when a mother does nothing else than care for children and household, or a father nothing else than work at a job he hates in order to pay his family's bills. And the burdensome aspects of these activities become all the greater when the person feels that the arrangement placing these burdens on her or on him is unjust, and that it is unfair to be required to bear them.

I shall consider in what follows only the obligations parents have to perform various tasks, not the activities they may share with their children for pleasure, and not the feelings with which the tasks are performed. Family and marriage texts generally assert that the mother's function is to provide emotional support, to "keep the family happy," to remain calm amid the noise and turmoil of the household, to sympathize, to be what is called the family's "heart.' The father's function, on the other hand, is to be efficient and strong in d' ing with the wider world, to be rational, impartial, just and firm in enf discipline, to be what is called the family's "head." I shall restrict th

sion that follows to the performance of specific tasks, without considering whether they include the supplying of adequate psychological or emotional benefits. And the tasks under consideration will be tasks that need doing, apart from whether or not they are done with an acceptable emotional tone or from an appropriate psychological stance.

It would certainly not be adequate to think of the relation between parents and children only or even largely in terms of obligations and rights. Children have rights to care and support, and parents have obligations to supply these when the society does not do so, but it is obviously better for children to receive more from their parents than what the mere fulfillment of the parents' obligations requires. A parent who gives love, concern, and attention to a child because it is a joy to do so is obviously a better parent than one who merely grimly meets his or her obligations to feed and safeguard the child. And it is surely of more value to the child that there be a genuine relationship of mutuality, of shared concern and respect, between the child's parents, than that such a relationship be absent.[10] But I am going to limit discussion here to obligations and their equality. Parents cannot have obligations to feel emotions beyond their control, or to give children everything that would be of value to them. They can be expected to meet their equal obligations.

I shall also not discuss how parental obligations to children arise in the first place. For instance, in a case where birth control measures have failed, where neither parent wants a child, but where society compels them to become parents against their wills through laws forbidding or social practices preventing abortion, do parents have any obligations to this child, or does society alone have them? Or, if one parent wants a child and the other does not, does the parent who wants the child have greater obligations to care for the child if they have one? Possibly, in such a case, the parents might make an agreement specifying their unequal obligations to the child, which child they otherwise might not have. I shall deal only with cases where both parents voluntarily become the parents of a child, are equally responsible for becoming parents, and recognize that they are equally responsible for the child.

What Does Equality Require?

Children are entitled to support and care. To the extent that, under given social arrangements, the moral obligation to provide these falls on the parents, it falls on them collectively. From the point of view of the child, it may often not matter which parent provides what aspect of support and care, or in what proportion.

Parents should first agree on what the child's rights and needs are, and on the necessity and relative importance of the tasks to be done before they consider which parent should do which tasks. They should try to decide how much the child's preferences will count and in which domains they will count before they learn what the child's preferences are. They should not accept, for instance, the child's preferences that require the mother to bear more than her otherwise fair share of the burdens of fulfilling parental obligations, and discount those preferences that would require the father to do so, although this has traditionally been standard.

Then the parents should proceed from such judgments as "the parents have an obligation to provide w, x, y, and z" to such judgments as "parent A has an obligation to provide w and z," and "parent B has an obligation to provide x and y." How people move from the former judgments to the latter has traditionally not been a matter of reasonable argument, but of little more than social prejudice. Much rethinking and goodwill are needed to reconcile thinking about the obligations of parents with thinking about the obligations of mothers and fathers in ways that are morally plausible.

In trying to see what equality requires, it is sometimes helpful to consider its application in some other area, close enough to be relevant but different enough to be instructive. Let us consider another family context than the one of parental obligations, a context of two men able to earn incomes—brothers in this case—having an obligation to support an aged mother unable to be self-supporting.

If the brothers agree that their obligations are equal, what would this require? If one brother is very rich, the other very poor, it is unlikely that they would feel obligated to contribute exactly the same *amount* of money to their mother's support. Would this be a departure from their having an equal obligation? It would seem not, but rather that a requirement to contribute according to ability would be applied equally to each.

Perhaps they might consider that if one contributed more money, the other could contribute more time, visiting the aged mother more often, helping her in her garden, etc. But let us limit the debate to the question of an equal obligation to provide financial support, in terms of some monetary unit.

If, then, the brothers recognize an equal obligation to contribute to financial support, would they have to contribute an equal percentage of their income, if one is rich and the other poor? Or would equality require them to recognize a further aspect of proportionality in their ability to pay, since equality would seem to require rather than oppose a graduated income tax? There might be general agreement for the latter decision, although there might be some difficulty in specifying the amount. It would seem plausible that equality of obligation would require that the rich brother contribute a greater amount *and* a greater percentage of his income, because the ability to contribute is a relevant factor to consider, a greater ability requires a greater contribution, and as the ability to contribute rises, it is appropriate for the percentage contribution to rise.

The question of the brothers' obligation to earn an income in the first place might be more troublesome. Suppose that one brother has more income because he works many hours, and the other brother has less because he works fewer hours. Both find paid work equally available and equally unsatisfying, but one brother earns three times as much money as the other because he works three times as many hours a week. We would then have to distinguish actual ability to contribute at a given time, once income was in hand, and the effort expended, prior to this, to arrive at this actual ability. Then it would not seem that an equal obligation would require the brother who works many hours to contribute three times as much as, or a much higher percentage of his income than, the brother who works few hours, because with an increase of effort, the latter could meet the difference and himself contribute a sum that really would be an absolutely equal amount. If, after that, the brother who works few hours chose leisure over further labor, that would be his right, at least relative to his brother. Nevertheless, if the combined amount contributed by the two for the mother's support left her in extreme and painful poverty, the brother who works few hours might have an obligation to work longer, and the brother who works many hours an obligation to raise the total amount.

If we suppose the earning capacity of the two brothers to be equal and that they find the labor necessary to earn income equally unsatisfying, we might think that fulfilling their obligations on a basis of equality might require each to provide half of what can be taken to be adequate to fulfill their combined obligation. Then we would be back to an absolutely equal amount, even if one brother is relatively rich and the other is relatively poor.

In considering cases such as these, the following principles would seem plausible: (a) In meeting their obligations, the person with the greater actual ability to contribute ought to make a proportionately larger contribution. (b) Effort is an appropriate factor to consider in deciding on obligations, and obligations concerning effort take priority over obligations based on actual ability to contribute. Thus, as between two persons with an equal actual ability to contribute, one person should not be expected to expend far more effort to achieve this actual ability. And as between two persons making an equal effort, a greater resulting actual ability to contribute requires that this person make a proportionately larger contribution, but if he or she should choose to make a further expenditure of effort, this should not be penalized by a still further increase of contribution.

If we find these principles plausible in the case of the brothers, we might extend them to the case of parental obligations. If the parents decide that the needs of the child require them to earn, say, 30 additional monetary units a week; and if, as would be likely in American society at present, the mother would have to work at a paid job almost twice as long as the father to earn the 15 units that would seem her equal share; then equality of obligation would not require her to provide half of the 30 units. Yet if the mother wishes to work, her contribution should not be discounted because her equal effort brings in less money. Again, if the work the mother would have to do, even if equally paid, would be significantly less satisfying than the work the father would have to do and thus be more of an effort to perform, an equal contribution would not require the mother to expend as much time at such work, or to provide as much money for the child as the father.

In a different aspect of their obligations, if the parents decide that on a typical day the child should be given breakfast, taken on a two-hour outing, given lunch, a rest, a bath, a story, and that the objects the child has scattered about the house should be put away, then equal obligations would not be fulfilled if the mother, because of greater effort, did (or, when appropriate, got the child to do) all these things on the days it was her turn, while the father, because of a lesser effort, managed to get done only two or three of the five on the days, an equal number, it was his turn. But if it really was, at least temporarily, significantly more difficult for him to do these things than for her, he might be required to do fewer of them.

In making these determinations, we could raise the question of whether it is intention or success that should count in establishing when two persons are making an equal effort. In childcare, one person may succeed with modest effort in keeping a baby satisfied and occupied, while the other may try much harder and fail. In trying to improve one's position in outside employment, one person may try and repeatedly suffer defeat, and the other may move steadily forward with little effort. But despite the possibilities it may create for deception and self-deception, in the case of meeting one's obligations, it seems to be intention, not success, that should count.[11] But then we must assume sincerity, and that statements such as "but I *am* doing the best I can" will not be used to mask willful inefficiency.

Whenever differences of interpretation arise as to what importance to attach to what, and what guidelines to use to weigh obligations, devices to cut down distortions of perception may be helpful. Parents can try to apply the "roommate test" suggested by Sandra and Daryl Bem, and ask how the tasks would be divided if, instead of being a male/female couple, they were roommates of the same sex.[12] Parents can acquaint themselves with all the tasks and devise arrangements and divisions of them before knowing which tasks they themselves will perform. They can, for instance, decide whether feeding the children their evening meal should count for more or less than doing their laundry before deciding which parent will do which task. And they can decide whether a typical hour of outside employment is more burdensome or more rewarding than a typical hour of childcare before they decide how the hours will be divided, and so on.

Differences of competence can be brought in at a later stage of discussion, but here again procedures to aid impartiality may be helpful. For instance, the parents might agree to evaluate each other's competence rather than their own, and to do so before knowing what arrangements their discussions will recommend. And differences of preference that make some tasks more burdensome to one parent than to the other should be considered only to the extent that the preferences of both parents are considered to an equal degree, including higher-order preferences, such as when a woman might say, "I do not now like to give lectures, but I want to get practice at it because I would like to like to."

To the objection that such counting of hours and calculation of who is doing how much will spoil the spontaneous and harmonious relation between parents and with children, or will turn family affection into the pursuit of selfishness and turn children into products, one can point to centuries of experience. Such charges have always been leveled against workers—factory workers, teachers, secretaries—who have calculated how many hours they were working overtime or without pay instead of failing, out of "loyality," to notice. And such charges have routinely been used against women who have finally begun to recognize that, in addition to working all day like their husbands, whether at home or at paying jobs, they have been doing nearly all of the evening housework. Those who have been taken advantage of have always been asked by the beneficiaries to be trusting and altruistic,[13] but the result of acquiescence to unfair arrangements is the growth of resentment and mistrust. The response must be that when respect and equality become habitual, calculation becomes unnecessary. Mutuality and sharing are to be sought, but on a basis of equality, not exploitation.

Can Work Be Different but Equal?

Equality of obligation would certainly not rule out *all* differences in the tasks performed by mothers and fathers. We now have, I think, no reliable empirical knowledge of any genuine differences of talents and tendencies between mothers and fathers (except the dispensable and brief capacity of mothers to nurse their infants). We should be very wary of accepting any division of labor between mothers and fathers based on their differing talents at the time they become parents, since these may be due to years of sex-stereotyped preparation, in which boys are encouraged to study and work at various jobs and girls to babysit and do housework. One significant feature of parenthood is that *neither* parent has had much previous training for the work, although this is often overlooked, as it is assumed that the mother will know what to do and hence, since it is supposed to be so much easier for her, that she should take care of the children. Anyone who has studied, or experienced, the anxious and helpless feelings of women with a first newborn baby to care for, or the feelings of guilt and incompetence of mothers not able to handle smoothly the outbursts and demands of small children, has every reason to believe that fathers would be equally capable of preparing themselves for childcare and of learning fast on the job.[14]

Still, we cannot preclude altogether the possibility that differences of parental ability and preferences between men and women may be significant. It was suggested in a recent article by David Gutmann, a psychologist, that the differences are particularly acute among young parents, and that these differences are more cultural. He wrote:

> the vulnerability and helplessness of infants and young children seem to arouse a sense of chronic emergency in parents even under relatively affluent conditions, and fathers and mothers respond to this sense of emergency in sex-specific ways. Thus, the young father forces even more deeply into his psychic underground the receptive sensuality that might be distracting to him in his instrumental role, and hence potentially lethal to his children . . . the wife becomes an external representation of the "passive" yearnings her husband must give up in order to provide for his family. By the same token the wife concedes to her husband—and figuratively sends out of the house with him—the agression that might be deadly, in the emotional and even in the physical sense, to her vulnerable offspring. The standard reaction for each sex is to surrender to the other the qualities that might interfere with the provision of its own special form of security. Men, the providers of physical security, give up the sensual dependency that might inhibit their courage and endurance; and women, the providers of emotional security, give up the aggression that might frighten or hurt a vulnerable and needful child.[15]

Even if one were to accept such "facts," one might suppose that they result more from the early upbringing of the parents than from innate psychological dispositions. Or perhaps, faced with the awesome and demanding responsibilities of new parenthood, both parents make extra efforts to conform to what society expects of them—to be, that is, what they have been induced by traditional roles to think of as "good" parents. But Gutmann considers the case for connecting different responses to parenthood with sexual differences to be strengthened by a consideration of what he calls "the sexual reversals that take place in middle-age, as children grow up and take over the responsibility of providing for their own security." As he sees it,

> A massive involution takes place in which men begin to live out directly—to own, as part of themselves—the passivity, sensuality, and tenderness, in effect the "femininity," that was previously repressed in the service of productive instrumentality. By the same token, we find (again, across a vast range of societies) the opposite effect in women, who generally become domineering, independent, and unsentimental in late middle life. . . . Grandpa becomes sweet, affable, but rather vague, Grandma becomes tough-minded and intrusive.[16]

One must say this is a ludicrous description of our social situation since, as one observes the leading positions in every important social structure—governmental, economic, legal, educational, etc.—one notes the almost total absence of anyone who is or ever will be a grandmother. So long as the society rewards the outside work of young fathers with promotions, pay raises, seniority, tenure, and career advancement, and asks young mothers to pay so heavily for their years of caring for children at home, to pay for the rest of their working lives with dismally restricted chances for occupational and personal development, the division of function suggested by Gutmann and those sympathetic to his point of view hardly appeals to our notions of equality.

But if, in fact, it suited our empirically given natures better for most of us to be, at different stages of our lives, successively either tenders of children or earners of income, rather than to try to keep the two in balance or to yield to one activity over the whole of our lives, then possibly more mothers than fathers *would* be suited to care for small children, *and* more grandmothers than grandfathers would be suited to run the world. And the requirements of equality between parents would not seem to be violated by life cycles that might be significantly different.

Equality of obligation, then, does not require that both parents perform exactly the same tasks, any more than equal opportunities for occupational attainment require that each person spend his or her working life at exactly the same kind of work. But it does require a *starting presumption* that *all* the tasks connected with supporting and bringing up children should *each* be divided equally. Dividing the tasks equally might be done by having both parents engage in the same activities for the same periods of their lives, as when they both split their days between childcare and outside work. Or, dividing the tasks equally might be achieved through taking somewhat longer turns, one parent working away from home for a few years for instance, while the other stayed home, and then, for the next few years, reversing the roles. These latter divisions may be especially appropriate for parents who are separated, or who must live separately at times for professional or other reasons. But women should be cautious about relying on agreements to have their years of child care "made up for later." A recent study shows that two-fifths of the divorced, separated, and single mothers legally eligible to receive child-support payments from the fathers of their children "have never received even a single payment," and many of those fathers who do provide support do so irregularly and in trivial amounts.[17] Furthermore, fathers who take little part in raising their children in the early years may not be able to develop close relations with them, suddenly, later on. And it may be very difficult for children to adjust to a complete shift of care from one parent to the other at different stages of their childhoods.

Equality of obligations *does* require that every departure from each parent performing the same tasks be justified in terms of relevant criteria and appropriate principles. There must be good reasons, and not merely customs and social pressures, for such departures. Simply being male or female is not a relevant ground for such departures and cannot be the basis for justifiable differences in parental roles. And equality of obligation requires that the choices to perform given tasks at given stages of our lives should be no less voluntary for one parent than for another.

For this principle to be recognized, we would have to abandon not only the view that the obligations of mothers and fathers are unequal, but also the view that they are in *any* way different. *Any* differences in tasks performed would have to be the result of voluntary agreement between the parents, arrived at on the basis of initial positions of equality, such agreements to include provisions for any later reversals of roles equality would require.

Taking care of small children for a few years of one's life is an incredibly interesting and satisfying kind of work, full of joyful as well as exhausting times. If mothers were not expected to pay so heavily in terms of their chances for self-development for choosing this kind of work, few would wish to miss out on it. In fact, women would probably, if given the choice, be glad to agree to more than an equal share of childcare work temporarily in exchange for more than an equal share of occupational opportunity and career advancement later on. But fathers should not be expected to be so foolish as to let mothers get more than their fair share of the best work of young adulthood, and to let grandmothers get more than their fair share of the best work of late middle age. If fathers *would* be that foolish, they would still be *entitled* to equality, and mothers would have an obligation to help them realize it.

Notes

I am grateful to Sissela Bok, Sandra Harding, Onora O'Neill, William Ruddick, and Mary Vetterling-Braggin for their helpful comments.

1. Nancy Chodorow, *The Reproduction of Mothering: Psychoanalysis and the Sociology of Gender* (Berkeley: University of California Press, 1978), p. 7. See also Dorothy Dinnerstein, *The Mermaid and the Minotaur* (New York: Harper Colophon Books, 1976).

2. Chodorow, *The Reproduction of Mothering,* p. 214.

3. Homer H. Clark, Jr., *The Law of Domestic Relations* (St. Paul, Minn.: West Publishing Co., 1968), p. 181.

4. See Georgia Dullea, "Joint Custody: Is Sharing the Child a Dangerous Idea?" *New York Times,* 24 May 1976, p. 24; and Charlotte Baum, "The Best of Both Parents," *New York Times Magazine,* 31 Oct. 1976, pp. 44-46.

5. It is ironic, or appropriate, that the quotation comes from an article called "The J-Curve of Rising and Declining Satisfaction as a Cause of Some Great Revolutions and a Contained Rebellion," by James C. Davies, in *The History of Violence in America,* edited by Hugh Davis Graham and Ted Robert Gurr (New York: New York Times Book, 1969), pp. 693-94.

6. See Ann Crittenden Scott, "The Value of Housework," *Ms.,* 1, no. 1 (July 1972) pp. 56-59.

7. See John Stuart Mill and Harriet Taylor, *Essays on Sex Equality,* edited by Alice S. Rossi (Chicago: Univ. of Chicago Press, 1970), esp. pp. 74-75 and 179-80.

8. On the distortions of Plato's argument to which his interpreters have sunk, see Christine Pierce, "Equality: *Republic V,*" *The Monist* 57, no. 1 (January 1973): 1–11.

9. See Virginia Held, "Men, Women, and Equal Liberty," in *Equality and Social Policy,* edited by Walter Feinberg (Urbana: Univ. of Illinois Press, 1978).

10. See Virginia Held, "Marx, Sex, and the Transformation of Society," in *Women and Philosophy,* edited by Carol C. Gould and Marx W. Wartofsky (New York: Putnam, 1976).

11. For a discussion, see Michael A. Slote, "Desert, Consent, and Justice," *Philosophy and Public Affairs* 2, no. 4 (Summer 1973): 323–47.

12. Sandra L. Bem and Daryl J. Bem, "Homogenizing the American Woman," reprinted in *Feminist Frameworks,* edited by Alison M. Jaggar and Paula Rothenberg Struhl (New York: McGraw-Hill, 1978).

13. See Larry Blum, Marcia Homiak, Judy Housman, and Naomi Scheman, "Altruism and Women's Oppression," in Gould and Wartofsky, *Women and Philosophy;* and Virginia Held, "Rationality and Reasonable Cooperation," *Social Research* 44, no. 4 (Winter 1977): 708–44.

14. For a perceptive discussion, see Angela Barron McBride, *The Growth and Development of Mothers* (New York: Harper, 1973).

15. David Gutmann, "Men, Women, and the Parental Imperative," *Commentary,* December 1973, p. 62.

16. Ibid.

17. *Search* (Washington, D.C.: The Urban Institute), Spring 1977.

2

Why Men Don't Rear Children: A Power Analysis

M. RIVKA POLATNICK

Introduction

The starting point for this essay is a simple fact of contemporary social life: in our society (as in most societies familiar to us), women rather than men have the primary responsibility for rearing children. Of course, fathers are not devoid of obligations vis-à-vis their offspring, but the father who accepts the routine day-to-day responsibility for supervising his children and servicing their needs, at the expense of outside employment and activity,* is a rare bird indeed.

In examining why this is so, I plan to steer clear of two potential pitfalls. First, I will make no attempt to unravel historical causes in pursuit of a primeval "first cause." Anthropological evidence about the origin of male and female behaviors is inconclusive and sheds little light on the contemporary situation, where the conditions of life are substantially different. This essay will deal only with current reasons why men don't rear children. Second, I have no intention of discussing individuals and their personal motivations. I treat men as a gender and women as a gender, and my conclusions will be generalizations about groups and group relations.

The choice of who rears a society's children and the implications of that choice for the whole social structure seem to me extremely fruitful subjects for sociological examination. Yet social scientists have shown little inclination to consider the allocation of childrearing responsibility as a matter of social

---

*Let this suffice as my definition of childrearing responsibility, with the qualification that outside employment and activity are possible if children spend part of the day with babysitters, at day-care centers, in school, or alone.

This essay is a large excerpt of a paper that originally appeared in *Berkeley Journal of Sociology* 18 (1973–74): 45–86. Copyright © 1973, 1982, by M. Rivka Polatnick. Reprinted by permission of the author.

choice. Instead they have been surprisingly willing to lay things at nature's door and ask no more: men don't rear children because women are the natural rearers of children.

For social scientists to rest so content with biological determinist explanations is at best intellectually unproductive, and at worst politically suspect. Elsewhere I have discussed in detail how the use (primarily misuse) of "nature" arguments has obscured the sociological understanding of childrearing as a social job.[1] My own explanation for why men don't rear children rests upon a basic premise about male/female relations: in our society (as in most societies familiar to us), men as a gender enjoy a superior power position in relation to women as a gender. That is, they are in control of the major sources of societal power (political, economic, social, physical),[2] and their superordinate position and the subordinate position of women are buttressed by an ideology of male supremacy and female inferiority.* It is not my purpose here to "prove" the existence of an overall power inequality between the sexes; by now there is a sufficient corpus of Women's Liberation literature that documents painstakingly the subordinate status of women in the various spheres of societal life.[3] I am interested instead in demonstrating how the assignment of childrearing responsibility to women articulates with a general pattern of male domination of our society. My analysis will illuminate and illustrate certain aspects of the gender power dynamic, but those unhappy with the basic premise will simply have to suspend misgivings and come along for the ride.

If, as I will argue, the current allocation of childrearing responsibility to women must be understood in the context of their subordinate position in society, then two different causal relationships suggest themselves:

1. Because women are the rearers of children, they are a powerless group vis-à-vis men.
2. Because women are a powerless group vis-à-vis men, they are the rearers of children.

The first proposal is of course wholly compatible with a biological determinist position. If those who regard females as the biologically designated rearers of children had at least examined the implications of this "fact" for the overall societal status of women, I would already have an important ingredient of my "power analysis." Unfortunately, biological determinists have been largely

---

*Modern democratic ideology requires that groups be defined as "different" rather than unequal, but the essence of a power relationship shines clearly through most of the basic decrees about male and female natures: women are soft, weak, passive, helpless, compliant, in need of care and protection; men are strong, active, assertive, commanding, suited for leadership and managerial roles.

associated with the "different but equal," "complementary," "separate spheres" school of thought about male/female relations, in which power is a foreign concept.

Women's responsibility for childrearing certainly contributes to their societal powerlessness, but this is only one component of the total "power picture." It will be my contention in the rest of this paper that the second causal relationship is operative as well. Thus, the causal model that will inform my discussion can be represented best by a feedback arrangement:

Women are a powerless group vis-à-vis men.

Women are the rearers of children.

My task will be to explain, elaborate, and justify this "power analysis."

Two final cautionary comments are in order. First, the subordinate position of women is rooted in multiple causes and is reinforced by many different institutions and practices. The causal model above is by no means intended as a complete statement about women's powerlessness; many other variables besides childrearing responsibility would have to be included in the picture. Freeing women from childrearing duties would not in and of itself eliminate the power differential between the sexes. For example, if domestic responsibilities didn't bar women from most influential jobs, discrimination in education, training, hiring, and promotion would. When I isolate the effects of any one variable upon the position of women, keep in mind that many other variables are left behind.

Second, I will be unable to do justice here to the complexities of social class. The gender dynamic of male superordination/female subordination operates across the entire range of socioeconomic status, but different realities and norms in each socioeconomic group produce variations in the basic pattern. Some of my specific statements, and some of the quotations I use, will be slanted toward middle-class realities; nevertheless, the essentials of my argument apply equally well to all social classes.

Social Advantage: The Power Analysis

Having elsewhere addressed and dispenced with the argument that men don't rear children because of "biology," I can now present and defend the central thesis of this essay: men (as a group) don't rear children because they don't *want* to rear children. (This implies, of course, that they are in a position to enforce their preferences.) It is to men's advantage that women are assigned childrearing responsibility, and it is in men's interest to keep things that way.

I should emphasize at once that I have no intention of measuring the "inherent worth" of childrearing as compared to other pursuits. On some "absolute" scale of values, childrearing would probably rank higher than many a work-world job. But my topic is not "the good life," it is power advantages. Thus my view of childrearing must be unabashedly pragmatic: will it get you ahead in the world? Does it even get you power in the family?

I will discuss the undesirability of the childrearing job under two general categories: (a) the advantages of avoiding childrearing responsibility (which are, primarily, the advantages of breadwinning responsibility), and (b) the disadvantages attached to childrearing responsibility.

Breadwinning Beats Childrearing

Full-time childrearing responsibility limits one's capacity to engage in most other activities. However, the most important thing, in power terms that childrearers can't do is to be the family breadwinner.[4] This is the job that men prefer as their primary family responsibility. It offers important power advantages over the home-based childrearing job.

MONEY, STATUS, POWER

First, and of signal importance, breadwinners earn money. "Money is a source of power that supports male dominance in the family. . . . Money belongs to him who earns it, not to her who spends it, since he who earns it may withhold it."[5]

Second, occupational achievement is probably the major source of social status in American society.

> In a certain sense the fundamental basis of the family's status is the occupational status of the husband and father. [The wife/mother] is excluded from the struggle for power and prestige in the occupational sphere [while the man's breadwinner role] carries with it . . . the primary prestige of achievement, responsibility, and authority.[6]

Even if one's occupation ranks very low in prestige and power, other tangible and intangible benefits accrue to wage earners, such as organizational experience, social contacts, "knowledge of the world," and feelings of independence and competence. Moreover, the resources that breadwinners garner in the outside world do not remain on the front porch; breadwinning power translates significantly into power within the family. This is in direct contradiction to the notion of "separate spheres": the man reigning supreme in extrafamilial affairs, the woman running the home-front show. (I'll return to this theme later.)

The correlation between earning power and family power has been substantiated concretely in a number of studies of family decision-making.[7] These studies show that the more a man earns, the more family power he wields; and the greater the discrepancy between the status of the husband's and wife's work, the greater the husband's power. When the wife works too, there is a shift toward a more egalitarian balance of power and more sharing of household burdens.*

Lois Hoffman has proposed four explanations for the increased family power of working wives, which convey again some of the power resources connected with breadwinning:

1. [Women who work have more control over money] and this control can be used, implicitly or explicitly, to wield power in the family.
2. Society attaches greater value to the role of wage earner than to that of housewife and thus legitimizes for both parents the notion that the former should have more power.
3. An independent supply of money enables the working woman to exert her influence to a greater extent because she is less dependent on her husband and could, if necessary, support herself in the event of the dissolution of the marriage.
4. Working outside the home provides more social interaction than being a housewife. This interaction has been seen as leading to an increase in the wife's power because of: (a) the development of social skills which are useful in influencing her husband; (b) the development of self-confidence; (c) the greater knowledge of alternative situations that exist in other families; and (d) the more frequent interaction with men, which may result in the feeling that remarriage is feasible.[8]

Not only does the woman's working modify the power relation between husband and wife, it also affects the gender power distribution in the whole family: when the mother works, daughters are likely to become more independent, and sons more dependent and obedient.[9]

POWER STRUCTURE OF THE "NORMAL" FAMILY

It is worth noting, in this connection, how sociological definitions of the "normal" family situation and "normal" personality development for sons and daughters sanction the status quo of male power and female powerlessness. Healthy families are those that produce strong, independent *sons,* ready to take on strong, independent "masculine roles." (Strong, independent daughters are not a goal; they're a symptom of deviance.) For the proper "masculine" upbringing, boys must have "male role models." What little importance academics have attached to fathers' playing a greater role in childrearing has been largely motivated by this concern. Lest they develop "nurturant" personalities, boys, brought up by "nurturant" mothers, should

---

*This should not imply, however, that women who earn more than their husbands necessarily have superior power, since the subordinate position of women stems from multiple causes.

have strong male role models close at hand, but not too actively involved in childrearing, for "a child whose father performs the mothering functions both tangibly and emotionally while the mother is preoccupied with her career can easily gain a distorted image of masculinity and femininity."[10]

Precisely.

MEN WANT TO BE THE BREADWINNERS

Men have good reason, then, to try to monopolize the job of principal family breadwinner (much as they may appreciate a second income). Husbands' objections to wives working "stem from feelings that their dominance is undermined when they are not the sole or primary breadwinners."[11] There is also

> the feeling of being threatened by women in industry, who are seen as limiting opportunities for men, diminishing the prestige of jobs formerly held only by men, and casting a cold eye on masculine pretentions to vocational superiority.[12]

These feelings are quite justified; as Benson so neatly understates it, "The male fear of competition from women is not based solely on myth."[13]

Where outright forbidding of the wife to work is no longer effective, the continued allocation of childrearing responsibility to women accomplishes the same end: assuring male domination of the occupational world. Should all other barriers to economic power for women suddenly vanish, childrearing responsibility would still handicap them hopelessly in economic competition with men.

Of course, children are not just a handy excuse to keep women out of the job market. Most people—male and female—want to have them, and somebody has to rear them. Men naturally prefer that women do it, so that having children need not interfere with their own occupational pursuits.

> Since housewife and mother roles are preferred for women, it is considered distasteful and perhaps dangerous to upgrade their occupational status. Apparently there is a fear of mass defections from maternal responsibility. Perhaps there is also a hidden suspicion that the woman's employment is symptomatic of a subversive attitude toward motherhood.[14]

Both these motives, therefore—the desire to limit females' occupational activities, and the desire to have children without limiting their own occupational activities—contribute to a male interest in defining childrearing as exclusively woman's domain. Thus,

> there has been consistent social effort as a norm with the woman whose vocational proclivities are completely and "naturally" satisfied by childbearing and childrearing, with the related domestic activities.[15]

One of the controls operating to restrict women's breadwinning activities is the social pressure against mothers who "neglect their children." Where financial need compels mothers with young children to work, their absence from the home is accepted as a "necessary evil." (Welfare departments, however, will generally support mothers of young children without pressuring them to seek work.) In the middle classes, sentiments about male/female responsibility are less obscured by immediate economic considerations:

> Some public disapproval is still directed toward the working mother of young children and the mother who devotes her primary attention to a career; the feeling persists that a mother who creates a full life for herself outside the home may be cheating her children, if not her husband.[16]

Fathers, on the other hand, have public license (in fact, a veritable public duty) to devote primary attention to job or career. Sandra and Daryl Bem have illustrated the existent "double standard" of parental responsibility with the example of a middle-class father who loses his wife:

> No matter how much he loved his children, no one would expect him to sacrifice his career in order to stay home with them on a full-time basis—even if he had an independent source of income. No one would charge him with selfishness or lack of parental feeling if he sought professional care for his children during the day.[17]

MEN WANT WOMEN TO BE THE CHILDREARERS

By propagating the belief that women are the ones who really desire children, men can then invoke a "principle of least interest": that is, because women are "most interested" in children, they must make most of the accommodations and sacrifices required to rear them. Benson says that "fatherhood . . . is less important to men than motherhood is to women, in spite of the fact that maternity causes severe limitations on women's activities."[18] My own version would be that fatherhood is less important to men than motherhood is to women *because* childrearing causes severe limitations on the childrearer's activities.

In a discussion of barriers to careers for women, Alice Rossi cites some very revealing findings about which sex advocates a more rigid standard of "mothering responsibility."

> On an item reading "Even if a woman has the ability and interest, she should not choose a career field that will be difficult to combine with childrearing," half of the women but two-thirds of the men agreed. Again, although half the women thought it appropriate for a woman to take a part-time job if a child was a preschooler, only one-third of the men approved. A quarter of the men, but only 14% of the women, thought a full-time job should not be taken until the children were "all grown up."[19]

Women too imbibe the ideology of motherhood, but men seem to be its strongest supporters. By insuring that the weight of childrearing responsibility falls on women's shoulders, they win for themselves the right of "paternal neglect." As Benson observes, "The man can throw himself into his work and still fulfill male obligations at home, mainly because the latter are minimal. [Men have] the luxury of more familial disengagement than women."[20]

Of course, men as family breadwinners must shoulder the *financial* burden involved in raising children: they may have to work harder, longer hours, and at jobs they dislike. But even factory workers enjoy set hours, scheduled breaks, vacation days, sick leave, and other union benefits. To the extent that men *can* select work suited to their interests, abilities, and ambitions, they are in a better position than women arbitrarily assigned to childrearing. And to the extent that breadwinning gains one the resources discussed earlier (money, status, family power, etc.), financial responsibility is clearly preferable, in power terms, to "mothering" responsibility.

CHILDREARING RESPONSIBILITY HANDICAPS WOMEN

From the perspective of women—the more affluent women faced with "mother/career conflict," the poorer women faced with "mother/any job at all conflict"—men possess the enviable option to "have their cake and eat it too," that is, to have children without sacrificing their activities outside the home. A woman knows that becoming a parent will adversely affect her occupational prospects. "For a period, at least, parenthood means that . . . whatever vocational or professional skills she may possess may become atrophied.[21] During this period of retirement the woman

> becomes isolated and almost totally socially, economically, and emotionally dependent upon her husband. . . . She loses her position, cannot keep up with developments in her field, does not build up seniority. . . . If she returns to work, and most women do, she must begin again at a low-status job and she stays there—underemployed and underpaid.[22]

Not only during the period of childrearing do women become economically or professionally disadvantaged vis-à-vis men; most women's lives have already been constructed in anticipation of that period. "Helpful advice" from family, friends, and guidance counselors, and discriminatory practices in the schools and in the job market steer women toward jobs and interests compatible with a future in childrearing.

With the assistance of relatives, babysitters, or the few day-care centers that exist, women can hold certain kinds of jobs while they're raising children (often part-time, generally low-status). Women without husbands, women with pressing financial needs, women who can afford hired help, may work fulltime despite the demands of "mothering."[23] But to an important extent, occupational achievement and childrearing responsibility are mutually exclusive. A 40-hour work-week permits more family involvement than did a 72-hour work-week, but it's still difficult to combine with primary responsibility for children (given the lack of institutional assistance). Furthermore, the higher-status professional jobs frequently demand a work week commitment closer to the 72-hour figure. Men can hold these jobs and also father families only because they can count on a "helpmeet" to take care of children and home. Thus it is said that the wages of a man buy the labor of two people. Without this back-up team of wife/mothers, something would have to give.

Alice Rossi has suggested that the period of women's lives spent at home rearing children is potentially the peak period for professional accomplishment:

> If we judge from the dozens of researches Harvey Lehman has conducted on the relationship between age and achievement, . . . the most creative work women and men have done in science was completed during the very years contemporary women are urged to remain at home rearing their families. . . . Older women who return to the labor force are an important reservoir for assistants and technicians and the less demanding professions, but only rarely for creative and original contributors to the more demanding professional fields.[24]

The woman who tries to work at home while raising children finds that this is not too practicable a solution. Writer/critic Marya Mannes noted with regard to her own profession: "The creative woman has no wife to protect her from intrusion. A man at his desk in a room with closed door is a man at work. A woman at a desk in any room is available."[25]

MAINTAINING THE STATUS QUO

If working hours and career patterns were more flexible, if childcare centers were more widely available, and if "retired mothers" reentering the workforce received special preference rather than unfavorable treatment,* childrearing would exact a less heavy toll on women's occupational achievement. Because men benefit from the status quo, they ignore, discourage, or actively resist such reform proposals. Alternative arrangements for rearing children, for balancing work commitment with family commitment, are not pressing concerns for men; the structural relegation of women to domestic service suits their interests very well.

Women's responsibility for children in the context of the nuclear family is an important buttress for a male-dominated society. It helps keep women out of the running for economic and political power. As Talcott Parsons states:

---

*Consider how the reentry of veterans into the workforce is eased by special benefits and preferential treatment.

It is, of course, possible for the adult woman to follow the masculine pattern and seek a career in fields of occupational achievement in direct competition with men of her own class. It is, however, notable that in spite of the very great progress of the emancipation of women from the traditional domestic pattern only a very small fraction have gone very far in this direction.* It is also clear that its generalization would only be possible with profound alterations in the structure of the family.[26]

I have chosen to focus upon breadwinning (economic activity) as the most important thing, from a power perspective, that childrearers can't do. Moreover, other activities—educational, political, cultural, social, recreational—suffer when one's life becomes centered around children and home.** The "on call" nature of "mothering" responsibility militates against any kind of sustained, serious commitment to other endeavors. A full-time mother loses

> the growth of competence and resources in the outside world, the community positions which contribute to power in the marriage. The boundaries of her world contract, the possibilities of growth diminish.[27]

While women are occupied with domestic duties, men consolidate their resources in the outside world and their position of command in the family. By the time most women complete their childrearing tenure, they can no longer recoup their power losses.

Childrearing: Not an Equal Sphere

By my explicit and implicit comparisons of breadwinning with childrearing, I have already asserted that the former is the more desirable "sphere" of action. Now I will discuss more directly the disadvantages of the childrearing job.

MONEY, STATUS, POWER

Once again, let's begin with the simple but significant matter of money. Money is a prime source of power in American society, and tending one's own children on a full-time basis is not a salaried activity.

> In sheer quantity, household labor, including child care, constitutes a huge amount of socially necessary production. Nevertheless, in a society based on commodity production, it is not usually considered "real work" since it is outside of trade and the market place. . . . In a society in which money determines value, women are a group who work outside the money

---

*One might well inquire what this "very great progress" is, if "only a small fraction" of women are actually involved.
**Here again, there's been little effort, for the sake of *female* childrearers, to develop more flexible programs of higher education and professional training.

economy. Their work is not worth money, is therefore valueless, is therefore not even real work. And women themselves, who do this valueless work, can hardly be expected to be worth as much as men, who work for money.[28]

Performing well at the job of childrearer may be a source of feminine credentials, but it is not a source of social power or status. Of all the possible adult roles for females, "the pattern of domesticity must be ranked lowest in terms of prestige," although "it offers perhaps the highest level of a certain kind of security."[29] When a woman bears and raises children, therefore, she is fulfilling social expectations and avoiding negative sanctions, but she "is not esteemed, in the culture or in the small society of her family, in proportion to her exercise of her 'glory,' childbearing."[30]

The rewards for rearing children are not as tangible as a raise or a promotion, and ready censure awaits any evidence of failure: "if the child goes wrong, mother is usually blamed."[31] Thus the male preference for the breadwinner role may reflect (among other things) an awareness that "it's easier to make money than it is to be a good father. . . . The family is a risky proposition in terms of rewards and self-enhancement."[32]

FAMILY POWER

If childrearers don't accumulate power resources in the outside world, do they at least win some advantage in the family balance of power? I have already cited the evidence that family power is directly related to earning power. It is not surprising that researchers have also found that the wife's power declines with the arrival of children; an inverse relationship exists between number of children and the wife's power vis-à-vis her husband.[33]

Two major theories of conjugal power suggest explanations for this effect. Blood and Wolfe's "resource theory" posits that "power will accrue to the spouse who has the more imposing or relevant resources, and thus has the greater contribution to make to the family."[34] If one considers occupational status and income as the most imposing of resources, then this explanation is little different from the "earning power equals family power" thesis. Yet Blood and Wolfe don't illuminate why breadwinning should be a "greater contribution" to the family than childbearing.

David Heer's "exchange value theory" postulates that "the spouse who could most likely marry another person who would be as desirable as or much more desirable than his (her) present spouse"[35] enjoys the superior power position. When a woman has children and becomes a full-time childrearer, she grows more dependent on her husband, her opportunities to meet men decrease, and her prospects for remarriage decline. The husband thus possesses the more promising alternatives outside the marriage, and his power increases.

The woman's power is at its lowest point during the preschool period, when childrearing responsibilities are most consuming.

> When her children start school, the mother can be more autonomous and exercise more power because she is better able to handle outside employment; the children can now take care of themselves in many ways and are supervised to a greater extent by the school and other community agencies.[36]

CHILDREARING: NOT A SEPARATE SPHERE

Despite the empirical evidence that women lose family power when they become mothers, one is still tempted to believe that by leaving childrearing to women, men have surrendered a significant area of control. This belief is based on the erroneous notion that women preside over childrearing as a separate sovereign domain. On the contrary, men's authority as family provider/family "head" carries right over into childrearing matters. Men may have surrendered the regular responsibility and routine decision-making, but they retain power where important decisions are concerned (including what the routine will be).

> In a sample of adolescents studied by Charles Bowerman and Glen Elder (1964), the father was reported to be the dominant parent in childrearing matters as often as the mother, in spite of the fact that mother does most of the actual work; apparently she often finds herself responsible for doing the menial chores without having the stronger voice in "childrearing policy."[37]

Constantina Safilios-Rothschild found that American men delegate to their wives many of the minor decisions related to rearing children and running a home—"those decisions, the enactment of which involves time-consuming tasks." This suggests to her that

> American husbands do not wish to take on "bothersome" decisions which are not crucial . . . and take too much of the time and energy that they prefer to dedicate to their work or leisure-time activities.[38]

Fathers may default from the daily childrearing routines but, much like male principals supervising female teachers, they still tend to wield the ultimate force and the ultimate decision-making power. Consider these statements of Benson's on the nature of paternal authority:

> The father as threatener is superimposed upon the mother's more basic pattern and is therefore more likely to appear as a terrorizing intruder, but one who speaks as authority and therefore ought to be obeyed. [page 14] . . . Family members can forsee his judgments and are constrained to act correctly according to their conception of his wishes. [page 18] . . . Even the social pattern that mother establishes is typically

legitimized by the larger, more insistent parent lurking in the background. . . . Father is the embodiment of a basic form of social control: coercive power. . . . Father is an agent of both internal and external control, and the child responds to him in terms of both his respect for the man and his respect for the man's power. [pages 50–52] . . . But when order breaks down or is openly challenged the need for a new approach assumes an immediate, deliberative significance, and father is customarily expected to help meet the crisis. In fact, it is common for him to take charge. [page 59][39]

Taking care of children, therefore, does not provide women with any real power base. Men can afford to leave childrearing *responsibility* to women because, given their superior power resources, they are still assured of substantial childrearing *authority*.

THE NATURE OF THE JOB

Childrearing, I have argued, is not a source of money, status, power in the society, or power in the family. The childrearing job is disadvantageous in terms of these major assets, but there are also drawbacks inherent in the nature of the work itself. The rearing of children "involves long years of exacting labor and self-sacrifice," but

the drudgery, the monotonous labor, and other disagreeable features of childrearing are minimized by "the social guardians." On the other hand, the joys and compensations of motherhood are magnified and presented to consciousness on every hand. Thus the tendency is to create an illusion whereby motherhood will appear to consist of compensations only, and thus come to be desired by those for whom the illusion is intended.[40]

The responsibilities of a childrearer/homemaker are not confined to a 40-hour work-week. Margaret Benston estimates that for a married woman with small children (excluding the very rich), "the irreducible minimum of work . . . is probably 70 or 80 hours a week."[41] In addition to the actual hours of work, there is the constant strain of being "on call." Thus, another consideration in why the husband's power is greatest when the children are young "may be the well-described chronic fatigue which affects young mothers with preschoolers.[42]

Furthermore, women are adults (assertions that they have "childlike" natures notwithstanding), and they need adequate adult company to stimulate their mental faculties.

A lot of women become disheartened because babies and children are not only not interesting to talk to (not everyone thrills at the wonders of da-da-ma-ma- talk) but they are generally not empathic, considerate people.[43]

Although interaction with young children is certainly rewarding in many ways, childrearers can lose touch with the world outside their domestic circle. In addition, American society segregates the worlds of childhood and adulthood; adults who keep close company with children are *déclassé*.

Since the "less-than-idyllic childrearing part of motherhood remains 'in small print,' "[44] new mothers are often in for some rude shocks. Betty Rollin quotes some mothers interviewed in an Ann Arbor, Michigan, study:

> Suddenly I had to devote myself to the child totally. I was under the illusion that the baby was going to fit into my life, and I found that I had to switch my life and my schedule to fit *him*.

> You never get away from the responsibility. Even when you leave the child with a sitter, you are not out from under the pressure of the responsibility.

> I hate ironing their pants and doing their underwear, and they never put their clothes in the laundry basket. . . . Best moment of the day is when all the children are in bed. . . . The worst time of day is 4 P.M., when you have to get dinner started, and the kids are tired, hungry, and crabby—everybody wants to talk to you about *their* day. . . . Your day is only half over.

> Once a mother, the responsibility and concern for my children became so encompassing. . . . It took a great deal of will to keep up other parts of my personality.

> I had anticipated that the baby would sleep and eat, sleep and eat. Instead, the experience was overwhelming. I really had not thought particularly about what motherhood would mean in a realistic sense. I want to do *other* things, like to become involved in things that are worthwhile—I don't mean women's clubs—but I don't have the physical energy to go out in the evenings. I feel like I'm missing something. . . . the experience of being somewhere with people and having them talking about something—something that's going on in the world.[45]

AVOIDING THE JOB

When women are wealthy enough to afford it, they often hire nurses and governesses to relieve them of the more burdensome aspects of childcare. They can then enjoy the children's company when they want to, be active mothers when it suits them, but avoid the constant responsibility and the more unpleasant parts of the job (diapers, tantrums, etc.). The relationship between rich mother and governess resembles in significant respects the relationship between average father and average mother. The father "hires" the mother (by providing her with support), in the expectation that she will relieve him of the major burdens of childrearing. (However, even a rich mother is expected to pay a lot more personal attention to her children than any father is.)

From the perspective of an ambitious person, taking full-time care of your own children is rather like baking your own bread: it might be nice if one had the time, but there are more important things to be done. Thus you pay for the service of having someone else do it, increasing your financial burden but freeing yourself of a time-consuming task.

Fathers, with full social support, can buy a significant degree of freedom from direct family responsibility. They have a category of people at hand—women—constrained by social forces to accept that responsibility. Women have no such convenient group to whom they can pass the childrearing buck. For mothers, the price of escape from childrearing—financial, social, psychological—is usually too high.

"MOTHERLY SELFLESSNESS"

A final relevant feature of the childrearing job itself is that mothers are obliged to subordinate their personal objectives and practice "selflessness"—putting the needs of others first, devoting themselves to the day-to-day well-being of other family members, loving and giving "unconditionally."* Such domestic service may be deemed virtuous, but it isn't a path to power and success. Males primed for competitive achievement show no eagerness to suppress their personal ambitions and sacrifice their own interests to attend to others' immediate wants.

Furthermore, men desire from women the same services and support, the same ministration to everyday needs, that mothers are supposed to provide for children. ("I want a wife to keep track of the children's doctor and dentist appointments. And to keep track of mine too. . . . a wife who will pick up after my children, a wife who will pick up after me.")[46] "Mothering" behavior is not very different from "feminine" behavior. By grooming females for "nurturance," men provide a selfless rearer for their children and an accommodating marriage partner for themselves.

Several movies and television serials have been constructed around the situation of a father/widower with a son or two, all in need of a "nurturant" woman to take care of them. The fact that children and fathers "compete" for similar services from the mother may explain why the Oedipus Complex is more pronounced than the Electra Complex (if these concepts still have any credibility).[47]

Margaret Adams has discussed the negative effects of this obligatory "selflessness" upon women.

> Both family and professional commitments incorporate the insidious notion that the needs of others should be woman's major, if not exclusive, concern. Implicit in the role that derives from this notion is the supposed

---

*Erich Fromm, in *The Art of Loving,* waxes eloquent about mothers' "unconditional" love.

virtue of subordinating individual needs to the welfare of others and the personal value and supposed reward of vicarious satisfaction from this exercise. . . . Women must abandon the role of the compassionate sibyl who is at everyone's beck and call, because being permanently available to help others keeps women from pursuing their own chosen avocations with the concentration that is essential for their successful completion.[18]

Men have a stake in ensuring that women remain unable to "abandon the role of the compassionate sibyl." They derive double benefit—as husbands wanting wifely services, as fathers wanting childrearing services—from the "emotional indenture" of women.[49]

MORE EVIDENCE THAT MEN DON'T WANT THE JOB

Despite all the disadvantages of childrearing responsibility, men often protest that they'd love to be able to stay home with the kids. Nonetheless, two additional sources of evidence indicate that men don't really find the job desirable.

The first relates to the widely noted phenomenon that boys who behave like girls draw stronger negative reactions than girls who behave like boys. A "sissy" playing with dolls elicits unmixed scorn, while an adventurous "tomboy" (as long as she's not too old) gets a certain amount of approval. In overall social estimation, female activities and traits are not as worthy or desirable as those of males. "The fact that . . . both sexes tend to value men and male characteristics, values, and activities more highly than those of women has been noted by many authorities.[50]

All this suggests the essential hypocrisy of men who laud female achievements as "different but equal," or who claim they'd gladly switch. Studies have consistently shown that far fewer men than women wish they had been born the opposite sex. The work of women, including most prominently the "nurturing" of children, is socially devalued, and a minuscule number of men have actually taken it on.

The second source of evidence relevant here is the attitude of men toward working with children as a salaried job. The overwhelming majority of people in occupations involving close interaction with children (elementary school teachers, day-care and nursery school personnel, child welfare workers, etc.) are women.* Judging by the statistics, men have not chosen working with children as suitable employment for their sex.

However, men are willing to enter such "female" fields as children's education at the upper echelons. In 1968, 78 percent of elementary school *principals* were men.[51] Men dominate the top of the profession of child study[52] and

---

*The closer children approach to adulthood, the higher the percentage of males teaching them.

dispense highly professional advice on childrearing to the actual rearers of children (for example, Dr. Spock).

Thus, working with children might not be such an unattractive prospect for males if the rewards (money, status, power) could be made commensurate with their expectations. In fact, there seems to be a current trend toward increased male participation in elementary education. This development is probably the result of several causes: a tight job market; a new concern that men be present in schools as "male role models";[53] and a general societal shift toward evaluating early childhood as a crucial learning period, and early education as a more important business. If the last factor is the predominant one, it's possible that the occupation of elementary school teacher could undergo a sex change, with the improvements in salary, benefits, job conditions, etc., that result when males move into female occupations. But even with a radical change in the status of salaried work with children, it is doubtful that unsalaried rearing of children will ever attract many males.

Conclusion

The allocation of childrearing responsibility to women, I have argued, is no sacred fiat of nature, but a social policy which supports male domination in the society and in the family.

Whatever the "intrinsic desirability" of rearing children, the conditions of the job as it's now constituted—no salary, low status, long hours, domestic isolation—mark it as a job for women only. Men, as the superordinate group, don't want childrearing responsibility, so they assign it to women. Women's functioning as childrearers reinforces, in turn, their subordinate position. Thus we come back again to the causal model of my Introduction—

Women are a powerless group vis-à-vis men

Women are the rearers of children

—a vicious circle that keeps male power intact.

Notes

Much appreciation for the bloodcurdling critiques of Judie "Tenspeed" Gaffin, "Diesel" Dair Gillespie, Carol "Boss" Hatch, Ann "The Man" Leffler, Elinor "Bulldog" Lerner, Maria "Muscle" Mendes, and "Stompin'" Stacey Oliker; much indebtedness to the Women's Movement in general.

1. See the original, longer version of this essay in *Berkeley Journal of Sociology* 18 (1973–74): 45–86.

2. "The general definition of 'power' is 'a capacity to get things done.' Either resources (rights in things) or authority (rights in persons) increases the ability of a person to do what he decides to do." (Arthur Stinchcombe, *Constructing Social Theories* [New York: Harcourt, Brace, & World, 1968], p. 157).

3. See, for example, Caroline Bird, *Born Female: The High Cost of Keeping Women Down* (New York: David McKay, 1968); Cynthia Fuchs Epstein, *Women's Place: Options and Limits in Professional Careers* (Berkeley: University of California Press, 1971); Kirsten Amundsen, *The Silenced Majority* (Englewood Cliffs, N.J.: Prentice-Hall, 1977); and Simone de Beauvoir, *The Second Sex* (New York: Alfred A. Knopf, 1952).

4. Many women work during some of the childrearing years, but if they have husbands, they are vary rarely the principal breadwinner. In 1978, working wives contributed about 26% to family income (U.S. Dept. of Labor, *Monthly Labor Review,* April 1980, p. 48).

5. Reuben Hill and Howard Becker, eds., *Family, Marriage, and Parenthood* (Boston: D.C. Heath, 1955), p. 790.

6. Talcott Parsons, "Age and Sex in the Social Structure" in *The Family: Its Structure and Functions,* edited by Rose Laub Coser (New York: St. Martin's Press, 1964), pp. 258, 261-62.

7. For a full report, see Leonard Benson, *Fatherhood: A Sociological Perspective* (New York: Random House, 1968).

8. Lois Wladis Hoffman, "Effects of the Employment of Mothers on Parental Power Relations and the Division of Household Tasks," *Marriage and Family Living* 22 (February 1960): 33.

9. Benson, *Fatherhood,* pp. 302-3.

10. Norman W. Bell and Ezra F. Vogel, eds., *A Modern Introduction to the Family,* rev. ed. (New York: The Free Press, 1968).

11. Phyllis Hallenbeck, "An Analysis of Power Dynamics in Marriage," *Journal of Marriage and the Family* 28 (May 1966): 201.

12. Helen Mayer Hacker, "The New Burdens of Masculinity," *Marriage and Family Living* 19 (August 1957): 232.

13. Benson, *Fatherhood,* p. 293.

14. Ibid.

15. Leta S. Hollingworth, "Social Devices for Impelling Women to Bear and Rear Children," *The American Journal of Sociology* 22 (July 1916): 20.

16. Benson, *Fatherhood,* p. 292.

17. Sandra L. Bem and Daryl J. Bem, "Training the Woman to Know Her Place" in *Roles Women Play,* edited by Michele Hoffnung Garskof (Belmont, Calif.: Wadsworth, 1971), p. 94.

18. Benson, *Fatherhood,* p. 292.

19. Alice S. Rossi, "Barriers to the Career Choice of Engineering, Medicine, or Science Among American Women" in *Women and the Scientific Professions,* edited by Jacquelyn A. Mattfeld and Carol G. Van Aken (Westport, Conn.: Greenwood Press, 1965), p. 87.

20. Benson, *Fatherhood,* pp. 132, 134.

21. Robert F. Winch, *The Modern Family,* rev. ed. (New York: Holt, Rinehart and Winston, 1964), p. 434.

22. Dair L. Gillespie, "Who Has the Power? The Marital Struggle," *Journal of Marriage and the Family* 33 (August 1971): 456.

23. In 1960, 18.6 percent of mothers with children under the age of six were in the labor force in some capacity; 11.4 percent were working 35 hours or more per week. By 1970, the proportion of these mothers in the paid labor force at least part time or look-

ing for paid jobs reached 32 percent, and in March 1979, 45 percent. The percentage actually working full time, year-round, remains low, however (U.S. Department of Labor, *Monthly Labor Review,* April 1980, p. 49). The increase in those working at least part time can probably be explained by the economy's need for more service and clerical workers, families' needs for more income because of recession and inflation, the increase in the percentage of mothers who are single, and the effects of the Women's Liberation Movement. Ongoing research will reveal to what extent men have taken on more childrearing work (U.S. Bureau of the Census, *Statistical Abstract of the U.S.: 1971* [Washington, D.C.: U.S.G.P.O., 1971], Table 332,; and *A U.S. Census of Population: 1960, Subject Reports: Families* [Washington, D.C.: U.S.G.P.O., 1963], Final Report PC(2)-44, Table 11).

24. Rossi, "Barriers to the Career Choice," pp. 102-3, 107.

25. Quoted in Betty Rollin, "Motherhood: Who Needs It?" in *Family in Transition,* edited by Arlene S. Skolnick and Jerome H. Skolnick (Boston: Little, Brown, 1971), p. 352.

26. Parsons, "Age and Sex in the Social Structure," pp. 258-59.

27. Gillespie, "Who Has the Power?" p. 456.

28. Margaret Benston, "The Political Economy of Women's Liberation" in Garskof, *Roles Women Play,* p. 196.

29. Parsons, "Age and Sex in the Social Structure," p. 261.

30. Judith Long Laws, "A Feminist Review of Marital Adjustment Literature," *Journal of Marriage and the Family* 33 (August 1971): 493.

31. Benson, *Fatherhood,* p. 12.

32. Myron Brenton, *The American Male* (New York: Coward-McCann, 1966), p. 133.

33. David M. Heer, "The Measurement and Bases of Family Power: An Overview" in *Marriage and Family Living* 25; Robert O. Blood and Donald M. Wolfe, *Husbands and Wives: The Dynamics of Married Living* (New York: The Free Press, 1960); Lois Wladis Hoffman and R. Lippitt, "The Measurement of Family Life Variables" in P. H. Mussen, ed., *Handbook of Research Methods in Child Development* (New York: Wiley and Sons, 1960); and Frederick L. Campbell, "Demographic Factors in Family Organizations" (Ph.D. dissertation, University of Michigan, 1967).

34. Benson, *Fatherhood,* p. 149.

35. Constantina Safilios-Rothschild, "The Study of Family Power Structure: A Review 1960-1969," *Journal of Marriage and the Family* 32 (November 1970): 548.

36. Herr, "The Measurement and Bases of Family Power," quoted in Benson, *Fatherhood,* p. 152.

37. Benson, ibid., p. 157.

38. Constantina Safilios-Rothschild, "Family Sociology or Wives' Family Sociology?" in *Journal of Marriage and the Family* 31 (May 1969): 297.

39. Benson, *Fatherhood.*

40. Holingsworth, "Social Devices," pp. 20-21, 27.

41. Benston, "Political Economy," p. 199.

42. Hallenbeck, "An Analysis of Power Dynamics in Marriage," p. 201.

43. Rollin, "Motherhood," p. 353.

44. Ibid., p. 349.

45. Ibid.

46. Judy Syfers, "Why I Want a Wife," in *Notes From the Third Year* (New York, 1971), p. 13.

47. See Shulamith Firestone, *The Dialectic of Sex* (New York: Bantam, 1970) for an excellent analysis of these complexes in power terms.

48. Margaret Adams, "The Compassion Trap," *Psychology Today* 5 (November

1971): 72, 101. Reprinted in *Women in Sexist Society,* edited by Vivian Gornick and Barbara K. Moran (New York: Basic Books, 1971).

49. Ibid., p. 100.

50. Jo Freeman, "The Social Construction of the Second Sex" in Garskof, *Roles Women Play,* p. 126 (references included).

51. Epstein, *Women's Place,* p. 10.

52. Bird, *Born Female,* p. 102.

53. See Patricia Sexton, *The Feminized Male* (New York: Random House, 1969).

3

When Women and Men Mother

DIANE EHRENSAFT

In the late sixties the women's movement put the traditional nuclear family on trial and declared it oppressive to women. Entrapment as housewives and mothers was targeted as key to female oppression. A prime focus, both theoretical and strategic, was to free women from their iron apron strings. Some women, particularly radical feminists, called for a boycott of women's involvement with marriage, men, or motherhood. Others demanded universal childcare to free women from the home. Some opted for motherhood but no men. A minority of women within the movement, who were either already in nuclear families or still desired involvement with men and children, opted for a different solution in their own lives—the equal sharing of parenthood between mothers and fathers. Contrary to traditional heterosexual relationships in which men are reported to spend an average of 12 minutes a day on primary childcare,[1] this new model of parenting assumed that mothers and fathers would share the full weight of rearing their children.*

Ten years later, a combination of forces pressured those of us who chose this latter solution to talk about and assess our experience. Recognizing the confusion and turmoil experienced by people in this country around issues of personal life, astute new-right organizers have responded with the rallying cry of "save our families, save our future" as the road to surviving contemporary crises. The emergence of the new right is strongly marked by a bid for women to remain responsible for primary childcare. At the same time, more and more mothers are working outside the home to support themselves and their families. For many women, this means two full-time jobs. The popular press

---

*This model is often linked to a broader demand for fuller involvement not just by both biological parents, but by other "significant others" in the child's life, either housemates, relatives, or intimate friends. This essay will look specifically at the relationships of mother and father.

This is a major portion of an essay that originally appeared in *Socialist Review* 49 (January–February 1980). Reprinted by permission of the author and the publisher.

abounds with news reports, articles, and books attesting to the growing interest of men in family life, accompanied by a drop in male workaholism, while the women they live with no longer settle for being "just a housewife."

Simultaneously, feminist theory (in particular two recent books, Dorothy Dinnerstein's *Mermaid and the Minotaur* and Nancy Chodorow's *The Reproduction of Mothering*) has stressed that gender differentiation and sex oppression will exist as long as women continue to be totally responsible for mothering. The call for shared parenting by men and women moves those of us already involved in attempting such a reorganization of family life to reflect and analyze its potential and actual effects on the reorganization of gender and childrearing structures. We are further moved by pressures from the new right to develop this analysis within the larger project of a left counterprogram that more effectively addresses people's fears about crumbling family stability, lack of personal commitment, increased social violence, and dissolution of knowable social forms. This must come not as a romantic plea for a return to the good old days, but as a step forward to new social structures that provide the emotional and social intimacy and sense of community for which people are legitimately searching.

This essay examines the experiences of a small group of men and women. Most of us do not represent the mainstream of American society. We are, on the whole, white graduates of the new left of the sixties, which puts most of us in our thirties. Often we hold professional, nontraditional, or "movement" jobs with greater opportunity for flex-time than most people have. We tend to congregate in liberal communities such as Boston, the Bay Area, New York, or western Massachusetts. While most of us hold that, ideally, all mothers and fathers living together should share equally in the parenting process, this is not the ultimate solution for all people. Parenting by women alone, by men alone, in extended families, in lesbian and gay couples, in communal situations within neighborhood networks—all are models to be explored and understood. Economic necessity and social context will influence different parenting solutions. But the experiences of our small group are important not only because they reveal the parameters and possibilities of gender reorganization within the family at this point in history; they also simultaneously reflect and speak to the concern of growing numbers of both women and men who find they no longer survive in or accept traditional family roles.[2] Shared parenting exists not in isolation, but as part of the larger struggle facing contemporary adults in redefining their position in (and out of) the family.

The political meaning of this analysis is twofold. On one hand, if feminist theory stands correct in pinpointing enforced motherhood as a major source of women's oppression through confirmation and reproduction of their domesticity, shared parenting challenges that situation. If, as Dinnerstein and Chodorow respectively argue, misogyny and gender-divided personality structure have their roots in female-dominated parenting, shared parenting sets the stage for a new generation of men and women and challenges a universal structure in the organization of gender.

On the other hand, an examination of actual shared-parenting experiences confirms that " 'production' and 'reproduction,' work and the family, far from being separate territories like the moon and the sun or the kitchen and the shop, are really intimately related modes that reverberate upon one another and frequently occur in the same social, physical, and even psychic spaces."[3] The present article, which focuses on the experiences of men and women who have taken an equal share in parenting while also maintaining outside work identities, argues that equalization of parenting between men and women is problematic within American capitalism. The interpenetration of work and family makes it very hard to alter power and psychological structures in the family without a concomitant restructuring of power and ideology in the public world of work and politics. By looking at the general nature of shared parenting, the division of labor and male-female relationships between shared parents, and speculating about the outcome for children in these families, we can explore the tension between the tremendous political potential and the actual limitations of shared parenting today in the reorganization of gender.

Shared Parenting in a Capitalist Context

Who is engaged in shared parenting? Any two individuals both of whom see themselves as primary caretakers to a child or children. As defined by Nancy Press Hawley, elements of shared parenting include: (a) intimacy, both between sharing adults and between adults and children; (b) care of the child in a regular, daily way; (c) awareness of being a primary caretaker or parent to the children; (d) ongoing commitment; and (e) attention paid to the adult relationship.[4] In addition to daily caretaking functions, we are talking about two individuals who fully share responsibility for the ongoing intellectual, emotional, and social development of the child.*

In the late 1960s and early 1970s, some people, coming out of new left lifestyles, tried to establish a model of two parents each of whom would split their work time between part-time paid work and parenting responsibilities. Others had a vision of a "one year on, one year off" model, with mother and father alternating primary parent responsibilities from one year or so to the next: "We had fantasies of each of us getting half-time jobs while we had babies so we could share in their care and taking turns working once the children were older."[5] But economic downturn smashed that vision for many. With part-time jobs hard to come by and the sum total of one income insuffi-

---

*This framework differentiates shared *parenting* from shared *custody,* in which two parents, separated or divorced, share the children back and forth.

cient to support a family, in 1980 we are more likely to be talking about two parents absent for much of the day, using child-care facilities, and sharing parenting responsibilities.

We have no statistics on how many women and men in this country fit the above criteria of shared parenting. Those of us involved do know we are a rare phenomenon: in the left and in the women's movement, because so few of our contemporaries (until recently) were parents at all; in the world at large because of economic, social, and ideological realities which dictate that *women* mother.

At the same time we find ourselves in a new major category of two-working-parent families.* Why should shared parenting therefore be so rare? Despite the trend of growing numbers of women in the workforce, the lack of decent childcare for very young children (particularly breast-fed babies), inadequate maternity policies at the workplace, income and job inequalities between men and women, and lack of flexible job structures leave women moving cyclically between home and workplace, and men even more firmly planted as the primary breadwinner: "The sexual division of labor and society remains intact even with women in the paid economy. Ideology adjusts to this by defining women as working mothers and the two jobs get done for less than the price of one."[6]

Simultaneously, the ideology of motherhood remains strong. With even liberals and feminists such as Selma Fraiberg and Alice Rossi arguing for the primacy of women as mothers,[7] the pressures on women to maintain parenting responsibilities remain great. A 1977 article in the *Los Angeles Times* reports that women with both children and jobs see themselves as nearly twice as harassed as women with no children and no job. "The strange thing about the study," reports the investigator, "is that women don't seem to mind." In fact, they often shoo away their husband's attempts to help, not wanting encroachment on their defined territory by an inept assistant.[8] Years spent within female-dominated households and within other social institutions lead many to believe it could not be otherwise: motherhood is women's "natural" calling and her obligation, or her sphere of power and expertise.

The traditional socialist belief is that entry into the sphere of production is the ultimate road to women's liberation: Only through entering the socialized arena of paid work can women establish the collective political leverage to free themselves from their shackles of oppression. Instead, we find the reverse to be true. Women now have a double workload—as paid worker and as housewife and primary parent. While many fathers have come forward to help out with kids and housework, doing more work in the family than in our

---

*According to government statistics, 28 percent of American households consist of both a father and a mother who are wage earners, in contrast to 17 percent in which father is the sole wage earner and mother is a full-time homemaker.

parents' time, the full sharing of parenting between women and men remains a rare phenomenon. When we hear about mothers and fathers away all day at work, and dad coming home to plop in front of the TV while mom puts in her extra day's work as housewife and mother, we feel compelled to demand shared parenting as a mass phenomenon rather than the rare experience it is now. At the same time we recognize the ideological and power dynamics that maintain the status quo. Mom will be reluctant to shoo dad away from the TV if the consequence is that he and his larger paycheck walk out the door, leaving her to support three kids on her own.

What have the women's movement and the left offered as guidance in the solution of this parenting problem? It is interesting to note that left-feminist and left politics in the last ten years, which have argued against this dual oppression of women as paid and unpaid workers, have nevertheless been vague about or even blind to the demand for men's involvement in parenting. For example, in a document drawn up by the Mothers' Caucus at the 1975 National Socialist-Feminist Conference in Yellow Springs, Ohio, the demand that men and women share equally in the responsibility for childcare is not mentioned once. The closest statement is that "collective childrearing is an absolute necessity." The 1974 Principles of Unity of the Berkeley-Oakland Women's Union were also vague on this point, going only so far as to demand that unpaid work in the home be recognized as socially necessary, and that all productive human activity become the collective responsibility of the whole society. This lack of an explicit call for fathers to come forth is again repeated in Juliet Mitchell's *Women's Estate.* Remaining vague, she calls for the diversification of socially acknowledged relationships now rigidly defined in the nuclear family. As for the rearing of children, the dominant demand has been for universally available childcare for women, without an explicit concomitant demand that men and women also share equal responsibility for finding that childcare or parenting those children.*

It is true that much of feminist writing and politics in the last ten years, with the exception of sex-role socialization and childcare projects, has been focused specifically on *woman* and her oppression, and only tangentially on men and the needed changes in their gender-related experience ("leave it to the men to figure that out"). Radical and socialist feminists, in particular, identified the

---

*The alteration of family relationships between men and women has most often been translated into a direct demand for sharing of housework (see, for example, Pat Mainardi, "The Politics of Housework," in *Sisterhood Is Powerful,* edited by Robin Morgan, 1970). The lack of attention given to men as *fathers* in the family can likely be explained by the childlessness of most of the women involved in the feminist movement in the late sixties to early seventies. Parenting was an issue that did not hit home for the majority of the women in the movement. Those who were in fact parents were often afraid or ashamed to admit it. At that moment in history, motherhood became for many a politically incorrect act.

nuclear family as a patriarchal underpinning of women's oppression and therefore often shied away from solutions, such as shared parenting, that might ostensibly reinforce this abhorrent social institution. Some radical feminists have taken the extreme "matriarchal" position that men ought not to be involved in the rearing of children at all. It has been liberal feminists who have spoken most directly to the issues of fathers who parent. While socialist feminists have remained abstract (dealing with the larger issues of sex, race, and class), and radical feminists have tended to avoid male-female parenting issues, liberal feminists have tackled the structural reforms that speak most directly to the actual experiences of daily parenting life. Liberal feminism also claims among its ranks more mothers than any other feminist tendency. Nevertheless, as more left feminists have children in an atmosphere where it is no longer politically incorrect and recognize that, to be effective, socialist feminism too must connect more directly to people's daily lives, we, too, begin looking for analyses of parenting and male-female relationships.

The lack of attention to men in parenting is not simply a feminist problem, but the left's as well. In a 1978 article on the baby boom, Sidney Blumenthal, pinpointing changes in parenting in the eighties, never once mentions the willingness or need for fathers to share childcare responsibilities.[9] Instead, he identifies *women's* desire and need to work and *women's* increased acceptance of day-care centers as critical differences that will differentiate the new baby boom from that in the fifties. He does not mention men's increased involvement in family life. The lack of attention to men's involvement when addressing parenting issues, both by the left and by much of the women's movement (with the exception of a particular radical feminist counterideology that only *women should* mother), reflects a deeply entrenched ideology, not easily shed, that simply equates parenthood with mothers.

From a political point of view, shared parenting between men and women is a novel phenomenon. Most left approaches have called for the emancipation of women by freeing them from the house and providing entry into the public sphere of work and politics: "The emancipation of woman will only be made possible when women can take part in production in a large social scale and domestic work no longer claims anything but an insignificant amount of her time."[10] Traditional left-feminists, such as de Beauvoir, have argued a similar approach. Alice Rossi, in her "Immodest Proposal," could envision the freeing of (middle-class) women from their homes into the world of the professions only by calling on other (working-class) women to enter these homes as paid substitute mothers.[11] In contrast, shared parenting among heterosexual couples demands that men enter the feminine sphere of baby powder and diapers. Their doing so is the practical embodiment of the socialist-feminist demand that women's traditional work be socially recognized and shared. But rather than turning to the state or to the public sphere—as in the demand for wages for housework/mothering or for universal childcare—shared parenting challenges the mystique of motherhood and the sexual division of labor at another critical point of reproduction: the home. As stated by a sharing father, "For me, the equal sharing of child care has meant bringing the feminist 'war' home—from the abstraction it would have remained in my mind, to those concrete day-to-day realities that transform us as few other situations I can think of."[12] It is a demand that accepts the viability of heterosexuality as one, though not the only, structure for personal life, but insists on a radical transformation in male-female relationships.

At this moment, shared parenting has several social and political dimensions. We have already pinpointed the pressing need to relieve growing numbers of women from the dual oppression of paid worker and primary parent. Also, in theory shared parenting (1) liberates women from full-time mothering; (2) affords opportunities for more equal relationships between women and men; (3) allows men more access to children; (4) allows children to be parented by two nurturing figures and frees them from the confines of an "overinvolved" parent who has no other outside identity; (5) provides new socialization experiences and possibly a breakdown in gender-differentiated character structures in children; (6) challenges the myth buttressed by sociobiology that women are better equipped biologically for parenting and that women *are* while men *do*; and (7) puts pressure on political, economic, and social structures for changes such as paternity and maternity leaves, job sharing, and freely available childcare facilities.

What, though, do we know about the actual implementation of shared parenting today? We have few models from the past, and few reports of present experiences. A woman writing about "Motherhood and the Liberated Woman" urges that "if women's liberation is to mean anything for people who have children or want to have them it must mean that fathers are in this, too. But in what ways it must change, my husband and I don't exactly know."[13] What can we conclude about the viability and political significance of shared parenting from the experience of those men and women who are trying to share "mothering"?

The Dialectics of Pampers and Paychecks: The Sexual Division of Labor in Shared Parenting

CAN MEN MOTHER?

In this argument, the word "mothering" is used specifically to refer to the day-to-day *primary* care of a child, to the consciousness of being *directly* in charge of the child's upbringing. It is to be differentiated from the once-a-week baseball games or daily 25 minutes of play that characterize the direct parenting in which men have typically been involved. One mother aptly characterizes shared parenting thus: "To a child Mommy is the person who

takes care of me, who tends my daily needs, who nurtures me in an unconditional and present way. Manda has two mothers; one is a male, Mommy
David, and the other a female, Mommy Alice."[14]

According to recent psychological studies, anyone can "mother an infant
who can do the following: provide frequent and sustained physical contact,
soothe the child when distressed, be sensitive to the baby's signals, and respond promptly to a baby's crying. Beyond these immediate behavioral in-
dices, psychoanalysts argue that anyone who has personally experienced a
positive parent-child relationship that allowed the development of both trust
and individuation in his or her own childhood has the emotional capabilities to
parent. Although sociobiologists would take issue, there is no conclusive
animal or human research indicating that female genitals, breasts, or hormonal structure provide women with any better equipment than men for
parenting.[15] On the other hand, years in female-dominated parenting situations and in gender differentiated cultural institutions can and do differentially prepare boys and girls for the task of "mothering."[16] And in adulthood,
social forces in the labor market, schools, media, etc. buttress these differential abilities. To understand what happens when two such differentially
prepared individuals come together to parent, two issues have to be addressed:
parenting and power, and the psychic division of labor in parenting.

POWER AND PARENTING

Numerous items in the popular press have acclaimed a shifting in family structure: women have become more and more interested in and committed to
extra-familial lives, while men have fled from the heartless world to the haven
of the family. Knowing that theirs is not the only paycheck coming in, more
men walk off the job, come late to work, rebel against the work ethic. The articles speak optimistically of a new generation of "family men" and "career
women" and a greater sharing among men and women in both family and
work life.[17] But we who know the behind-the-scenes story take a moment of
pause. We women who have shared parenting with men know the tremendous
support and comfort (and luxury) of not being the only one there for our
children. We see the opportunities to develop the many facets of ourselves that
were not as easily afforded to our mothers, or to other women who have carried the primary load of parenting. We watch our children benefit from the
full access to two rather than to one primary nurturing figure, providing them
with intimacy with both women and men, with a richer, more complex emotional milieu, and with role models that challenge gender stereotypes. We see
men able to develop more fully the nurturant parts of themselves as fathers, an
opportunity often historically denied to them. And we develop close, open,
and more equal relationships between men and women as we grapple with the
daily ups and downs of parenting together. The quality of our lives no doubt

has been improved immensely by the equalization of parenting responsibilities between men and women.

Yet we also know another side of the experience, that shared parenting is easier said than done. Because it has remained so unspoken, it is this latter reality I wish to speak to here, while urging the reader to keep in mind the larger context of the successes, the improvements in daily life, and the political import that accompany the shared parenting project.

> Men and women are brought up for a different position in the labor force: the man for the world of work, the woman for the family. This difference in the sexual division of labor in society means that the relationship of men as a group to production is different from that of women. For a man the social relations and values of commodity production predominate and home is a retreat into intimacy. For the woman the public world of work belongs to and is owned by men.[18]

While men hold fast to the domination of the "public sphere," it has been the world of home and family that is woman's domain. Particularly in the rearing of children, it is often her primary (or only) sphere of power. For all the oppressive and debilitating effects of the institution of motherhood, a woman *does* get social credit for being a "good" mother. She also accrues for herself some sense of control and authority in the growth and development of her children. As a mother she is afforded the opportunity for genuine human interaction, in contrast to the alienation and depersonalization of the workplace:

> A woman's desire to experience power and control is mixed with the desire to obtain joy in child-rearing and cannot be separated from it. It is the position of women in society as a whole, their dependent position in the family, the cultural expectation that the maternal role should be the most important role for all women, that make the exaggerated wish to possess one's child an entirely reasonable reaction. Deprived and oppressed, women see in motherhood their only source of pleasure, reward, and fulfillment.[19]

It is this power and control that she must partially give up in sharing parenting equally with a father.

What she gains in exchange is twofold: a freedom from the confines of 24-hour-a-day motherhood, and the same opportunity as her male partner to enter the public world of work and politics, with the additional power in the family that her paycheck brings with it. But that public world, as Rowbotham points out, is controlled and dominated by men and does not easily make a place for women within it. The alteration in gender relations within the shared parent family is not met by a simultaneous gender reorganization outside the home. A certain loosening of societal gender hierarchies (e.g., the opening of new job opportunities for women) no doubt has prefigured and created the structural conditions that have allowed a small number of men and women to share parenting at this historical moment. But those structural changes are minor in contrast to the drastic alteration of gender relations and power necessary for shared parenting to succeed. So the world the sharing mother enters as she walks out her door will be far less "fifty-fifty" than the newly created world within those doors.

For a man taking on parenting responsibilities, the gain is also twofold: he gains access to his children and is able to experience the pleasures and joys of childrearing. His life is not totally dominated by the alienated relations of commodity production. He is able to nurture, to discover the child in himself. But he, too, loses something in the process. First, in a culture that dictates that a man "make something of himself," he will be hard pressed to compete in terms of time and energy with his male counterparts who have minimal or no parenting responsibility. In short, parenting will cut into his opportunities for "transcendence." Second, the sharing father is now burdened with the daily headaches and hassles of childcare which can (and do) drive many a woman to distraction—the indelible scribble on the walls, the search for a nonexistent good child-care center, the two-hour tantrums, and so on. He has now committed himself to a sphere of work that brings little social recognition—I'm *just* a housewife and a mother.

In *shared* parenting, the gains and losses are not equal for men and women. Mom gives up some of her power only to find societally induced guilt feelings for not being a "real" mother, and maybe even for being a "bad" mother. (Remember: for years she may have grown up believing she should and would be a full-time mommy when she was big.) The myth of motherhood remains ideologically entrenched far beyond the point when its structural underpinnings have begun to crumble. She gives up power in the domestic sphere, historically her domain, with little compensation from increased power in the public sphere. Discrimination against women in the labor force is still rampant. She will likely have less earning power, less job opportunity, less creative work, and less social recognition than her male partner. When push comes to shove, she is only a "working mother." (There is as yet no parallel term "working father.")

The power dynamic for a sharing father is quite different and more complicated. On one level he gains quite a bit of authority in the daily domestic sphere of childrearing, a heretofore female domain. But by dirtying his hands with diapers he also removes himself from his patriarchal pedestal as the breadwinning but distant father, a position crucial to men's power in the traditional family. He now does the same "debasing" work as mama, and she now has at least some control of the purse strings. Nonetheless, as the second "mother" the father has encroached on an arena of power that traditionally belongs to women, while at the same time he most likely retains more economic and social power vis-à-vis mom in the public world of work and politics.

The societal reaction is also double-edged for the sharing father. Given the subculture that most current sharing parents come from, in his immediate circles dad often receives praise for being the "exceptional" father so devoted to his children or so committed to denying his male privileges. In challenging a myth as deeply embedded as motherhood, the man who marches with baby bottle and infant in arm can become quite an anti-sexist hero. But in the larger culture reactions are often adverse. A man who stays home to care for children is assumed by many to be either disabled, deranged, or demasculinized. One father, pushing his child in a stroller past a school on a weekday afternoon, was bemused by a preadolescent leaning out the school window yelling, "Faggot, Faggot." Some time ago my grandmother, in response to my mother's praise of my husband's involvement with our children, snapped, "Well, of course, he doesn't work." But as pressures of shifting family structures increase, popular response is rapidly swinging in the sharing father's favor, at least among the middle classes; and the response to his fathering from his most immediate and intimate circles is most likely a positive or even laudatory one.

When the results are tabulated, the gains and losses for men and women are not comparable: women come out behind. Where does this newly experienced power imbalance leave mothers and fathers vis-à-vis their commitment to shared parenting? Women can feel deprived of status both at home and at work. The experienced sexual inequalities in the world outside the family can create a tension in the "sharing" mother to reclaim dominance as primary parent and establish control and autonomy *somewhere*:*

> I was angry and I was jealous. I was jealous because he not only had the rewards of parenthood, he was into work he could relate to. I think one reason I nursed as long as I did was to keep myself as Amanda's most special person. It was also difficult to share one area of competence I felt I had. . . . After all, if she prefers David, what else do I have. I am woman therefore mother. I held on to my ambivalent identity as student in order to have something of my own.[20]

Structural forces dictate that she'll be much more successful in claiming control in the family sphere than in the public sphere. For some women, particularly those who start as primary parents and then move to shared parenting, it is not a question of reclaiming, but of giving up control for parenting to men in the first place.

> Neither of us could find a satisfactory way to increase his involvement. The children would have nothing to do with him. This situation probably came about because he was home less often and also because for many years the

---

*In the public sphere of work, this is paralleled by the resistance of female childcare workers to allowing men in their field, as it is one area of paid work where women do have control (and can get jobs).

children were my own arena and thus my main base of power. At some level I probably did not want Ernie to be equally important in the lives of the children.*[21]

The reclaiming or unwillingness to give up a more primary role in parenting is not easy. It often culminates in frustration or anger (self- or other-directed) when a woman sees herself as doing more or too much parenting in comparison to her male partner.

The man, on his part, can feel a number of things when his female partner claims more parenting responsibility for herself: resistant to being shut out by mom, inadequate in his own seeming lack of parenting skills, relieved to relinquish 50 percent of control in a sphere that he was never meant or prepared to participate in anyway. This is not to say that father merely reacts to mother's power tactics. As we will discuss more fully in the next section, he is often quite active in "granting" women increased power in the sphere of parenting to give him the time he wants, needs, or has been conditioned to devote to extra-familial activities.

The underlying point is this: powerful tensions arise when the sexual divisions of labor and power in the family are altered without simultaneous sweeping restructuring of gender-related power relations outside the family. Women under advanced capitalism spend too much time feeling powerless to relish a situation where, under the auspices of liberation, they find themselves with less power. I have watched many a sharing mother—undervalued, sexually harassed, or discriminated against at the workplace—waffle on her outside work identity and refocus on the pleasure, reward, and fulfillment that one can find in identity as a mother. This is not to say that she relinquishes her paid work, but that, indeed, she becomes a *working mother*. Fathers, for their part, are not often prepared for the arduous, but undervalued task they're taking on in becoming the other mommy:

> I get an empty feeling when poeple ask me what I'm doing. Most of my energy in the last six months has focused on Dylan, on taking care of him and getting used to his being here. But I still have enough man-work expectations in me that I feel uncomfortable just saying that.[22]

Even if he, too, balks at the alienation of the workplace, the flight into parenthood is not a likely one.

The tension between men and women over this issue was illustrated by the marked female-male differences in response to the first draft of this essay. Women, whether mothers or non-mothers, urged me to emphasize how *rare* it is for men to involve themselves in parenting or for shared parenting actually

---

*This desire to maintain parenting within woman's sphere as a source of power might have some influence, conscious or unconscious, on the feminist movement's tendency to avoid demands for fathers' involvement in parenting.

to work. Men, on the other hand, wanted me to put more emphasis on the growing involvement of men in family life and the actual fathering than men have done historically *and continue to do*. Both are true, and both reflect the unresolved dialectic between women and men regarding responsibility.

PHYSICAL VERSUS PSYCHIC DIVISION OF LABOR IN PARENTING

The tensions in shared parenting cannot, however, be reduced to power politics in personal relationships. External expectations, attitudes, and ideology collide with deeply internalized self-concepts, skills, and personality structures to make the breakdown of the sexual division of labor in parenting an exciting but difficult project. Often the sharing of *physical* tasks between mothers and fathers is easily implemented—you feed the baby in the morning, I'll do it in the afternoon; you give the kids a bath on Mondays, I'll do it on Thursdays. What is left at least partially intact is the sexual division of the *psychological* labor in parenting. There is the question, "Who carries around in their head knowledge of diapers needing to be laundered, fingernails needing to be cut, new clothes needing to be bought?" Answer: mother, because of years of socialization to do so. Vis-à-vis fathers, sharing mothers often find themselves in the position of cataloguer and taskmaster—we really should change the kids' sheets today; I think it's time for the kids' teeth to be checked. It is probable that men carry less of the mental load of parenting, regardless of mutual agreements to share the responsibility of parenting; this leaves the women more caught up in parenting's psychic aspects.

The more significant division of psychological labor, however, is the different intrapsychic conflict men and women experience in integrating their parent and non-parent identities. We already looked at the power imbalance that pulls mothers back into the home and fathers away from it. Women often feel tremendous ambivalence or guilt in relinquishing full-time mothering responsibilities. This is common among all women who depart from full-time mothering, either by working outside the home or sharing parenting responsibility with other(s):

> The myth of motherhood takes its toll. Employed mothers often feel guilty. They feel inadequate, and they worry about whether they are doing the best for their children. They have internalized the myth that there is something their children need that only they can give them.[23]

> To have children but turn over their rearing to someone else—even their father—brings social disapproval: a mother who does this must be "hard," "unloving," and of course, "unfeminine."[24]

Numerous studies denying any ill effects to children who are not totally mother-raised tend to be overlooked in favor of sensationalist reports of the delinquency, psychopathology, and emotional deficiencies that supposedly will befall our children if they are not provided with the proper "mother-love." And this love is "naturally" *woman's* duty and domain. Raised in this culture, even the most committed feminist "sharing" mother will experience doubt. Doubts and fears are profound because the stakes are so high. By sharing parenting, we are experimenting with the growth and development of our children; we are adopting new childrearing structures in the face of reports from psychologists, pediatricians, and politicians that we will bring ruin to our young.

These fears are fueled by pressures from individuals in the sharing mother's immediate life. Her mother is often appalled or threatened by her daughter's deviation from her own parenting model. Relatives are often resistant to the notion that a man should hang around the house taking care of a kid. People will inadvertently (or deliberately) turn to mother rather than father in asking information about the children. Letters from school come addressed to "Dear Mother." From the point of view of the outside world, even though men are being given more and more attention for their participation in family life, father remains an invisible or minimal figure in the daily rearing of children. A feeling so deeply internalized as "mother guilt," constantly rekindled by these external pressures and messages, creates in the sharing mother a strong ambivalence. Our intellectual selves lash out at Alice Rossi's telling us that we as women are the best-made parents, but our emotional selves struggle hard to calm the fear that our feminist views on motherhood may be ill-founded.

If mother guilt were not enough, women are confronted with two additional conflicts. First, the traditional structures of childrearing have produced in a woman a psychological capacity to mother. With personal observations and experience to back her up, she may have a hard time believing that a father, with no parallel long-term preparation, is really capable of fulfilling "mothering" responsibilities. As she watches her male partner stick the baby with a diaper pin (even though she as a new parent may have done the same thing the day before) or try unsuccessfully to calm a screaming child, her suspicions are confirmed. Thus, internal forces pressure the mother to reclaim control over parenting, so she can be assured her children survive intact. Men are often accomplices in this process: "Some men act out unconscious resistance to shared parenting by accentuating their ignorance, asking a lot of questions they could figure out themselves."[25] Sometimes women are not willing to be teachers. In the short run, they find it easier to do it themselves.

The second conflict arises from a woman's establishment of an "extra-mother" identity. We've already mentioned that women do not accrue much social recognition at the workplace, that they are seen as mothers first and workers second, and that when attempting shared parenting, women sometimes retreat from the world of paid work back into the female sphere of family life. Within her own psyche the sharing mother has a hard time integrating a work identity with being a mother: "When you go out to work, the job is something you *do*. But the work of a housewife and mother is not just something you do, it's something you *are*."[26]

For men, however, the experience is quite different. Historically, since the advent of industrialization, fathers' daily involvement with the kids in the nuclear family has been peripheral—usually concentrated on evening, weekend, and holiday play or instructional activities. Fathers have always been important figures in their children's lives and socialization experiences, even if as a result of their absence. The traditional father is actively involved in his child's life as breadwinner, as role model, as disciplinarian, but not in the day-to-day nurturant fashion that shared parenting dictates. The challenge for the man in shared parenting is to move from being a "father" to a "mother."

Today the growing participation of men in the birth experience of their children often stops at the delivery room doors. Contrasted to mothers, the sharing father more likely enters the parenting experience with a notion that parenting is something you *do* rather than someone you are. In early preparation for this consciousness, preschool boys in a recent study not once reported "Daddy" as something they would be when they grew up, while a majority of girls named "Mommy" as a projected adult identity.[27] In popular writing today, involved fathering is often presented as a *choice*, "only if the man wants to."

Only this consciousness could yield an article in the *San Francisco Chronicle* about a football coach who "tossed in the towel" after a 68-day attempt at mothering: "Peters said yesterday he's convinced 'motherhood' is an imposible *task* [emphasis mine] for a normal human being."[28] If parenting is something you *do,* then it is something you can stop doing. But it is much harder to stop being someone you are.*

The guilt that the sharing father experiences is markedly different from the mother guilt reported above. Often he feels caught up in his own inadequacies, his own lack of socially molded "intuition" in handling the everyday intrapsychic and interpersonal aspects of parent-child relationships. It was mentioned earlier that men often resist shared parenting by accentuating their ignorance. But often they also genuinely feel ignorant, lacking the psychological skills to meet their children's emotional needs. Learning practical skills like changing diapers or administering nose drops is one thing. Developing traits of "empathy," "nurturance," "taking the role of the other" necessary to good mothering is a far more challenging task. These are the very traits that often remain underdeveloped or atrophy in the man's life history and are not easily reinstated at a later developmental period. The shared father's male

---

*In the general population, the large number of desertions or failures to pay alimony or child support by fathers testifies to the male-female difference in "parenting permanence"; the number of women who similarly desert their parenting role is infinitesimal in comparison.

guilt parallels the guilt felt more generally by men who feel accountable for the oppression of women (or a woman) and for the perpetuation of sexism. But within a relational context, it can become magnified in shared parenting because the object of the father's guilt is not just the women he lives with, but also the children he loves and feels responsible for. This is not to say father guilt is limited only to the *sharing* father. Any father who is involved in some parenting functions may feel he is shirking his responsibilities (not spending enough time with the kids, not providing enough of an income, etc.) and ex-perience guilt.

But the guilt is felt in relationship to something he *does,* in contrast to a more central and deep-seated guilt in mothers for something she *is.* Because of this the "sharing" man is less likely to be consumed by father guilt than the woman is by mother guilt. Instead, he feels caught between parenting respon-sibilities and extra-familial identity. When people ask him what his paid work is, nobody asks him, as they do his female partner, who takes care of the kids while he works. No one is awestruck by his dual responsibilities as worker and father. But people and institutions will put pressure on him to perform as if he had no childcare responsibilities. And as a child who grew up believing he should make something of himself, that aspiration can gnaw at him. In de Beauvoir's sense of "transcendence," being a successful parent does not qualify; being successful or fulfilled in one's paid work or in public life does. Even when a man repudiates the work or public success ethic, which has oc-curred in our generation, he seldom turns to parenting as the locus of fulfill-ment and positive identity. This is well illustrated in the *San Francisco Chroni-cle* account of a financial wizard on Wall Street, a father of three, who took a year off to find himself. He spent his time lying on the couch, talking on the phone, collecting tropical fish, setting himself a "schedule bristling with physical, intellectual, and cultural self-improvement projects," and "marvel-ing" at his wife's frantic schedule as homemaker and mother. His only paren-ting activity during this year was watching his son from behind a tree when his class had sports in the park.[29] Does this represent, at least in part, the actual content of "Men's growing involvement in the family" which is making such a media splash? Coming home to a haven where one's own psychological needs can be nurtured is a far cry from taking on new responsibilities for the nur-turance of others.

Gender-differentiated intrapsychic conflicts of sharing parents do not necessarily remain quietly within the mother's and father's heads. They appear in subtle male-female differences in actual parenting among sharing parents. The obvious difference often cited is that women will continue in our genera-tion to make better parents than men because of their preparation and social induction into parenting through years of dolls and playing house. Grappling with the repudiation of socially induced guilt that to mother less than full time is to abandon one's intimate relationship with the child, a mother often vacillates among three stances: (a) overinvolvement with her child, often to prove to the world, her child, and herself that she is "supermom";* (b) respectful human interaction with her children based on her ability to explore both her parent and non-parent self and not carry the whole weight of parenting on her shoulders; (c) tension and frustration, or underlying resentment, directed at the child (or other parent), reflecting her own struggle to integrate, in the face of institutional and ideological obstacles, her identity as both a mother and a non-parenting adult.

The sharing father is less likely to experience such a tension-ridden relationship or overinvolvement with the children. He is not consumed by guilt for not parenting enough; more likely, he is being raised to the level of sainthood in certain of his immediate circles for parenting at all. He can maintain effective boundaries between himself and his child and provide unconflicted warmth and nurturance. But with doing rather than being as the basis of day-to-day fathering, and with pressures to do something loftier than change diapers all day, the pull on the man may manifest itself instead in a psychic (or physical) disappearing act vis-à-vis the children, a phenomenon reminiscent of men's general coping style in other emotional relations. Instead of an overtly conflict-ridden relationship, the father's relationship with the children may be somewhat diluted in contrast to mother's, or it may periodically dissipate. Father, too, may feel the same frustration as mother in trying to integrate parenting with other parts of his life. But he has a safety valve not as accessible to women. With more power than women in the outside world and less indoctrination in the inevitability of parenthood as his primary adult role, he is freer to pull back from his parenting and direct more energy elsewhere. One mother reports she had to leave town to accomplish this same redirection of energy away from parenting. The gender-related differences in handling this conflict are further exemplified in the following account. A mother was responsible for arranging childcare for her child one year, while the father was responsible the next year. Because she didn't have a paid job and felt it would allow her time with her child, the mother deliberately limited the number of days her child would attend childcare that year. In handling childcare arrangements for the following year, with the option of three or five days of childcare per week, the father's response was: "Five days of childcare, of course. It's my freedom we're talking about."

The above mother-father differences are most representative of sharing couples who try to balance parenting and outside work. It is somewhat different for the "one year on, one year off" parenting pair. Here, when father is "on," he is more firmly planted in his parenting seat—mom is out working

---

*This is parallel to a phenomenon that many lesbian mothers feel even more strongly: to answer society's accusations that they are unfit mothers, they are constantly under pressure to be even better than the best moms.

and just isn't there to take over. And mom, by periodically finding herself structurally in the traditional fathering role, can theoretically make a cleaner break from being a hovering mother on her year "off."* But the advantages of this model must be weighed against its problems: (a) It is becoming increasingly difficult as more people discover a single income to be financially insufficient. (b) Often the mother's "year on" is during the child's infancy, when mother is recovering from pregnancy and also breastfeeding. But it is also when strong infant-parent bonding is developing, bonding that carries into later years and makes mommy more central than daddy in the child's psyche. (c) Even with the "on again, off again" parenting model, both parents are still integrally involved in the child's life and, for all the reasons cited above, mom is still often more involved in her children during her "off" periods than dad in his "off" times.

In sum, both women and men in shared parenting relationships find themselves in a dialectical tension between breaking away from and retreating back into gender-differentiated parenting. The challenge and success in breaking away from traditional fathering and mothering is one of the most exciting social projects for our generation. For those of us who come from second-generation left families, our parents look at our own shared parenting relationships with admiration and some sense of loss and frustration that their historical moment did not open up the same consciousness and opportunities for them. At the same time the difficulties we encounter in actually implementing shared parenting bring home to us the long-term nature of our project and the necessity of working on all three fronts at once—production, social reproduction, and ideology—in the reorganization of personal life.

In this project we remind ourselves that shared parenting is necessary not just for the development of healthier relationships between mothers and fathers. We also look to the elimination of destructive engenderment and the provision of healthier socialization experiences along socialist-feminist principles for our children.

Conclusion

We have analyzed the experiences of a very small group of people in this country. At the same time, all signs show a rapidly changing family structure in which parents do not live in nuclear families at all or, when they do, both continue in the labor market. Disequilibrium is great at present: the concurrent

---

*The importance of this structural position, often outweighing the saliency of gender, is highlighted in the account of a lesbian parent who holds a paid job while her partner, the actual biological mother of the child, stays home to care for the baby. She reports feeling just like a father when she arrives home, wanting to be cared for, attended to by her partner after a long day at work.

pressures of work and what is experienced as "family upheaval" overwhelm many. For these reasons a reorganization of parenting becomes for many not a choice, as it has been for many attempting shared parenting, but a necessity. This necessity gives us on the left the leverage to introduce a new concept of family structure that challenges both the sex-gender system and capitalist modes of reproduction. The new right has been built partly through addressing people's fears about the rapidly deteriorating quality of life. Recognizing people's concern for the future, particularly the well-being of their children, the new right offers reactionary programs which, retreating to old patriarchal forms, claim to save unborn offspring from murder, shield families from untoward homosexual influence, and put the dollar back in the family's pocket where it belongs. The left and the women's movement have to address the concerns that underlie these issues. Many of us have begun to look more closely at issues of family or personal life. Some have taken the tack of defending or rebuilding the family in the face of capitalist attack. Others of us feel wary of an approach that, by uncritically "defending the family," tends to reproduce the romantic, anti-feminist thrust of the new right. We need to demonstrate the ability of *new* social and family structures to provide the satisfactions that people legitimately long for—emotional and sexual intimacy, childrearing by caring people, a sense of community.

In the latter context, shared parenting is an important political effort. It challenges an oppressive feature of the family—the universality of motherhood. Shared parenting frees women from the dual burden of paid and unpaid work, affords men access to the growth and development of children and children access to the growth and development of men, and helps to eliminate gender-linked divisions between males and females that reproduce the sex-gender system. But shared parenting must also be seen as only one aspect of the larger demand for new forms of personal life to replace the decaying traditional nuclear family and to provide solutions to the problems of personal tension, violence, and loneliness experienced by so many. We need to restructure social responsibility for children so that not only mothers and fathers, but also non-family-members have access to and responsibility for the care of children. What is labeled by many as a crisis of the family should more aptly be approached as a historical shift in family structure. In this period of flux, we can try to create and sustain a new fluidity between family and nonfamily for the responsibility of children, a greater involvement of men in this process, new kinds of authority relations between parents and children, and forms other than the traditional nuclear family in which people can choose to live. These goals necessitate addressing the interpenetration of reproduction, production, and ideology. These goals will not be achieved overnight. Yet we know much *can* be accomplished, and such efforts will be an increasingly important part of political and social life in the coming years.

Notes

I want to thank Nancy Chodorow, Jim Hawley, Barry Kaufman, Gail Kaufman, Joanna Levine, Elli Meeropol, Robby Meeropol, David Plotke, Marcy Whitebook, and the SR West collective for their criticism and support in my writing of this essay.

1. Joseph Pleck, *Men's New Roles in the Family: Housework and Child Care* (Ann Arbor, Mich.: Institute for Social Research, December 1976).
2. See, for example, Betty Friedan, "Feminism Takes a New Turn," *New York Times Magazine,* 16 November 1979; Caroline Bird, *The Two-Paycheck Marriage* (New York: Rawson, Wade, 1979); Jane Geniesse, "On Wall Street: The Man Who Gave Up Working," *San Francisco Chronicle,* 11 November 1979; Lindsy Van Gelder, "An Unmarried Man," *Ms.,* November 1979.
3. Rosalind Petchesky, "Dissolving the Hyphen: A Report on Marxist-Feminist Groups 1-5," in *Capitalist Patriarchy and the Case for Socialist Feminism,* edited by Zillah Eisenstein (New York: Monthly Review Press, 1978), p. 376.
4. Nancy Press Hawley, "Shared Parenthood," in Boston Women's Health Collective, *Ourselves and Our Children* (New York: Random House, 1978).
5. Alice Abarbenal, "Redefining Motherhood," in *The Future of the Family,* edited by Louise Kapp Howe (New York: Simon & Schuster, 1972), p. 349.
6. Zillah Eisenstein, "Developing a Theory of Capitalist Patriarchy and Socialist Feminism," in Eisenstein, ed., *Capitalist Patriarchy,* p. 29.
7. See Selma Fraiberg, *In Defense of Mothering: Every Child's Birthright* (New York: Basic Books, 1977); and Alice Rossi, "A Biosocial Perspective on Parenting," *Daedalus,* Spring 1977, pp. 1-31.
8. Susan Stewart, "Working Women Don't Get All the Breaks," *Los Angeles Times,* 31 August 1977.
9. Sidney Blumenthal, "A Baby Boom in the 80's?" *In These Times,* 30 August-5 September 1978.
10. Frederick Engels, in *The Woman Question* (New York: International Publishers, 1951).
11. Alice Rossi, "Equality Between the Sexes: An Immodest Proposal," *Daedalus,* Spring 1964; reprinted in *The Woman in America,* edited by Robert J. Lifton (Boston: Beacon Press, 1967).
12. Kenneth Pitchford, "The Manly Art of Child Care," *Ms.,* October 1978, p. 98.
13. D. Baldwin, "Motherhood and the Liberated Woman," *San Francisco Chronicle,* 12 October 1978.
14. Abarbenal, "Redefining Motherhood," p. 366.
15. Cf. Ann Oakley, *Woman's Work,* ch. 8: "Myths of Woman's Place, 2: Motherhood" (New York: Vintage, 1974); Wini Breines, Margaret Cerullo, and Judith Stacey, "Social Biology, Family Studies, and Antifeminist Backlash," *Feminist Studies,* February 1978, pp. 43-68.
16. Nancy Chodorow, *The Reproduction of Mothering: Psychoanalysis and the Sociology of Gender* (Berkeley: University of California Press, 1978).
17. See, for example, the items cited in note 2.
18. Sheila Rowbotham, *Woman's Consciousness, Man's World* (Baltimore: Penguin, 1973), p. 61.
19. Oakley, *Woman's Work,* p. 220.
20. Abarbenal, "Redefining Motherhood," p. 360.
21. Quoted interview in Hawley, "Shared Parenthood," p. 134.

22. David Steinberg, *Fatherjournal: Five Years of Awakening to Fatherhood* (Albion, Calif.: Times Change Press, 1977), p. 37.

23. Oakley, *Woman's Work,* p. 211.

24. Ibid., p. 189.

25. Hawley, "Shared Parenthood," p. 139.

26. Rowbotham, *Woman's Consciousness,* p. 76.

27. Barbara Chasen, "Sex Role Stereotyping and Pre-Kindergarten Teachers," *Elementary School Journal,* 1974, pp. 74, 225–35.

28. "A Father Who Failed as a Mother," *San Francisco Chronicle,* 6 September 1978.

29. Geniesse, "On Wall Street." See note 2.

4

Against "Parenting"

SUSAN RAE PETERSON

Introduction

Recently, friends of mine began using a new term when discussing their childcare activities—the term "parenting." They would make remarks such as "I can't go to the meeting on Thursday because I'll be parenting Daniel," or "I very much enjoy parenting."[1] Upon first hearing this new turn of phrase I was confused. What was it that my friends were doing? Babysitting? Going to a PTA meeting? Taking a child to a ball game? Changing diapers? Any of those things? All of these things? The only thing clear to me was that "parenting" referred to some aspect of childrearing and that some of those using the term were not typical, conventional citizens, but intellectuals and liberals making efforts to lessen women's oppression. I guess they believe that using gender-neutral terms is always desirable; indeed, I can easily concur that at least *prima facie,* gender-neutrality is a desirable method of language reform. "Chair" is a much better, more feminist term than "chairman," and using "Ms." is certainly preferable to forcing women to designate their marital status merely to be addressed politely.

I believe, however, that the reasons justifying such language reforms as "chair" and "Ms." do not apply in the case of "parenting." In this essay I argue against the use of the term, at least until social reforms take place that considerably lessen women's oppression. One might think that such changes will not occur unless we make a conscious effort to reform language; but this, I believe, is simply mistaken. Feminists in particular ought to be very wary of simply adopting the term, for it only *appears* to have a feminist basis; many of its advocates are anti-feminist and reactionary with respect to alleviating social oppression. In particular, I am thinking of some members of the "men's movement," the new "fathering movement," and the loosely formed "parenting movement." Given the novelty of the word "parenting," together with the recent origin of social movements adopting it, it will not be easy to clarify the meaning of the term, let alone the rationales for its use. Nonetheless, I attempt to do so here.

I try throughout to make a comparative evaluation between "parenting" and the terms it appears to be meant to replace, i.e., "mothering" and "fathering." Using ordinary common sense, my own experience of progress made by the Women's Movement, and statistical information, I conclude that "parenting" ought not be used for four reasons. First, using "parenting" is ahistorical, since there is currently no set of social activities that can be called "parenting"; the term lacks a historical or material base. Second, encouraging this change in language does not further feminist goals, because language is relatively powerless to effect changes in material conditions of women's oppression, and because using the term can falsely create the impression that women's condition has improved more than it actually has. Third, using "parenting" in any given case may be morally wrong, insofar as it deprives those doing "primary childcare," i.e., the laborious, day-to-day nurturing of children, of the proper credit they deserve, whether they are men or women. Last, using "parenting" can have dire political consequences because it can disguise illegitimate and anti-feminist motives and social actions. Really, "parenting" is an elite, obfuscatory euphemism that does much more harm to women's condition than good. I prefer "mothering" to refer to day-to-day childcare whether done by women or men, but I also accept the compromise term "nurturing."

Gender-Neutral versus Gender-Specific Terms

Many people assume that gender-neutral language is always more feminist than gender-specific language. I believe this to be the case only when the latter inaccurately describes social reality by indicating that women do not have certain roles they in fact have, or when it implies that women cannot perform certain functions that actually lie within their reach (e.g., "chairman," "repairman"). It is true that some people use "parenting" rather than "nurturing" because, for them, "mothering" appears to imply that only women can perform primary childcare activities. Yet the term "mothering" is defined in Webster's as either giving birth to or "caring for another with maternal affection or tenderness,"[2] and clearly human beings of almost any age and of either sex can care for another with maternal affection (although I doubt whether men can do so as easily and well as women, generally speaking). Equally clearly, only women give birth to other humans. But only the biological determinist fallaciously argues that because women bear children they ought to rear them. By now, the women's movement has largely discredited that view, and I shall consider it no more.

One central sense of "fathering" is "to beget," frequently used in both a biological and a metaphorical sense (as in, "Frances Bacon was the father of modern science").[3] To say that men "beget" children not only denies women their equivalent biological role in conception, but also reminds women of the tendency of men throughout history to "beget and forget"—to leave women behind to care for the results of biological mating. Although men and women do participate equally in conception (though with the advent of "artificial" insemination, even this has been altered), I do not think the primary rationale for "parenting" is to re-characterize biological reproduction. Typically, "I am parenting" does not mean "I am procreating."

The metaphorical role of fathers as begetters has been a favorite analogy for centuries in what can be called the "gardening metaphor of family life." In this metaphor, men plant the seeds and women reap the crop, i.e., raise the children. Needless to say, this division of labor seems eminently unfair to women, not only because of the huge differential in time and labor involved in childbearing as compared to inseminating, but also because sexual intercourse is much more pleasurable than the 15 to 20 years of housework necessary for childrearing. The gardening metaphor implies that both men and women, mothers and fathers, are equally necessary to family life and therefore participate equally in it, though their roles are different. The appeal of this metaphor has persisted through the centuries, even to the present.[4] I have no quarrel with feminists' desire to disparage this image of family life, but I doubt very much whether using "parenting" will contribute to its destruction.

Consider the following case. Imagine a farming community in which the men's responsibility is to sow seeds each spring. The men sow the seeds and then disappear for the summer, only to reappear in the fall to sell the harvested crop to other men in a market context. The women's responsibility in this community is to bring the crop to fruition by tilling the fields, fertilizing the land, irrigating the ditches, pulling the weeds, chasing away varmints and pests, and finally harvesting the crop for the market. The men plant and the women cultivate, analogous to men "fathering" and women "mothering." The question is, is the claim "The men and women in this community farm for a living" preferable to the claim "In this community, the men sow the seeds and sell the crop, while the women cultivate and reap the crop"? It should be clear to the reader that the neutral "farming" does not accurately characterize what both the men and women in this society do with their lives (at least during the summer), nor does it give warranted credit to those doing the most work. Now of course, calling what both sexes do in this community "farming" is not entirely *in*accurate, although it is on a high level of generality. But using the more vague and general term falsely implies that both sexes participate equally, or at least equivalently, in a collective effort. However, this is precisely what is not the case; with respect to gender roles within the family, it is precisely the lack of equality of labor performed by men and women that has been the target of feminist reform. Sowers might be *necessary* for farming (though this may be brought about simply by the use of force or monopoly), but this does not make their contribution "equal." (To claim that it is an equal contribution calls to mind the capitalist claim that capital investment is an equal contribution, with labor, to the production of goods. Laborers have not, by and large, agreed with this assumption.)

I believe that as much progress is made by using "parenting" to refer to "mothering" and "fathering" as is made by using "farming" to substitute for "sowing" and "cultivating and reaping." In other words, very little progress indeed. By all means let us try to change unfair divisions of labor, but let us withhold changing our terminology until it reflects actual social reform. When men actually do perform primary childcare, "parenting" will not be objectionable, in my opinion, on feminist grounds. At present, the term "parenting" ought be avoided.

The Patriarchal Family and the New Fathering Movement

Another standard use of "fathering" refers not to procreation, but to patriarchal roles in which men are the founders and sole authorities of the family.[5] As feminist literature has pointed out, patriarchal family structures are inextricably bound up with male domination and control; it is from the patriarchal model of the family that the term "paternalism" derives, which refers to the practice of making choices for others, regardless of the others' choices, ostensibly for their own good. Both paternal and maternal roles within the patriarchal family are aptly described by Virginia Held:

> Family and marriage texts have generally asserted that the mother's function is to provide "emotional support" to "keep the family happy," to remain calm amidst the noise and turmoil of the household, to sympathize . . . the father's function, on the other hand, is to be efficient and strong in dealing with the wider world, to be rational, impartial, just and firm in enforcing discipline, to be what is called the family's "head."[6]

Although contemporary families appear in varied forms, many families in America today are still based on patriarchy.

The model of the patriarchal family is being reasserted by the new fathering movement, which advocates a return to ancient patriarchal forms of male domination. In the literature of this movement much is written about the need for a male authority figure, though the rationale is less the old puritanical desire to foster frugality, sobriety, and industry, than it is a new psychologically based desire to provide role models for gender identity and to counteract women's supposedly harmful influence on children. Most of the publications of the new fathering movement are little more than "primers in patriarchy," which adovcate a return of fathers to the armchair, the head of the table, and the role of decision-making and control.[7] Consider, for example, the following blurbs used to promote the book *Weekend Fathers:*

> In the stampede to help women, men are being trampled!

Are you tired of being a mere money machine for your ex-wife and children?

Do you feel virtually cut off from the everyday lives of your children, unable to maintain authority, positive influence and control over them?

Divorced fathers comprise the most oppressed minority in the country—economically, socially, and emotionally.[8]

Feminists should be loathe to ally themselves with such advocates of "parenting."[9]

Although men in the fathering movement may express an apparently new-found fondness for their children, I cannot help but be skeptical about their real interest in childcare. A recent estimate by sociologists puts the average amount of time spent by fathers with their very young children at about 38 seconds per day.[10] At any rate, it is evident that in many cases men want custody at least in part to avoid child support and alimony payments. The fact is that the vast majority of men pay neither alimony nor child support after separation or divorce.[11] Custody of their children would relieve them from even the obligation to pay, as suggested in the advertisement quoted above:

The reality of divorce is that where the children go, so goes the property.

The Divorce-Domino Theory: Mom gets the kids, and of course the pets stay with them too. Since she has the family, she needs the house. One cannot have a house without furniture, so it goes to Mom. Now she must pay for all this, thus the need for large alimony and child-support payments. And so the dominoes fall, one after another.[12]

These fathering advocates commonly use the term "parenting" in making claims against wives and mothers, falsely implying that each parent has contributed equally to the fostering of the children's growth. But for the vast majority of families in the United States today, this is not the case.

Breadwinning and Homemaking

A third sense of "fathering" may be supposed to be "breadwinning." In typical modern families (which are growing less common), fathers have a job or career requiring their absence from the household for a large portion of the week, while wives have the responsibilities of homemaking. On this modern, industrial, and urban model of family life, men contribute by providing financial support to the family, while women perform time-consuming and tedious work usually classified as "consumption" by economists. On this model, a particularly good husband and father will babysit occasionally for the mother (one must note that the term "babysitting" already implies sex-specific norms, for no one says that mothers babysit their own children).

Perhaps some "parenting" advocates think that using this new term will reform this type of family structure and encourage men to participate more in primary childcare. I doubt, however, that this is so. First, the bulk of work connected to primary childcare is drudgery and not attractive to anyone, including women. Second, the workplace outside the home is so structured that it does not allow time for full-time workers to contribute equally to housework performed by those not working in the public market. We would need a 20-hour workweek to accomplish such a goal.

Notice that in the rare cases when the gender roles are reversed, we use a term such as "househusbanding" to indicate that a man is doing mothering activities usually performed by wives. The advantages of "househusbanding" over "parenting" are, in my view, considerable. For one thing, it gives us a clearer picture of what such a man is doing, namely, the household and childcare tasks usually reserved for women.

Further, using "parenting" implies that women and men are equally competent to care for children, a claim not supported by the evidence.[13] Recent work by feminist theorists emphasizes the importance of early socialization in enabling people to become competent nurturers,[14] indeed, men who do primary childcare often find that their nurturing abilities and skills are sorely lacking, even where their motivation is not. So men, lacking the socialization required for good mothering, may in fact not contribute to the well-being of the children they care for. For example, some evidence indicates that men tend to enforce gender roles more strictly than women.[15] My point here is not that men should not do mothering, but rather that we should not assume, as using the term "parenting" may lead us to do, that men are as capable as women of caring for children.

Some may object that because there are so many single people as heads of households these days, my arguments miss the point, for in many cases single parents are responsible for breadwinning *and* household and childcare; so why not say that they are parenting? But although mothers may perform both breadwinning and childcare tasks, their work outside the home is not the same as a man's because they do not command the economic power and control that men do. Hence it is inappropriate to suggest that the role of a single mother is equivalent to that of a single father. The single father is usually not "parenting" either. He is likely to be following the advice of Michael McFadden, one of the spokesmen of the new fathering movement, who suggests that men should perform childcare tasks and take custody of children during divorce on the grounds that "It's not that big a deal to take care of your small child. Most of us are able to figure out some kind of arrangement."[16] McFadden's suggestion is to hire a pretty, 22-year-old au pair girl at $200 a month! Men who hire women to perform primary childcare should certainly not be described as men who are "parenting." They are doing traditional fathering activities, and are still shoving off onto women's shoulders the painstaking and time-consuming tasks demanded by primary childcare.

"Parenting" advocates may object that I have mischaracterized them as reactionary and anti-feminist. In some respects, this is true. As Diane Ehrensaft said of mothers and fathers who share the responsibilities for children more or less equally,

> Most of us do not represent the mainstream of American society. We are, on the whole, white graduates of the New Left of the sixties, which puts most of us in our thirties. Often we hold professional, nontraditional, or "movement" jobs with greater opportunity for flex-time than most people have. We tend to congregate in liberal communities such as Boston, the Bay Area, New York or western Massachusetts.[17]

It is to be hoped that those involved in such social groups have a sincere desire to make feminist reforms in society. However, we should not forget that such drastic changes as would further feminist goals cannot be brought about by individuals in the radical fringes of society. The numbers of people involved in such groups are too small to constitute a true social reform, nor can the goals of such groups (of which I count myself a member) be considered representative of either "parenting" advocates generally or society as a whole.

Conclusion

Let us not become complacent by pretending that social roles and family structures have changed so drastically that women are oppressed no more, and that there is now a sex- and gender-neutral social role that could be characterized as "parenting." I do not say that this is an impossible eventuality, merely that until it occurs the term "parenting" is ahistorical. Putting our reformist efforts into deceptive language legislation only retards the goals of feminists, not only by creating an overly optimistic assessment of women's advances and a sense of complacency concerning continuing feminist activism, but also by dangerously disguising the motives and goals of those opposed to feminist values. It also deprives women of the credit they deserve for the hard work they perform in primary childcare.

To those who are unable to disregard traditional gender connotations of the term "mothering," I would suggest the use of "nurturing" as a compromise equivalent. And I sincerely hope that more men will become competent at nurturing. I just do not think that concocting a phony social role called "parenting" will accomplish this.

Notes

1. This essay originated in discussions with my friends Alice and David Sprintzen, both of whom both mother and father their son, Daniel. To this day, I want to commend David for mothering Daniel, while he wishes to be considered as one who is "parenting." Our discussions have been enjoyable and fruitful, as have discussions with Barbara Ehrenreich and Mairi MacRae Cohen. Also, the comments and criticisms

I have had from this volume's editor, Joyce Trebilcot, and the discussions I have had with her have been so largely responsible for the final formulation of my arguments that she should be considered a co-author.

2. *Webster's New Collegiate Dictionary* (Springfield, Mass.: G. & C. Merriam Co., 1974).

3. See Evelyn Fox Keller, "Baconian Science: A Hermaphroditic Birth," *The Philosophical Forum* II, no. 3 (Spring 1980): 299–308. (The suggestive language used by Bacon's account of "taming nature" and "penetrating her to learn her secrets" may reveal the true nature of scientific enterprise as primarily masculinist and phallocentric.)

4. A contemporary philosopher, William Ruddick, is sufficiently enamored of the farming/gardening analogy of the family as to actually advocate it as a normative model for childcare. See William Ruddick, "Parents and Life Prospects," in *Having Children: Philosophical and Legal Reflections on Parenthood* (New York: Oxford University Press, 1971), pp. 123–37.

5. *The Shorter Oxford English Dictionary,* 3rd ed. (Oxford: Clarendon Press, 1973).

6. Virginia Held, "The Obligations of Mothers and Fathers," this volume, p. 11.

7. Many of the books referred to here are included in James A. Levine's review of the new fathering literature in *Psychology Today* (December 1978), p. 152.

8. Advertisement for Gerald A. and Myrna Silver, *Weekend Fathers* (Beverly Hills, Calif.: Stratford Press, 1981) in *The New York Times,* 16 August 1981.

9. I am not the only one who is suspicious of the motives of enthusiastic advocates of the fathering movement. Molly Haskell (*New York Times,* 11 February 1982) says:

What distinguishes this latest cycle of noble movie daddies is the implication that they herald a new era: that at last men are reclaiming the emotional and domestic terrain they have so long neglected. So why am I griping? Isn't this precisely what women have been pleading for—a greater sharing of the joys and burdens of the home? I guess I'd be more encouraged if I felt these fables really did represent a deeper and more long-term commitment by men. Are divorced men really prepared to go beyond the weekend Santa Claus routine? . . . These fables smack of "what if" fantasies. Their protagonists have the self-congratulatory air of tourists who have discovered a new vacation spot.

10. See Adele Hendrickson and Joanne Schulman, "Don't Count on Winning: The Myths and Economics of Custody," *Aegis: Magazine on Ending Violence Against Women* 33 (Winter 1982): 7–13.

11. Ibid.

12. *The New York Times,* 16 August 1981.

13. See, for example, Betty Holcomb, "Confessions of Domestic Men," *Ms.* 11, no. 4 (October 1982): 39–40; and Letty Cottin Pogrebin, "Growing Up Free: Raising Your Child in the 1980s," *Families* 1, no. 4 (November 1981), esp. 43–47.

14. Chodorow, *Reproduction of Mothering;* further references are found in her bibliography.

15. See Miriam Johnson, "Sex Role Learning in the Nuclear Family" in *Child Development* 34 (1963): 319–34; and "Fathers, Mothers and Sex-Typing" in *Sociological Inquiry* 45, no. 1 (1975): 15–26.

16. Levine review, *Psychology Today* (see note 8.)

17. Diane Ehrensaft, "When Women and Men Mother," this volume, p. 42.

5

If All Else Fails, I'm Still a Mother

LUCIA VALESKA

What I have to say about women and childraising is harsh. I know of no other way to get the message across, so mucked up are we in fear, myth, romance and historical ignorance of the world's oldest and most significant female vocation—motherhood. The harshness comes from a sense of urgency. Unless we untangle the real features of childraising, the feminist movement will fail to jump its most difficult hurdle.

Three years ago in the midst of the contemporary lesbian rebellion, as a mother I turned to my lesbian sisters and said: "Mothers will be next and lesbians will look like silly putty in comparison." Mothers outweigh us in numbers, rage, and immobility. When they strike we will come up with them or they will take us down. That is how I felt. Two years later in an impatient surge toward individual liberation I gave up custody of my three children. As a result, I am a mother and then again I am not. Non-mothers or the childfree measure their words in my presence, and since I've left the fold, most mothers find me fundamentally suspect. But the view from renegade bridge is enlightening.

I see three distinct but occasionally overlapping political camps: (a) the childraisers, (b) the children, and (c) the childless or childfree. These camps share a common oppression, but they are also in direct conflict with one another. Each situation carries a series of contradictions and concomitant ambivalencies, complicated by the separate realities of sex, race, and traditional class divisions. The job of untangling the conflicts, of forging a common struggle is nearly beyond comprehension, but we must start digging somewhere.

This essay first appeared in *Quest: a feminist quarterly* 1, no. 3, (Winter 1975). Copyright © 1975 by Lucia Valeska. Reprinted by permission of the author.

The Childraisers

Mothers are not the only childraisers. Included in this group are lovers, housekeepers, babysitters, nursery, elementary, and secondary school teachers, communal mothers, relatives, friends, feminist aids, and an occasional father. They can be broadly defined as primary and secondary childraisers, with much variety and several degrees in between. A primary childraiser is the primary source of emotional and economic support for her children. The secondary childraiser is only one of a group of people who is economically and emotionally responsible for the children.

Whether you are a primary or secondary childraiser and what else you do with your time makes a big difference. The myth tells us simply that you are a mother or you are not. But the facts cast the deciding vote, especially regarding the strength or poverty of the self-image you derive from childraising. Ethel Kennedy affords a ready illustration. Tennis, horsebacking riding, golf, a huge houseful of surrogates, and the Washington cocktail circuit can uniquely influence the self-concept of your basic mother of eleven. The single mother who works a nine-hour shift to support her four children will have a different self-image. What we do well tends to create a solid self-concept; what we do poorly results in the opposite. How well we do anything directly depends on the economic and social environment in which we do it. The crunch in childraising comes when you realize that poor mothering and faulty childcare are currently built-in givens in the North American social and economic system.

Specific signs of decay are readily apparent. To begin with, we are all familiar with the dreaded question: "And what do *you* do?" (a) "I'm a mother" (b) "I'm a lawyer" or (c) "I'm a pig farmer." As a mother I was always tempted to answer with (c) because there are some interesting historical parallels. The primary difference boils down to the fact that pig farming went out a little earlier than motherhood, and so you pick up an extra point or two on its antique value. Not even the middle-class American supermom with the greatest resources at her private command can beat the inevitable failure. As the feminist movement legitimizes rebellion, supermom after supermom throws in the towel of her discontent and, as often as not, returns to school.

If being with children is a joy, why aren't we fighting harder for the privilege? Why is it, when you ask for childcare volunteers, that everybody in the room contemplates their boot laces? Why are the mothers and a handful of political stalwarts inevitably left with the job of consciousness raising (children are human beings too) and organizing childcare for meetings, jobs, community, wherever?

The signs are real. The message is clear. If you're looking for a solid self, don't be a mother, or an elementary school teacher, or a childcare center aid at all. Since failure is built into childraising in our society, there is no such thing as a good mother and no such thing as a good self-concept emerging from this work. The situation goes beyond the sole dictates of male supremacy. It has nothing whatever to do with any individual childraiser's advanced skill at maneuvering. The more privileged work out for themselves a number of ingenious, if partial, escape routes. But there you go; it is an *escape*—something to get away from. That *something* transcends good or bad mothering. What is it?

THE CHANGING ECONOMY OF MOTHERHOOD

Early one morning everybody in the world woke up and decided in unison to hate children. Hence the cure: we all wake up tomorrow morning and decide to love children. Stripped of its rational facade, this is the kind of solution which too often prevails. Many contemporary writers (Jill Johnston, Shulamith Firestone, Germaine Greer, Jane Alpert) talk of returning to the good old days when children were "integrated" into adult society, when they were treated as "small adults" and were a constant presence in the daily life of the community. It's not a bad idea. We could gather up all the children and go marching through the factories, business offices, medical schools, cocktail lounges, libraries, college administrations, board meetings, and nuclear laboratories, saying: "Here's three for you and three for you and three for you; keep them safe, happy and intelligent; we'll be back for them in 25 years."

The description of an integrated society these writers present resembles an historical truth, which in many parts of the world still prevails. But it is the entire social, technological, and economic fabric of these periods and places that makes the integration of children a viable reality. Many of these integrated children vitally contribute to the economic life of the community: they work from sun-up to sun-down. But most significant, their relationship to their mothers is relatively casual.

In any economic setting with an extended family, the mother's relationship to her children is automatically secondary. That is, the children will be raised and *economically supported* by a group of people of which the biological mother is simply one member. This is generally true for all classes, races, and cultures.

The economic settings that maintain a secondary relationship between mothers and children cover an enormous range and variety in lifestyle. They include nomadic communal gathering and hunting peoples, agrarian societies, feudal societies, and early industrial societies. Since these economic forms have prevailed for most of human history, many of the contemporary expressions of motherhood are outgrowths of an economic existence now obsolete in most parts of the United States and generally in any advanced industrial setting.

Here's the deal: the nuclear family is the result of an economic system that has come to depend upon small, tight, economically autonomous, mobile units. It is essential to capitalism because it not only meets the peculiar production needs of our economy, but also fits the requirements of capitalistic consumption. Thus, the ideal nuclear family boasts one producer and several (but not too many lest the labor force explode) consumers. It is a middle-class ideal and the norm held out for all classes. Even though the working-class family rarely achieves the ideal, it too believes this is the way life is supposed to be. In the "good" family, the man "works"; the woman is wife, mother, and homemaker.

The nuclear family provided stable family units for the advanced industrial state for a number of years. Now, the very mobility it arose to feed is turning around and killing it. The means of stabilizing and sustaining the old family have progressively disintegrated: neighborhoods, churches, ministers, relatives, etc. New institutional buffers have taken their place: TV, psychiatrists, psychologists, social workers, family counselors, school counselors, and a huge educational system.

By keeping the nuclear family limping along, these adjustments have eased the new primary relationship between mothers and children. But short of total fascistic control (no divorce, no abortion, no childcare) the attempt is economically doomed. The U.S. government has failed to salvage an institution that served it well. The stopgap adjustments have not been sufficient. Psychiatrists no longer even attempt to "save" marriages: they help people through "transitions." The divorce rate soars, giving the nation a new choice and women and children a new deal. Either the old nuclear provider supports two, three, or four families, which most men can't or won't afford, or middle-class women join the labor force with unmatched vengeance, at a time when the number of jobs is rapidly shrinking.

Meanwhile, back at the homestead, the children are waiting to go to school to make this new deal possible. A mother of three has a wait of at least nine years on diaper duty before she is free to look for "work." Upon finding that job, she also finds she must be away from home for at least eight hours a day, not including travel time. Most children's school days run two to four hours short of this requirement. Talk about credibility gaps; here we have a possibility gap. Welcome, ladies, to the working class.

But long ago, they moved middle-class women out of the extended family, Mexican, Irish, Italian, Jewish neighborhood. Mother still lives in Pocatello, Aunt Jean is in an institution up in Rhode Island, so who now will watch the kids? Arise the new childcare center: haphazard, unfunded, disorganized, and expensive. A college-educated woman earns less than a male with two years of high school training. If you even find a job, do you grasp the size of the paycheck coming in, minus babysitting, childcare, groceries, moving, housing, and medical costs? This is a framework for built-in failure.

Take a good look at the rhetoric surrounding the issue of motherhood. The term "childless" represents our society's traditional perception of the situation. Since motherhood was the primary and often *only* route to social and economic well-being for women, having children was a material asset, and to be "childless" was historically negative. Indeed, the term was often directly equated with "barrenness." Few women were autonomous; survival depended on marrying and bearing children. No man wanted a barren woman. So under these circumstances no "sane" woman *chose* not to have children. To be childless still carries a negative stigma, even though the social and economic reality has drastically changed. Consequently the question, must we be childless, is loaded.

The term "childfree" represents a new perception of reality in the United States. Not only is motherhood no longer the only route to social and economic well being, it has become a real detriment—a detriment which is clearly visible when a mother looks for a job, a place to live, babysitters, or childcare, whenever she tries to *take* her children any place she goes.

Women must for the first time in herstory leave the nest in order to gain an identity and a living wage. Yet a mother cannot leave the nest because she is the children's sole remaining legal, economic, and emotional representative. When children are barred from any productive role until they are 25 years old, it makes the job of representative tenfold what it was in the past. To be a good representative you must be economically solvent, have a solid self-concept (gained elsewhere), and have a great deal of time on your hands.

On another level, the debate between "childless" and "childfree" is purely rhetorical. With or without children, women clearly are not free in our society. Even more important, as long as children exist it is a delusion to speak of being free of them. They are still all out there, impatiently clamoring for recognition and support.

Meanwhile the government takes its own stand. It has already paid farmers not to grow food and workers not to work past a certain magical age. It pays students not to join the labor force and fathers to stay away from home. Now the government is implicitly paying women not to have children. It refuses the necessary funds for childcare in order to "preserve the American family." The new deal for children and mothers amounts to no deal at all. They are forced into an economic and social transition that is doomed to failure from the start.

CONSEQUENCES AND STRATEGIES

The situation portrayed presents distinct consequences and strategical possibilities for the three political camps: mothers, children, and the childfree. We must recognize the contemporary condition of women and children as a complex product of economic history. The problem is far more complicated than just the result of bad men in places of power. The grim fact that women in feminist collectives refuse to deal with the dilemma, unless mothers literally put them up against the wall, is one indication that our situation is not a simple by-product of the ideology of male supremacy.

Think. In general the feminist movement has benefited its members. It has given them a collective identity which, in turn, has made them stronger as individuals. Women have given of themselves freely and deeply, in order to develop this new strength. Of course we've had our casualties, but in general the prize has been worth the cost. In the case of childraising the prize does not yet equal the cost. We reflect society's perception that mothers, children, and childcare are expendable. The "expendability" is often expressed in statements such as: "Childcare is a reformist issue." But this expendability of mothers and children is built into the economic system that controls us all.

Mothers

Mothers must militantly make it clear that they are not expendable. The economic changes that have made motherhood a national disaster area can be changed. National and local budget priorities and consciousness can be rearranged to suit job, educational, and childcare needs. Of course the privileged, be they men in power or your so-called childfree sisters, will *never* give up their advantages out of the goodness of their hearts. They need to know that the price of not dealing with your situation is greater than the cost of dealing with it—that whatever endeavor they are involved in simply cannot proceed without meeting your needs. You are raising their children; they must provide the resources to do the job adequately. Mothers everywhere must caucus, organize unions, and put an end to their isolation through collective action. There is a lesbian mothers union, based in California, and mothers should use this as a beginning model for collective effort.

In the meantime, if an individual mother's situation is unbearable, and if the option of custody transfer is remotely feasible, she should give this option serious consideration. It is the surest, quickest, most effective strategy available for personal survival. It is also a political statement. It says in no uncertain terms: "If my community will not provide me with the freedom I need to rebuild my life, then I will take it for myself." For a growing number of women, custody transfer is more than an option. It is a necessity.

The potential tragedy is not that children and mothers are lost to each other, but that the decision is made in a social vacuum. There is virtually no community support. The so-called experts—psychologists, counselors—paint an invariably gloomy future for you. Even the most liberal, non-judgmental therapist tends to lose her cool at the mention of custody transfer. The one I consulted rose up out of his chair and shouted: "You can't do that." Fortunately, I disregarded this "advice" and proceeded. What women need is someone or group to share positively both the decision and the transition with them.

No mother makes this choice easily. Both the social taboo and the mother's entire conditioning conspire to keep it out of the realm of serious possibility. Another obstacle is the false assumption that the decision will be complete and irrevocable—a "here today, gone tomorrow" finality. Such is not usually the case. The details, including psychological consequences for both mothers and children, will vary with the individual situation.

Whether a child is raised by her uncle, her grandmother, two people or a group of people, and what kind of people they are makes all the difference in the world. My own three children have two sets of parents (one lesbian, one heterosexual), and four functioning grandmothers. They spend summers with my lover and me, and the school year with their father and another mother. The transition was gradual. My oldest child moved in with his father three years ago. A year later the two younger ones joined him.

In our case the change was a necessity, economically and emotionally. Perhaps we could have scraped by economically, although I had no vocational skills and was still working on a college degree. But emotionally the situation for me as a single mother was disastrous. My two-year stint in the women's movement had allowed a vast reservoir of rage to surface. The open resentment at being trapped began to far outstrip the pleasures of mothering, and the daily burden was too great for me or my kids to bear. That a healthier situation was available was a stroke of luck and privilege for which I shall be forever grateful.

Children

A key feature of industrialization is that the "workplace" is far removed from the home, which gradually leads to the segregation of children from the "business" of the world. As industrialization and technological development proceed, the discrepancy between adult and child spheres grows. Children must be set aside for longer and longer periods of their lives before they can play any integral, responsible role in the life of the community. At the same time, increased mobility combines with super media to expose children to a constant flow of new situations and a complex environment, which demands that they grow up more quickly than ever.

In essence, we have mass-produced a nation of young people who are extremely sophisticated, while we have simultaneously denied that sophistication any serious expression. Because children are segregated and constantly held down, they have developed their own culture, with values, codes of honor, and means of social control that clash with the adult ones. Even though children are packed neatly away in their ghetto—the American Public School System—we cannot avoid bumping into them, because trouble is brewing in the ghetto.

Like other oppressed peoples, children have begun to organize, to demand basic rights and responsibilities commensurate with their abilities. As with other oppressed groups who begin to rebel, society has reacted negatively to these initial efforts. Just as rape has become a national sport, razor blades and arsenic in halloween treats, and armed guards in the corridors of our best middle-class junior highs have become standard. These reinforce the children's own conclusion that they live in a state of siege.

Segregation of children has had one potentially liberating consequence: it significantly dilutes the impact of where they lay their heads at night. It is no longer possible for adults to stamp out pint-sized replicas of themselves through the nuclear or traditional family. The individual child's destiny is increasingly determined by her own community. In this respect, children are in part seeing to their own liberation. But their situation is still unique for two reasons. First, their condition is temporary by definition. Second, they are by nature dependent to some extent on the adult community. That's where we come in.

A well-developed industrial system changes children from an advantage to a deficit. Under other economic systems, children materially contribute to a family's wealth and well-being, and eventually the young take care of the old. Not so today. This change has tremendously influenced both our perception and treatment of children. No amount of sweetness and light, innocence and charm can outweigh the fact that they are a pain in the ass and cost a lot of money. Since our perception of children comes from a specific social and economic environment, it can only be changed by altering that environment. The cost of childraising can no longer be shouldered by private individuals. Childraising must move from the private to the public sphere, from the individual to the local and national community. *My* children must become *our* children.

We have begun this transition—witness the education industry. But we are dragging our heels all the way. If we compare need with designated resources, the educational establishment today is a mere welfare program. By and large its treatment of children is comparable to the treatment of welfare recipients. Imagine how different the funding for education and childcare would be if the grandchildren of our national legislators were in public childcare from the age of three months!

In making the transition from *my* children to *our* children, we can and must change the consciousness of our sisters first. And then, we change the nation. But society's perception of children will not change until we create a viable role for children and give them the resources to fulfill that new role.

In the meantime, childhating must go. It should not be replaced with old platitudes on the natural virtues of children or life with them. Rather, it should be replaced with a firm understanding of why children are "unacceptable" in our society, and a concrete strategy to include children in our thoughts and actions.

Any organization or gathering is practicing childhating if it does not arrange for quality, feminist childcare by the "childfree." Furthermore, any person who says "But I don't particularly like children" is practicing childhating. She is letting society's negative stereotype of children take over her mind. There is as much variety among children as there is among individual women. How can you dislike all of them? The statement comes from one who perceives children as an *inferior* group that is not worthy of her personal recognition or time. Struggles against racism and sexism have set our minds bolt upright on these issues. The casualness with which childhating statements are made and received is a measure of our lack of consciousness of this issue.

The Childfree

All women who are able to plot their destinies with the relative mobility of the childfree should be encouraged to take on at least one existing child, part time or full time. Love that child, teach her something she might otherwise never learn, show her respect she might not find elsewhere. Oh yes, and be consistent. Let one child in your community grow to expect and rely on your coming just as she relies on the air she breathes. You should not do so because the experience will be joyful, but because it is politically necessary for the growth of all women and children. Then if joy comes, halleluja!

To have our own biological children today is personally and politically irresponsible. If you have health, strength, energy, and financial assets to give to children, then do so. Who then will have children? If the childfree raise existing children, more people than ever will "have" children. The line between biological and non-biological mothers will begin to disappear. Are we in danger of depleting the population? Are you kidding?

Right now in your community there are hundreds of thousands of children and mothers who desperately need individual and community support. It is not enough for feminists to add to this population and then help out in their spare time. A growing number of young women are indeed beginning to resist having their own biological children, mostly from a sense of self-preservation. But the new childfree must not only take conscious control of their reproductive organs, they must also see that true self-preservation depends upon the survival of their entire community—one that includes living children.

We must develop feminist vision and practice that includes children. We must allow mothers and children a way out of the required primary relationships of the nuclear family. This can only be done by forging new relationships, with economic and emotional underpinnings, between children and the childfree. At this historical moment the goal is a moral imperative only. Moral imperatives have a habit of hanging out there in thin air until hell freezes. It *is* the responsibility of non-mothers to end the twin tyrannies of motherhood and childhood as they are lived today, but the childfree will not do so until mothers and children light a big fire of their own.

PART TWO

Mothering and the Explanation of Patriarchy

6

Reproduction, Mothering, and the Origins of Patriarchy

AZIZAH AL-HIBRI

Introduction

This essay is an attempt to explain the origins, development, and forms of patriarchal behavior and institutions. The essay accepts as its starting point the general human fear of death and the desire for continuity or immortality. It places this fear and desire in the context of the male's experience of the world, and argues that it is this context which ultimately leads to the emergence of patriarchy.

Three different theses about males are introduced, examined, and used at various stages of the discussion. In asserting each thesis is true of the male, it is not simultaneously denied of the female. However, it is argued that there is an important difference between the male's experience of being in the world, and the female's. If these theses are true of females as well as of males, they are not true of them in the same way or to the same degree.

The discussion is based mainly on data obtained from western culture, since the reader of this essay will be more familiar with such data. But what is presented here is not an account of the western female-male relationship; rather it is a speculative account, cast in western mold, that provides a structural or symbolic framework for understanding the female-male dialectic of opposites.

THESIS I: THE MALE DESIRES IMMORTALITY

Aristotle puts it this way: "But we must not follow those who advice us, being men, to think of human things, and being mortal, of mortal things, but must, so far as we can, make ourselves *immortal*."[1]

Hannah Arendt argues that

> imbedded in a cosmos where everything was immortal, mortality became the hallmark of human existence. . . . by their capacity for the immortal deed, by their ability to leave non-perishable traces behind, men, their individual mortality notwithstanding, attain an immortality of their own and prove themselves to be of a "divine" nature.[2]

Arendt defines immortality as "endurance in time, deathless life on earth."[3] Put in this way it becomes clearer that men generally desire immortality. The promise of an afterlife can also be seen as a way of allaying the anxieties of people about their mortality, which helps to explain the increased religiosity of people as they approach death. During the SALT II talks, the seriously ill leader of the U.S.S.R., Leonid Breshnev, was heard to say, "*God* will not forgive us if we fail."[4]

THESIS II: THE MALE CONSIDERS REPRODUCTION A PATH TO IMMORTALITY

There is an Arabic saying that "he who reproduces does not die." The importance to the male of having children is well known. But we need to keep in mind that the desire for offspring is directly connected to the desire for *immortality*. Fathers try to live their lives all over again through their sons. In the *Symposium,* Socrates introduces Diotima of Mantineia, a wise and revered woman with whom he has a most interesting dialogue about immortality and love. In that dialogue Diotima argues that

> to the mortal creature, generation is a sort of eternity and immortality. [For] the mortal nature is seeking as far as possible to be ever-lasting and immortal: and this is only to be attained in generation, because generation always leaves behind a new existence in place of the old.[5]

When Socrates shows astonishment at her words, she elaborates, adding at one point, "Marvel not then at the love which all men have of their offspring; for that universal love and interest is for the sake of immortality.[6] Later, Socrates concludes his account of Diotima's views saying that he was persuaded of their truth, "and being persuaded of them, I try to persuade others."[7]

The desire for a son to carry on the family's name is one of the patriarchy's ways of giving immortality to the male ancestor whose name is immortalized through the generations of his male descendents. Women rarely immortalize their own male (or even female) ancestors in patriarchal societies. More often, they only get the chance to participate in immortalizing the male ancestors of their husbands. For instance, my family can trace its family tree back several centuries, but all the names on that tree are male. It was a shocking experience to me when I realized that I cannot trace my matrilineage back for more than two generations. It appears that women have been characteristically less obsessed with immortality than men.

THESIS III: THE MALE CONSIDERS PRODUCTION A PATH TO IMMORTALITY

Production can be of words, as in poetry; or of deeds, as in society; or more generally of tools, as in technology. But the key requirement is to produce that which reflects a person's individual talent (or essence) and consequently to objectify it in the outer world, giving the producer an illusion of permanence. This mode of immortalization is seen as superior to that obtained through reproduction (perhaps because it can last longer than one's immediate offspring and is not dependent on the wish or ability of others to participate). Even Diotima concurs. According to Socrates, she wonders, "Who, when he thinks of Homer and Hesiod and other great poets, would not rather have their children than ordinary human ones?"[8] And Arendt, too:

> The task and potential greatness of mortals lie in their ability to *produce* things—works and deeds and words—which would deserve to be and, at least to some degree, are at home in *everlastingness,* so that through them mortal souls find their place in a cosmos where everything is immortal except themselves.[9]

Even Marx, in his discussion of alienated labor in capitalist societies, utilizes terminology more befitting the description of reproduction than production. The product of labor is seen by Marx as the objectification, not only in consciousness, but in the real world, of the specified character of the individual. It is duplication, it is creation, and its alienation is "begetting as emasculating."[10] And why not, since in appropriating the product of the worker's labor, the capitalist is doing to the worker what the patriarchal male has done to the female? Diotima is quite straightforward about it—for her, the product is also a child, but not a mortal one.

A Feminist Theory on the Origins and Development of Patriarchy and (Male) Technology

Early man must surely have perceived the female as the being in nature most similar to him, and yet quite different. The component of identity between male and female contributed to the centrality of this relationship in the lives of humans. The difference complicated that central relationship.

The most obvious difference between the male and female is the genital difference and related phenomena. One such phenomenon is that females can bleed suddenly and heavily without dying. (Perhaps this is the earliest reason for associating women with magic, since few men would have survived such bleeding.) Another is that the bleeding can stop just as suddenly as it starts. Furthermore, a woman's body can change shape and then produce a miniature human being, which is subsequently nourished by the female body and grows to start another full life. Meanwhile, the male body does not change, it does not reproduce, it has no nourishment for children even after they are brought into the world by females. In terms of life changes, the male body may have seemed barren and boring. The anthropologist Leo Frobenius quotes an Abyssinian woman commenting on the complexity and richness of the female's body relative to that of the male: "His life and body are always the same. . . . He knows nothing."[11]

Such differences between male and female provide adequate foundations for the male to develop the notion of the female as an Other. Nevertheless, the female Other is not a diffused Other, that is, merely something different from Self. Rather, it is a most focused, specific, and special Other, by virtue of the fact that it is another consciousness with a basic underlying similarity. It is thus understood as a complementary Other; and for this reason it occupies a central position in man's concern with Otherness.

It is reasonable to assume that during early times human knowledge of biological functions was so primitive that the male did not know his role in reproduction. Since intercourse and childbirth (or even visible pregnancy) are separated by such a significant time lag, the development of the notion of causality here could not have been either immediate or simple. Bronislaw Malinowski lends credence to this conclusion. Commenting on the beliefs of the Trobrianders concerning conception, he says,

> The primeval woman is always imagined to bear children without the intervention of a husband or of any other male partner; but not without the vagina being opened by some means. In some of the traditions this is mentioned explicitly. Thus on the island of Vakuta there is a myth which describes how an ancestress of one of the sub-clans exposed her body to falling rain, and thus mechanically lost her virginity.[12]

The following dialogue with a male native of the Trobriand Islands is recounted by Malinowski:

> "What then, is the cause of pregnancy?" He answered: "Blood on the head makes child. The seminal fluid does not make the child. Spirits bring at night time the infant, put on women's heads—it makes blood. Then, after two or three months, when the blood [that is, menstruous blood] does not come out, they know: 'Oh, I am pregnant!' "[13]

Thus, at the dawn of history the male had ample reason to experience the female Other as a substantial ego threat. In contradistinction to the male, the female exhibited a greater permanence. Not only did she constantly recover from her bouts with bleeding, but more significantly, she constantly reproduced herself—she had the key to immortality and he did not. The male, then, had cause to experience himself as inferior and mortal, as excluded and cut off from the cycle of ever-regenerating life.

It is understandable that under such a state of affairs, substantial amounts of alienation and frustration are generated in the male that culminate in feelings of inadequacy, jealousy, or hostility toward the female. Philosophical questions of the sort raised by Plato and Aristotle may well have found their primitive roots in this situation. The questions facing a male dissatisfied with his being in the world would be of the following sort: "What is my significance?" "What am I good for?" "What is my role in life, my destiny?" "What kind of being am I?"

The male's negative experience of his being in the world was also reinforced by the fact that the male has always been dependent in his early childhood on the female for his very existence.

MOTHERING AND THE GROUNDS FOR BREAST JEALOUSY

It is reasonable to assume that before the appearance of the nuclear family, mothering was quite a different experience for the male. Even today, in some non-western societies, traces of that old relationship of mothering continue to exist. In places where extended families or tribes continue a communal style of living, it is not unusual for women other than the mother to pick up a crying child, clean it up, or even nurse it with their own milk if they are new mothers themselves. As a result, it is not unusual for the child to develop attachments to some other women that are stronger than those it has toward its biological mother. I have a friend whose child refused to rejoin the family in the United States because it had become more attached to its grandmother. The mother submitted to the will of the child (not the grandmother), reasoning that when she herself returns to her homeland she will be living again with the grandmother and the child, so that the problem will be resolved.

But such a model seems to invoke an order in which women were already the nurturers. Let me explain how I see this to have come about. First, it is reasonable to assume that the male, feeling cut off from the cycle of life and lacking knowledge of his role in it, would resent not only the childbearing capacity of the female but also its final product—the child. In fact, such resentment can be detected in the male even today when the male's role in reproduction has been more than adequately asserted. Such feelings of resentment are not conducive to a nurturing attitude. Second, the child itself learns quickly that only a human being with breasts can satisfy its most pressing need for food/milk. Given a choice, the child will elect the arms of a (potential) mother/nurser. This, of course, does not improve the male's attitude toward the child. Thus, rather than assuming that only a female, because of her biology, is "naturally" suited for the role of nurturer and thus "condemned" to it, I am saying that the male, who became increasingly alienated from the child, withdrew from the nurturing process.

THE MALE'S RESPONSE TO HIS HUMAN CONDITION:
THE EMERGENCE OF PATRIARCHY AND (MALE) TECHNOLOGY

As a free human being whose essence is defined by his choices, the male had, since early times, the option of setting out to meet this challenge. At least two courses of action were available to him. First, he could appropriate the gifts of the female and her offspring; this action would integrate him into the cycle of life, if only indirectly. Hence the male appropriated the female's womb and breasts, making them his and divorcing them from their biological functions. As a result, they no longer appeared as valuable potential natural resources for humanity. Instead, they became problems to be dealt with: how can one ensure that the womb grows only the "right" patriarchal child? Even the breast, the property of the husband, must be protected not only from the world (public exposure), but even from the child (nursing causes breasts to sag, so give the baby bottled milk).

Later discoveries concerning the role of the male in conception may have further reinforced this mode of immortalization for him, and prompted the shift of male dominance from the brother and father of the female and child to the mate or husband. For, the appropriation of offspring would have been given for the first time a biological, or objective justification. The male could then see himself for the first time as appropriating what was already his, his immortalization becoming more direct than ever. Furthermore, this could partly explain why the male has gone to great lengths in minimizing the obvious and substantial contributions of the female to reproduction. He has often described the female as a mere container, an incubator, while he held that his sperm supplied the life principle. If this analysis is correct, then it was not private property, not natural law that made the male appropriate reproduction from the female. Rather, it was his unabashed desire and struggle for immortality in a world that seemed determined to deny it to him.

But the male wanted to appropriate from the female not only her powers of reproduction, but also her powers as a provider. Until recently, mothers were the sole providers of the milk that was the fountain of life and without which the cycle of life could not go on. By appropriating the female's breasts, the male appropriated symbolically her role as a natural provider. Thus in patriarchal society, patriarchy reverses reality, and the natural provider becomes the dependent/provided for while the dependent is declared the provider. This reversal carries through in capitalist societies to the workers and people of Third World countries. These true providers of labor and resources are now cast as those who are to be provided for by the capitalist—the "white man's burden."

A second course of action available to the male was that of making himself useful (and later perhaps indispensable). This approach, unlike the first, was not necessarily based on the notion of domination, but could easily be integrated with it. Historically, the most salient male application of this approach may be found in the area of technology, an area which captured specifically the male imagination. Tools that the male produced were useful in simplifying and securing certain processes in life. Thus they were ideal as compensation for a perceived inadequacy. It also gave the male for the first time some feeling of power. As Freud and others were quick to observe "with every tool man is perfecting his own organs."[14] The male was no longer helpless; he was no longer stuck with his human condition. Through technology he discovered that he could improve his condition by artificial means of his own creation. Therefore, this technological endeavor was particularly suited to the feelings of inadequacy or hostility in the male. It supplied both the possibility of liberation from his perceived inferiority to the female, and also the possibility of a better, more effective foundation for her domination. But most important, in production, the male finally gave concrete expression to his urge for having offspring, i.e., for immortality. The product, as Diotima, Marx, and others reveal, became the child. Production became an imitation of reproduction. The male's minimizing the importance of reproduction in favor of production could be interpreted as the male's way of emphasizing his own significance and of forcing himself deeper into the cycle of life.

Thus, one may conclude that both male technology and patriarchy are based on the male's feeling of inadequacy and mortality vis-à-vis the female, and his desire to transcend his human condition by forcing himself into the cycle of life from which he *perceived* himself to be cut off through no fault of his own. That this is indeed the case has become even more obvious recently. Not only did the male develop patriarchal technology as a tool for compensation and domination, but as a way for duplicating the very powers of the female he coveted. Thus in recent years, bottled milk and baby foods were developed. Doctors told women that their milk was inadequate nourishment for babies and must be supplemented or eliminated altogether. An advertisement points out that the whole family is happier when mothers use baby food, since now the father can participate in feeding the baby. In Third World countries babies continue to suffer and die as a result of the misuse of bottled milk by mothers who have been convinced by bottled milk companies that it is the best for their babies.[15] But the final straw in the attempt to supercede women's powers and make women superfluous is clonal research.[16]

THE GROUNDS FOR REGARDING NATURE AS AN OTHER

There is another dimension associated with the male's feeling of being cut off from the cycle of life. The male has often observed that the female is somehow at one with the rhythms of the universe, of nature. Her bodily rhythm is attuned to it, and nature, like the female, reproduces and nourishes its "children." Nature thus became "Mother Nature" and the connection between the female and nature became exaggerated and magical to the human eye. The belief in the affinity of the female to nature was accepted (though to different degrees and in different ways) by both males and females with interesting results. During the very early stages of technology:

> Agriculture was invented by people living within a magical world view and *by virtue of* that world view. Most likely it was . . . an invention of women, who perceived in the fecundity of seed and soil an image of their own sexuality. From that initial poetic insight the technics of cultivation burgeoned into a splendid variety of sexual-spiritual symbols. The new agrarian cultures saw the earth as a mothering womb, the seed and rain as sperm, the crops as a bearing of offspring.[17]

But it is perhaps this view of nature as female that finally led to the male's attempt at extending his domination to nature itself. The category of female Other was enlarged to engulf nature as well. For it too had the gifts of immortality, of reproduction, and mothering. On Nature too the male was dependent, and against it his feelings of inadequacy were confirmed. Thus while initially nature like woman was dreaded and respected, it later became, like the female, the target of male domination and hostility through male technology. Tools, which were initially produced for constructive purposes, became agents of subordination and destruction for both women and nature. Man had tasted power and immortality through domination and production. He defied woman and nature; and domination through production seemed to have paid off.

THE FEMALE RESPONSE AND HER GRADUAL EXCLUSION FROM POWER

It is reasonable to believe that the female did not keep up with this technological twist of events for two reasons. First, her experience of the world was substantially different from that of the male. She was planted deeply into the cycle of life and the womb and bosom of nature. Thus she had no reason to feel cut off, frustrated, or shortchanged. If she was anxious about mortality, her anxiety was not exaggerated by those feelings. So she had good reason to relate to the world in a more relaxed fashion. For example, she had no reason to be driven to produce, although she did produce. (Note that later she was driven by patriarchy to reproduce in order to retain her social position, etc., and that came to be interpreted as an expression of her "mother instinct"!) Nor did her production need to be (initially at least) tainted by hostility and frustration. It was instead oriented primarily toward improving the quality of life (agriculture, for example), and not toward enhancing her powers of domination. With the male's concentration on the latter orientation, a male power-base was gradually formed with no effective parallel female opposition. Second, the male who understood the extent of power conferred upon him by technology understandably denied woman access to his technology. Thus while patriarchy served male efforts in denying the female access to technology, technology was used by the male to reinforce patriarchy. We may also note that technology provided an answer to the male's original philosophical questions. For he had found a function that characterized his contribution (or function) in life. While women reproduced and mothered, men produced and provided (and that, the male said, was more important). This was a balance of division of labor that the male could live with. It would hardly have been acceptable for him if women reproduced, mothered, produced, and provided, while men only produced and provided. Hence to preserve the fragile male ego it became desirable, among other things, to exclude women from production (housework notwithstanding).

THE ROLE OF RELIGION

It is important at this point to note that man's attempt to gain immortality through production did not go totally unquestioned in the course of history. As Arendt points out,

> The fall of the Roman Empire plainly demonstrated that no work of mortal hands can be immortal, and it was accompanied by the rise of the Christian gospel of an everlasting individual life to its position as the exclusive religion of Western mankind.[18]

Various historical events served to reveal the inadequacy of the male's attempt to gain immortality through production. Together, they made two facts quite clear: (1) as Arendt observed, the products fabricated by males themselves disintegrated in time; and (2) even when these products temporarily escaped the onslaught of time, they ended up immortalizing either themselves or someone other than the producers. More often than not, the individual identity and life story of the producers were lost.

Religion provided a timely solution to this crisis. If man behaved in accordance with certain values, he could gain, not immortality, but better yet, an everlasting life in heaven. But again such a solution would not do if women were equally capable of gaining everlasting life. For then again, women would have the possibility for both immortality and everlasting life; while men would have the possibility of the latter only. This problem was solved along lines similar to those used in the realm of production. God was declared male, and man was declared created in his likeness. Eve became the symbol of temptation and sin; and woman was consequently judged a less likely candidate for salvation and everlasting life in heaven than man. Mary Daly summarizes these and related developments as follows:

> The infamous passages of the Old Testiment are well known. I need not allude to the misogynism of the church Fathers—for example, Tertullian, who informed women in general: "You are the devil's gateway," or Augustine, who opined that women are not made in the image of God. I can omit reference to Thomas Aquinas and his numerous commentators and disciples who defined women as misbegotten males. I can overlook Martin Luther's remark that God created Adam lord over all living creatures but Eve spoiled it all. I can pass over the fact that John Knox composed a "First Blast of the Trumpet against the Monstrous Regiment of Women." All of this, after all, is past history.[19]

One result of the substitution of the goal of everlasting life for that of immortality is that technological activity slackened considerably during this period and became a secondary concern. St. Augustine, for example, argued that the ideal state of affairs was one where the person attended chiefly to the development of his contemplative knowledge (of eternal things) while at the same time directing his reason to the good use of material things "without which this life cannot go on."[20] Clearly then, during St. Augustine's days society had become sufficiently dependent on technology and its artifacts as to be unable to do away with them without substantially threatening the quality of life; but they no longer occupied a central position in society.

One problem with religion's promise of everlasting life was that it could not be substantiated. The promise had to be accepted in faith. Slowly, man started exhibiting restlessness about entrusting such a major concern to the unknown. At the same time, accumulated scientific theories in the West continued to present ever-stronger reasons to doubt the biblical accounts of creation and of man himself. The Copernican revolution, the Newtonian revolution, the Darwinian revolution, and later psychoanalysis, all inflicted deep wounds on the male ego.[21] They also shook his faith in religion.

The process of secularization allowed the male to overthrow God-the-Father and replace him with the image of *Ubermensch*. The major attribute of this *Ubermensch* is his ability to be hard against himself by overcoming his passions and human limitations. It is this patriarchal image, presupposing a new "height" in the development of patriarchal ideology, that made possible such events as the Holocaust, the bombing of Hiroshima and Nagasaki, and the Sabra and Shatila massacres in Beirut.

Indeed, as I have argued at length elsewhere,[22] the whole history of political oppression (e.g. colonialism, imperialism, etc.) is conceptually tied to shifts and developments in the patriarchal world- (and self-) views. Specifically, racism is simply one offshoot of a particular patriarchal ideology. This fact suggests that feminist world (and self-) views are invaluable for Third World liberation struggles.

Conclusion

This theory is another "just so" story. But to describe it in this fashion is not to minimize its significance or to take it less seriously. All theories are essentially "just so" stories, and yet no discipline can do without them—not even science, that patriarchal paradigm of objectivity. I do not intend to argue that this is exactly and precisely what happened historically between males and females. Instead, I merely wish to present the reader with a story which has at once significant powers of prediction as well as explanation of patriarchal behavior. To the extent that this theory works, one can accept it.

The ramifications of this theory are many, and only some of them have been described here. Readers can reflect on the ramifications in their areas of concern. For example, this theory sheds a new light on the real threat of lesbianism to patriarchal society. It is not that of women loving women; it is women reappropriating their own bodies from men, and hence threatening to cut them from the cycle of life—from one important way in which patriarchal men attempt to immortalize themselves.

The theory outlined in this article provides a solid basis for formulating strategic as well as tactical feminist policies for dissipating male control. Essential to that dissipation is the elimination of obsessive desires for immortality. This is not an easy task. It is a painfully slow one. Nonetheless, since I am arguing that the root of the problem lies in patriarchal ideology, triggered by an obsessive desire for immortality, it becomes essential to strike at the heart of the problem and eliminate it once and for all. This goal is educational and can be achieved in a variety of ways in the home, schools, and mass media. It demands healthier attitudes toward death and dying, as well as the coming to terms with one's own being. Feminist educators, psychologists, etc., should concern themselves with devising the best possible ways for achieving this goal. Feminists should recognize, much more than they do today, the crucial role of mass media (especially television) and pour their energies into using these powerful tools in the service of liberation. This approach is meant to liberate primarily female victims of patriarchal ideology who have contracted the same obsessive desire for immortality, and have adopted the patriarchal view of children as future extensions of one's self. This "need" for children has traditionally chained women to the monogomous family and contributed significantly to their oppression. Thus, to liberate women from unrealistic patriarchal desires for immortality is to give them the freedom of really choosing the style of life they prefer.

Clearly, coupled with such efforts, we must attempt to alter society's view of children as extensions of their parents. This means that part of our task is to struggle for children's liberation. For, so long as children are seen as tools for immortality, they shall continue to be used along with their mothers.

Another major task facing women in the next few decades is, in a temporal sense, the most urgent one. It involves reproductive research conducted by men and threatening to make women's reproductive powers obsolete. This research is much more advanced than is generally believed (see note 16). If my theory of "womb/breast jealousy" is correct, then women may very well be devalued with the success of the research, and technology will replace the womb as the "civilized" way to reproduce. With the existing power structure, and the male's historic jealousy toward the female, this may result in total separation. At that point total separation will keep women from reproducing, while men clone themselves. In short, women may become extinct.

Thus, the male's attempt to seize (in a new technological way) the power of reproduction from woman must be faced today before it is too late. This means that women should organize and claim supervision and control of such research projects. They should also be developing adequate technological sophistication to run their own reproductive research that could protect them from future catastrophies. (For example, under what conditions can one egg fertilize another? It doesn't look possible now, but neither did cloning before substantial research was devoted to it.)

Finally, feminists should study the history of Third World struggles as a way of understanding how vicious the enemy can get when he thinks his victims are dispensable. Such a study should then inform both feminist theory and practice, opening up to a more dynamic and seasoned approach. To this day, many Third World women have not closed ranks with the American feminist movement because it is seen as white. Its whiteness stems partly from the middle-class issues the movement has traditionally been identified with. But that whiteness also stems from the understandable complacency of many white women who never had to run for their lives. Most Third World women do. Thus it is imperative that the American feminist movement work hard at attracting American women of color, and at integrating their perspective into the heart of feminist ideology. Only then will women of all colors be prepared for the coming onslaught.

Notes

1. Aristotle, *Nicomachean Ethics,* 1177b 31; in *The Works of Aristotle,* volume 9, edited and translated by W. D. Ross (London: Oxford University Press, 1944) (emphasis mine).

2. Hannah Arendt, *The Human Condition* (Chicago: The University of Chicago Press, 1969), pp. 18, 19.

3. Ibid., p. 18.

4. *Time,* 25 June 1979, p. 15 (emphasis mine).

5. Plato, *Dialogues,* translated by B. Jowett, edited by J. D. Kaplan (New York: Pocket Books, 1951), pp. 212, 213.

6. Ibid., p. 213.

7. Ibid., p. 219.

8. Ibid., p. 215.

9. Arendt, *The Human Condition,* p. 19 (emphasis mine).

10. Karl Marx and Frederick Engels, *Collected works,* vol. 3 (New York: International Publishers, 1975), p. 275.

11. Quoted in Adrienne Rich, *Of Woman Born* (New York: W. W. Norton, 1976), p. 126.

12. Bronislaw Malinowski, *The Sexual Life of Savages* (New York: Harcourt, Brace and World, 1929), p. 182.

13. Ibid., p. 188.

14. Sigmund Freud, *Civilization and Its Discontents,* edited and translated by James Strachey (New York: W. W. Norton, 1961), p. 37.

15. For more on this, see *Technology and Human Affairs,* edited by Larry Hickman and Azizah al-Hibri (St. Louis: C. V. Mosby, 1981) pp. 575-80.

16. For more on this, see my paper "Reproductive Technology and the Future of Women," forthcoming.

17. Theodore Roszak, *Where the Wasteland Ends* (New York: Doubleday, 1972), pp. 373-74.

18. Arendt, *The Human Condition,* p. 21.

19. Mary Daly, *Beyond God the Father* (Boston: Beacon Press, 1973), p. 3.

20. Frederick Copleston, S. J., *History of Philosophy,* vol. 2 (New York: Image Books, 1962), Part 1, p. 73.

21. See similar remarks made by Sigmund Freud, *Collected Papers,* vol. 4, edited by J. Riviere and J. Strachey (New York: The International Psycho-Analytical Press, 1924-50), pp. 351-55.

22. See my "Capitalism Is an Advanced Stage of Patriarchy," a longer and older version of this paper, in *Women and Revolution,* edited by Lydia Sargent (Boston: South End Press, 1981).

7

Womb Envy: An Explanatory Concept

EVA FEDER KITTAY

"Gack, gack, gack, I have laid an egg," sang the hen. "Cock-a-doodle-do," crowed the cock for he was as proud as if he had laid the egg himself.

Hans Christian Andersen

It is certain that envy is the worst sin that is; for all other sins are sins only against one virtue, whereas envy is against all virtue and against all goodness.

Chaucer

Toward a Concept of Womb Envy

The facts of sexual desire and the apparent need for two distinct sexes to perpetuate the species have given rise to that sense of "incompleteness" so amusingly represented by Plato's Aristophanes in the *Symposium*. In his portrayal, Aristophanes speaks of mankind's original nature, in which each individual was composed of man-man, woman-woman, or man-woman. These "whole" individuals were split in half, creating forever the longing for "the other half," the longing we now experience as sexual desire. Such a sense of "incompleteness," as well as the curiousity our species manifests, makes plausible the view that among both sexes we would find a curiosity concerning, and even a desire to possess, the genital organs and functions of the other sex.

Freud claimed that women felt such desires and that they envied man his penis. Indeed, Freud claimed that this envy was a "primary narcissistic wound" for the woman and as such constituted a central element in her personality formation. The question arises as to whether there might not be a parallel envy on the part of men which similarly might constitute a primary narcissistic wound for them. Freud never argued for or against this view, although his silence spoke loudly against such a thesis. The notion of penis envy and the significance Freud accorded it have not gone unchallenged, both by feminists and other critics of psychoanalysis. Although the notion of a parallel envy is suggested by the Freudian concept, we can independently raise the question of whether men, generally, might not envy women's distinctive sexual apparatus and functions and whether such envy might constitute a significant element in their personality development having explanatory force with regard to both individual actions and cultural institutions. Such envy I designate "womb envy," meaning by the term not merely envy of the specifically named organ but of the complex of a woman's organs and capacities, particularly as it relates to her distinctive childbearing functions.

A great deal of clinical, anecdotal, anthropological and cultural data suggest that men, in various cultures and through diverse historical periods, have desired to possess woman's capacities and functions. Some of Freud's own case studies document fantasies on the part of men and boys for woman's organs and functions. Similar fantasies and expressed wishes have been recorded by other analysts and psychotherapists. Bruno Bettelheim (1954), for example, writes of the schizophrenic young boys and adolescents in his school who expressed the desire to be able to bear children and felt "tormented by the desire to possess female breasts," which the boys generally regarded as sources of power (p. 32).

Anecdotal data concerning seemingly normal boys and men are available to the intrepid inquirer. Mothers have described the various antics of their "pregnant" young boys, who stuff pillows under their shirts (including one who used instead a puppy wrapped in a sheet, which he then dramatically unveiled at "birth"). They also tell of daughters who taunt their brothers with the fact that only girls can give birth. One young boy, between three and four years old, who asked when he would develop breasts, was disappointed to learn that he would not and repeatedly asked when he would bear his own children, although it was often explained to him that only women give birth. When, at age six, he had a mild stomachache, he remarked, wistfully, that it felt as if a baby was moving around in his belly. Ross (1974) conducted a study with young boys and recounts many anecdotes of a similar nature.

In college classrooms where I have discussed the question of womb envy, there have always been at least some men who were willing to admit feeling jealous of woman's childbearing capacity. Many men, after hearing me describe my own favorable childbearing experiences, have spoken openly of their envy.[1]

Anthropological research is a rich source for data suggesting that, in cultures very different from our own, men express similar desires. Margaret Mead, speaking of the initiation rites of New Guinea societies, says that their basic theme is that:

> Women, by virtue of their ability to make children, hold the secrets of life. . . . Man has hit upon a method of compensating himself for his basic

inferiority. . . . They can get the male children away from the women, brand them as incomplete and themselves turn boys into men. Women, it is true, make human beings, but only men can make men. (Mead, 1949, p. 103)

Within our own culture we find persistent metaphors and images of procreation where the one who is "birthing" is male, not female. Consider the birth of Eve from Adam's rib or the male poets and scientists who speak of their "brainchild," as well as the pervasive use of the procreative female powers as metaphor for men's creativity.

Suggestive as such data may be, they do not constitute *evidence* for the existence of womb envy as an underlying psychological reality having explanatory force. Two sorts of considerations enter here: one conceptual, concerning the nature of envy; the second methodological, concerning the nature of evidence. With respect to the first, not all our wishes or desires are envious. We need to ask what is required for a desire to be envious. With respect to the second, we need to show that materials such as those cited above are not merely surface phenomena reducible to or explanable by other psychological concepts.

The concept of envy. Let us consider first the conceptual question. Although most would agree that the spontaneous flight of birds is something humans find desirable, no one would seriously propose "wing envy" as a significant psychological component of human personality formation. Why not?

It might appear at first that we do not envy the bird because we recognize the impossibility of acquiring the desired characteristic. But if this were sufficient to forestall envious feelings, then penis envy would have to take its place next to "wing envy." Unfortunately, we can feel envious even when we know it is impossible to acquire what we desire; witness the short man's envy of the tall man's height.

We do not envy the bird its flight, not because we recognize spontaneous flight as an impossibility, but because the bird is too dissimilar to ourselves for us to begrudge it the joy we imagine in flying. We only envy someone the possession of a desired object if we can *identify* with that individual, that is, if we regard the other as sufficiently similar to ourselves that we may imagine the other's qualities or possessions as our own. If we can perceive ourselves as sufficiently similar, the fact that the other possesses that object and we do not seems unduly arbitrary.[2] To say that we do not identify sufficiently with a bird to be able to envy it is to say that we do not, except perhaps in rare poetic fantasies, project onto a bird those qualities we subjectively deem to be our essential qualities. We do not regard it as an accidental property that we are human and not birds, while it does appear accidental that we are, let us say, short-limbed rather than long-limbed. As different as men and women are from one another, they are not so different that they cannot identify with one another and to some extent view their gender as "accidental." As I specify what I mean by the term "identification," I will claim that the young boy's identification with his mother plays a prominent role in the formation of womb envy.

Envy is an essentially negative and destructive emotion. Spinoza defined it as "hatred, insofar as it induces a man to be pained by another's good fortune and to rejoice in another's evil fortune."[3] Melanie Klein (1957) defines envy as "the angry feeling that another person possesses and enjoys something desirable—the envious impulse being to take it away or to spoil it" (p. 187). The desire to fly may be a desire stimulated by the flight of a bird, but there need be no attendant ill-will toward the creature who naturally possesses that capacity.

Were man always and everywhere to have treated woman with equality, we could scarcely believe that such desires were envious. But since mankind's history is one in which men have acted contemptuously, condescendingly, and abusively toward women (although periodically *woman's image* has been glorified and sanctified), it appears worth pursuing the question of whether this depreciation and concomitant exploitation might not have at its root some deeply felt envy. Since woman's most distinctive difference lies in her procreative capacities and related functions and characteristics, and since so many theories concerning her supposed inferiority center on matters sexual, it seems not unreasonable to look for the source of such ill-will in envy of those very differences and those unique powers.

The methodological consideration: What is to count as evidence? How can we establish that womb envy is a concept with explanatory value? If Freud is correct with regard to the mechanism of repression in matters we do not easily admit to, we must look for our evidence not in straightforward declarations, but in the circuitous expressions psychoanalysis has so well described, e.g., conversion formations, displacements, reversals, etc. However, these can be regarded as symptoms of an underlying and repressed womb envy only if we have some antecedent reason for believing that there is such a thing. Compare the case of penis envy. Its presumed validity as a fundamental psychological phenomenon is guaranteed, not simply by "clinical observations," but by the place it occupies within Freudian theory and therapeutic practice. To deny the existence of penis envy one must offer another theoretical interpretation of the phenomenon that it purports to describe and explain, and one must necessarily strike a significant blow to the Freudian picture of the female personality. Similarly, to establish the validity of the concept of womb envy, we need to secure for it a place in a theoretical framework.

A logical candidate is Freudian psychoanalysis. Beyond the fact that the phenomenon received some attention in the early history of psychoanalysis

(Ross, 1975), some central doctrines in Freudian psychology would seem to demand an inclusion of such a notion; in particular, his doctrine of an inherent bisexuality and the positing of an "ancient symbolic equivalence" between penis and baby.[4]

We know that Freud himself never developed any of these theoretical considerations favoring the inclusion of womb envy into the heart of psychoanalytic theory. The main trend of psychoanalysis continues to ignore womb envy and to exclude it from serious consideration. Following Freud's lead, apparent clinical manifestations of womb envy are considered indications or autoerotic or homosexual desires; i.e., they are considered only in terms of *male* sexuality.[5] But the Freudian reduction of womb envy to concepts of a male-centered sexuality is faulty; Freudian theory is seriously defective insofar as it fails to recognize anything intrinsic in woman's sexuality.[6] Freud made what he took as the genuinely feminine wish for a child compensatory only, replacing the wish for the valued genital organ, the penis. In the concept of penis envy, a woman's sexuality becomes defined exclusively in terms of man, for she adapts her sexuality to receive the penis and to transform it into a baby.

On this account, the idea of womb envy is incomprehensible, even incoherent, for although the physiological organs exist in women and not in men, there is *psychologically* nothing to envy: the woman bears a child to compensate herself for the penis the man already possesses. It is incoherent to speak of an envy for the *compensation* for something that one *already* has. It is as if a rich man who owned an original Picasso were to envy a poor man's cheap reproduction of the same Picasso. As for a woman's sexuality, it is nothing but what is adapted for men—for a man to envy it is to covet that which is already for his use. Men's wishes to possess aspects of a woman's body can then only be expressions of homosexual longings for the father, and pregnancy wishes must be forestallings of castration fears along with regressions to an earlier pregenital stage (anal eroticism). Given Freud's view of femininity, there is no room for womb envy. This is why Freud, astute observer and theoretician that he was, remained blind to the significance of womb envy and why orthodox Freudian psychoanalysis still cannot incorporate this concept.

The notion of penis envy, as many feminists have argued, has force only in the situation of woman's subordination to man. Within the context of patriarchical male dominance, where Man is the Essential and Woman the Other, sexual differences cannot be simply differences. They take on symbolic significance as hierarchical differentia so that features of men are positively marked and those of women are lacks, defects, or excesses. But then, ought we not to argue that womb envy is subject to the same social circumstances; those which value what is male and devalue what is female? Freud might then, after all, be justified. Just as there is no room in his theory for womb envy, the possibilities of the "womb" may be so devalued that there is no place for envy. We only envy what we value.

If boys learned of women's sexual characteristics only after they had learned what Freud called "the normal male contempt for women," we might expect this to override any natural curiosity about what it must be like to possess the female anatomy. But clearly boys learn about breasts early in life—from birth, if nursed. Even when placated with stories about storks, children still connect a child's arrival with mother—it is mother to whom the stork bestows the gift. For boy and girl alike, the wonder of woman precedes her symbolic "castration."

Beyond curiosity there is the fascination and awesome quality of creation itself—the transmutation performed by the parturient woman from nothing to an existent. The creation of a baby must seem to the child, as indeed it seems to many adults still, the most wondrous of all magical acts. The girl grows up knowing that she is in possession of the physiology that holds this secret. As she becomes a woman, this knowledge is part of who she is and how she lives her life. If she loses or is deprived of this capacity, that loss may have significant impact on her, but the deprivation will not have been a structure of her personality in the way in which, I will argue, it is so for men. In *this sense* no woman can have womb envy.[7]

Ultimately, more important is the child's intense early relation to the woman who mothers, and who is the first external object with which the child identifies. It is in terms of this relationship that womb envy gains its force, particularly in light of aspects of the child's emotional and cognitive development which shapes her or his conception of sexual identity and gender-related aspects of power.

An Account of Womb Envy

In the following pages I will attempt to develop a theoretical framework from which to derive the notion of womb envy. I will argue that such envy does not simply emerge from a man's perception of the species similarities between the two sexes, but that it first arises before the boy child understands that the differences between men and women are such as to preclude his bearing a child, in fact before he perceives any relevant difference between himself and his mother. Further, I will argue that the force of the child's affectional ties to the mother creates a sense of identity with her that fuels the subsequent envy. Finally, I will claim that the general societal devaluation of woman renders this identification, along with the desire to bear children, far more problematic than the bare biological, procreative difference would warrant. That is to say, I will argue that just as "penis envy" derives its force not from mere biological difference—although that difference is a potential source of envy—but from the context of cultural male supremacy, so "womb envy" assumes its strength and fury within this same context.

PRIMARY IDENTIFICATION AND THE DESIRE TO MOTHER

The notion of identification I will employ for this discussion approximates that of Lawrence Kohlberg (1966). It involves "a perceived conceptual similarity between the self and the model" but may also rest upon "the existence of a strong emotional attitude or tie to the other, i.e., upon a relationship of love for, or of control by, the model" (p. 125).

A child's identification with its mother is grounded in its earliest relationship to her. Out of that relationship grows the child's own sense of self, from its initial total dependency to its sense of separateness of and love for the mother's person. The sense in which a child identifies with its mother is a complex one, based in part on cognitive recognitions of similarity, but more basically on affective ties such that the boundary relations between oneself and one's mother and between aspects of oneself and of one's mother shift about. We identify with our mother because, ultimately, the self we recognize is forged in relation to her; aspects of her relation to us are experienced by us as aspects of our own identity.[8] It is an identification crucial both to our sense of who we are and to our efforts at mastering our world. Ruth Mack Brunswick (1940) writes that "each bit of activity is based to some extent on an identification with the active mother" (p. 298).

In this identification we can find the germination of parenting impulses in children as young as ten months, according to some writers (see Ross, 1977). Although the child is still too young to formulate, much less to articulate wishes for a baby, it behaves in relation to what Winnicott (1953) has called "transitional objects" (e.g., a blanket, a toy, a set of babbling sounds) in ways which are distinctly imitative of the mother's relation to the child; the child sometimes adopting the role of mother, sometimes of child. The behavior in regard to the early transitional objects may be less an expression of a desire to have a child than of an effort toward what Ross and others call "self-parenting."

The child's awareness of the mother as the one who fulfills needs and offers gratification and love increases as the child moves from a situation of total dependence to partial independence. Chodorow writes, "Felt dependence increases as real dependence declines" (p. 68). The object love for the mother, which replaces the early narcissistic love for her, comes with this felt dependence. But so does an appreciation of her power and control. As we recognize her separate existence, we recognize that only her compliance with our wishes, and not our wishes alone, are responsible for the fulfillment of our desires. The love we grant our mothers is not only a gratitude for her satisfaction of our needs, but also an appreciation of her power to withhold gratification and a gratitude that this power was used instead to fulfill needs and give pleasure.

We can presume that for the child, the special relation the mother bears to it must have an equally special warrant—and what else would serve as such a warrant if not the awesome power to create life itself? We could perhaps reconstruct the thought along the following metonymic sequence: what we create out of our own self is a part or extension of ourselves; what is an extension of ourself belongs to us; this is then our possession; our possession is ours to dispose of or care for as we wish. That the child regards itself as the mother's possession, and that her love and control are somehow grounded in her birth-giving capacity may be seen in children's sexual hypotheses: e.g., that babies are made from milk, or are born of breasts or carved out of the mother's body. These theories indicate "a young child's initial confusion and equation of nurturance with birth and productivity" (Ross, 1977, p. 331).

That the warrant of the special relation of mother and child is somehow rooted in the mother's childbearing is also expressed in Freud's case of Little Hans. When the boy, at age five, finally assimilated the information that only women can give birth, he was puzzled by the father's role and the father's relation to him. His confusion was expressed in questions directed at his father such as, "I belong to *you* too, don't I?"

Ross's research, as well as my own inquiries and Freud's description of young Hans, seems to confirm that between the ages of two-and-a-half and four, boys appear to be particularly expressive and insistent about their beliefs and desires that they will bear children. At this time children have the requisite cognitive skills needed for such representations, and while they have some conception of gender and genital differentiation, these are not yet fully formed. It is also a time of special importance in the process of separation and individuation and marks, particularly for the boy, the period intermediate between the pre-Oedipal attachment to the mother and the Oedipal conflict. I propose that the confluence of cognitive and psychosexual affective factors renders the child's wish to bear and nurture children especially important at this juncture in the lives of both boys and girls.

A study by Rabban (1950) supports the view that these years are salient ones for boys' desires to adopt the parenting of the mother. Rabban investigated the gender-identification of middle- and working-class children, ages three to eight. In each social group there were fifteen girls and fifteen boys of each age. He asked the children whether they would like to be mothers or fathers when they grew up. In the middle-class group at age three, only four of the boys wanted to be fathers, while the rest wanted to be mothers; eight of the girls wished to be mothers. Among working-class three-year-olds, nine girls and eight boys responded that they wanted to be mothers. The figures clearly favor the choice of the mother.[9]

It is significant that Rabban found among the three-year-olds some confusion as to their own sexual identity. Although most three-year-olds answered correctly when asked whether they were girls or boys, by age four all but two answered correctly, and over age five no one erred. Further, when presented, at age four, with dolls whose sex they were to identify, all correctly identified the sex of the dolls. At age three, the responses were far less consistent. One may infer that while most three-year-olds have some conception of their own sexual identity, they do not as yet have a clear conception of gender as a category nor a sense of what characteristics differentiate men and women.

By age four, children appear to have developed cognitive capacities to recognize gender as a category, i.e., as having distinctive properties that remain fixed through time and constant through a variety of changes. This development parallels other cognitive advances. Before the age of four, children have not yet acquired a conception of quantitative constancies that enables them to understand that it is possible for a volume of liquid, for example, to remain constant when it is poured from a short, stout container to a long, thin container. A nice example of the difficulty a young child has in understanding constancy through change is provided by a two-and-a-half-year-old. Confronted with a large mushroom in the identical spot where a week earlier a small mushroom had been, and asked by his father how the large mushroom had gotten there, the boy answered: "the little mushroom died and the big one grew (or came) in its place."

Until four years of age, a boy may know that he is a boy, but may no more understand that this means that the male characteristics which now qualify him as a boy will develop into those which will then make him a man, than this child understood that it is the same mushroom which is small when young and large a week later. Until the child understands qualitative constancies, the boy can express his desires to have breasts and bear children unimpeded by the knowledge that such wishes are impossible. At this point, for boys as well as for girls, such desires are less envy for what they do not possess than projections into the future of ways in which they expect to be able to emulate mother. Notice that children's ignorance on these points need not be due to adults' failures to sufficiently enlighten them, because even when enlightened, children appear unable to assimilate such information.

Once the cognitive capacities have developed, the child is far less confused about its sexual identity, the sexual identity of others, and projections of its future parental role. In Rabban's study, the sex appropriateness of parental choice improved dramatically in the fourth-year children. In the working-class group, 11 boys and 12 girls chose appropriately; among the middle class, 13 boys and 13 girls chose appropriately.

THE NARCISSISTIC WOUND

Given these empirical and theoretic considerations of the formation of a child's gender identification and differentiation we can postulate that sometime after the age of four, the young boy must relinquish his aspirations to imitate and perhaps compete with his mother in her childbearing capacities. The realization that his body does not contain such possibilities would be affectively equivalent to the sense that these capacities were now irretrievably lost. Because he expected to be able to bear children and perhaps nurture them from his own substance—feats to which he attached immense importance, for they were the basis of his "belonging to" his mother—the relinquished expectations constitute a *loss*, indeed a narcissistic wound (and grounds for a lifelong sense of inferiority; see Freud, 1928) at the very least comparable to the girl's vis-à-vis her "absent penis." With the lost capacities must come as well a sense of lost power, or better, belief in a serious limitation to one's power and hence a loss of self-esteem.

The full sense of loss most likely does not come until a few years later, for what is of further significance is that around age four, children also gain an awareness of a hierarchical ordering of the newly apprehended sexual differences. Kohlberg presents data that by ages four to five, American children, almost without exception and regardless of the particularities of the home situation, regard men as greater than women along parameters of both (a) violence, danger, and aggression and (b) size and strength. Kohlberg points out that "the general concreteness of young children's thought leads them to define social and behavioral attributes in concrete body terms," and that "size becomes a basic indicator for all important age-status differences, e.g., differences in strength, in knowledge or smartness, in social power and in self-control" (p. 102).

By age four or five, then, children have established discriminations and hierarchies which their subsequent understanding of male-female roles and relations of social and economic power will reinforce and stabilize into an assignment of superior social power and prestige to the man. According to a number of studies cited by Kohlberg, "While children under five do not seem to differentiate roles by social power, . . . by age six–seven almost all of a sampling of American children are aware that high power roles are assigned to men" (p. 102).[10]

It appears that the ages of four through seven are years in which the child sees the early power of the mother eroded, a power which the father may or may not have shared with her, and the supremacy of the father and his sex established. Freud assigns to this period the child's realization that the "phallic mother" is in fact a castrate. If one interprets the phallus as a concrete and masculine symbol of power, we have a perfect coincidence with the children's dawning awareness of gender-related power differentials. But most pertinent here is the boy's awareness that the person with whom he identified before he understood the gender-relevant ways in which he differed from his mother, that the mother to whom he attributed so much power by virtue of their relationship and her procreative capacities and whose powers he so wanted to share, is in the wider view of society (and even religion) a devalued person.

In *The Reproduction of Mothering,* Chodorow claims that the need for the boy to repress not only the Oedipal love but also the early pre-Oedipal identification with the mother, a repression which is required of him for the appropriate gender identity to take place, carries a substantial emotional cost for the male child and importantly decreases his affective relational (including nurturant) capacities in his future development. Chodorow's account needs to be supplemented with a discussion of the fate of those desires that pertain to the pre-Oedipal identification of the child with the mother's childbearing capacities, particularly in light of the concomitant recognition of the higher status men possess. We have already argued that the boy experiences a loss with regard to such capacities. It becomes a more acute loss as he understands that genital differences are the source of gender differences which both render him incapable of bearing children and qualify him as a member of the superior caste. In the studies cited by Kohlberg, it appears that this does not happen until age five to seven.

Before the boy understands the nature of genital difference in the exclusive division of the sexes into two genders, he can continue to desire to be androgynous, i.e., to concretely and symbolically retain his penis, but wish for woman's childbearing anatomical features as well.[11] He may even be willing to sacrifice the actual penis for the desired procreative power of women: one little boy asked his mother, "If I cut off my penis, then could I have a baby?" But his full comprehension of sex and gender differentiation makes him realize that he would possess mother's birth-giving powers only at the expense of his superior position which is equivalent to his masculinity, and which, in turn, stands in direct opposition to the femininity of his mother, which makes her at once capable of giving birth and a devalued person. To the extent that he does not want to relinquish the desire to bear a child, he finds himself desiring what only an inferior being may possess and indeed the very thing that clearly marks her as inferior, even though in the child's not very distant past it had marked her special potency. This must be a baffling and difficult situation for the young boy. His superior position vis-à-vis women should enable him to possess whatever they possess that he deems desirable—such are the prerogatives of superior status, or else what good is it? But here is a desired capacity which only an inferior being can possess, and her inferior status is intimately tied to her unique possession of that capacity. Is it then that he learns that such desires are unworthy of him (as are the tears he sheds as he learns, within our culture at least, that such tears are womanly and unworthy of a "little man") and that he must revalue and devalue birthgiving (and related nurturing) if he himself is not to be devalued and thought "unworthy" of his manhood?

How is the young boy to resolve his dilemma? Most likely he will take up some defense against his envious feelings, one which is made available to him within his cultural setting and which answers to the way in which the problem presents itself to him. In the following section, I will argue that the defenses ultimately fail to compensate for the sensed loss, but not without, in the wake, causing harm to women who become the objects of the envy. In the final section, I shall suggest directions in which to look if we are to dissipate the envy itself.

The Consequences of Womb Envy

The groundwork for "womb envy" is laid in early childhood. While I have made my discussion concrete by employing data and studies that draw primarily from what is known of the early childhood in western, industrial societies where the norm is presumed to be the white middle-class heterosexual nuclear family, I have attempted to stay as close as possible to considerations with recognized universal validity: women's mothering, women's subordinate status, and a developmental approach to cognition. The distinct shapes and expressions of these factors will importantly determine the outcome of womb envy. The cultural forms and material life of the society in which the boy matures and reaches adulthood will determine the possible defenses available to him and their effectiveness in handling the envy. Cross-cultural study reveals a multitude of ways in which men arrange to soothe the narcissistic wound inflicted by their perceived inferiority. Some institutions may be established primarily for this end, while others, serving independent purposes, become employed to help defend against womb envy. In the discussion that follows I suggest that womb envy contributes importantly to the behavior or cultural institutions that I cite,[12] particularly as they exhibit the destructive aspects of envy, and that some of the phenomena can be better understood if we recognize the contribution of womb envy to their establishment or continuance.[13] My discussion here is essentially speculative and suggestive and I hope that it will serve as a stimulus to others to demonstrate why, given the significant variables within distinct cultural settings, womb envy expresses itself in one form or another.

Once we grant that womb envy is a genuine phenomenon, it becomes strikingly apparent that our entire culture and heritage are pervaded by men's envy of women's procreation. That Eve is born of the rib of a man no longer seems a simple endorsement of masculine prerogative, but an expression of the envious fantasies of the patriarchs who wrote the Bible. That male gynecologists deliver unconscious women of their offspring, that Plato repeatedly used childbirth as a metaphor for philosophical activity, that the Muses which inspire men poets are female, and that male circumcision during initiation rites heralds the birth of a man, all receive new insight when we recognize in them elements of womb envy.

In discussing the effects of womb envy, we must bear in mind that envy is a destructive emotion that tends to spoil the very thing it covets and from which it seeks gratification. Because envy tends to wreak its destructiveness on what

Klein calls "the good object," envy tends toward ever more destructiveness, since only gratification from the desired object can soothe the anger felt at not having that object.[14] For this reason, defenses against womb envy are rarely effective in blocking angry and destructive feelings and actions which ultimately are directed against the possessors of the desired object, women. In identifying some of these defenses we will be able to recognize the devaluation and hostility to which women are subject as they possess the desired object.

To gain some insight into the workings of envy, it will be useful to recognize parallels to be drawn between womb envy and what Melanie Klein claimed to be primal envy, envy of the mother's breast. For the infant, the mother's breast is the source of relief from hunger and the pleasure of sucking, yet even the best mother is not always available to the infant. The infant wants the breast for itself and envies the mother this valued possession. To protect against the feelings of envy and of anger at not having the breast when the infant desires it, the baby "splits" the breast into a "good object," the one which is there when wanted and gives gratification, and the "bad object," the one which is absent when desired and which causes pain and frustration. To the extent that the good object yields satisfaction and is secure for the child, to that extent it can dissipate the envious feelings. The envious impulses are either to gain possession of the desired object or to spoil that object. They arouse guilt and anxiety, which further despoil the "good object" and render it incapable of giving the gratification which could dissipate the envy. The infant tries to find ways of defending against the envy, often creating further splits in the object.

For the young boy who is aware of his gender but not yet aware that he cannot give birth, there is a split between a woman and her procreative capabilities, abilities which the boy expects to appropriate for himself. When he learns that these capacities are not his, that the woman is devalued and, moreover, that she is a woman by virtue of these same capacities, he creates further splits and attempts to reconcile his desires with his valued manhood.

Klein describes six defenses against envy that she has encountered in clinical work. If what I call "womb envy" is a genuine and deep-seated form of envy, then the application of these defenses to the appropriate behaviors should help explain them (in part, at least) as manifestations and defenses against womb envy. Thus, we will also be demonstrating the fruitfulness of the concept. The defenses Klein discusses include idealization, devaluation of the object, devaluation of the self, a greedy incorporation of the object (which I term "appropriation"), stirring up envy in others, and stifling the feeling of love while increasing feelings of hate. These are not mutually exclusive categories, and all in some way partake of attempts to spoil the object and to take possession of it.

Idealization. Exaltation of "the object and its gifts" can be used to make the object beyond our ken—we say, colloquially, "It is too good for the likes of us." Here the idealization, "The Mother, source of angelic love and forgiveness . . . the feminine, leavening, emotional element . . . the symbol . . . of moral values and tenderness in a world of wars" (Rich, 1976, p. 35) involves a sentimentalizing of motherhood and establishing what Rich has called "the institution of motherhood" as distinct from the experience of motherhood.

Alternatively, it can take the shape of the idolatry of Mother as Nature and fertility, as in periods of vitalistic romanticism, which Simone de Beauvoir (1946) captures in the following passage: "The mother is the root which, sunk in the depths of the cosmos, can draw up its juices; she is the fountain whence springs forth the living water, water that is also a nourishing milk" (p. 164).

But the gifts of maternal nature are for men: periods of romanticism have not been periods in which women have made advances toward autonomy. In idealizing the maternal aspects of women, men reduce the full scope of woman's human capabilities to her reproductive functions; by sentimentalizing an ideal mother, men can vent their envious anger on the actual woman who fails to meet the measure of the ideal. To see such idealizations as manifestations of men's womb envy is to understand why they of necessity go hand in hand with the actual oppression of women, the more direct expression of the envy which manifests itself when the defense of the idealization breaks down.

Devaluation of the object. This is an obvious strategem, since what is devalued need no longer be coveted and therefore no longer envied. The devaluation may be of childbearing per se, or of particular aspects of woman's physiology, or generalized to human corporeality, often all at once. Some devaluations involve direct dispersion cast on the object, others involve an indirect devaluation implicit in the high valuation placed on some activity opposed to or compared with childbirth. This consideration offers an interesting counterpoint to women's envy of the male role in western cultures, which Mead (1949) notes, "can come as much from an undervaluation of the role of wife and mother as from an overvaluation of public aspects of achievement which have been reserved for men" (p. 92).

The direct devaluation of childbirth often coexists with a devaluation of the physical, or the fleshly. Childbirth is an unfortunate reminder of our animal nature. Whereas Athena could spring forth full-grown from the forehead of Zeus, we must emerge from bodily cavities of the lower regions of the body. To those who regard childbirth as a messy, perhaps even revolting affair, the glowing excitement of the man who has witnessed the birth of his child in prepared childbirth is hardly comprehensible. The pregnant woman is uncomplimentarily characterized as a "cow," and nursing is regarded as "uncivilized" or "animallike." Man, de Beauvoir writes, "sees himself as a fallen god: his curse is to be fallen from a bright and ordered heaven into the chaotic shadows of his mother's womb" (p. 164).[15] The form of devaluation may be less direct in that childrearing activities may be regarded as unworthy, but on-ly relative to some comparable but exclusively male activity. Concomitant with or alternative to the direct devaluation of our corporality, we often find that childbirth is conceived to be split into a spiritual and a physical compo-nent, wherein men are responsible for the former and women for the latter. We find examples of all these strategies in the writings of such foundational figures of western civilization as Plato, Aristotle, and Aquinas.

In Plato (the least misogynist of the triumvirate), we find the least direct form of devaluation, wherein childbirth is used as symbol or metaphor for ex-clusively male activities considered superior to the female activity after which they are modeled. In Plato's *Theaetetus,* Socrates, a son of a midwife, ex-plicates the role of philosopher-teacher on the model of his mother's profes-sion. While the midwife aids the mother in bringing forth children, Socrates aids young men in bringing forth their ideas: the domain of the midwife is ex-clusively female, that of the philosopher is exclusively male (see Kittay and Lehrer, 1981). As it is dependent on the higher value placed on what is idea-tional rather than sensible, the devaluation is largely implicit. The indirect devaluation is similar to the defense of appropriation of which another Platonic use of the birth metaphor, Diotima's speech in the *Symposium,* is ex-emplary.

Both Aristotle and Aquinas apply the strategem of splitting childbirth into a valued and a devalued component, attributing the former to men and the lat-ter to women. Aristotle, in his theory of generation, maintained that man's semen contributes the Form of the being, the "principle of the soul," which is active and causative, while the woman contributes the Matter, which is merely passive. To be certain that no one mistake as equal the two distinct sexual con-tributions, Aristotle writes that, "the Form is *better* and more divine in its nature than the Matter" (included in Mahowald, 1978, p. 62).

Aquinas, in the *Summa Theologica,* both attributed the superior compo-nent of procreation to men, and posited another parallel activity, reserved for men, which he took to be "a still nobler work of life" than childbirth: "and that is intellectual operation" (in Mahowald, 1978, p. 80).

The general devaluation of childbirth may account for the fact that, unlike other heralded moments that involve "rites of passage"—puberty, marriage, and death—relatively little public ceremony surrounds childbirth. The initial "passage," the child's birth, and the one marking parenthood receive scant ceremony.[16] Couvade rituals provide an exception, but these focus on *men* rather than on women.

Devaluation of the object as a defense is rarely sufficient to ward off envy, for although the object may have been devalued, the desire to possess it usual-ly remains. A tentative solution, one we have already encountered and will see more of, is to split the object: what is devalued is identified with woman, and what is valued belongs to man. Another possibility is that the man who continues to experience envy regards himself as devalued: he thinks himself un-worthy if he desires that which is unworthy of his manhood.

Devaluation of the self. Klein suggests that this defense is utilized when it is felt to be less painful than the guilt and persecutory anxiety roused when the object is spoiled or greedily incorporated. As a defense against womb envy it is particularly inadequate in a culture of male dominance, where masculinity is importantly related to positions of power or to physical domination (e.g., in our own culture a man who loses a position of importance or some form of power says that he "no longer feels like a man"). Where a man's self-devaluation results in a questioning of sexual identity, then docility, non-competitiveness, or effeminacy may be an aberrant response to excessive womb envy; when confronted with his wife's or lover's pregnancy and delivery, such self-devaluation may lead to depressive and suicidal tendencies. A contrary but alternative response is extreme aggressivity and hostility, which might be used to cover the sense of inferiority.[17] In this disguised devaluation is the potential for an explosive anger which may make women victims. This man despises women for a power he cannot have and which he perceives as directly impeding his own, and also for this powerlessness that renders his own sense of impotence so much more acute. In a dreadful but telling account of the rape and mutilation of a 15-year-old girl who had hitched a ride from a man who was later accused of the crimes committed against her, we see the anger and fear a 51-year-old merchant marine felt in the presence of an unarmed young girl (whom he literally un-armed). In his mind it was he who was kidnapped and threatened with mutilation and he who begged to go free (see Spake, 1980). Likewise, the manifest hatred in pornography's contrary images of woman as castrating bitch and willing victim is explained, at least in part, by viewing that hatred as a defense against a self-devaluation resulting from men's envy of women's sexuality.

Appropriation. Klein says that to defend against envy, the infant greedily in-ternalizes the breast, so that "in the infant's mind it becomes entirely his possession and controlled by him, he feels that all the good that he attributes to it will be his own" (p. 218). Such a process I call "appropriation." It is a prime manifestation of womb envy, on a cultural level.

   Among its most conspicuous forms is the initiation cult of New Guinea. This structure "assumes that men become men only by men's ritualizing birth and taking over—as a collective group—the functions that women perform naturally" (Mead, 1949, p. 98). These cults are so central to the societies in which they are found that when they break down, as in the case of missionary influence, the entire social order is threatened. The initiation rites involve the symbolic death of the boy, who has been within the maternal domain, and his rebirth as a man, a birth effected by men. The rituals are in some ways imitative of birth. The initiate may, for example, be "swallowed" by the crocodile who represents the men's group, be reborn at the other end, and then may be confined to womblike huts and be tended by "male mothers," who treat him as a just-born babe who must be taught everything anew. Also involved are rites in which initiates participate in transforming their bodies in ways imitative of female procreative functioning. Particularly fascinating are the rituals of "male menstruation." Here, selected older men and the initiates are made to bleed, either from the genitals or from the nose or tongue, and this bleeding is referred to as male menstruation. These rituals are practiced in societies where menstrual blood arouses great fear, where it is embued with terrible powers and is thought to purge the body of evil and sickness. The purgatory efficacy of menstruation, as well as its ability to mark the girl's transformation into a woman with true childbearing capacity, is appropriated by men through arduous and painful rites.

The claim is made that the secrets of male menstruation were stolen by men from ancestral females. So also, it is claimed, are the highly prized sacred flutes that accompany the rituals. The possession of these flutes, which symbolizes men's creativity and connection with the fertile powers of the ancestral females, is often touted as the source of male superiority.

Within initiation rites in New Guinea and elsewhere, circumcision is often practiced and spoken of as means by which the boy is reborn as a man or by which the penis is reborn as the potent phallus. Subincision, the ritualized practice of incising the penis along the penile urethra, found primarily among the central tribes of Australia, renders the penis more vulvalike in appearance. Not only is the wound itself called "vulva," but the blood from the wound is considered blood from the "menses of the old Wawilak women" (quoted in Bettelheim, p. 105). Here again is the notion that men's theft of the powers of ancestral females becomes the source of male superiority.

In societies where men and women live separately and boys reside with the mother until they are nine or ten, the emotional separation from the mother and identification with men is differently effected than through the Oedipal model. Having observed and studied initiation rituals in New Guinea, Ruth and Ted Lidz remark:

> Any tendency of the boy to be a woman is countered by providing equivalents of what in a woman a man might envy—the ability to purify the self through menstruation, and her natural creativity that man attains by playing the sacred flutes. *Then, the status of the male is elevated and that of the female degraded* [Lidz and Lidz, 1977, p. 29, emphasis mine].

In the initiation cults, men create representations of the birth of men from men, based on the procreative powers of women. These representations are their "greedy" appropriations of women's powers: the "greed" is found in the male exclusivity and posited superiority, while the "appropriation" is attested to by the mythological theft common to these male births.

In the couvade rituals, men whose wives are about to or have just given birth engage in some prescribed behavior generally attributable to the parturient woman. In appropriating the good which men attribute to women's powers, men symbolically lay claim to the infant's birth itself, rather than construct a symbolic birth of the adolescent male. The couvade is a widespread practice, found globally in preliterate and peasant societies. It includes the simulation of labor pains during the actual birth of the child, a period of lying-in on the part of the father while the mother goes about her usual business, and dietary restrictions imposed on the expectant father and the father of the new-born. Where the couvade ritual is practiced, it is presumed that the expectant father's conduct affects the child as much as or even more than the behavior of the pregnant mother. Where the mother goes about her usual affairs immediately after childbirth while the husband, catered to by wife and kin, takes to bed with child for a period of a month or two, the justification is sometimes given that "the woman has had a hard bout of it, and 'tis but fair that the man should have his share of the suffering" (quoted in Reik, 1931, p. 29). Such a justification is rather like the joke in which a man says that he and his friend *together* moved a boulder, for while his friend did the pushing, *he* did the grunting.

Other justifications are somewhat more honest: "the life of the man is more valuable than that of the woman, and the husand [is] the more important factor in the birth of the child" (quoted in Reik, p. 29). Lest it be thought that these women are so hearty that they have no need of a lying-in period, among some of the same peoples it is thought that the man's lying-in is a means of transferring to the husband what is *recognized* as the woman's weakness after childbirth.

The couvade has been variously analyzed and interpreted, although it is rarely interpreted as a manifestation of womb envy. Of course, to a male interpreter who denies that there is anything to envy in childbirth, other explanations must be sought. Reik, with his characteristically Freudian orientation, claims that among the social purposes of the couvade is the protection of the woman against the latent hostility and sexual aggression of the man, hostility engendered by her sexual unavailability during the pregnancy and postpartum period. Prohibition against sexual intercourse during this period is, however, itself a social institution, and not a natural and inevitable fact. Why should men institute such prohibitions if they engender a hostility which must then be protected against by the elaborate proceedings of the couvade? Most likely, the best case for the couvade as a positive institution can be made on the grounds that it encourages a bonding between the father and the child. But this takes place at the cost of denying the mother her needed postpartum recuperation and her rightful recognition as one who has just participated in an arduous and marvelous feat.

As we move closer culturally to our own western industrial society, appropriations are no longer of this symbolic or imitative sort. Instead of ritualized symbolic births and symbolic menstruation, we find men employing birth as a metaphor for more valued activities. Instead of men mimicking the behavior of the laboring mother to aid, to upstage, or to displace her altogether in the postnatal period, we find the actual intervention of men into the childbearing process. Instead of symbolic appropriations which are clearly at the center of social organization, we find scattered evidence of men conceptualizing their work or creating roles so as to give them access to the good they attribute to women's powers. While womb envy may not be less significant in our own culture, its effects are more dispersed and less directly experienced.

Within our own culture and its historical antecedents, forms of appropriation are most evident in creative intellectual and artistic endeavors and in the theories of generation and the practice of childbirth itself. We have already mentioned the biblical and mythological births performed by Adam and Zeus, the metaphoric births conceived by Plato, and the scientific theory of procreation postulated by Aristotle; all deserve more attention as instances of appropriation. But I will here confine myself to a brief discussion of the passage in Plato's *Symposium* where Socrates expounds the wisdom of Diotima. In Diotima's view procreation serves as the model for all human endeavor. In the misogynist and homophilic Greece of Socrates, a man's union with a woman is thought of primarily in terms of offspring, while love between men issues in no such birth. But the sterility of these relations is compensated for in the metaphor of artistic and intellectual birth.[18] Socrates has Diotima say:

> Those who are pregnant in the body only, betake themselves to women and beget children. . . . But souls [of men] which are pregnant . . . conceive that which is proper for the soul to conceive or contain. And what are these conceptions?—wisdom and virtue in general. And such creatures are poets and all artists who are deserving of the name inventor. [In Plato, 1892, p. 333]

But, we may wonder, if this speech reflects an appropriation by men of what they take as "the good" in procreation, why is it spoken by a woman? We should bear in mind that Diotima speaks of these as the "mysteries of love" which are to be productive of the birth of "many fair and noble thoughts." Socrates, like the men of New Guinea, must have the secrets of love and fertility revealed to him by a woman, for the secrets of birth are hers. Men have access to them only through theft and appropriation. That these secrets are uttered by a woman guarantees their validity and truth, just as Socrates invokes the authority of his mother for his own practice of "midwifery."

The metaphor of artistic and intellectual creation as birth is traditionally reflected in the Muse, always female, so that male creators could have intercourse with them and produce a "brainchild" (Ong, 1967, p. 252).[19] A contemporary instance of a similar appropriation surfaces in a study (Simenauer, 1954) of "pregnancy envy" in the poet Rilke. Rilke's intimate friend Lou

Andreas-Salome, herself a writer and psychoanalyst, speaks of Rilke's "uncommunicable longing for pregnancy," saying that he considered his work as "something ejected from himself" which "he brought forth from his internal self" (p. 240). Rilke speaks of "those who come together in the night and are entwined in a rocking delight [who] do an earnest work and gather depth and strength for the song of some coming poet" (p. 239).

This passage from the "Book of Hours" is perhaps particularly telling:

> Give the last proof unto us . . . and bestow on us man's real motherhood (not of the kind of woman's labor), install the he-man in his right as he who giveth birth; birth to Death—Messiah; fulfill his longings, for they are greater than the dream of the virgin giving birth to God. [Quoted in and trans. by Simenauer, p. 242]

The passage reveals that Rilke placed high valuation on pregnancy and motherhood only as these are appropriated by the male artist. Simenauer points out that in the *Tuscan Diaries,* Rilke attempts to convince women not to compete with men artists, indeed to forego motherhood itself and to remain virgins and die young! Rilke himself apparently feared and distrusted sexual love and had a "morbid horror" of childbirth.

Within our traditional sex stereotypes, we tend to regard the poet and the creative artist as often associated with more feminine ideals and values, so that expressions of envy of women from these quarters are perhaps not unexpected. The scientist and physician are within intellectual spheres that are more rigorous representatives of masculine supremacy. Yet scientific theories of procreation from Aristotle onward bear unmistakable signs of a refusal to grant women even an equal share in this apparently feminine domain. Not until the latter part of the 19th century was there sufficient understanding of the role of both egg and sperm to commend to the scientific community the view that both sexes contribute equally to their offspring. Harvey, who is often cited as the founder of modern biology and who is credited with discovering that all animals are born of eggs, nonetheless believed in the greater potency of semen. So great was the power of semen, thought Harvey, that impregnation was a sort of contagion which did not require contact between the sperm and egg, and which could effect a woman's brain as well as her body.

Although scientists of the 17th and 18th centuries believed that the egg nourished the seed contained in the semen, Harvey and others believed that the semen alone contained the fledgling human being. Some claimed to have detected the miniscule homunculus in the spermatozoa with their microscopes (see Merchant, 1979). The woman was merely the vessel that housed and nourished the seed of man. The 17th-century men of science used their microscopes to attribute to themselves the prerogative of creating life; to advance the same view, Aeschylus, centuries earlier puts in the mouth of Apollo:

> The mother to the child that men call hers
> Is not true life-begetter, but a nurse
> Of live seed. 'Tis the sower of the seed
> Alone begetteth . . .'
>
>   (from the *Oresteia*)

Contemporary western science has, of course, relinquished such theories, but in their place has been substituted what may, in fact, be a more pernicious form of appropriation. If science did not succeed in having the man "alone beget," it did succeed in allowing males unprecedented control over women's procreative functions. Since the 17th century, in Europe and later in the United States, through the ruthless purging of midwifery, male practitioners with their forceps, their "hands of iron," replaced the "hands of flesh" of the midwives (Ehrenreich and English, 1973; and Rich, 1976).

Male control of the process of pregnancy and childbirth in the United States today is exercised by the physician who habitually treats maternity as a "disease" (an association which Lomas, 1966, compares to that of societies in which the newly parturient woman is regarded as unclean and taboo). The physician's control and "patient's" passivity are encouraged and reflected in the fact that the gynecologist/obstetrician's is the one medical office where the patient is characteristically and habitually referred to by her first name, while the doctor is addressed with the honorific title. The hospital procedure for the laboring woman reduces her to an inert piece of suffering flesh. She is manipulated, wired, drugged and as Lomas correctly points out, encouraged to behave in a generally regressive and helpless fashion. Even in the case of a completely normal birth, she may be so anaesthetized that she is incapable of participating in the expulsion of the child and must be delivered with forceps—the same tool which first gained men entrance into the chamber of the confined woman. After birth, whether or not the woman has been sedated, her child is whisked away and she is left alone or with other women who, moaning and weeping, are recovering from their anesthesia. Although the hospital attendants are mostly female nurses, the reigning sovereign is the male physician. In this way, the woman is deprived of her active participation in the birth of her child and of the first glorious and joyful moments after a hard but fruitful labor. The male physician has taken over the event.

As more women become anxious to recover their lost powers and insist that the physician is the servant and not the master of the moment, women may find ways, such as prepared childbirth, which will enable them to gain from medical science its life-saving capabilities without being deprived of their life-producing prerogatives.

To speak of medicine as "life-saving" suggests that the entrance of men into the healing professions, professions which in Europe and the United States had traditionally been in the hands of women, is itself a form of appropriation. "If we men cannot *produce* life in childbirth, we can monopolize the skills needed to *save* life." The extent to which female healers were wiped out and women still today remain largely excluded from the medical profession lends some credence to such speculations.

Men's intervention in women's procreative functions is not limited to childbirth itself. I want to suggest that behind the controversy surrounding abortion, sterilization of women, and birth control devices for women only, as well as in vitro fertilization, there is a strong element of man's attempt to control and hence appropriate those powers he envies in women and which he feels he can never truly call his own.

In all the appropriating activities of which I have spoken, it is important to see that it is not the activity itself which, inherently, is womb envying. Cultures may want to mark the passage of a child into adolescence and adulthood, human beings may want to create poetry and philosophy, find healing methods and ways of controlling their procreative functions, without necessarily being envious of women's childbearing capacities. These activities serve such envious impulses when they exclude woman or deny her agency, so that they can be thought of as exclusively or primarily male domains in which men outdo women with respect to that which they envy in women's power.

Stirring up envy in others. What I have called forms of appropriation also serve this particular defense. Two additional examples come to mind. Freud, in his theory of penis envy, does not so much stir up envy as postulate the existence of a very powerful envy in women for what only men can possess. Yet if, as I have suggested before, penis envy has largely symbolic significance while womb envy has a reality beyond a symbolic value (it is not only the power signified by the womb but its actual capacities and those of related organs which is coveted), Freud's postulation may well be a theoretician's equivalent to exciting another's envy.

The initiatory cults of which we have spoken provide another example of how men defend against womb envy by directing envy towards themselves. Among the Chuga, the men claim that during initiation their anus is "plugged up." After this they pretend not to defecate until they are old when, "for their son's sake," they have the plug removed (Bettelheim, 1954, p. 130.) We may note here the equation between control over feces and control over babies. The Chuga designate pregnancy by the cessation of menses, saying "the woman closes herself up." The setting of the *ngoso* [plug] provides men with a counterpart to displaying their manhood. But beyond this, *"So that even greater honors were given to men . . .* these men arrived at the pretense of claiming that men, on reaching sexual maturity, are able to digest totally and do without elimination" (B. Gutman, quoted in Bettelheim, p. 130; emphasis mine). The acknowledged deception upon which their manhood is based is surrounded with the most extreme secrecy from women and children—

although the women are aware of the fakery and either mock or indulge their men. Upon their initiation, young Chuga males learn that the touted capacity is a fiction and are taught the means by which to perpetuate it.

We see here what appears to be a fairly clear example of a way in which the men of Chuga both appropriate birth, the "birth" of men, and attempt to draw the envy of women by claiming access to an even greater natural feat than that of the body's production or putting forth (of babies), namely the ability to hold in, to voluntarily suppress production (of feces). Implicit may be the thought that if man can so suppress production—stop the (natural—inertial) flow out of the body (of feces), he could produce such output (of babies).

The awareness that it is all a fake is congruent with the experience of defending against envy by attempting to draw the envy of others. If the sole purpose of our purported achievement is to defend against the envy of another, then since the object we tout is for us but a mere substitute and inferior to what we envy, it invariably feels like a sham, whether the achievement is genuine or not. The ineffectiveness of such a defense, as Klein points out, is that envious people are felt to be the worst persecutors. As woman has control of childbearing, man may additionally fear that she will consider him superfluous or deprive him of his offspring. By drawing woman's envy to them, man hopes to fool women into thinking that he is endowed with such powers that those of woman are insignificant. In thus gaining her respect and, moreover, gaining ascendency, he hopes to make himself indispensable. But in the process he has endowed her with potentially still more power, i.e., the power to see through the pretense, thus making for himself a precarious reign and turning woman into a feared persecutor.

The stifling of feelings of love and corresponding intensifying of hate. Womb-envying behaviors may be seen as manifesting themselves in men's avowed hatred toward or apparent indifference toward infants, nursing mothers, or pregnant women, as well as expressing itself in an hostility directed toward female organs. Much of the derision directed toward pregnant women may be seen as part of this defense. The intense hatred and fear directed against the vagina is undoubtedly fed by men's envy of the organ of birth and of expulsion.[20]

Indifference is discussed by Jacobson in speaking of a young boy's experience of the arrival of a sibling:

> Gratifications gained from his participation in the baby's care help to reduce his envy of the infant. But mostly we see that, after a period of great emotional concern with the infant, little boys will lose much of their interest in the newcomer. It seems that they renounce or repress their envy of the infant-mother relationship most successfully by withdrawing interest from both. [Jacobson, 1950, p. 143].

She also suggests that "the absence of a longing for children in men until they approach marriage is also due to firm defenses against envy of woman's reproductive functions" (p. 144). Extreme envy, having taken such defenses, can result in men delaying and denying wives' demands for having children. She writes of her clinical experience: "In the course of analysis, their conspicuous disinterest in having children of their own regularly proves to be a stubborn defense against a deeply repressed envy of woman's reproductive abilities" (p. 144).

Under the heading of this defense we can consider the glorification of destruction as opposed to creation. The intensified hatred is put into the service of displacing value from life-creating powers onto life-destroying powers. While the former are universally (although not exclusively) vested in women, the latter are universally (although, again, not exclusively) vested in men (see Sanday, 1981).

A hatred of women that might well be linked with womb-envying defenses, and which I have previously mentioned briefly, is pornography, especially violent pornography. The joining of sexuality and violence characteristic of much pornography is defended as an intrinsic aspect of human sexuality by George Bataille, himself a novelist, philosopher, and pornographer. In *Death and Sensuality,* a philosophic attempt to justify pornography, Bataille argues that in both death and eroticism the distinct, individual barriers between persons, which constitute the profound discontinuity between persons, are broken down, satisfying our yearning for "a primal continuity linking us with everything that is" (Bataille, 1962, p. 9). Bataille's thesis is that reproduction brings about discrete existences, while death violates the barriers of individual existents. Eroticism should not be identified with reproduction, even if that is its eventual outcome under certain circumstances, but with violence, with violation.

I want to suggest that in views such as Bataille's we have, in fact, an inversion of life and death, birth and destruction (or violence), love and hate—not merely a theoretic inversion, but an experientially felt inversion of values. My claim is that Bataille's views exemplify a "stifling of feelings of love and intensification of hatred" both toward women and toward their special life-giving capacities. The results in a supervaluation of sexual violence, particularly toward women, and of destruction and death as the means by which men achieve what Bataille values in woman's powers. The special virtue of merger and continuity which Bataille seeks in violence is indeed what Bataille would want to appropriate from the childbearing woman.

Although I do not argue it here, I believe a case could be made for the view that the metaphysical urge for, as well as the fear of, merger and continuity has its origins in the dim memory of both the delights and comforts and the threat of loss and fear and anger we experienced with our mothers in our early symbiosis with her and later identification and dependency on her. These delights and fearful vulnerability may be called forth once again in lovemaking. The child emerging from dependency also experiences the expectation and anticipation of recreating that symbiosis with a child of one's own—again experiencing the merger, only this time with greater control and without the painful dependency.

Bataille, we will recall, attributes to reproduction the creation of distinct individuals with distinct boundaries. While he may be correct in that the outcome of reproduction eventually issues in relatively distinct individuals, the process of reproduction is a succession of experiences in which merging and continuity are foremost and far more pronounced than in most other moments. The continuity between oneself and the child one carries within (so knowing oneself as two beings in one), the experience of feeling oneself continuous with immense natural forces during the birth itself, the joining of two bodies during nursing, accompanied as it is by the separate existence yet complete emotional and physical dependency of the newborn—these experiences, as much as the sexual act that brings the new being into existence, break down the barriers that define otherwise discrete individuals.[21]

It is pertinent to point out also that the actual experience of childbirth, at least when carried out in favorable circumstances, is *par excellence* an experience of merger and continuity with all of creation. I speak now of an unproblematic birth for the woman who is willing, awake, and aware, and not terrorized by fear. During her labor and especially in its final moments, the laboring woman feels herself at once overtaken by and working along with overwhelmingly powerful forces—forces she never imagined her body capable of generating—to bring about the birth of the child. We know that the sexual act can overwhelm us and introduce to us new possibilities of our physical and emotional selves. It can bind us to another and bring us into contact with inherent capacities we possess which normally are concealed from us. Moments of sexual excitation may bring with them a sense of larger nature, indeed the sense of merger and disruption of our discrete existence of which Bataille speaks. But childbirth is still more powerful—the uterine contractions that are needed to expel the baby are far more intense than orgasmic contractions; and the tiny head emerging from within us remains a magical conjuring act which discloses our continuity amid discreteness as completely as any sexual encounter.

In all this, I do not want to obscure the fact that childbirth generally is painful, difficult, and potentially hazardous to mother and child. But so are many intense experiences in which we recognize our powers and our limits. When such experiences are carried out in unfavorable circumstances and when the agency of the principals is denied, these experiences cannot bring the principal actors moments of revelation and happiness, but only abject misery. It is unfortunate that much of women's childbearing has been conducted under these adverse conditions. The adversities are due not to biological factors alone, but to the political and economic conditions under which women suffer, not a few of which may be traced to men's envious despoiling of woman's capacities. In this light, the biblical injunction that women will bear children in toil and in pain seems less a comment on the strength of the uterine contractions than on the manmade conditions under which women labor.

In the devaluation of birthgiving and the confinement of women's sexuality to men's gratification, we forget the inherently sexual nature of procreative functions and are surprised, even scandalized, at the possibility of sexual gratification in the expulsion of the fetus and in breast-feeding. Again, under conditions of material and emotional deprivation, where the child was not desired or threatens to confine the woman to a narrow and perhaps difficult existence, such joys are extracted only rarely. But where the birth and early nursing escape the invasive oppression of sexual, racial, and material injustices, these experiences answer the desires to extend beyond our own discrete boundaries and merge with larger forces.

Violence and destruction may indeed obliterate boundaries, but such merging is desirable only paradoxically (and perhaps this reveals the "bad faith" of the proponents of this course) for those who remain agents in the process (whether the agency is doing the violating or the choosing to be a "willing victim"). By remaining agents they may savor the continuity as they experience their own or another's obliteration. For the unwilling victim, as for the drugged or terrified laboring woman, there is no exaltation.

Such distinctions are not made by Bataille, for whom the "beloved woman" and "the sacrificial victim" are almost indistinguishable. This, he would have us believe, is both intrinsic to the nature of eroticism and allows the woman to have bestowed on her "the limitless, infinite nature of sacred things." But then, why is man generally the sacrificer and (in the heterosexual relations of which Bataille speaks) woman generally the victim? Why should love, in its violent aspect, be so gender-specific with respect to who does the violating and who is violated? Moreover, to female sensibilities, Bataille's descriptions of love seem less like loving encounters than like rape; but the rapist's hapless victim is not embarked on a metaphysical quest in her torments, regardless of what they may provide for her persecutor. Bataille's arguments seem rather like ratiocinations for an anger, doubtless mixed with erotic feelings, and we must wonder where this rage originates.

If sexuality promises/threatens merger and if that merger harkens back to the primal symbiosis and identification with the mother, then all the feelings directed to the woman, both as beloved and as object of the anger and fear stemming from feelings of powerlessness, along with man's frustration at not being able to recreate this relationship with a child of his own, are understandable in their often-disastrous ambivalence. In Bataille's endorsement and glorification of violent sexuality we find an expression of a resentment and anger at woman for her capacity to recreate and re-experience life-creating and life-sustaining connectedness. The achievement of such connectedness and continuity through the violation of woman in intercourse is, in part at least, an envious striking out at she who has within her the capacity to achieve this, not through destruction, but through birthgiving.

The valuing of destruction rather than creation, of death rather than life, is a defensive, compensatory transposition of values and is particularly pernicious if Klein is correct in her analysis of the relation between envy and other destructive forces. She points out that as "envy spoils the primal good object," it impedes the future enjoyment of the object's goodness and the gratitude that accompanies such enjoyment. This only increases the destructive feelings toward the good object. When the object is felt as "good after all, it is all the more greedily desired." (For example, in spite of his devaluation of childbearing, the envious man insists on keeping his woman pregnant and is increasingly brutal toward her—increasingly accusing her of bearing him another man's child, etc.) According to Klein, "Greed, envy and persecutory anxiety, which are bound up with each other, inevitably increase each other." This might help to explain why destruction escalates, why there is so rarely any sense of satiation with violence. Klein writes: "For it is *enjoyment* and the *gratitude* to which it gives rise that mitigate destructive impulses, envy and greed" (p. 187). Envy of the woman interferes with the gratification of seeing life emerge and empathetically reliving the best moments of the symbiosis and the experience of parental power and generosity available in nurturing a child. But the destruction of life does not yield the sought-for gratification. Since the transposition of values has been accomplished to deal with the envy, and since there is anger at the failure of gratification, the destruction is renewed, fueled now with greater anger.

The Politics of Womb Envy

The significance of womb envy as an explanatory concept has its place within a feminist program which believes that a feminist transformation of society must occur on several fronts at once: most particularly, economics, sexuality, and mothering. It is at their interfaces that we must seek strategies to dissipate womb envy.

The economic power men wield is undoubtedly decisive. Without a redistribution of wealth and earning power, reforms aimed at woman's autonomy remain a cruel hoax. Recommendations one might make to counter womb envy remain utopian visions without the material conditions needed to support such efforts. Yet the very economic power man wields resonates with manifestations of a womb envy that overvalues the productivity reserved for man and devalues that to which woman alone is biologically fit.

The question of womb envy emerges out of a consideration of the nature of female sexuality. Female sexuality has been rendered a thing defined and even experienced by women themselves in terms of men's desires and needs. That women generally eroticize men they take to be their superiors (while men eroticize women they accept as their inferiors—regardless of the chosen parameters) is taken to mean that man's sexual domination over women is intrinsic to the nature of female sexuality. Through such sexual domination the material power men have over women is solidified and threatens to vitiate whatever economic independence they might otherwise have achieved. In the preceding pages, I have claimed that the prevailing theory of personality formation, Freudian psychoanalytic theory, has failed to recognize the significance of womb envy, because its conception of female sexuality renders the concept incoherent. A challenge to such a conception of female sexuality necessitates an examination of womb envy as an important explanatory concept of individual and cultural male behaviors and institutions through which women are oppressed and exploited.

Finally, mothering, as Chodorow so brilliantly exhibits, is at once a source of woman's strength and the means by which the reproduction of male domination occurs. While womb envy relates importantly to economic and sexual considerations, it is in the area of mothering, in the context of male domination, that womb envy originates. The apparently universal conditions of women's mothering and women's subordinate status, along with a cognitive psychosexual account of early boyhood, provide ample ground for the claim that not only do young boys want to be able to bear children, but that they perceive their incapacity as a loss and a narcissistic wound which results in a subsequent womb envy. Although the resultant womb envy certainly has a basis in a biological difference, *it does not reduce to biological fact*. Rather the sexual difference in procreative contributions is elaborated into a gender difference regarding the continued nurturance of the baby, once outside the womb.

To defend against womb envy, I have claimed, the boy may devalue himself or devalue life-giving. He may maintain the high valuation on creation but displace the creative capacities from woman, appropriating them to man and to his exclusive domains. Such appropriation, in its many manifestations, is probably the most likely outcome of womb envy. For the child, this means forming ambitions in which he can outdo women in their productivity, accepting ideologies in which men play the "really" important part in procreation and the family and, in general, fiercely adopting the stance of male superiority.

The most felicitous resolution would involve an understanding on the part of the boy that women do not procreate alone, but that men play an equally critical role. However, such abstract considerations of paternity can only gain affective force if the child has had experience with male nurturance. For womb envy, I have argued here, is significant not only because the power to give life is intrinsically desirable and awe-inspiring, but because it is closely fused in the child's mind with the special love and power he accorded to his mother. The man's biological role in creation can be a genuine salve for the narcissistic wound created by womb envy only where the child can feel that the father's role in procreation gives him the same warrant for a special relation to the child that the mother's more obvious and dramatic role does. In this way the boy would not need to repress childbearing wishes as much as transform them into the very nurturing ones from which these wishes themselves emerged; the boy could then look forward to his own future role as a parent, to recapturing all that was warm and comfortable, and to rectifying that which was fearsome and painful.

Such possibilities can be envisioned as concrete only in a social and economic environment in which male nurturance is socially expected (not merely socially accepted) and is economically plausible—where men and women have access to the same earning capacity, where maternity and paternity leaves are institutionalized, where early childcare is well paid and attracts talented men and women to staff readily accessible centers, etc.

But there is the rub. The conditions of woman's oppression partake of the self-reproductive character Chodorow describes for mothering, making definite strategems which are not merely utopian difficult to devise. For example, as much as one would want to recommend an increased participation of men in early childcare as the way to dissipate womb envy, the material support must be available. But the fact that women do not have an earning power commensurate with men's is itself partly due to the womb-envying behavior that confines women to the more devalued and hence poorly paid occupations. Again, womb envying devaluation of nurturance, for both psychological and economic considerations, similarly keeps men away from the early nurturance of their own child or from employment in early childcare. Moreover, if Chodorow is correct, the nurturing qualities we value in women have been suppressed in men—though fortunately the socialization process is not always perfect. To entrust our children to men who have not developed the necessary virtues may be to subject young children to undesirable behaviors. Women have already paid a high price for allowing men to replace the previously female prerogative of midwifery. Before wholeheartedly endorsing male nurturance, women must carefully examine the concrete realities they face to see what steps need to be taken to break out of a viciously circular entrapment, one which transmutes our strengths into our limitations.

Lacking the fruits of such investigations, I can better conclude this discussion with a vision rather than with definite strategems. Without the context of male supremacy, in a world in which men and women together nurture their offspring from birth onward, the bare biological fact of women's childbearing would not give rise to the hostile and destructive defenses men attempt in order to guard against their envy; defenses against the repetition of what Freud referred to as one of the painful disappointments of childhood, the child's "own attempt to make a baby himself, carried out in tragic seriousness [which] fails shamefully" (Freud, 1928, p. 43). She who would give birth would not be a devalued person over whom man has to assert his superiority. The knowledge of the young boy that his procreative contribution is of equal significance and that he, as well as his sister, will have the opportunity to recreate and create anew infancy and childhood in an intimate relation with a child, may dissipate what envious desires he might feel vis-à-vis the biological distinction. If the gratification from "the good object" is what will dissipate envy, while each defense constructed out of envy ultimately fuels that envy, then only empathetic involvement with pregnancy and childbirth, and most important, involvement with early childcare, will successfully provide for men the gratification needed to dissipate womb envy.

Because biological difference per se is not sufficient to give womb envy its force, we can draw no inferences—however inviting they may be—concerning its causative role in the original fact of woman's subordination. Such claims would be speculative in the worst sense. Speculation that opens avenues for more systematic inquiry of either a theoretical or empirical kind is necessary and valuable. But speculation that merely posits claims that can in no way be further examined becomes fodder for polemical debate. To infer that man originally subordinated woman because he envied her her capacity to bear children would lend itself to the view that as long as woman will bear children, man will attempt to dominate her; moreover, if she wants equality she must either wait in vain or she must applaud a technology that will render her womb a vestigial organ. But this speculation is futile, and its conclusions for woman's liberation serve the envy they purport to dissipate.

To move away from a position of biological determinism, to see the role of cultural factors shaping what appears so otherwise inevitable, is to open the way for change and genuine liberation. Womb envy, regarded in light of cultural factors and psychosocial development, may be seen to both contribute to and result from woman's subordinate status. For woman to attain autonomy she need not renounce her biological capacities, but gain control over them. The decision to bear a child must be hers; and it can be a true decision only when woman gains control over her procreative capacity, sheds the burden of exclusive mothering, and shares with men the hardships and joys of nurturing children.

The distinctive childbearing capacities of woman must be reclaimed from men's envious impulses to appropriate or despoil them. Women within western industrial society, at least, have come to regard Eve's inheritance as their unjust biological burden. But I venture that they have become such burdens in the course of men's appropriations and despoilings. To reclaim childbirth is to understand the conditions under which it can empower and enrich so that women do not regard their physiology as a prison, but as a source of strength. I spoke earlier of the difficulty, pain, and danger of childbirth, as well as its potential as an exhilarating and awe-inspiring experience. The mountain climber, the competitive athlete, the adventurer similarly face danger, pain, and difficulty in their quest for the momentous experience. Yet we do not think of their hardships as merely suffered; they are embraced as part of the mastery of the activity. If woman did not have motherhood thrust on her, if pregnancy and childbirth were freely undertaken where other desirable options were available and where motherhood did not mean a foreclosure of all other possibilities (just as fatherhood signifies no such closure for men), and if both men and women thought how to aid the laboring mother, recognizing her agency, then while much of the pain, difficulty and hazard might remain, they would be, for many, challenges to be mastered rather than ordeals to be suffered. Under these conditions woman could enjoy potential rewards of participating in the creative action of nature, rather than suffer the present situation in which her special capacities are turned into the instruments of her own oppression.

The womb-envying behavior of which I have spoken in this essay contributes to and underlies some of the hostility and aggression against women. It results in the exclusion of woman from the appropriating activities of man, and it makes of woman passive suffering flesh in the one activity that is exclusively her prerogative. None of this arises out of biological necessity alone. Womb envy and the defenses men erect against it are the result of and sustain man-made constructs and structures which woman must de-construct, destruct and restructure if she is to liberate herself and the issues of her womb.

Notes

I must thank Jeffrey, our children Sesha and Leo, and Margaret Grennan. Each one in their special way, without confining my work or limiting my capacities to motherhood, has made giving birth and mothering such joyful and profound experiences that I could understand women's distinctive capacities as indeed enviable. I also want to thank Katherine Wolpe of the New York Psychoanalytic Society Library for her help in locating bibliographical sources and Ken Itzkowitz, Susan Petersen, and Edward Casey for their helpful editorial comments.

1. A reflective colleague related that while he was writing his dissertation, he felt competitive toward his pregnant wife, with whom he saw himself in a race as to who would give "birth" first.
2. The "aura" privileged classes pretend to, e.g., the "blue blood" of the nobility, the "divine right" of kings, the intellectual elitism of the highly paid professional, helps protect them from the envy of those to whom the privileges are denied.
3. Spinoza, *The Ethics,* Bk III, Definition of the Emotions, Definition XXIII.
4. See Freud (1933): "Femininity," p. 13; also see "Anxiety and the Instinctual Life," same volume, p. 89, and Freud (1908), p. 34.
5. See Freud's treatment of the Wolfman (1918), Little Hans (1909), and Dr. Schreber (1911). His stress on penis envy in favor of womb envy has long been criticized

as part of his androcentric or phallocentric bias. See, for example, Zillboorg (1944), Bettelheim (1954), and Fromm (1951).

6. I have argued this point in some detail in Kittay, "Why Not Womb Envy?—A Reading of Freud's 'Femininity' " (unpublished).

7. While a woman might envy the pregnancy of another (the reverse envy is also possible), or one who has had a hysterectomy or has passed menopause might envy one who still is fertile, neither constitutes *womb envy* in the sense I mean to use the term. There exists a chromosomal disorder, Turner's Syndrome, which makes girls genetically incapable of bearing children, though with hormonal treatment they can mature into otherwise normal women. Prior to recent advances in genetic screening procedures, misdiagnosis was the rule until the girl was grown, so that the Turner Syndrome girl grew up believing herself capable of giving birth. Whatever impact the discovery of her condition may have on her personality development, it will differ from that of someone who was raised thinking that childbirth was not possible for her or him. That is, she would not have womb envy in the same sense a boy would have womb envy. Today, more Turner Syndrome girls will be raised knowing that while they are girls they are limited in a way that boys are. Accordingly, it is theoretically possible for such girls to develop a womb envy, but qualified and complicated in many ways hard to ascertain here.

8. My account is based on Chodorow's (1978) interpretation of the work of Mahler (1968), Jacobson (1964), and other object-relation theorists.

9. The discrepancies between middle- and working-class boys may be explained by a more thorough delineation of sex roles early in the lives of working-class children and a greater professed equality between the sexes in middle-class homes.

10. Notice that the middle-class girls in Rabban's study made more appropriate parental role choices at age five than at age six, although at age eight all made appropriate choices. The suggestion is that it is around six when the differences in social power between men and women becomes most apparent to the girls who have been raised in an atmosphere of sexual equality within the home—or more likely a pretense at sexual equality.

11. Perhaps this is still another significance of Freud's phallic mother: it is the male child's projection onto his mother of his desire and belief in such androgynous possibilities.

12. Note that I do not claim that these behaviors simply reduce to womb envy; human institutions and behaviors are generally overdetermined. Furthermore, womb envy is so intimately related to women's inferior status that it will often be impossible to separate out the contributing factors.

13. I am not treating womb envy as an individual pathological state, although some culturally aberrant behavior may be related to an ineffective routing of womb envy into the culturally approved avenues. For some psychoanalytic case studies, see Lacoursiere (1972), Eisler (1921), Boehm (1930), Evans (1951), van Leeuwen (1966), Wainwright (1966), Eylon (1967), Trethowan (1968), Knight (1971). Even such aberrant, unacceptable behavior takes shape according to culturally determined options.

14. The term "object" refers to a person or an aspect or symbol of a person.

15. De Beauvoir, as an existentialist, is in sympathy with this antipathy toward the fleshy—her critique is directed toward its identification with woman or rather the reduction of woman to the flesh. She does not recognize the extent to which this attitude itself is part and parcel of the devaluation of woman as childbearers and that this devaluation serves as a defense against men's envy.

16. This may be due to the precariousness of the infant's life in places where the infant mortality rate is great although, on the contrary, high mortality might have been reason for added protection through ceremony.

17. For the former, see Boehm (1930), Van der Leeuw (1958), Knight (1971) Lacoursiere (1972). For the latter see Van Leeuwen (1966), Lacoursiere (1972), Jaffe (1968).

18. A very different theory that is also a belief in some fecund outcome of male homosexual encounters may be found in the belief among young black homosexual men that anal intercourse can produce a "blood baby" to which a man "gives birth" anally (in J. Money and G. Hosta, 1968).

19. Note that in women, with the notable exception of Mary, intercourse with nonhuman powers results only in malevolent powers of witchcraft; many a woman has met torture and death through the accusation that she copulated with the devil, while men win accolades for the offspring they produce through their relations with the Muses.

20. Personal communication from a female psychologist, who remarked on clinical experience of the intense hatred focused on the vagina by those men who at the same time are extremely attracted to the same organ. See also Horney (1932). Bettelheim reports that among the boys in his school were ones of varying ages who "have many fantasies about cutting off and tearing out breasts and vaginas" (p. 31).

21. We need only look at the moral complexities concerning the pregnant woman and abortion to see the extent to which such distinct individual barriers are problematic in experiences relating to childbearing. See Whitbeck (forthcoming) for one of the few treatments of this subject.

Bibliography

Bataille, Georges. 1962. *Death and Sensuality*. New York: Ballantine Books, 1969.

Bettelheim, Bruno. 1954. *Symbolic Wounds*. New York: Macmillan, 1971.

Boehm, Felix. 1930. "The Femininity-Complex in Men." *International Journal of Psychoanalysis* 11: 444–69.

Brunswick, Ruth Mack. 1940. "The Preoedipal Phase of the Libido Development." *Psychoanalytic Quarterly* 9: 293–319.

Chodorow, Nancy. 1978. *The Reproduction of Mothering*. Berkeley: University of California Press.

de Beauvoir, Simone. 1949. *The Second Sex*. New York: Random House, 1974.

Ehrenreich, Barbara, and English, Deirdre. 1973. *Witches, Midwives, and Nurses: A History of Women Healers*. Old Westbury, Conn.: The Feminist Press.

Eisler, Michael Joseph. 1921. "A Man's Unconscious Phantasy of Pregnancy in the Guise of Traumatic Hysteria." *The International Journal of Psychoanalysis* 2: 255–86.

Evans, William N. 1951. "Simulated Pregnancy in a Male." *Psychoanalytic Quarterly* 20: 165–78.

Eylon, Yizhar. 1967. "Birth events, appendicitis, and appendectomy." *British Journal of Medical Psychology* 40: 317–31.

Freud, Sigmund. 1908. "On the Sexual Theories of Children." *The Sexual Enlightenment of Children*. Edited by Philip Rieff. New York: Macmillan, 1976.

———. 1909. "Analysis of a Phobia in a Five-Year-Old Boy." *The Sexual Enlightenment of Children*. Edited by Philip Rieff. New York: Macmillan, 1976.

———. 1911. "Psychoanalytic Notes Upon an Autobiographical Account of a Case of Paranoia (*Dementia Paranoides*)" ("The Psychotic Doctor Schreber"). In *Three Case Histories*. Edited by Philip Rieff. New York: Macmillan, 1968.

———. 1918. "From the History of an Infantile Neurosis" ("The Wolf Man"). In *Three Case Histories*. Edited by Philip Rieff. New York: Macmillan, 1968.

———. 1925. "Some Psychological Consequences of the Anatomical Distinction Between the Sexes." *Collected Papers*, vol. 5. London: Hogarth Press, 1950.

———. 1928. *Beyond the Pleasure Principle.* Translated by James Strachey. New York: Bantam Books, 1967.

———. 1931. "Female Sexuality." *Collected Papers,* vol. 5. London: Hogarth Press, 1950.

———. 1933. *New Introductory Lectures on Psychoanalysis.* Translated by James Strachey. New York: W. W. Norton, 1965.

Fromm, Erich. 1951. *The Forgotten Language.* New York: Holt, Rinehart & Winston, 1967.

Horney, Karen. 1932. "The Dread of Woman." *Feminine Psychology.* Edited by Harold Kelman. New York: W. W. Norton, 1973.

Jacobson, Edith. 1950. "Development of the wish for a child in boys." *The Psychoanalytic Study of the Child* 5: 139-52. New York: International Universities Press.

———. 1964. *The Self and the Object World.* New York: International Universities Press.

Jaffe, Daniel S. 1968. "The Masculine Envy of Woman's Procreative Function. *Journal of the American Psychoanalytical Association* 16: 521-48.

Kittay, Eva. 1983. "Pornography and the Erotization of Power." *Beyond Domination.* Edited by Carol C. Gould. Totowa, N.J.: Rowman & Allanheld.

Kittay, Eva, and Lehrer, Adrienne. 1981. "Semantic Fields and the Structure of Metaphor." *Studies in Language* 5, no. 1: 31-63.

Klein, Melanie. 1957. "Envy and Gratitude." *Envy and Gratitude and Other Works: 1946-1963.* New York: Delacorte, 1975.

Knight, James A. 1971. "Unusual Case: False Pregnancy in a Male." *Medical Aspects of Human Sexuality.* (March): 58-67.

Kohlberg, Lawrence. 1966. "A Cognitive-Developmental Analysis of Children's Sex-Role Concepts and Attitudes." *The Development of Sex Differences.* Edited by E. Maccoby. Palo Alto: Stanford University Press.

Lacoursiere, Roy B. 1972. "Fatherhood and Mental Illness: A Review and New Material." *Psychiatric Quarterly* 46: 109-23.

Lidz, Ruth W., and Lidz, Theodore. 1977. "Male Menstruation: A Ritual Alternative to the Oedipal Transition." *International Journal of Psychoanalysis* 58: 17-31.

Lomas, Peter. 1966. "Ritualistic elements in the management of childbirth." *British Journal of Medical Psychology* 39: 207-13.

Mahler, Margaret. 1968. *On Human Symbiosis and the Vicissitudes of Individuation. Vol. I: Infantile Psychosis.* New York: International Universities Press.

Mahowald, Mary Briody. 1978. *Philosophy of Woman: Classical to Current Concepts.* Indianapolis: Hackett Publishing Company.

Mead, Margaret. 1949. *Male and Female.* New York: William Morrow.

Merchant, Carolyn. 1979. *The Domination of Nature.* San Francisco: Harper & Row.

Money, John, and Hosta, Geoffrey. 1968. "Negro Folklore of Male Pregnancy." *The Journal of Sex Research* 4: 34-50.

Ong, Walter. 1967. *The Presence of the Word.* New Haven and London: Yale University Press.

Plato. *Symposium. The Dialogues of Plato* (1892). Edited and translated by Benjamin Jowett. New York: Random House, 1937.

Plato. *The Theaetetus. The Dialogues of Plato.* Translated by Benjamin Jowett: London: Oxford University Press, 1968.

Rabban, Meyer. 1950. "Sex-Role Identification in Young Children in Two Diverse Social Groups." *Genetic Psychology Monographs* 42: 81-158.

Reik, Theodor. 1931. *Ritual.* Translated by Douglas Bryan. New York: W. W. Norton.

Rich, Adrienne. 1976. *Of Woman Born.* New York: Bantam Books, 1977.

Ross, John Munder. 1974. "The Children's Children: A Psychoanalytic Study of Generativity and Nurturance in Boys." Ph. D. dissertation, New York University.

———. 1975. "Paternal Identity: A Critical Review of the Literature on Nurturance and Generativity in Boys and Men." *Journal of the American Psychoanalytic Association 23: 783–818.*

————. 1977. *"Towards Fatherhood: The Epigenesis of Paternal Identity During a Boy's First Decade." International Review of Psychoanalysis* 4: 327–47.

Sanday, Peggy Reeves. 1981. *Female Power and Male Dominance: On the Origins of of Sexual Inequality.* New York: Cambridge University Press.

Simenauer, Erich. 1954. " 'Pregnancy Envy' in Rainer Maria Rilke." *The American Imago* 11: 235–48.

Spake, Amanda. 1980. "The End of the Ride." *Mother Jones* 5, no. 3. Page 34.

Spinoza. *The Ethics.* Translated by R. H. M. Elwes. New York: Dover Publications, 1951.

Trethowan, W. H. 1968. "The Couvade Syndrome—Some Further Observations." *Journal of Psychosomatic Research* 12: 107–15.

van der Leeuw, P. J. 1958. "The Preoedipal Phase of the Male." *The Psychoanalytic Study of the Child* 13: 352–74.

van Leeuwen, Kato. 1966. "Pregnancy Envy in the Male." *International Journal of Psychoanalysis* 47: 319–24.

Wainwright, William H. 1966. "Fatherhood as a Precipitant of Mental Illness." *American Journal of Psychiatry* 123: 40–44.

Whitbeck, Caroline. 1982. "The Moral Implications of Treating Women as Persons." *The Concept of the Person and Its Implications for the Use of the Fetus in Medicine.* Edited by Stuart Spicker and Tristam Engelhardt. Dordrecht, Holland: D. Reidel Publishing Company (forthcoming).

Winnicott, D. W. 1953. "Transitional Objects and Transitional Phenomena." *International Journal of Psychoanalysis* 34: 89–97.

Zilboorg, Gregory. 1944. "Masculine and Feminine." *Psychiatry* 7: 257–96.

8

Is Male Gender Identity the Cause of Male Domination?

IRIS MARION YOUNG

In this essay I assess the place of Nancy Chodorow's theory of the development of gender personality with respect to the overall project of a feminist social theory. Without doubt Chodorow's theory has made a vital contribution to a feminist understanding of the meaning and production of gender identity. Chodorow herself, as well as a number of other writers, however, has suggested that this gender theory can ground a theory of male domination as a whole, as well as other relations of domination. I will argue that such a use of Chodorow's theory is illegitimate.

I examine passages in Chodorow's writing which suggest that she takes her theory as a theory of male domination. I examine as well the accounts of Nancy Hartsock and Sandra Harding, who use Chodorow's theory to account for male domination more explicitly than Chodorow herself does and who also go farther to claim that male personality is a foundation for all domination relations. All three writers tend to claim that the social relations of women's mothering and the gender personalities they produce are a crucial foundation for male domination. I should emphasize that this is only a tendency in their work, and in focusing on this tendency I shall to a certain extent not be doing justice to the subtlety of their arguments. The precise status of the explanatory power they claim for the theory of gender is ambiguous, I argue, because they fail to distinguish adequately the categories of gender differentiation and male domination. Once these categories are distinguished and their reference formulated, it becomes clear that a theory of gender personality at best can provide only a small part of the description and explanation of institutions of male domination. By failing to distinguish explicitly these categories and focusing primarily on phenomena relating to gender, these accounts divert the attention of feminist theory from questions of the material and structural bases of power.

I

Nancy Chodorow's theory of the development of gender personalities, along with similar work by Jane Flax and the related but rather different work of Dorothy Dinnerstein,[1] has opened a rich territory of theorizing previously only slightly explored by feminist thinkers. In this feminist psychoanalytic theory we have an approach to conceptualizing typical differences in the behavior and experience of men and women that avoids the disadvantages of the only two alternatives we have had until recently for understanding these differences: a biological account or a role-learning account. Chodorow's theory shows the gender characteristics that are stubbornly typical among men and women in our society to be determined by social factors. Unlike a biological account, then, feminist psychoanalytic theory of gender reveals this structure as changeable. But Chodorow's theory also explains why gender identity is so deep-seated as to be virtually impossible to unlearn, and why so much anxiety surrounds gender issues, even for adults. Socialization theory of gender, which conceptualizes gender characteristics as no different in principle from any other learned role norms, cannot account for the uniquely central place of gender in self-identity.

Briefly, the account that Chodorow gives of the development of gender personality in *The Reproduction of Mothering* is as follows.[2] She starts with the fact that the primary person in the life of both men and women is their mother. The significant stages of psychological development that lead to the formation of a separate sense of identity, personality characteristics, the acquisition of gender identity, and sexual orientation, in her theory, play out for both boys and girls in the context of their relation to their mothers. She explains how this exclusive female parenting produces gender identities and personality characteristics that predispose women to be nurturant and cuts off these dispositions in men.

Because of her own gender identity, the mother identifies with her girl child more than with her boy child. In relating to her daughter she unconsciously replays many of the ambiguities and identifications she experiences with her own mother. The mother thus often tends to relate to her daughter more as an extension of herself than as a separate person. The infant girl also experiences herself as identified with her mother, as does the infant boy. The mutually reinforcing identification of mother and daughter results in the girl's acquiring a sense of separate identity later than boys, and never acquiring a sense of separation from others as strong as the boy's. Feminine personality, Chodorow argues, entails the development of relatively permeable "ego boundaries." The normal woman does develop a sense of identity distinct from other people, an ego. But she tends more than the man to fashion her identity by reference to her relation to other people, and to empathize more easily with other people.

For the boy the story is rather different. Due again to her own gender identity, which usually includes a heterosexual identity, the mother of the boy does not identify with him as much as with a girl. She often tends unconsciously to sexualize her relation to him, thus pushing him into a relation of opposition with her. Unlike the girl, then, the boy is encouraged in his effort to separate his identity from his mother. When the boy himself begins to acquire an understanding of gender, his project of separating from the mother becomes one not merely of defining himself as a different person, but a different *kind* of person. In separating from the mother and developing a distinct identity, then, the boy sets himself in opposition to the mother and all that is feminine. Chodorow concludes that from this process the masculine personality typically develops rigid ego boundaries. A man's sense of separate identity, that is, entails cutting off a sense of continuity and empathy with others.

Chodorow is ambiguous about the explanatory status of her theory. On one reading, her theory accounts for no more than how persons accommodate to gender-divided and male-dominated social relations in our society. Her theory explains only how the gender division of labor in the modern nuclear family, which gives exclusive responsibilities for early childcare to the mother, produces gender-differentiated persons with desires and capacities that particularly suit them for continuing that gender division of labor.[3] On this reading, the structures of male domination in our society are presupposed. A separate explanation is required to account for the origin and maintenance of these structures themselves, such as the relations of authority, dependence, and coercion that define this or any other male-dominated society, or the differential access to important resources that underlies gender inequality.

The dominant strain in Chodorow's book, however, suggests that she thinks that at least the basic form of her theory applies to an explanation of male domination in all societies that have existed. Following Gayle Rubin's idea of the "sex/gender system,"[4] Chodorow defines the social organization of gender as the social construction of sexuality, procreation, and kinship which differentiates by gender. She asserts that while logically a society could be gendered without being male-dominated, no such society has ever existed. Thus she seems to conclude that gender differentiation is identical to male domination in at least all hitherto existing societies, and that her theory of the development of gender personalities by women's mothering is a theory of this male-dominated gender system.[5] Hartsock and Harding also tend to collapse the categories of gender differentiation and male domination, at least insofar as they appear to make inferences about male domination directly from claims about gender differentiation.

Alongside passages which suggest that this theory of gender accounts for the motivation of individuals to act in accordance with the institutions of male domination, there are passages such as the following in which Chodorow appears to claim that the theory accounts for male domination itself.

We can define and articulate certain broad universal sexual asymmetries in the social organization of gender *generated* by women's mothering. Women's mothering *determines* women's primary location in the domestic sphere and creates a *basis* for the structural differentiation of domestic and public spheres. But these spheres operate hierarchically. Kinship rules organize claims of men on domestic units, and men dominate kinship. Culturally and politically, the public sphere dominates the domestic, and *hence* men dominate women.[6]

In my reading of this and similar passages, Chodorow claims that her theory explains the basic causes of male domination in all societies. Following Rosaldo and Lamphere,[7] she assumes that the subordination of women is a function of a universal public-domestic division. This public-domestic division, she says, originates in and is reproduced by the social relations of women's mothering that produce distinctive gender personalities. While a direct argument for this set of claims does not appear in Chodorow's writing, one can be reconstructed from what she does say.

Chodorow argues that in developing a masculine self-identity, boys must not only develop a sense of self distinct from the mother, but a sense of being a different kind of self. Since the mother provides him with his first model of what it is to be a person, the boy defines masculinity negatively, as what the mother is not. To have a positive sense of masculinity, therefore, boys must denigrate and dissociate themselves from the female. Boys develop a dread of women and a desire to have power over them through this process, because mother poses a threat to their separate masculine identities.[8]

To secure his masculine identity, the boy rejects the mother and joins with other boys and men in a positive, exclusive sphere without the attributes of nurturance and dependence associated with the feminine. This masculine realm takes on a more highly valued character than the domestic, because men must affirm their masculinity by denying and denigrating the female. This would appear to be the argument for Chodorow's above-quoted claim that women's mothering "creates a basis for the structural differentiation of domestic and public spheres" and sets up a hierarchical relation between them.

Women's mothering also creates gender personalities that particularly suit women and men for the domestic and public realms respectively. The relative stability of her identification with the mother gives to the girl's gender identity a personality oriented toward affective relations with others. This suits girls for the particularistic relations of the domestic realm. Women's mothering creates in boys, on the other hand, a more bounded, instrumentally oriented, and abstract personality. This suits them particularly for the formal and instrumental character of the relations in the public realm. This presumably is the argument for Chodorow's above-quoted claim that "women's mothering determines women's primary location in the domestic sphere."

In a paper entitled "The Feminist Standpoint: Developing the Ground of a

Specifically Feminist Historical Materialism," Nancy Hartsock uses Chodorow's theory of the development of gender personalities as a central element in her account of the "abstract masculinity" she claims underlies Western culture.[9] Abstract masculinity is a mode of conceptualization that emphasizes mutually exclusive dualities. These dualities—such as same-other, identity-difference, negation-affirmation, life-death, body-mind—have a crucial ground in the structure of the masculine personality which creates in men an oppositional attitude in human relations, a polarity of self and other.

Hartsock uses the notion of abstract masculinity primarily to account for the logic of much of western metaphysical and political thought. More relevant for the issues of this paper, she also appeals to abstract masculinity to account for the nature of institutions. Abstract masculinity, she claims, accounts for hierarchical dualism in the institutions of society, which underlies relations of class domination and gender domination. She argues that "male rather than female experience and activity replicates itself in both the hierarchical and dualist institutions of class society and the frameworks of thought generated by that experience.[10] A primary determinant of this experience is the self-other dichotomy produced in masculine personality by women's mothering.

It is difficult to tell just what sort of causal relations Hartsock asserts, or how strongly. As I interpret her claims, she asserts that masculine personality causes institutions of domination in the following way. Being mothered by women produces in men a propensity to approach relations with others in an oppositional and competitive way. Thus, men produce institutions defined by opposition, hierarchy, and competition. The masculine personality generated by women's mothering also produces the oppression of women because men tend to denigrate and repress activities associated with the body, and women are most linked to such activities.

Sandra Harding asserts an even stronger and more explicit relationship between women's mothering and institutions of domination. In a paper entitled "What is the Real Material Base of Patriarchy and Capital?" she answers that the social relations of women's mothering are the most fundamental material base of all forms of oppression—not only gender oppression, but also class, race, lesbian and gay oppression. The theory of the production of gendered personalities, she claims, explains "why it is that *men* control and thus have material interests in maintaining both patriarchy and capital." The social relations of women's mothering "create patterns of dominating social relations which are more general than class oppression and gender oppression."[11]

A later paper by Harding specifies more precisely the nature of her causal claim. The social relations of women's mothering determine the form or structure common to male personalities, institutions of domination, and the ideas associated with them.[12] The social relations of women's mothering constitute the material base of classism, racism, heterosexism, and sexism insofar as they are all structured by a dualistic hierarchy of dominance and subordination.

Like Chodorow and Hartsock, Harding does not clearly and explicitly lay out the argument for this claim. As I reconstruct her argument, it appears to be the following: Harding theorizes that women's mothering produces a self-other dichotomy in the masculine personality. Because boys have particular separation problems, their search for a separate identity leads them to form rigid ego boundaries and to tend to regard other persons, especially women, as in antagonistic opposition to themselves. This self-other dichotomy is not merely an opposition, but a heirarchy in which self is of greater value. Men thus have a psychic interest in dominating, in setting themselves up as master in relation to other men, to nature, and of course to women. Since men design and control all of society's institutions, according to Harding, these institutions reflect this psychology of self-other domination. Thus class oppression, racial oppression, gender oppression, and homosexual oppression have a common formal cause in "the stereotypically masculine modes of structuring social relations between self and other which originate *in individuals,* in the psycho/physical labor required to become masculinely gendered social persons."[13]

II

Nancy Chodorow appears to identify gender differentiation with male domination, and thus tends to argue that her theory of the development of gender personalities is a theory of male domination. Hartsock and Harding also tend to collapse the categories of gender differentiation and male domination, at least insofar as they appear to make inferences about male domination directly from claims about gender differentiation. In contrast, I perceive and defend a distinction between these two categories. While gender differentiation is a phenomenon of individual psychology and experience, as well as of cultural categorization, male domination refers to structural relations of genders and institutional forms that determine those structures. Any complete account of a male-dominated society requires an account of gender, but also requires an account of the causes and reproduction of structures not originating from gender psychology. For these reasons a theory of gender cannot, as the three writers here treated think, be used as the basis for a theory of male domination. The failure to distinguish the category of gender differentiation from male domination is not uncommon among feminist theorists, especially those who rely on psychoanalytic theory.[14] Thus the significance of the theoretical remarks in this section extends beyond the three thinkers I focus on to the whole project of feminist social theory.

Gender differentiation refers primarily to phenomena of individual psychology and experience. Chodorow shows how the unconscious inner life of men and women is differently structured because they have different infant relations to their mothers, and Harding follows Chodorow on this. Hartsock defines the phenomena of gender less in terms of personality structure and more in terms of the different experience men and women have of the world because they are mothered by women and because the sexual division of labor allocates to them different sorts of activities.[15] Whether interpreted primarily in terms of personality structure or mode of experiencing the world, gender differentiation also includes propensities of both men and women to behave in certain typical ways. All three of the writers under discussion here appear to think that psychological dispositions associated with gender can themselves explain social structural phenomena, such as a distinction between public and private spheres, or relations of hierarchy in institutions, and I shall argue below that such reasoning is inappropriate.

Gender is not merely a phenomenon of individual psychology and experience. In most cultures it is a basic metaphysical category by which the whole universe is organized. Most languages, for example, are elaboratedly gendered, with gender-differentiated modes of address, verb and noun forms, and so on. In most cultures, moreover, all the significant elements of the social, natural, and spiritual world are differentiated by gender. This usually means more than merely designating animals, weather phenomena, abstract concepts, and so on, as masculine or feminine; it entails as well that the entities categorized carry a rich set of genderized attributes and relationships. The integrating mythologies of most cultures rely heavily on gender symbols, as do most legitimating ideologies.[16]

As a category, then, gender differentiation is primarily a phenomenon of symbolic life, in both the individual consciousness and the general metaphysical framework and ideologies of a culture. Psychoanalytic theory of gender is the most adequate theory, because more than any other type of theory it can make the connections between individual affectivity, motivation, and desire, on the one hand, and the symbolic and categories of culture, on the other. A psychoanalytic account of gender can explain why gender meanings are so deep-seated in individual identity and cultural categorization, and why discussion of alteration in gender meanings or gender relationships causes most people great anxiety. As a theory of symbolism, and of the unconscious mechanism for symbol substitution and transference, moreover, psychoanalysis can provide a framework for understanding the pervasiveness of gender meanings throughout a culture's categorical and symbolic systems. The feminist theories of gender developed by Chodorow, Flax, Dinnerstein, and others no doubt need more elaboration and refinement, particularly with regard to questions of cross-cultural and historical variation. There is little doubt, however, that they have already contributed significantly to the development of feminist social theory.

To regard male domination as identical with or derivable from gender differentiation, however, is to overpsychologize the social phenomena of male domination.[17] As a category, male domination refers not primarily to psychological and cultural phenomena, but to a different aspect of social reality, institutional structures.[18] This structural aspect of social reality includes at least the following: (a) what the major institutions in a given society are, how differentiated they are from one another, and how they reinforce or conflict with one another; (b) how material resources are produced and distributed within and among these institutions, and how these patterns of production and distribution provide differentiated capacities and satisfactions for different individuals and groups of people; and (c) the rules according to which the institutions are organized and the means of their enforcement, especially as these define relations of authority and subordination.

Male domination refers to the organization of a particular institution or the pattern of institutional organization in a whole society, in which men have some degree of unreciprocated authority or control over women, and/or men have greater control than women over the operations of the institutions or set of institutions. Male domination exists within an institution or in a whole society when one or more of the following conditions obtain: (a) men have the power to control aspects of women's lives and actions and the means to enforce their will, and women do not have complementary control over men's lives; (b) men occupy institutionalized positions of social decision-making from which women are excluded, and women do not have their own spheres with comparable privilege or control over men's lives; (c) men benefit from the labor and other activity of women to a greater degree than women benefit from that of men.[19]

It is possible to conceive of a gender-differentiated society, I suggest, in which none of these conditions of male domination exist. It may be true that all hitherto existing societies have been male-dominated as well as gender-differentiated, although this is a matter of some dispute. Even if it were true that male domination in fact has always existed along with gender differentiation, that would not mean that they are identical, or that the former derives from the latter. Unless we make a clear distinction between these two categories and develop clear criteria for what counts as male domination, we will not be able to discover how culturally and historically widespread male domination is, or how it varies in degree and kind. Only by keeping the distinction clear can we ascertain whether there is any regular relation between phenomena of gender differentiation and phenomena of male domination.

Before continuing the examination of the theories of Chodorow, Harding, and Hartsock, it might be useful to illustrate the categorical distinctions I have been making with an example of phenomena of male domination that cannot be explained by appealing to gender theory.

Evelyn Fox Keller presents a very interesting account of the origins of the style of modern scientific inquiry in the masculine personality women's mothering generates. She argues that the rigid notion of scientific objectivity that excludes all affectivity, value, and human meaning derives from the rigid character of masculine ego-boundaries. She argues that the metaphors of

Bacon and other founders of modern science that depict the scientist as conquering and mastering a female nature, moreover, arise from a masculine self-
other opposition that identifies the other as female.[20] Her account reveals
much about the cognitive styles of modern and contemporary science, and the
degree to which we can understand these as bound to the identities of the men
who have founded and dominated that science.

It does not itself account for why, since the early modern period, men have
dominated scientific activity, however, as Keller suggests it does. Nor does it
show how male domination of scientific and technological activity has had
crucial implications for the specific forms of women's oppression in the
modern world. Explaining why men dominate science, and why that fact
enables them to dominate women, entails reference to more structural aspects
of social life and their changes.

Important among these structural aspects is specific change in the gender
division of labor that accompanied the rise of science. During the time that
Bacon defined science as the domination of nature, men were appropriating
from women many of the practical arts whose union with traditional intellectual science Bacon saw as the key to the new method. For example, feminists
have most researched the male appropriation of the healing arts, which before
that time were dominated by women. An account like Keller's can explain
why, once men had dominated medicine and defined it as science, the concep-
tualizaton of the body by medicine became more objectified, the use of instruments increased, and so on. The gender theory cannot explain, however,
how men were able to take over the formerly female-dominated professions,
or even why they wanted to.[21]

III

I have argued that attempts to develop a general theory of women's oppression
from gender theory fail to distinguish clearly between gender differentiation
and male domination. As a result, as I will show in this section, this use of
gender theory tends to divert the attention of feminist social theory from questions of the bases, conditions, and exercise of power.

Chodorow's theory of the development of gender personalities exhibits a
curious lack of reference to male power. Unlike earlier feminist attempts to
reinterpret psychoanalytic theory, such as those by Firestone, Rubin, and
Mitchell,[22] Chodorow does not at all appeal to the power of the father in the
family to account for the development of different personalities in boys and
girls. On those earlier accounts, which follow Freud more closely than
Chodorow does, the boy gives up his attachment to his mother in exchange for
the promise that one day he can accede to the power of the father. Thus, when
the boy despises the mother and gives up identification with her, he does so
not simply because he is uncertain about who he is, but because he despises her

powerlessness. For the girl, on the other hand, the discovery that she lacks the phallus as does her mother is a discovery that she belongs to the class of the powerless. Penis envy is her desire to belong to the class of the powerful. The girl drops her desire for her mother and turns her affection to the father as her only avenue to power. Chodorow's theory has an advantage over these accounts in the specific attention she gives to the positive relation the infant has to the mother. This emphasis on the relations of mothering, however, leads her to ignore the power of the father in accounting for gender personality. In her account, the father is primarily an absence, not a power.

This deemphasis of male power in Chodorow's theory carries over into the uses made of it for general feminist social theory. All three of the thinkers summarized above, of course, claim to be concerned with explaining the sources of male power and the oppression of women. The most they explain, however, is a masculine *desire* for power. The social relations of infant care, they argue, produce men with more of a propensity than women to instrumentalize relations with others. Men also emerge from the mothering process with a hierarchical self-other dichotomy that allows them to view all persons as potential subordinates. The three thinkers account for a specific male desire to dominate women, moreover, by appeal to an unconscious dread of women resulting from male insecurity of self as different from the other.

Unless a psychological propensity to wield power itself makes men powerful, however, their accounts do not touch on the question of the sources of male power. Neither Chodorow, Hartsock, nor Harding sees that their theories ignore concrete relations of domination, and as I have already pointed out, they tend to draw conclusions about the latter from arguments about the former. Other elements of gender theory also contribute to a tendency to deemphasize concrete relations of power. In particular, uses of gender theory to found a theory of male domination tend to (a) ignore historical and cultural specificity, (b) to focus on ideational forms, and (c) to assume incorrect social ontology.

OMISSION OF HISTORICAL AND CULTURAL SPECIFICITY

All three of the theorists under discussion abstract from the cultural and historical specificity of concrete social structures. They pose their claims in terms of what is common to all (male-dominated) societies. As a consequence of this universalizing tendency, they make controversial claims about the universality of certain social phenomena. Chodorow and Harding assume, for example, that in all societies women have exclusive responsibility for primary infant care, and that in all societies women have been devalued. Both assumptions, however, would be disputed by many anthropologists.[23] Chodorow appears to assume that all societies have a public-private split, which allocates men to the public and women to the private. Many anthropologists and historians would take issue with this, as well.[24] Finally, many anthropologists and historians would dispute the assumption made by all three writers that in all societies women are oppressed, or at least have a lesser status than men.

From a methodological point of view, this universalizing tendency has several problems. First, claims about the universality of gender structures are usually made without empirical warrant. On most questions about what is common to all societies, the data simply are not in. Second, trans-historical or trans-cultural claims too often carry over assumptions based on the historically specific structures of modern European society to other societies and periods.[25]

The attempt to make universalistic claims about male domination, finally, requires taking a very abstract approach to social reality. For concrete observation shows that there is extraordinary variability in the causes and degree of male domination in different societies, or even among different subgroups in one society. Since the concrete social relations of gender vary enormously in content and structure, then, gender theory can only make trans-historical or trans-cultural assertions by abstracting from these concrete relations. For Chodorow to regard the public-private distinction as a cultural universal always connected with women's mothering and women's status in the same way, for example, she must conceive it as an abstract and purely formal distinction empty of specific content. Harding says explicitly that gender theory is concerned not with the content of social phenomena, but rather with the formal similarity she claims exists among masculine personality, patriarchal social institutions, and the belief systems that arise within those institutions. These all have in common, she suggests, the formal structure of hierarchical dualism.[26]

EMPHASIS ON IDEATIONAL FORMS

Relations of power and domination drop out of consideration in the accounts we are examining here precisely because of the level of abstraction at which they operate. The bases, structure, and operation of power and domination are necessarily concrete, and are extraordinarily variable in both form and degree.[27] The inability of this formalism to deal with power becomes apparent in the way that Hartsock and Harding conceptualize domination itself. They do not refer to concrete material conditions to describe the enactment of power and domination, but rather only to the relation among categories. For both, social relations of domination appear to be defined as nothing more than a hierarchical dualism of self and other.

Hartsock, for example, appears to define class society as a social structure in which there is a hierarchical dualism, a ruling group standing in opposition to a ruled group.[28] This merely defines the abstract categorical relations of class society, and excludes reference to the social structures and material relations that also ought to define class society. Class society is indeed hierarchical but, more specifically, it involves relations of power and dependence in which one sector of society enforces the appropriation of the products of the labor of other segments of society.[29]

Despite the fact that the gender theorists claim to be materialist in their account of the bases of male domination, their accounts are idealist in the strict sense. They claim that the nature of institutions is determined by a relation among ideas. To be sure, they attempt to ground the self-other dichotomy they attribute to the masculine personality in the material relations of infant care. They do not argue, however, that material relations determine the institutional structure. They argue, rather, that a certain logical or metaphysical structure determines the structure of social institutions, namely, a conceptualization of experience in terms of a rigid self-other dichotomy.

If I have offered a correct analysis of the categories of gender differentiation and male domination, phenomena related to gender differentiation cannot by themselves explain structures of male domination, because the former category refers to ideas, symbols, and forms of consciousness, and the latter refers to the appropriation of benefit from women by men in a concrete material way. Gender theory can plausibly be used to argue that certain forms of conceptualization that appear in western theories and ideologies have a root in the masculine personality generated by women's mothering.[30] For here the account grounds one set of forms of consciousness in another.

Gender theory surely can contribute a part of the explanation of the nature and relation of social institutions, moreover. But the explanation of any institutional form, especially those relating to power and domination, requires in addition reference to the relation of institutions to one another, and an account of the material means of access, control, enforcement, and autonomy that agents have within those institutions. In not recognizing the categorical difference between gender differentiation and male domination, gender theory ignores these explanatory requirements.

Let me give an example of this sort of confusion. Chodorow's arguments, as well as Harding's, focus on the deviation of women rather than directly on the question of male domination. In explaining devaluation of women they appear to think they have thereby explained male domination, when in fact no such inference is warranted.

As summarized above, Chodorow explains the source of the devaluation of women by men in a dread of women and anxiety about their masculinity caused by the social relations of mothering. Inasmuch as it argues that one form of consciousness—masculine personality—grounds another, masculine attitude toward women, this is a plausible argument. One cannot pass from such an argument directly to a conclusion about the causes of male domination, however. Even if we find that devaluation of women and male domination always occur together, we cannot conclude that the explanation of one is also the explanation of the other. Description and explanation of male domination still require reference to material relations of dependence and autonomy, access to resources and the material means of coercion, as well as to the structural relations among institutions which reinforce or change these.

ASSUMPTION OF INCORRECT SOCIAL ONTOLOGY

A final element of the accounts of Hartsock and Harding contributes to their lack of specific attention to the concrete causes and operation of power. They both assume that the institutions of male-dominated society reflect masculine personality, and only masculine personality. Harding most explicitly argues that the nature of institutions of domination is determined by the self-other dichotomy of masculine personality because men design and control all institutions in patriarchal societies, and make them in their own image.[31]

This argument falsely assumes that the nature of institutions in patriarchal societies is solely or primarily a product of male action. Even in the most male-dominated societies, many spheres of social life exist in which women's action and temperament have a significant influence. The problem of male domination is not that women are prevented from acting upon and within institutions, but that the benefits of their contribution are systematically transferred to men.

More important, that institutions of domination reflect the structure of masculine personality is an argument that rests on a questionable assumption about the relation of individuals and social structures. It assumes that the nature of institutions is determined by the nature of the individuals whose actions produce and maintain them. There are several problems, however, with this assumption.

While acting persons are indeed the only concrete human entities that exist in the social world, it does not follow that the nature of institutions is isomorphic with the nature of individuals. The assumption mistakes the fundamental unit of institutions, which is not individuals but *interactions* among individuals.[32] Most institutions relevant to a theory of male domination are products of interactions between men and women, and not merely among men. The characteristics of personality, the motives they influence, and the interpretations of events they color are surely important elements in these interactions. But the structure of the institutions cannot be read off from the structure of individual personalities.[33]

Actions and interactions, moreover, are not the only determinants of institutional structures and practices. Individuals always act situated within and oriented toward natural and geographical givens, the possibilities and limits of available technologies and artifacts, and the cultural traditions to which they are heir. Perhaps even more important, the actions and interactions of social life almost always generate unintended consequences. One cannot foresee or control the interpretation others will give to one's actions or how they will respond, nor how others will respond to the response, and so on. Social events are often the result of the cumulative effect of a great many individual actions and interactions, moreover, bringing results neither intended nor predicted by any of the actors. Economic events like depressions, for example, often have this character.

The argument that the nature of institutions of domination is determined by the self-other dichotomy of the masculine personality created by women's mothering, then, erases the complex material and social structural factors involved in the causes, maintenance, and operation of relations of power and domination. These arguments fail to distinguish male domination from gender differentiation insofar as then tend to reduce social structural phenomena to psychological causes. Thus they fail to give adequate focus to those structures of male domination in a particular context which cannot be reduced to individual psychologies.

In sum, gender theory diverts feminist thinking from specific focus on power because it tends to be universalistic, hence to couch its claims in terms of abstract relations of categories, and to reduce social structures to products of individual personality.[34]

IV

Chodorow's theory, as well as Dinnerstein's, has received much discussion and has been absorbed quickly into feminist theorizing, at least partly because it seemed to offer a concrete and workable strategy for transforming gender relations. The theories suggest that exclusive parenting of infants by women is a key cause of male domination and the oppression of women. Thus, if the social relations of infant care were to change such that men participated as much as women, it seems to follow that the whole edifice erected on the base of exclusive female parenting would topple.

Parenting shared by men and women is the key step in eliminating the oppression of women. When that strategy was first put forward, it sounded simple and straightforward. It has not taken feminists long, however, to see that the matter is not simple. Many wonder whether men with their present masculine personalities, complete with their insecurities and hatred of women, should be anywhere near children. Others have pointed out that in contemporary society, mothering is one of the only activities in which most women have some autonomy and from which they derive a measure of self-respect. If men were encouraged to participate in that sphere as well, under present conditions, it could mean a loss of status for women.

It quickly became apparent, moreover, that to really change the social relations of infant care entails monumental changes in all institutions of society. For shared parenting to be possible, the whole structure of work outside the home would have to change and become more flexible. To encourage men to be childcare workers, outside the home as well as in it, the value of childcare would have to be significantly increased. Without alteration in other elements of male domination, moreover, shared parenting, even if it happened, would not be likely to change greatly the patterns of socialization or the resulting masculine and feminine personalities. If men were to continue to occupy positions of authority, for example, and the idea of authority continued to be associated with masculinity, then children raised by both women and men would be likely to maintain that association. If media images continued to sentimentalize and sexualize women while presenting men as tough and emotionally distant, children and adults of both sexes would be likely to internalize and reproduce those images.

When we ask about feminist strategy, the error of collapsing the categories of male domination and gender differentiation and attributing the key cause of male domination to women's mothering becomes apparent. Gender division in parenting is only one among the many institutional structures that produce and maintain the oppression of women. If the above arguments are sound, moreover, women's mothering may be less fundamental than other institutions of male domination, since it appears that relations of parenting cannot be changed without first changing other structures.

What does it mean, then, for feminist theory to pay attention to issues of power and domination? I have suggested that it entails a structural analysis of relations of authority and dependence, and a description of the transfer and appropriation of benefits of labor. To describe and explain male domination as concrete relations of power, feminist theory must ask questions like the following. Which gender has access to what social resources as a result of performing its gender-differentiated activity, and what do the resources give members of the gender the capacity to do? How much and by what means are members of each gender organized in networks of solidarity?[35] How do the structural relations among various institutions—state and family, for example—affect the concrete relations of dependence and autonomy in which women stand?[36]

If it does not offer us a very full strategy for feminist revolution, what can gender theory offer that will aid in undermining the oppression of women? Gender theory can provide us with an important understanding of the power of symbols, and the bases of motivation and desire. It can help sensitize both women and men to the deep sources of some of the ways of experiencing that are particular to each gender. It can also help us understand, as Flax has argued, how in the women's movement itself we may tend to reproduce our relations to our mothers in our relationships with each other. Perhaps most important, gender theory can be an enormous aid in consciousness raising about contemporary masculinist ideologies, by showing some of the sources of their misogyny. All this needs to be supplemented with a concrete analysis of the social structure, however, which cannot be provided by gender theory. To fight against male domination we need to understand how the institutions work in such a way as to promote women's working for men, how the current arrangements are enforced, and who controls the resources that produce and maintain them.

Notes

I began research for this paper while participating in a National Endowment for the Humanities Summer Seminar Fellowship on "Themes in Cross-Cultural Analysis of Women and Society" directed by Eleanor Leacock, City University of New York, in the summer of 1980. An earlier version of this paper was presented at the Caucus for a New Political Science, American Political Science Association meetings, New York City, September 1981; and at a meeting of the society for Women in Philosophy, Western Division, Fort Wayne, Indiana, October 1981. I am grateful to women at those meetings for their responses and suggestions. I am also grateful to Nancy Hartsock, Muriel Dimen, Linda Nicholson, Sandra Bartky, Roger Gottlieb and David Alexander for their helpful suggestions.

1. Jane Flax, "The Conflict Between Nurturance and Autonomy in Mother-Daughter Relationships and within Feminism," *Feminist Studies* 4, no. 2 (1978); Dorothy Dinnerstein, *The Mermaid and the Minotaur: Sexual Arrangements and Human Malaise* (New York: Harper & Row, 1976).
2. Nancy Chodorow, *The Reproduction of Mothering* (Berkeley: University of California Press, 1978).
3. Ibid., pp. 185, 208-9.
4. Gayle Rubin, "The Traffic in Women: Notes Toward a Political Economy of Sex," in *Toward an Anthropology of Women,* edited by Rayna Reiter (New York: Monthly Review Press, 1976).
5. Chodorow, *Reproduction of Mothering,* pp. 8-9.
6. Ibid., pp. 9-10 (italics mine).
7. Michelle Zimbalist Rosaldo and Louise Lamphere, Introduction to *Woman, Culture and Society* (Stanford: Stanford University Press, 1974), pp. 1-16.
8. Chodorow talks most explicitly about dread of women as an element in masculine personality in her paper "Being and Doing: A Cross-Cultural Examination of the Socialization of Males and Females," in *Woman in Sexist Society,* edited by Vivian Gornick and Barbara K. Moran (New York: Basic Books, 1971); see also Chodorow, *Reproduction of Mothering,* pp. 181-83.
9. Included in *Discovering Reality: Feminist Perspectives on Epistemology, Metaphysics, Methodology, and Philosophy of Science,* edited by Sandra Harding and Merrill B. Hintikka (Dordrecht: Reidel Publishing Co., 1983).
10. Hartsock, "The Feminist Standpoint," p. 20.
11. Sandra Harding, "What is the Real Material Base of Patriarchy and Capital?" in *Women and Revolution,* edited by Lydia Sargent (Boston: South End Press, 1981), p. 139.
12. See Sandra Harding, "Gender Politics of Infancy," *Quest* 5, no. 3, p. 63.
13. Ibid., p. 62.
14. For example, Juliet Mitchell, in her book *Psychoanalysis and Feminism* (New York: Vintage Books, 1975), clearly identifies patriarchy with the psychodynamics of gender. See my critique of her failure to make this distinction in "Socialist Feminism and the Limits of Dual Systems Theory," *Socialist Review* 50/51, Summer 1980.

15. Nancy Hartsock, in a personal communication, has pointed out this difference in emphasis between her account and the others. This distinction raises the question, which I do not intend to answer here, of what the relationship is between the concepts of "personality" and "experience."

16. For an incisive definition of gender in these terms, see David Alexander, "Gender Labor and Occupational Segregation by Sex," (unpublished, University of Massachusetts).

17. Susan Bourque and Kay Barbara Warren make this point in *Women of the Andes: Patriarchy and Social Change in Two Peruvian Towns* (Ann Arbor: University of Michigan Press, 1981), pp. 58 and 83. They do not give very thorough reasons for their claim that an understanding of patriarchy requires analysis of the institutional context of sex roles independent of psychology.

18. For an account of the logic of social analysis which distinguishes between psychological and structural aspects without falling into the polarization typical of other sociological frameworks, see Anthony Giddens, *Central Problems in Social Theory* (Berkeley: University of California Press, 1979), Chaps. 2–5.

19. Very few feminist theorists have discussed how to define criteria of male domination. Peggy Reeves Sanday has a useful discussion of the way certain anthropologists have defined the concept, and offers an alternative formulation of her own, one somewhat narrower than the one I have articulated. See *Female Power and Male Dominance* (New York: Cambridge University Press, 1981), especially pp. 163–79.

Naomi Rosenthal has developed a useful notion of the measures of male dominance and female autonomy based on the ability to mobilize resources, including political and ideological resources, which she applies to five Amazonian societies. See her "Women in Amazonia," (unpublished, SUNY at Old Westbury).

Lisa Leghorn and Katherine Parker, in *Woman's Worth* (New York: Routledge & Kegan Paul, 1981), develop criteria for distinguishing three levels of male-dominated societies: those in which women have no power, those in which women have token power, and those in which women have negotiating power. They measure women's power within three areas: (a) valuation of women's fertility and physical integrity; (b) women's access to and control over crucial resources, including property, paid and collective labor, training and education; and (c) women's networks (p. 22).

20. Evelyn Fox Keller, "Baconian Science: A Hermaphroditic Birth," *Philosophical Forum* II, No. 3 (Spring 1980).

21. To my knowledge, Alice Clark's 1919 book, *The Working Life of Women in the Seventeenth Century* (New York: E. P. Dutton & Co.), is still the best single source on this process of change in women's economic status.

22. Shulamith Firestone, *The Dialectic of Sex* (New York: William Morrow, 1970), Chap. 3; Rubin, "The Traffic in Women"; Mitchell, *Psychoanalysis and Feminism.*

23. Sanday, *Female Power and Male Dominance,* Eleanor Leacock, "Women in Egalitarian Society," in *Becoming Visible: Women in European History,* edited by Renate Bridenthal and Claudia Koonz (Boston: Houghton Mifflin, 1977).

24. In an article published shortly before she died, Rosaldo argued against her earlier position that discussion of a universal public-domestic split tends to rely on cultural assumptions based on that particular form of the public-private split that dates from the 19th century in western Europe. See Michelle Rosaldo, "The Use and Abuse of Anthropology: Reflections on Feminism and Cross-Cultural Understanding," *Signs* 5, no. 3 (1980): 389–417. Linda Nicholson suggests that feminist theory should conceptualize public-domestic divisions in historically specific ways in "Feminist Theory: The Public and the Private," (SUNY at Albany).

25. Mina Davis Caulfield, "Universal Sex Oppression? A Critique from Marxist Anthropology," *Catalyst* 10/11 (Summer 1977): 60–77.

26. Harding, "Gender Politics of Infancy," p. 63.

27. Rosaldo, "The Use and Abuse of Anthropology," passim.

28. Hartsock, "The Feminist Standpoint," p. 20.

29. It is indicative that in her account of the social relations of class society as grounded in a self-other dichotomy, Hartsock appeals to Hegel's master-slave account. This provides some support for my claim that her conceptualization of the basis of social relations is essentially idealistic.

30. Hartsock and Keller have arguments to this effect in the papers already cited. See also the papers by Jane Flax and Naomi Schemen in Harding and Hintikka, eds., *Discovering Reality*.

31. Harding, "What is the Real Material Base of Patriarchy and Capitalism?" p. 139; here Harding asserts quite strongly that *all* institutions in society are controlled by men. On page 150 Harding gives the argument that institutions reflect male psyches because men design and control them.

32. Cf. Rosaldo, "Use and Abuse."

33. Cf. Giddens, *Central Problems in Social Theory*, pp. 73-95; Sartre conceptualizes the notion of social structure as the result of individual actions that nevertheless do not have attributes that can be assigned to individuals in his concepts of *totalization* and *counter-finality*. See his *Critique of Dialectical Reason* (London: New Left Books, 1976).

34. Harding specifically disclaims that her theory is psychologically reductionist, on the grounds that it says that the psychic structures that cause institutional forms are themselves caused by the social relations of mothering. See "What is the Real Material Base," p. 149. This does not answer my point, however, since I am claiming that she reduces the attributes of institutions to attributes of individuals.

35. Rosenthal, in "Women in Amazonia," takes gender solidarity as a major factor in accounting for male domination or the lack of it. In examining Amazonian societies she concludes that collective solidarity among men, where such collective solidarity is lacking among women, accounts for the only significant inequality between the genders in those societies.

36. Harding, "Gender Politics of Infancy," p. 68; cf. Chodorow, *Reproduction of Mothering*, pp. 218-19.

9

Review of Chodorow's The Reproduction of Mothering

PAULINE BART

If a computer were programmed to analyze texts, it would print out that *The Reproduction of Mothering* was written by two authors. The first author, Nancy Chodorow *A*, is the socialist feminist who speaks of institutionalized male dominance, of the primary emotional importance of women for women, who is anti-capitalist, who tries to be careful about heterosexist bias, who does not use "he" generically, and who is critical of the misogyny in Freud, albeit not in the mother-blaming of the psychoanalytic writers she quotes. This is the Chodorow who wrote two articles on mothering before she apparently fell under the thrall of psychoanalysis and whose presence is felt in the first and last sections of *The Reproduction of Mothering.*

The computer would also report that the book was written by Nancy Chodorow *B*, who starts her chapters with pithy quotes from Freud and other psychoanalytic mavens.* This author does not quote important feminist analysts of motherhood such as Adrienne Rich (*Of Woman Born*) or of incest, such as Florence Rush ("Freudian Cover-up," *Chrysalis* 1, 1977) and Judith Herman and Lisa Hershman ("Father-Daughter Incest," *Signs* 2, no. 4, 1977). Chodorow *B* assumes the necessity for adults of two genders for socialization and thus reinforces heterosexuality and the nuclear family. She joins with Philip Slater (*Glory of Hera*) in blaming mothers for psychosis in ancient Greece. She herself speaks of mothers' *collusive* bonding, echoing psychoanalytically oriented writers who traditionally refer to mothers' collusion when describing the dynamics of incest. This Chodorow has written a book on motherhood that few mothers can read. In the hope, presumably, of

---

*Yiddish term for "experts."

This review first appeared in *Off Our Backs* 11, no. 1 (January 1981). Reprinted by permission of the author and publisher.

adding a sociological suit to the psychoanalytic house of cards, she contributes to our mystification rather than to the demystification of the female experience that is the goal of feminist scholarship.

This is the time of the backlash: abortion rights are rapidly eroding, the ERA is stalled, our old costume of skirts, high heels, and nylons has returned.* We are told that now we are "liberated" and can return to being "feminine." This is the year when "Kramer vs. Kramer," a backlash film, received the Academy Award, and when a bill the press called "the Kramer bill" that allowed joint custody was introduced in the New York State legislature. It is the year when the U.S. government spoke of drafting women to protect the right of the Afghan rebels to prevent "their" women from becoming literate, the event that sparked the men's revolt against the Marxist central government. It is the year that Nancy Chodorow's psychoanalytically conceptualized *The Reproduction of Mothering* won the award named for the feminist sociologist Jessie Bernard from the American Sociological Association. The patriarchy has additionally rewarded Chodorow with a coveted fellowship to the Institute for Advanced Study in the Behavioral Sciences at Palo Alto. The first printing of the book has already sold out, an unusual event in academic publishing, particularly for a book as difficult to read as Chodorow's. Dorothy Dinnerstein, author of *The Mermaid and the Minotaur,* a similar book, has been sanctified in the pages of *Ms.* magazine and was extravagantly praised by Gloria Steinem in her invited talk to the American Psychological Association.

One must ask why the Dinnerstein and Chodorow books are so honored at this particular time, while Rich's brilliant and moving *Of Woman Born* was viciously attacked in 1976 in both *The New York Times* and *The New York Review of Books*—and attacked by women because, since the women's movement, men now find women to do the hatchet jobs that were previously done by men. We've come a long way, baby.

In the past few years the women's movement has discovered that mothers are women and that motherhood is an appropriate, even compelling feminist issue (cf. special issues of *Frontiers* 3, no. 2 and *Feminist Studies* 2 [June 1978], courses and conferences addressing the issue, and a number of books and articles). Is this because women who belonged to the radical groups within the women's movement in the late 1960s are now confronting decisions about whether or not to have children, or because they have had children and have learned that previously apparently egalitarian relationships collapse under the stress of childcare? Is it because we are now seeing the results of the ideology of androgyny which permeated feminism, an ideology which ignored the structural factors that constrain androgyny? In fact, we are now seeing that we

---

*This review was written in 1979 [Ed. note].

have given up our right, gained in the 20th century, to raise our children when we are divorced, without gaining the power to control the patriarchal judicial institutions. Thus women are losing their children if they are lesbians, if they work outside the home, if they earn less money than their former husbands, and if they cannot provide a traditional nuclear family relationship for their children as their remarried husbands can. Caroll Smith-Rosenberg's brilliant description of female bonding in the 19th century, of friendship not only between age mates but between mothers and daughters ("The Female World of Love and Ritual," in *Signs* 1, 1975) teaches that the ambivalences and sometimes anger we feel toward our mothers is not *inherent* in the mother-daughter relationship but is a product of a particular historical era.

I will focus on Chodorow in this review, although much of what I say applies to Dinnerstein (see my review of *"The Mermaid and the Minotaur,* a Fishy Story that's Part Bull" in *Contemporary Psychology* 22, no. 11, 1977). Both works attribute problems between the genders to socialization by mother, and they both have the same solution—bring men in.

These books violate patriarchal academic conventions both stylistically and methodologically. They are non-linear, and their "data" do not meet the criteria ordinarily used by sociologists and psychologists to justify their conclusions. Other women, for instance Phyllis Chesler (*Women and Madness*), who have violated these norms have been severely condemned. So, when these books and the authors of these books are honored by the establishment, one has to ask the sociology of knowledge question *cui bono*—in whose interest are these books? The answer is not difficult to find. Radical feminist approaches to motherhood such as Adrienne Rich's *Of Woman Born* and Judith Arcana's *Our Mother's Daughters* suggest women bonding as a solution to the oppressive nature of motherhood as an institution. But Chodorow and Dinnerstein claim that most of our difficulties are caused by socialization by mothers; thus, they maintain, most of the problems we face will wither away like the state after the revolution if men, whom they have previously described as inadequate to the task because they were socialized by their mothers, are brought into childrearing. It is clear which solution is less threatening to the status quo. After all, it was, as Marcia Westcott notes in "Mothers and Daughters in the World of the Father," (*Frontiers* 3, no. 2, 1978), our fathers who played us off against our mothers and thus prevented many of us from mother-daughter bonding. And it is our academic fathers (of both genders) who see to it that woman bonding is discredited as a solution because it is so much more threatening than bringing men in. But the socialist and liberal feminists, who have been praising these books, have never been able to deal adequately with the misogyny endemic in society. Betty Friedan ran off a stage in tears when confronted with this issue. And certainly it is not in men's interest to support women bonding as a solution to male misogyny.

Moreover, requiring adults of both genders to raise children reinforces heterosexuality and the nuclear family. When I asked Chodorow if her theory implied that children being raised by two lesbians should be removed and put into a situation where there was a man present, she replied that the man did not have to be there all the time or be the biological father. But her theory does not suggest it could be the mailman.

Has such dual parenting caused the necessary transformation in the male psyche? Does infant care, like music, have charms to soothe the savage beast? Chodorow herself says that her theory is a contribution to the feminist effort and "demonstrates" that women as mothers produce daughters with mothering capacities and a desire to mother, and that "these capacities are built into and stem from the mother-daughter relationship." But she states that mothers produce sons *without* such nurturant capacities. So why should we turn over our children to men even half the time?

Who among us does not know women who thought they had egalitarian relationships with men with whom they were coparenting, only to see it all fall apart and the male sense of entitlement reemerge when they wanted to divorce? Anna Demeter's *Legal Kidnapping* is an example of such a case.

If, as Chodorow claims, we are given our mothering capacities and desires to mother by our mothers, what about the women who do not want to be mothers, who either have no children or reject those they have? Did they spring full-blown from their fathers' foreheads, like Athena? Chodorow's central hypothesis is that women have symbiotic relationships with their daughters but not with their sons, and that "the clinical and cultural examples . . . discussed point to the conclusion that pre-oedipal experiences of girls and boys differ" as a result of these relationships. She states that "because they are the same gender as their daughters . . . mothers of daughters tend not to experience their infant daughters as separate from them in the same way as do mothers of infant sons." She also thinks that because mothers have exclusive care for children and are isolated from other adults, they may sexualize their relationships to their infant sons. She cites Barbara Deck's remark that the mother is excited by the infant male "as a little man with a penis." Sure. I could scarcely contain myself every time I changed my son's diaper. Especially when he peed in my face. It is not the mothers who commit incest. It is the fathers, and indeed several pages later she reports that fathers sex-stereotype their daughters, encourage "feminine behavior," and label their daughters "flirtatious." Clearly it is the *fathers* who sexualize, but she does not draw this obvious conclusion from these data.

Since she is a sociologist, one might expect her to turn to what is ordinarily considered evidence in sociology. However, she does not examine the many structural reasons why women are the primary childrearers. She could have looked at the well-known labor force statistics and noted that it is clearly in the family's interest to have men devote their time and energy to paid work because women are paid so much less than men. Judith Lorber critiqued Chodorow on these grounds at the 1979 American Sociological Association meetings. Rather, her "evidence" rests solely on psychoanalysts' reconstructions of patients' reconstructions of how their mothers treated them. She neither interviews mothers nor observes mother-child interaction, especially interaction with children of different genders, to support her position. She ignores the child's birth order, activity level, and the mother's situation—her class, race, ethnicity, to say nothing of her politics.

In order to see if indeed there was this difference in relationships, I asked every woman I knew who had children of two genders. Birth order and activity level seemed more important than gender for the blurring of ego boundaries and the other manifestations she discusses. In my own case (and our lives are our data), my son is always perceived by others and by me as like me, and my daugher as "the other"—better in math than in languages, closed rather than open, having mechanical aptitude and, unlike her brother and me, not a "luftmensch" with feet firmly planted in the air. But Chodorow did not conduct such a survey. As a sociologist, she should know that people who go to psychoanalysts and provide the "clinical evidence" on which psychoanalytic writings are based differ on almost every important demographic variable from the general population. So she uses examples from psychoanalysts Robert Fliess, Christine Olden, Klaus Angel, and Alice Balint, stating that "the patterns of separateness they describe are more likely to happen in early mother-daughter relationships than in those of mothers and sons." That, to Chodorow, is evidence. But she claims that Eleanor Maccoby and Carol Jacklin's review of the experimental research on the psychology of sex differences, which did not support this contention, is not data.

Chodorow refers to differences of nuance and tone quality that are revealed in "a small range of clinical case material." She notes that she relies on "extensive accounting and quoting" because a "simple assertion of the distinctions I wish to demonstrate would not be persuasive without the clinical illustrations." They would not be persuasive *with* the case studies either. Rejecting Maccoby and Jacklin and accepting therapists' accounts of adults' accounts of their mothers' behavior when they were "pre-oedipal" is like rejecting evolutionary explanations of the origin of the species even though aspects of it are still open to question, and accepting the unprovable and less parsimonious "creationism" as an explanation. One would have to make a leap of faith into the psychoanalytic religion. She agrees with sociologists in stating that biology and instinct do not provide adequate explanations for how women came to mother, but she also believes that socialization theories "rely inappropriately on intention," that is, girls and boys are *taught* appropriate behavior and *learn* appropriate feelings. She's wrong in both beliefs. Socialization theory does not rest on the assumption of intentions; much of what goes on is not consciously intended. But socialization theory rather than how I was mothered certainly could account for my deciding to have children in the first place. Every institution, every media presentation, every significant other spoke as with one voice, saying, "Aren't you pregnant yet? You won't be really happy until you have a baby, and you'll regret it later if you don't." My mother said, "People who don't have children are selfish." It is not true, as Chodorow claims, that notions of correct behavior cannot in themselves produce parenting.

Chodorow's theoretical position is grounded in what psychoanalysts call "object relations" theory, rather than in the more parsimonious symbolic interaction theory that could provide her with an account to explain many of the relationships she is discussing. For those not familiar with object relations theory, the first thing to understand is that *people are called objects.* Thus, when she speaks of female genital object choice, she does not mean what vibrator you prefer, but what gender you prefer sexually.

Psychoanalytic theory has been notorious for mother-blaming—one would think that children were produced by cloning. Psychoanalysts are those wonderful people who brought you the vaginal orgasm and penis envy. Chodorow, thank the Goddess, does not believe these are *biological* in origin. She says that little girls have a castration complex, but their penis envy (sic) may be because they think they need the organ in order to win their mother's love. Not to worry! The "transference" of pleasurable sensations from the clitoris to the vagina does not have a biological base. So what kind of a base does it have? The phrasing implies that it is a fact and therefore has a base. Thus she says, "Once we deny the biological, instinctual component of the clitoral-vaginal shift and of the activity-passivity distinction, then the way these phenomena are experienced, or enter as psychological fantasy elements into relationships, can be investigated." She states that they "derive from special social relationships, and from normative definitions of the sexual situation imposed on and learned by members of particular societies."

It is 13 years since the second wave of the women's movement started and women who call themselves feminists are still writing about penis envy and vaginal orgasms, and citing the very authors whose works contributed to the Freudian hegemony of the fifties, which came close to destroying an entire decade of women, myself among them. The rehabilitation of psychoanalytic theories in the women's movement here and in Britain and France makes my blood run cold.

10

On Conceiving Motherhood and Sexuality: A Feminist Materialist Approach

ANN FERGUSON

Analytic Categories

> The cathexis between mother and daughter—essential, distorted, misused—is the great unwritten story. Probably there is nothing in human nature more resonant with charges than the flow of energy between two biologically alike bodies, one of which has lain in amniotic bliss inside the other, one of which has labored to give birth to the other.

> The "childless woman" and the "mother" are a false polarity which has served the institutions of both motherhood and heterosexuality . . . We are, none of us, "either" mothers or daughters; to our amazement, confusion, and greater complexity, we are both.
>
> Adrienne Rich, *Of Woman Born*[1]

Every woman has had at least one mother, and the overwhelming majority of women have had the experience of being mothered. Many women, like me, are also mothers. Having been mothered and being a mother give one some insights into the mothering relationship. But by itself, the experience of mothering can tell us little about the *conception* of motherhood prevalent in a society at a certain time, or differences in the conception of motherhood that are prevalent in different economic classes or different racial and ethnic groups.

To understand conceptions of motherhood and sexuality, their connections and interactions, the changes they undergo in different historical periods in a society, and the differences between conceptions of motherhood and sexuality in different cultures, we require an analytic framework of categories. As a feminist social theorist, I focus on the connections between motherhood and sexuality because I wish to develop a general paradigm of the cross-cultural persistence of male domination based on the two cross-cultural constants common to all or most women: (a) that we are or can become biological mothers and (b) that the vast majority of us were primarily "mothered" rather than "fathered," i.e., socially cared for in infancy and early childhood by mothers/women. These cross-cultural constants ensure that women's experience of parenting and sexuality will be different from men's. Does the sexual division of labor in parenting and the different consequences of sexuality for men and women also suggest a base for the persistence of male dominance cross-culturally?

To answer this question, which is actually a question of power, i.e., the relative power that the relations of parenting and sexuality give to men vs. women, we must introduce an analytic framework of categories that does not attribute a falsely universalist and static quality to male dominance. The relations of motherhood and sexuality, and the relative power of men and women in these relations, vary not only in different societies, but in different societies at different historical periods, and in the same society across class, ethnic, and race lines.

A MULTI-SYSTEMS APPROACH TO DOMINATION RELATIONS

My approach to understanding motherhood and sexuality is a *multi-systems* feminist materialist (or socialist-feminist) approach. By "multi-system," I mean an approach that is not reductive, that is, one that does not attempt to reduce male domination to a function of capitalist or commodity production economic systems (classic marxism), nor to reduce race and class domination to a function of patriarchy (classic radical feminism). Rather, I assume that much of human history can be understood only by conceiving societies in terms of interacting but semi-autonomous systems of human domination, three important ones having been class, race/ethnic, and sex/gender. These domination systems may not always support each other, particularly in periods of rapid change or social crisis. One way to understand the social movements of a particular historical period, such as the black civil rights movement of the '60s or the Women's Movement of the '70s in the United States, is to conjecture that a dialectical undermining of one domination system by the historical development of another, e.g., race and sex domination undermined by capitalist development, has provoked a social crisis. A multi-systems theory, unlike a reductivist approach, does not posit that social crises are automatically resolved by the development of a new social "equilibrium" that guarantees the same level of class, race, or male domination.

What distinguishes my particular multi-systems socialist-feminist theory of male domination from others is the concept of "sex/affective production."

The concept of sex/affective production develops Gayle Rubin's point (Rubin, 1975) that every society has a "sex/gender system" that arranges a sexual division of labor, organizes sexuality and kinship interactions, and teaches sex/gender. It also is connected to Habermas's insight (Habermas, 1979) that what is distinctive about humans as a species is the way human societies construct human nature through different types of family and kinship networks. My theory, unlike one tendency within classic marxist theory, does not privilege the economic realm (the production of *things* to meet human material needs and the manner in which the social surplus gets appropriated) as the material base for all human domination relations. Rather, I conceptualize the production and reproduction of *people* in family and kinship networks as a production process that may take different *forms* or *modes,* depending on the historical relations between parenting, kinship, and sexual structures and economic modes of production. Just as marxism postulates distinctive "logics" (structural rules) that are characteristic of different modes of class production, so I suggest that each mode of sex/affective production will have its own distinctive logic of exchange of the human services of sexuality, nurturance, and affection, and will therefore differently constitute the human nature of its special product: human children. Because I think that infancy and early childhood form a crucial period in the formation of gender identity and attendant masculine and feminine personality structures, I privilege family and kin networks as the material base for sex/affective production. It does not follow, however, that sex/affective production is limited to family and kin networks. On the contrary, I argue that modes of sex/affective production specific to capitalist economic development create problematic and contradictory gender identities in both boys and girls in childhood, identities which then make subsequent experiences in peer interaction in schools and communities, and later in workplaces, very important in determining sexual preference, sexual practices, and the ultimate content of one's gender identity.

The separation between the public and the private, the realm of economic production and the realm of domestic life specific to capitalist society, should not lead us to the error of conceptualizing sex/affective production, or the production of people, as a process occurring in a place or realm different from that where the production of things takes place. The sexual division of wage labor, sexual harassment in the workplace, male decision-making and female obedience roles, and high-status male work vs. low-status female work are all specific aspects of the capitalist production process which are its sex/affective production component. In the same way the power of the male wage earner vs. the non-paid housewife and class differences in women's ability to pay for childcare and thus obtain leisure time for themselves as mothers are specific examples of the capitalist aspect of sex/affective production. The production of things and the production of people thus interpenetrate. The point of conceptualizing them as separate production systems is that they have different logics, logics which must be understood historically and specifically if we are to understand possibilities for change and strategies of resistance to domination relations embedded in both sorts of production.

Before the specific types of sex/affective production are analyzed, the concepts involved and the underlying assumptions about affection, parenting, and sexuality need to be examined.

THE CONCEPT OF SEX/AFFECTIVE PRODUCTION

The conceptual category *sex/affective production* is a way of understanding the social organization of labor and the exchange of services that occur between men and women in the production of children, affection, and sexuality. Every human society has its particular mode or modes of organizing and controlling sexuality, affectionate interactions (e.g., friendships, social bonding, alliances), and parenting relationships. Complex class and race/ethnic-divided societies like our own may have a number of different modes centered in different organizations of family households and kin networks.

Central to all previous modes of organization of this work and service has been a sexual division of labor in the performance of the tasks and the distribution of the services involved. The sexual division of labor in the production and exchange of these sex/affective services (sexuality, affection, parenting) is a central key to the social production of people as "sex/gendered," i.e., as having the consciousness of self as male or female. This consciousness is always relational (i.e., what is male is not-female, and what is female is not-male), thus connecting one to a social sex/gender class which is expected to have certain ideal masculine or feminine characteristics. One of these ideal characteristics is, usually, a sexual attraction for the opposite sex.[2] It is important to note, however, that there is no automatic (merely a strong contingent) connection between sex/gender identity and sexual identity (i.e., sexual preference): one is a deviant male if one is sexually attracted only to men, but one is still a male (and similarly for females who are attracted to females).

In stratified class and caste societies, different economic classes and racial/ethnic groups may hold different sex/gender ideals, although when this happens the lower classes are usually categorized as inferior male and female types "by nature." Often, split categories stereotype the good and bad woman—e.g., the Madonna [Mother]/Whore—exemplifying the hegemony of dominant classes' ideals for men and women, which allows their members (but not those of subordinate classes) to fulfill those preferred ideals.

Many different modes of sex/affective production are male-dominant (or patriarchal).[3] In general, they all have in common an unequal and exploitative production and exchange of sexuality, affection, and parenting between men and women; that is, women have less control over the process of production (e.g., control of human reproductive decisions) and the services exchanged; and men characteristically get more than they give in the exchange of these services. They differ in the specific sexual divisions of labor and the social mechanisms by which men dominate and exploit women, as well as in the female strategies of resistance, escape, and sabotage of male power in parenting, sexuality, and affectional bonding.[4]

In order to understand the "unity" of sex/affective production, we need to explore further its philosophical underpinnings. Why, for example, is it assumed that sexuality, affection, and parenting are intertwined in a way that the production of goods to meet material survival needs are not? What underlying theories of sexuality, affection, and production are assumed? What implications are there for the concepts of human agency, domination, and exploitation that are used in the classification of different modes of sex/affective production? Why link *sexuality* and *affection* in sex/affective production? The underlying assumption is that both sexuality and affection are *bodily* as well as *social* energies, and that they are each specific manifestations of a general type of physical/social energy we can call "sex/affective" energy.[5] We tend to think of affectional bonds as emotional rather than bodily and of sexual bonds as bodily rather than emotional or social. In fact, however, I would claim that this is a distortion that comes about because of western dualistic thought patterns. It may be more helpful to conceive of sex/affective energy as a spectrum ranging from the affectional/spiritual/not-specifically-physical interactions, at one pole, to genital sexual exchanges that are physical but not specifically affectional, at the other. A second way to conceive of sex/affective energy is as presenting two different dimensions or aspects which can admit of degree: a dimension of *physical* involvement, attraction, and interconnection of a human being with (an)other human being(s) or objects symbolizing human beings, and a *social/emotional* dimension of involvement, attraction, and interdefinition of self with (an)other human being(s).

We need now to consider some of the insights and problems of the sex/affective production paradigm.

First, a thesis about human nature: humans do not reproduce themselves (i.e., have children) merely as a means to guarantee that their material needs for physical survival will be met (e.g., that they will have children to care for them in old age). Rather, humans are a social species whose needs to connect to one another in some form of sexual and/or affectional interaction are as basic as their material needs as an animal species to produce a material livelihood. Heterosexual mating leads, intentionally or inadvertently, to human procreation, which leads to parenting. Thus, the sexuality and affection that heterosexual mates give each other requires the social development of parenting systems in which nurturance/affection, socialization, and physical maintenance of the young are organized. Since patriarchal parenting systems also organize adult sexuality (most often by compulsory heterosexuality in marriage arrangements which impose double-standard monogamy), an interaction exists between the type of sexual exchanges engaged in by adults and the nature, amount, and control of parenting work engaged in by each sex/gender.

A second thesis is that the position of sex/affective production systems as a base for male dominance is a feminist *materialist* approach in two specific senses. First, we know that human babies require affection and nurturance in order to survive. Thus, mothering or caretaking that involves more than simply feeding and clothing is a material requirement for the reproduction of the human species. Second, human young, unlike other animal species, have bodily energies (e.g., affectional, sexual, nutritional) that are initially without specific objects. The fact that humans are without instincts with fixed goals requires a period of care and socialization of the young that make some system of parenting, and the organization of sexuality and affection around these tasks, a material necessity for the human species.

We need thus to widen the concept of production as socially necessary labor to satisfy basic human material needs that Marx and Engels introduced in *The German Ideology* to include not merely a transformation of nature to meet human needs, but also the production and reproduction of new life, i.e., the production and transformation of *people* via various historical parenting and sexual systems embedded in family and kin networks.[6]

Let me take a moment to contrast the concept of sex/affective production with other feminist revisions of classical marxist categories. Some marxist-feminists attempt to revise the classical marxist emphasis on the primacy of the economic sphere in human social organization (particularly in systems where the production of things involves the creation and distribution of a social surplus). They argue that every economic system involves both production and reproduction, and therefore that modes of reproduction of a system (including the reproduction of labor power and thus modes of procreation) are just as important to the total operation of the system as the production of things. They argue either that we should reject the concept of the social primacy of the economic (the base/superstructure distinction), or that modes of reproduction in family and kin networks are just as much a part of the economic base of a social formation as is the production of things.

The problem with the concepts of modes of reproduction (Brown, 1981) and modes of procreation (McDonough and Harrison, 1978) is that either (a) they ambiguously mean both human biological and human social reproduction, or (b) they emphasize the production of children as the goal and aim of this form of social relations. Neither approach is satisfactory. The former case allows confusion with the marxist categories of production/reproduction (Barrett, 1981), where the mode of social reproduction of an economic system can be said to occur simultaneously at every site of social relations—e.g., in the factory, state, and schools as well as in the family. This concept of social reproduction does not give us any non-functionalist way to conceive of, for example, the relationship between capitalism and patriarchy.

In the second alternative (modes of procreation), human biological reproduction and the regulation of fertility rates would be seen as the goal of these systems. Such an emphasis marginalizes the human incentives to experience the pleasures of sexuality not as reproductive instruments, but as intrinsic energizers. We would also miss the ways that affectional and sexual same-sex relations, which develop for their own sake in sexual divisions of labor, are used as mechanisms both to cement (if dominant male) or to resist (if subordinate or deviant male or female) patriarchal sex/affective production processes (Hartmann, 1981).

The sex/affective production paradigm is superior to these other approaches because conceiving of a semi-autonomous system of the organization of sexuality, affection, and the production of children in family and kin networks can allow us to understand how patriarchal relations can persist (since embedded and reproduced in family and kin networks) through changes in modes of production of things (feudalism, capitalism, state socialism). It can conceptualize how changes in family structure due to capitalist development might weaken certain forms of patriarchal sex/affective production while allowing for the possibility that other adaptive forms are developing.

A serious philosophical problem that the concept of sex/affective production raises is how we can distinguish between childcare and sexual or nurturant activities that are work or *labor* and those that are *leisure* activities. Using the concept of production assumes one can empirically distinguish between labor (activity socially necessary to meet human material needs) and activity which may be work (not thought of as leisure by its agent) but not labor per se, and activity which is play. Childcare is an aspect of housework that mothers perform at home while caring for infants and small children, yet we know that the very idea that childcare and housework are separate work activities is a historical development caused by the separation of the homes from economic production with the development of capitalist production. Ehrenreich and English (1975 and 1978) have documented how the combined effect of the domestic science movement, the development of the medical establishment, child development experts, and consumer capitalism in the early 20th century expanded rather than reduced the tasks thought socially necessary in parenting work.

A parallel historical argument would challenge the view of some feminists that sexual exchanges between men and women in patriarchal societies involve work on the part of women that is not repaid, since the control and sexual satisfaction involved are not equal for both male and female partners. How can we make this argument if we accept recent historical arguments (Foucault,

1980; Weeks, 1979, 1981) that our very conception of sexuality, its exchange and deployment, as at the center of bodily and mental health, is a recent social construction of discourses developed by bourgeois sexologists and therapists? And, if the conception of sexual satisfaction and sexual health itself is historically relative, how can we defend the claim that there is an exchange of socially necessary labor in parenting, sexuality, and affection? Or the claim that patriarchal parenting and sexual systems allow men to control and exploit the productive process of parenting and sexual exchange by contributing less (labor or services) and receiving more (leisure, services, pleasures)?

Even if one admits that there are no ahistorical universal requirements for good parenting, sexuality, or friendship, it does not follow that there is no empirical and historical way to compare male and female inputs, rewards from, and control of these production processes. Marx's concept of socially necessary labor has a "historical and moral element" which in part depends on what has come to be accepted as a decent minimal standard of living, given the available resources and expectations of a society at a particular historical period. Similarly, women's expectations of acceptable sexual satisfaction have changed since the 19th century, in part because of the writings of sexologists and in part because of the second wave Women's Movement.

The inequality of patriarchal forms of sexual exchange lies not simply in the fact that men characteristically experience more orgasms and sexual satisfaction than women, although this is certainly relevant and can be empirically measured. It is the aspect of domination, the fact that men usually control the nature of the interaction itself as the sexual initiators, that perpetuates the image of women as the sexual objects of men, and women's bodies as the instruments of men's pleasure. In such a situation it would seem that a woman has less agency in the sexual encounter, even though she may experience more orgasms than the man she relates to.

We will not really be able to measure the relative equality or inequality of sexual exchanges until we have a physical model of sexual satisfaction and sexual agency that allows us to make connections between certain bodily states such as body blocks, orgasms, complete orgiastic release (Reich, 1970), and the experience of sexual agency vs. sexual patiency. But that we have no complete theory suggests merely the need for further empirical sexual research rather than a dead end for the sex/affective production paradigm. No matter how we ultimately measure equality in sexual exchange, we do have some intuitive criteria we can use in the meantime: for example, most would agree that any sexual exchange in which one partner but not the other enjoys orgasms regularly and in which the enjoying partner also controls the sexual process is an unequal exchange.

Finally, the question of one's power or control/agency in sexual and parenting exchanges cannot be separated from the economic, political/legal, and cultural constraints that may limit women's freedom of choice more than men's. Such constraints as economic dependence, legal restrictions on reproductive control, lack of strong female bonding networks that support sexual freedom for women or parental responsibilities for men, and physical violence by one's partner are all empirical factors that make women less free in parenting and sexuality than men. This shows the way in which sex/affective production systems are not autonomous from the economic mode of production, the nature of the state, etc.

In determining which parental interactions with children are labor and which are leisure, we can agree that this is historically relative to social (and perhaps class and ethnic) expectations of parents and still find a way to compare the equality or inequality of the exchange between women and men in parenting work. No matter how the line between parenting labor and leisure is culturally drawn, it remains clear that most mothers in patriarchal modes of sex/affective production do more direct and indirect parenting work than men in terms of total labor hours spent (where "indirect parenting work" would include wage-earning as well as unpaid productive work which produces, or exchanges for, goods necessary to the physical maintenance of infants and children). Folbre (1980a) is developing an economic model to compare the waged and nonwaged work (parenting and housework) in the family economy so as to develop a way to measure the relative exploitation of women vs. men, and parents vs. children. Delphy (1976) argues that the male-dominated family economy continues after divorce, since mothers are saddled with much more direct and indirect parenting work and few fathers provide much in child support funds. Thus, in this sense male exploitation of women who are mothers increases with divorce, which suggests that the rise of single-mother families should be seen not simply as a decline in husband-patriarchy, but rather as the rise of a new patriarchal sex/affective form, which we might call "single-mother–absent patriarchy" and which is connected to the shift from family-centered patriarchal forms to more impersonal forms of state-patriarchy (Hooks, 1981; and see below).

A final question concerns the relativity vs. universality of the connection between affection, sexuality, and parenting. The analytic categories of sex/affective production would seem to suggest a universal connection (hence a mate-self-child sex/affective triangle) which has historically specific forms. Nevertheless, Ariès (1965) and Shorter (1977) argue that affectionate interaction between children, kin, and spouses is characteristic neither of peasant nor of aristocratic families in the medieval period. Rather, it develops as a part of the bourgeois sentimental family, which develops a new conception of childhood and an increased emphasis on affection.

I would agree that we need to conceptualize a different form of patriarchal sex/affective production for aristocratic and peasant families than for bourgeois families. The interpersonal dynamic between parents, children, and mates will obviously be different when affectionate connections are present, or absent, or not exclusive (as when children are cared for by wet nurses, nannies or extended kin networks). It is obvious that sexual intercourse to produce heirs has a different dynamic than when the resulting children and sexual energy are valued for their own sake.

Despite the relativity of who performs nurturant/affectionate services to children, a caretaker must provide a minimal affection quotient for the child to survive. Thus, the procuring of someone to perform these services is a necessary part of sex/affective production even in aristocratic families. Furthermore, it may be argued that courtly love ideals for extramarital relationships among the medieval aristocracy, idealized homosexual love relationships among ancient Greek male aristocracy, and close same-sex bonding among peasants are evidence that affectionate interactions will come to be institutionalized in some form in human societies where they are lacking in parenting and marriage interactions.

DOUBLE CONSCIOUSNESS AND THE SEX/AFFECTIVE TRIANGLE

In this section I will explore a mechanism for perpetuating male dominance through motherhood in specific modes of patriarchal sex/affective production, particularly nuclear family forms as they develop with the growth of capitalism and the breakdown of feudalism. I call these forms "bourgeois patriarchal family forms," where this is understood to include families in independent rural production (as in the colonial United States), working-class nuclearized families, and families of the bourgeois classes. These are the dominant family forms of the period of American history that I will consider later.

The family form involves a sex/affective triangle of father-mother-child(ren) that creates a structural contradiction of sex/affective interests for mothers but not fathers, which explains a psychological mechanism through which male dominance is internalized by women: the phenomenon of women's double consciousness. On the other hand, the structural triangle also sets the conditions for mothers' internal resistance to patriarchy and the progressive development of successively less strong patriarchal family forms in American history.

The structural situation is this: the sexual division of labor in childrearing in which women mother, i.e., perform primary infant and childcare, gives the mother a greater, because longer and more intense, affectionate relationship with the offspring. This situation tends to make her identify with the sex/affective interests of the child more than does the father.[7] In addition, the situation of childbirth and breastfeeding, plus the greater physical nurturance the mother gives the young child, arouse maternal erotic and sexual feelings toward the child that are repressed due to the weight of the patriarchal incest taboo. Nonetheless, the persistence of these feelings creates a much stronger mother-child than father-child sex/affective bond (Contratto, 1980; Person, 1980; Rich, 1980).

The greater absorption of mothers than fathers in the sex/affective interests of children may not only be because of the psychological investment of time and energy in the child. Some feminists have argued that the metaphysical and psychological indeterminacy over the boundaries of one's body vs. the child's in childbirth and breastfeeding give mothers a special "epistemological standpoint" different from men's (Hartsock, 1981).[8]

The potential contradiction of the sex/affective triangle for the mother is highlighted by her involvement as well in the other leg of the mate-self-child sex/affective triangle, i.e., that as the present and/or former mate of the father, she is also identified with his sex/affective interests. Thus the woman's, but not the man's, own sex/affective interests as a rational agent are bound up with promoting both a woman/mate bond and a woman/child bond. She is forced into the position of negotiator of the sexual and emotional jealousies (conflicts of sex/affective interests) between children and father.

What this imbalance in parenting work creates for mothers is a *double consciousness:* a consciousness of the potential conflict between their own interests as sexual agents/partners in a peer/mate relationship and their interests as mothers in a nonpeer mother/child relationship. Women's sex/affective energy is consequently more bound than men's into adjudicating actual and potential conflicts of interests in the sex/affective family triangle. The relatively greater absorption of energy this involves often occurs at the expense of their other needs. Consider, for example, the routine sacrifices undergone by women for children and mates: given up are leisure time, job-training possibilities, access to greater economic productive resources, political liaisons, and sexual liaisons with other mates.

The structural double consciousness created by the imbalance in parenting work between men and women explains how women internalize the oppression of male domination as long as they are engaged in such a patriarchal parenting process. Double consciousness creates a double or split self-image for women. On the one hand, most mothers have a positive image of themselves and positive gratification from their mothering work with children. On the other hand, most women have a negative self-image when father and child jealousy is a factor. Women feel both more responsible than men for adjudicating this conflict and more to blame when they do not succeed in negotiating it.

One implication of this sex/affective triangle in bourgeois patriarchal family forms is the possibility of father/daughter incest as a response by the father to the divided loyalty of the mother (Herman, 1981). Incest is a patriarchal tool of domination by the father which disrupts the strength of the mother-daughter bond by a possessive sexual relationship that forces the daughter's sex/affective involvement away from the mother. Incest occurs when fathers, jealous of the attention that mothers give to daughters and/or angry at the lack of sex/affective attention from mothers, sexualize their relations with their daughters. This turns the daughters into substitute mothers, turns daughters against mothers, and makes mothers feel themselves to be the guilty accomplices of their daughter's sexual abuse. Mothers, on the contrary, are more sensitive than fathers to the power imbalance between adults and children, and are often powerless themselves to escape from the father. Thus, mothers are more likely to refrain from sexual relations with their children, not only for the child's good and from guilt feelings about the father's needs, but also from a powerlessness to escape the oppressive economic, political, and psychological structures of the family household engaged in patriarchal sex/affective production.

We have already alluded to the difficulty of drawing the line between parenting labor and parenting leisure activities with children. For the mother this is due in part, again, to the phenomenon of double consciousness: after all, if cooking and serving a meal to husband and children increases the sex/affective energy available to everyone—mate, self, and children—how can one see it as *work*? Thus many women do not experience unequal sexual division of labor in parenting as exploitative. It is often only when one is forced to change one's social relations of parenting (by divorce, by step-parenting, by a change to lesbian parenting, etc.) that one experiences an alternative arrangement allowing for a higher level of sex/affective energy in both mating and mothering due to a more egalitarian organization of parenting work. On hindsight, one can then see the previous organization of sex/affective production as exploitative.

If the mother's absorption in both legs of the sex/affective triangle immerses her in a self-sacrificing negotiator role vis-à-vis the sex/affective interests of father-mate and child(ren), we could expect to see in history various forms of female resistance to this self-sacrificing role. Women may be oppressed within patriarchal structures, but they are also always partial agents within these structures and, as such, can try to alter the power relations within the structure, often in favorable historical conditions thus altering the structures themselves. Some of the forms of historical resistance we might expect to find to bourgeois patriarchal family forms include the following: (a) women could refuse marriage altogether (in the contemporary period, this includes the possibility of choosing a lesbian relationship); (b) women could marry yet resist childbearing; (c) women could favor one leg of the triangle (e.g., relation to child or relation to mate) at the expense of the other; or (d) women could emphasize outside kin and friendship networks with peers as a way of withholding energy, either to male mates or to the mother/child bond; (e) if economically viable, women could engage in serial monogamy and several marriages, which would tend to diminish loyalty to the mate bond and expand loyalty to the mother/child bond (the one that lasts).

I have argued in this section that unequal relations of childrearing create in bourgeois family forms a double consciousness in women due to their structural inequality in the mate-child-self sex/affective parenting triangle. This analysis I find superior to Chodorow's neo-Freudian approach to understanding the way that the reproduction of mothering perpetuates male dominance. In the next section, I will provide a brief historical sketch of changes in patriarchal sex/affective production in American history which will indicate the sex/affective production paradigm's usefulness in explaining historical change in parenting patterns and ideologies.

Historical Applications

I have maintained that a multi-systems approach to analyzing male dominance is best; i.e., one that takes account of the economic *class* structure of a given historical period (the mode of economic production), the *racial/ethnic* dominance patterns of the period (what we could call the mode of community relations—Albert and Hahnel, 1978), and the *sex/gender* dominance patterns of the period (the mode of sex/affective production). To understand the relative strengths of each domination system, we will also have to consider other aspects of a society, such as the form of the state and its relation to the economy. The relationship between the three domination systems is dialectical rather than functional: there is no automatic fit between different systems of dominance. Nonetheless, those on top in various domination systems will attempt to maintain their positions. Historical alliance will be created by various representative elements of dominant groups, alliances that during periods of social crisis or protracted change may be undermined or superceded. Ongoing developments in one mode of social organization may undermine social dominance patterns in another, and this will create an intersystemic social crisis. It is at these historical junctures that social change of appreciable dimensions is likely to occur. The structures of sex/affective production as they are reconstituted after a period of major social change will depend in large part on the consciousness and collective power of existing social movements of subordinate groups: women, nonwhites, and subordinate economic classes.

PERIODS OF SEX/AFFECTIVE PRODUCTION
IN AMERICAN HISTORY

Since colonial times, there have been three main periods of patriarchal sex/affective production in American history.[9] Each of these periods involves a different sort of patriarchal relationship between men, women, and children, and each of them has its different basic mechanisms for maintaining (or, in marxist terminology, "reproducing") male dominance. In the colonial period, Father Patriarchy was reproduced by father's legal/economic control of inheritance through family property vested in sons, not daughters. In the romantic/Victorian period, Husband Patriarchy was reproduced by the institution of the "family wage," which was vested in husbands who were the family breadwinners. And in the present period of the consumer economy, Public Patriarchy has been reproduced through a number of mechanisms; these include laws restricting birth control and abortion, state welfare support of single mothers, the growth of the advertising industry and the manipulation of women's images (Ewen, 1976), and market mechanisms encouraging repressive desublimation (Marcuse, 1964) such as pornography, media violence against women, and sexual advertising, which promote the sexual objectification of women.

Let us consider each period in greater detail.

Period I: Father Patriarchy. White European settlers, primarily English religious Puritans, established a mode of agricultural production based in family households in the New England states that lasted from about 1620–1799. The mode of economic production was characterized by farm households producing primary for use and not for market; and was consolidated by force against existing Native American economies which were hunting/gathering, nomadic societies. Dominance relations between men and women were perpetuated by Father Patriarchy, a combination of economic, political/legal, and childrearing structures in which the father owned property and dispensed it at will to his children, the land to sons and a lesser dowry to daughters. The father was the religious/moral head of the household. Children needed their fathers' permission to marry and were completely dependent on his largesse in inheritance.

The father in a Puritan household was not only the supreme authority in sex/affective production relations with wife and children; he was usually also master to indentured servants and young relatives who were apprenticed from adjacent family households. Thus, class relations were internal family household relations as well. Although a small artisan class grew with the rise of commercial capitalism and urban centers, which afforded an escape for men of the subsumed servant class from the family patriarchal domination in the rural family household, it was not possible for a woman, regardless of economic class, to have any economic independence nor any escape from Father Patriarchy, unless she was a widow and could take over her husband's business, trade, or land.

The conception of motherhood in the Puritan era was derived from Old Testament beliefs that women were weaker in reason and more emotional and therefore in need of practical moral and intellectual control by men. This, in turn, was due to the conception of motherhood as a natural, nearly automatic consequence of women's bodies. Since bodies themselves had evil lusts, women were thought to be more innately subject to sin than men. The ideal standard of parenthood was the same for both sexes, and both men and women were conceived to be innately sexual beings as well as feeling beings. But since feelings uncontrolled by reason were suspect, maternal feeling itself was dangerous and without moral authority, and thus had to be subjected to father authority for appropriate correction. Women were often chastized for showing their offspring too much natural affection. Since children were thought to be sinful, depraved creatures in Calvinist ideology, which lacked a developmental theory of the human ego, there was little distinction between appropriate punishment for a child and for an adult. The key feature of the Puritan ideology of childrearing was to break the child's will as soon as possible to create a proper fear of those in authority, i.e., the hierarchy of patriarchs who controlled sinful desires and affections—individually in their homes and collectively as church/state elders (Stewart, 1981).

Some authors have argued (Ryan, 1975) that the Puritan emphasis on women as helpmates to men, the absence of an ideology of romantic love, and a more egalitarian sexual ideology, which posited sexual drives in both men and women, were indications that women were more equal as sexual partners in the Puritan period than in the subsequent Romantic era. It certainly is true that there was less of a sexual double standard in the Puritan period than subsequently: men could be punished for raping wives or for fornication outside of marriage. Nonetheless, I think some authors overplay "egalitarian" implications of sexual practices in Puritan society (Mitchell, 1973): sexual double standards still persisted with respect to adultery, and a woman who became pregnant by rape outside of marriage could still be flogged or fined.

Three distinctive features of Puritan sex/affective production indicate that women had *less* power over mothering than in subsequent periods. First, children were regularly sent at young ages (around seven) to live on relatives' farms. This was in part to counter the excessive affection which was thought to permeate natal families (Stewart, 1981). Thus, an intense mother-child bond was not only ideologically suspect but difficult to maintain because of physical distance. This meant that mothers not only had less control over the dispensation of nurturance and discipline than in subsequent periods, but also less ability to "corner the market" on the positive satisfactions of an intense affectionate relationship with children.

Second, the pervasive presence of the father and his ideological hegemony over childrearing undermined an independent authority of mothers over children. Fathers, not mothers, seem to have been the major enforcers of the "breaking of the will" practices that were used on children particularly during the separation/individuation period around the age of two. (This shows that it is not simply shared childrearing which is necessary to overcome gender-differentiated personality development in childhood.)[10]

Third, Demos (1970) presents a fascinating sketch of Puritan weaning practices which suggests that mother/child identification was rudely severed by the abrupt weaning of the 18-month-child at the moment of the birth of the next child. This abrupt separation, in connection with "breaking the will" practices to stifle the child's attempts at separation/autonomy, created an authoritarian (repressed but dependent) individual particularly subject to male-domination structures.

Period II: Husband Patriarchy. American society went through a period of rapid social change after the American Revolution and through the Jacksonian period. The shift from rural production to commercial capitalism, the beginning of industrial capitalism, and the expansion of slavery in the south occurred in the context of the creation of a new political entity, the national state of the United States. These changes also meant changes in the family, mothering, and sexuality.

A new ideology of motherhood and sexuality came into existence at this time in American history: the moral motherhood/cult of domesticity paradigm. In this ideology which, as we shall see, did not refer to all women, women were no longer conceived as inferior helpmeets to men. Rather, women were "moral mothers." The domestic world was now conceptualized as a separate sphere and motherhood as a chosen vocation, one that required specialized skills (moral perception, intuitive and emotional connection). Men could not achieve these skills, for they were constrained to act within the public sphere of the capitalist marketplace, which required that they develop the skills necessary to survive there: egoism, individualism, cunning, and immorality. Instead of *natural* (sinful) mothers who subjected themselves to the superior moral authority of men, women had become the *chosen* mothers, the moral and spiritual superiors of men in their protected sphere of the home.

My explanation of this shift in the practices and ideology of parenting differs from those theories (Zaretsky, 1976; Benston, 1969; Douglass, 1977) that suggest that moral motherhood ideology was a sentimental response that sought to hide from consciousness the actual devaluation of women's role with the developing split between home and commodity production (i.e., the public/private split). What is wrong with the sentimentalist hypothesis is the assumption that middle-class women were the *victims* of an ideology meant to hide their parasitical dependence on men. Rather, I would argue from the multi-systems approach that the reformation of parenting and sexual practices as reflected by the moral motherhood ideology was the result of a dialectical struggle between middle-class men, women, and ministers/writers; i.e. social groups whose roles were in transition. The evangelical ministers involved in the Great Awakening spiritual revival movement made common cause with middle-class women, who formed the majority of their congregations, to elevate women's spiritual status in the Church. Thus, middle-class women were partial agents in a reformation of bourgeois patriarchal sex/affective production in order to gain greater power as mothers than they had in the Puritan period, while they nonetheless preserved some aspects of men's power in the family as husbands.

Daniel Scott Smith argues for this perspective in an important paper in which he dubs as "domestic feminism" the underground social movement by women in the 19th century, in which women increased female control over reproductive sexuality and increased their autonomous control over childrearing (Smith, 1974). He dubs as "maritarchalism" the weaker form of patriarchy that developed during this period, in which men as fathers lost power but women were still controlled by men's economic and legal power as husbands.

Smith's evidence that women essentially gained rather than lost power in 19th century maritarchal sex/affective production rests primarily on the declining fertility rate. From the sex/affective production paradigm, we can further develop Smith's insight that women, by reducing fertility, increased their control over mothering work. Reduced fertility not only means less risks of maternal mortality, but the possibility of increased attention to each child. Thus, the emphasis on new theories of childhood as a distinctive stage of human life and the conceptualization of childhood through the notion of developmental stages suggest the need for an increased intuitive-affective understanding of each child (possible for women but not for men, since the latter are absent from the home in commodity production). The stage is set for the theory of childrearing that emphasizes the internalization of values through identification and guilt, rather than through the imposition of values by external force (shame). Each of the elements of the romantic view of childhood can be seen as legitimizing the priority of the mother-child bond *over* the father-child bond. In terms of the father-mother-child parenting triangle, sex/affective energy between mother and child is increased at the expense of sex/affective energy between father and mother, thus giving women increased bargaining power in sex/affective power relationships.[11]

The connection of moral motherhood with asexuality is important for understanding 19th-century sex/affective ideology. How can conceptualizing good women as asexual (vs. men who are naturally lustful) and bad women as sexual (whores) have been used as a tool to increase women's power in the family?

First, the voluntary motherhood and social purity movements of the late 19th century used the notion of the morally pure, asexual woman to insist that sexuality needed to be controlled by women. As Linda Gordon has pointed out (Gordon, 1976, ch. 5), this was not necessarily because advocates of social purity were opposed to sexuality per se. Rather, they argued that sexuality needed to be controlled by women in order to bring men under the same standard of sexual morality as women, thus eliminating the double standard. Not only was this designed to allow women to control the timing and frequency of genital intercourse so as to give more control over reproductive sexuality; it was also used as part of the campaign to eliminate prostitution as its perceived source, i.e., male sexual promiscuity.

The reversal of the emphasis prevalent today in sex/affective relationships seems to have characterized middle-class women's lives in the 19th century.

Given that genital sexual relationships were unsatisfactory and men's and women's work worlds so different, it is not surprising that the affectionate relations that women had with other women most often contained higher levels of erotic energy than did relations, whether genital or affectionate, with men (Sahli, 1979; Faderman, 1981). And as we have argued, the primacy of the mother-child bond over the heterosexual couple bond prevalent during this period no doubt involved a similar concentration of sex/affective energy. Thus, we need not assume that Victorian women's lives were devoid of sex/affective gratification in comparison with Puritan women or contemporary women; or that women had "given up" sex in order to get control of mothering. What is needed is a further amplification of the concept of sex/affective energy in order to conceptualize more clearly the conditions under which it is expressed/satisfied vs. conditions under which it is frustrated. For example, Victorian women may have gained power in sex/affective production, compared to Puritan women, by emphasizing nonsexual but intensely affectionate relations with children and other women. But in changed historical conditions it also seems true that the 20th-century sexual revolution, particularly the lesbian-feminist validation of sexual relations between women, contains a revolutionary potential for increased sex/affective energy gratification for contemporary women (Ferguson, 1981b). This is true despite the fact that much of the theory and practice of sexologists and advocates of sexual freedom have been male-dominant (Simons, 1979; Campbell, 1980).

Class and race differences in motherhood and sexuality. I have argued that the romantic/Victorian ideology of moral motherhood was a tool used by northern, white, middle-class Protestant women to aid in the transformation of sex/affective production in a way that increased their power over the production and distribution of sex/affective energy and also increased the relative quantity of sex/affective energy they received from children and homosocial networks. But by the end of the 19th century, the moral motherhood ideology was almost universally accepted by white working-class families as well. This was ironic, since the emphasis that the romantic/Victorian ideology placed on women being at home where their standards of sexual purity could be enforced on husbands and taught to children legitimized sexual violence against working-class women who were forced, for economic reasons, to work outside their homes.

For black women the moral motherhood ideology has two dimensions of racist control: the background of slavery, and economic necessity. The historical background of slavery in which black women were raped by white owners in order to produce more slaves created the material base for a racial-sexual stereotype of black women as bestial and sexual. Motherhood for them was not, like that for "full" (white) humans, a chosen career, but a natural, involuntary process as it is for all beasts of burden. The image is created of black people mating like dogs. Under this stereotype, black women could not be expected to be moral authorities like white mothers. Rather, they could care for the white mistress's children under her moral supervision. The second part of the slavery stereotype of black women as mothers, then, is as servants caring for (white) children, rather than as mothers in authority caring for their own children. The racial/sexual stereotype thus sets up the dichotomy *white* (good, virginal mother) vs. *black* (evil, sexual, bestial, whore).

One explanation for working-class acceptance of the moral motherhood/ cult of domesticity is provided by Hartmann (1981). According to her, late 19th-century organized trade union movements led by skilled male workers attempted to create a "family wage" in order to protect their challenged interests as family patriarchs. A family wage, i.e., a wage which allowed a wage-earning husband to support a non-wage-earning wife and children, performed two functions for patriarchal control: it cut competition from women wage workers, and it allowed men to keep their wives at home to provide personal services, services that are not so easily forthcoming when women have to deal with the problems of the second shift. The family wage and protective labor legislation for women and children were a "bargain" struck by male capitalists, upper-middle-class women reformers, and workers, which served each group's interests—the capitalists' because their new concern to reproduce a skilled labor force led them to emphasize public schooling and home childcare for children, care most economically provided free by working-class mothers.

It is important to note that contemporary changes in the married women wage labor force have changed the historical dynamic in which women could in fact gain power as mothers by remaining home with children. Working-class white women historically gained power as mothers by the institution of the family wage and protective legislation, but they also lost the power that being economically independent/less dependent on men brings to women who are waged. Black women, however, never gained any power from family wage legislation, for black men were largely excluded from unions. So black male unemployment and/or low wages was one of the reasons so many black married women worked in wage labor.[12]

Period III: Public (Capitalist) Patriarchy. Our contemporary American society is a social totality containing a mode of economic production, welfare state corporate capitalism, and a patriarchal mode of sex/affective production we can call "masculinist" (Ehrenreich and English, 1978). The shift between the first phase of industrial capitalism and our present stage began to occur during the progressive period of the 1890s and has been increasingly consolidated since then by the growth of the welfare state.

In terms of sex/affective production, the content and social relations of women's mothering in the home have changed significantly with the advent of the consumer economy. First, many of the tasks associated with "mothering" maintenance work (e.g., sewing, mending, cooking, gardening, nursing children and old people) are now no longer done primarily at home by mothers. Readymade clothes, store-bought foods, and fast food restaurants have lessened mother's domestic work in these areas, although the increasing drain on the male breadwinner's wage that consumerism brings has caused a steady rise in women's wage work in the 20th century.

The fact that mothers' work as health care workers and isolated mothers in the home has been diminished by the shift to public schools, hospitals, and nursing homes has not brought women a greater equality or control in the societywide sexual division of labor providing these services. Rather, as Ehrenreich and English note, the rise of the male-dominated medical profession in the late 19th and early 20th centuries diminished the control women had in health care, childbearing (by eliminating midwifery), and child nurturing. As male experts came to define what was healthy medicinally (the proliferation of the drug industry), emotionally (child development "experts"), and sexually (Freud and the sexologists), women lost the "moral expert" status *re* children they had gained with the adoption of the moral mother ideology.

Contemporary childbirth and reproductive practices are increasingly a form of "alienated labor" in the market sense, as a male-controlled medical technology is used to limit women's reproductive control (e.g., involuntary sterilizations, and making mothers passive, drugged objects in childbirth (Rich, 1976; Jaggar, 1981).

The increasing dominance of the public school system and the growth of suburban and urban living patterns has meant the isolation of mothers from supportive networks of other women. This has meant an increasing loss of control over their children's emotional and social environment. The 19th-century concept of children as private property of their parents is increasingly unbelievable (Ferguson, 1981a). Not only do major socializers of children beside the family (teachers, peers, TV, and the mass media) contribute to personality formation of young people, but the welfare state with its social workers of all kinds has increasing legal power to intervene in family affairs (McIntosh, 1978; Donzelot, 1979).

Contemporary motherhood creates an ambivalent relationship between mother and child that is extreme. Children are no longer apprentices to parents nor may their adult lives be much like those of their parents, so it is hard for mothers to see their children as products reproducing their interests and skills. From the child's point of view, parents become increasingly outmoded authorities whose only value lies in their access to money to pay for children's wants. Children form intense social bonds with their peers that often supplant parents as the objects of sex/affective energy.[13]

Within the nuclear family context itself, the influences of the sexual revolution for women have not so much increased the sexual satisfaction afforded to women as undermined their power as mothers. The late '20s and '30s saw the popularization of Freudian ideas by the development of a new liberal ideal of the "companionate marriage" (Simons, 1979). This involved a new domestic ideal of "mom" as sexy housewife. Mental health within the family required that mothers balance their affectionate involvement with their children by an equally intense, sexually intimate, and affectionately involving relationship with their husbands. Women who attempted to resort to 19th-century methods of controlling sexual intercourse by resisting husbands' advances could now be labeled "frigid" and "castrating women." Women who preferred the company of their children to that of their husbands were "narcissistic," had "separation problems," were causing sons to become homosexuals by tying them to their apron strings, and in general were damaging their children's health by excessive "momism" (Ehrenreich and English, 1978). Finally, women who prefer homosocial friendship networks to social time with their husbands, a practice taken for granted in the 19th century, can now be stigmatized as "sexually repressed" or, even worse, as *lesbians,* a concept which didn't exist in the 19th century (Ferguson, 1981b; Weeks, 1979, 1981).

It is not surprising that motherhood has become devalued in late 20th-century capitalist countries. Now that the percentage of women in the United States who are wage workers is over 50 percent and the number of married mothers with children under 18 who do wage work has increased dramatically in the last ten years, the second shift problem has become acute for working mothers. The United States in particular has handled the problem of working mothers in a totally inadequate way: only one out of six children whose mothers seek public childcare are able to find an available slot. Why have the problems of motherhood increased while its consequent social status has decreased?

One explanation is provided by Carl Brown (1981), who argues that since children are no longer economic assets to the family, due to the development of public schooling and child labor laws, men have lost interest in economically supporting children. Thus, what seems to be an advance or even a victory for women, the change from "father right" characteristic of 19th-century divorce law to the "mother right" typical of 20th-century cases (lesbian mothers of course not included!) is, in actuality, a breakdown of paternal obligations toward children. Women have won a "right" to child custody that merely guarantees an added unequal burden compared to fathers: not only the total burden of the sex/affective work involved in raising children, but in addition being the "breadwinner" (if only via welfare payments) as well.[14]

Carol Brown's argument has a rather excessive economistic emphasis on the economic costs and benefits of children. From the sex/affective production paradigm we can frame an additional explanation of why fathers have ceased to accept the "family wage" bargain of the 19th century and the role of primary breadwinner for wives and children. This is that the "victory" of the 19th-century mothers using the moral motherhood ideology in gaining control of the sex/affective energy exchange between parents and children disassociated fathers from direct control and production of this sex/affective good. Thus men don't want to contribute to the support of children to whom they do not experience a close sex/affective connection.

Another reason why the status of motherhood has declined under Public Patriarchy is, ironically, the partial success of the sexual revolution for women. Women's increasing economic independence from men and increased sexual permissiveness (partly as a result of the commoditization of sex through the influence of consumerism) has weakened men's ability to impose sexual double standards on women.

A frustrated male backlash to greater sexual freedom for women has been male recourse to sexual violence (rape, incest, domestic violence) (Easton, 1978) as well as the increased sexual objectification of women (pornography, sexual advertising) (Dworkin, 1981). In sharp contrast to the 19th-century split between the moral mother and the whore, many men now experience women simultaneously as both mother and whore, thus devaluing motherhood (Hooks, 1981).

The increasing crisis of motherhood in the United States is exacerbated by the phenomenal increase in the divorce rate in the 20th century (up to two-fifths of all marriages) (Bureau of the Census, 1977). Since marriage is no longer for life, women cannot rely on a stable family household and support from a male breadwinner in exchange for mothering and housework. Even though it is easier for divorced women to remarry now that the social stigma of divorce is lessening, many white mothers find divorce creates a crisis in self-identity, in part because single motherhood has been so devalued in white culture. This is an important difference between black and white culture, for American black culture has always valued motherhood, married or not, more than white culture has.[15]

The major increase in alternate families, particularly single motherhood and families formed by remarriage, is creating new social problems. Step-children often resent their new social parent (or mother's new lover), and lack of social precedents for how to facilitate conflicts often keeps the new family from developing equitable decision-making processes. This creates special problems for women, for as mothers and step-mothers (despite the patriarchal image of the "wicked step-mother") women are expected to be the ones to heal the conflicts within the family and to nurture everyone involved.

Racism has kept motherhood a very different experience for American white and black women in the past. Nonetheless, 20th-century changes in multi-systems domination relations are developing a particular form of white-supremacist capitalist patriarchy. Non-capitalist class white and black women's lives as wage workers, welfare recipients, single mothers, and sexual objects are much more similar with regard to sex/affective production than they used to be. Four key factors are the rise in single motherhood for both black and white women; the general rise in impersonalized violence against all women (rape); the rise in physical mobility of families and individuals, which causes the loosening of extended family networks; and consequently, the increasing isolation of motherhood for all women.

Political strength and emotional survival under these conditions requires for both black and white women a *chosen* as well as a blood kinship networking with other women to handle the fact of motherhood. This is not to deny that racism and classism oppress women differently. Rather, it suggests that with respect to motherhood, issues of sex/gender class in sex/affective production (e.g., conflicts between men and women over parenting, sexuality, and nurturance) are becoming structurally similar. Black and Third World feminist organizations are thus developing within different racial and ethnic communities as an attempt to resolve intra-community the social crisis of the family and personal intimacy presently occurring across racial/ethnic lines. Influential members and groups within the white women's movement are presently seeking to make coalitions with black feminists, in part by dealing with the racism within the white women's movement.

The Women's Movement has created a rising consciousness of the social inequalities forced on mothers by our current social arrangements of parenting (masculinist sex/affective production). Lesbian-feminism arose in the early '70s as one way to turn the sexual revolution toward egalitarian sexual relationships for women. As a result, many young women who might have married and had children in an earlier era have become lesbians. Many women, lesbian and heterosexual, have coped with the problem of motherhood today by choosing not to become mothers. For them, the problem becomes how to challenge the patriarchal ideology that a woman is not successful (indeed has not achieved adult status) until she becomes a mother. Other women are resorting to nontraditional ways of becoming mothers: artificial insemination, the "one night stand," adoption, etc. In addition to the economic, legal, and social difficulties that single women face in trying to become mothers, there are continuing legal problems of child custody rights faced by lesbian mothers.

It would take another paper to develop in detail the political implications of conceptualizing motherhood as a part of a sex/affective production process. Briefly, however, we can say that, failing a fascist takeover of state capitalism, the New Right will not be able to reconstruct the patriarchal nuclear family of 19th-century Husband Patriarchy. Families of choice, viz., social families with alternate egalitarian structures, are here to stay. Rather than accept the terms of the debate posed by the New Right (the family *vs.* lesbian/gay rights, traditional mothers vs. career women, etc.), the Women's Movement needs to continue to build an oppositional culture and politics that validates social, egalitarian parenting (parenting characterized by chosen, non-possessive social networks of women and children [social motherhood], or men, women, and children [social parenthood] (Ferguson, 1981a; Allison, 1980). Only in this way can we strengthen ourselves as women and mothers to use the current contradictions between masculinist sex/affective production based in the family and the ongoing development of state capitalist society in a struggle to challenge public patriarchy as a system of male domination.

Conclusion

I have argued that male domination can best be understood as perpetuated by the social relations of parenting, affection, and sexuality. These social relations involve different modes of the production and exchange of "sex/affective energy" and the production of gendered producers of this energy (modes of "sex/affective production"). Although different societies have had different modes of sex/affective production at different times, a cross-cultural constant is involved in different modes of bourgeois patriarchal sex/affective production. This is that women as mothers are placed in a structural bind by mother-centered infant and small child care, a bind that ensures that mothers will give more than they get in the sex/affective parenting triangle to which even lesbian and single parents are subjected. The ensuing double consciousness explains the internalization of oppressive structures of parenting in a way that avoids the static, deterministic emphasis of feminist neo-Freudian analyses like those of Nancy Chodorow. Furthermore, the concept of modes of sex/affective production can be applied to historical changes in parenting in American history to pinpoint changes in the concepts of motherhood and consequent strategies of resistance to male domination.

Historically, there are three main modes of sex/affective production in modern American history: Father Patriarchy (the colonial period), Husband Patriarchy (the romantic/Victorian Period) and Public Patriarchy (the twentieth century). The multi-systems approach shows that each of these periods is characterized by different power relations between men and women in parenting and sexuality, relations which also vary by race and class. Consequently, the *meaning* of motherhood, as a strategy of resistance to male domination or as a capitulation to it, varies in different periods, classes, and races. Further analyses are needed of areas within capitalist patriarchy where different domination systems functionally support each other and where they are in contradiction. Only by such concrete analyses can we develop specific feminist strategies for change in motherhood that make it clear what sorts of families of choice (social families) rather than birth (biological kin networks) we must conceptualize.

Notes

Thanks to many friends who gave me criticisms of earlier drafts of this essay, including Sam Bowles, Barbara Ehrenreich, Nancy Folbre, Sandra Harding, Annette Kuhn, Elaine MacCrate, Linda Nicolson, Francine Rainone, and Iris

Young. Special thanks to Liz, Francine, Kathy, Connie, Sarah, Lisa, and all the mothers and daughters who have provided the nurturance in which this article was born.

1. Adrienne Rich's classic *Of Woman Born* (1976) raises important issues for further thought. I chose these two quotes to begin this article not because I totally agree with them, but because they raise important theoretical questions. The first quote privileges the *biological* bond between mothers and daughters, thus raising the question of whether *social* mothering (adoptive mothers, step and foster mothers, older sisters, other mother surrogates) involves a secondary or different kind of mother-daughter bond. The second quote is ambiguous on the question of whether the actual *process* of mothering a child, as opposed to having been a child, makes an important difference to one's self-concept and perspective on life. I disagree with one of the implications of this quote, which suggests that actual mothering is irrelevant to one's self-concept. Rather, I maintain that actual mothering, whether biological-social or non-biological social (e.g., adopting, communal living, etc.) does make a difference to one's self-concept, which is not simply one of status in patriarchal societies.

2. The connection between gender identity and sexual preference (sexual identity) is problematic. While some theorists seem to assume an automatic connection (Chodorow, 1978), the gay and lesbian liberation movements of the 20th century have hypothesized sexual identity as quite separate from gender identity (Ferguson, 1981b). Compare also the view of sexologists and gays of the late 19th and early 20th century that gays constituted a "third sex": "Uranians" (Weeks, 1979).

3. I use the word "patriarchal" in a generic sense to refer to many types of male-dominant sex/affective production processes, and not in the specific sense in which it refers to a *father* patriarchal family where wife and children are economic and legal dependents.

4. In an earlier paper (Ferguson, 1979) I argue that in patriarchal sex/affective production systems, unequal labor time exchanged by men and women in housework, sexuality, nurturance, and childcare is exploitative in the classic marxist sense: men appropriate the surplus labor time of women in appropriating more of the human goods produced. In a subsequent paper (Ferguson and Folbre, 1981) the argument is advanced that increasing contradictions between patriarchy and capitalism are creating women as a new sex/gender class that cuts across family economic class lines. I owe many of my ideas on the analogies between economic and sex/affective production to Nancy Folbre (Folbre, 1980a, b).

5. I develop the concept of sex/affective energy to improve on the concept of libido introduced by Freud and further developed by Reich (1970, 1974). I have two objections to classic libido theory as developed by Freud and Reich: (1) They posit it as a bodily *drive* or type of *instinct* rather than an *energy*. This suggests a fixed quantity of energy held in check by the psychological mechanisms of repression. Foucault (1980), among others, has creatively criticized that image of sexuality and has suggested, to the contrary, that sexuality is an energy that can be brought into existence, focused, and augmented by social discourses. On this point I tend to agree with Foucault. (2) Freud and Reich's use of the concept of libido seems to assume that *genital sexuality* is the highest expression of this drive: that other forms of sexuality are either stages of arrested development or sublimated forms. I do not wish to assume that any one form of sexuality or affection is a "higher" or more basic expression of the generic form, nor do I wish to imply that affection is simply sublimated genital sexuality. Hence, I hyphenate the concept: sex/affective energy.

6. A much-quoted passage from Engels' *Origin of the Family* is richly suggestive yet

ultimately ambiguous on the question of how to conceptualize sexuality, nurturance, and human reproduction:

> According to the materialistic conception, the determining factor in history is, in the final instance, the production and reproduction of immediate life. This again is of a two fold character: on the one side, the production of the means of existence, of food, clothing and shelter and the tools necessary for that production; on the other side, the production of human beings themselves, the propagation of the species. The social organization under which the people of a particular historical epoch and a particular country live is determined by both kinds of production; by the stage of development of labor on the one hand and of the family on the other (Engels, 1972: 71-72).

The quote would seem to suggest that modes of the family are part of the material base of a society. Unfortunately, neither *Origins* nor *The German Ideology* deals seriously with changes in the "production of people" except as a direct function of the production of things (viz., the economy). So, other passages from *The German Ideology* suggest that Marx and Engels thought that the family in capitalist production is no longer part of the material base of society but has become part of the superstructure. This is a position which *reduces* the domination relations involved in the patriarchal production of people to a straight function of the domination relations involved in the production of things. The concept of sex/affective production, on the contrary, is meant to avoid this consequence.

7. Sara Ruddick argues (1980) that the maternal perspective involves a constant adjudication of one's own needs in reference to the child's because of three features of mothering work: concern for the physical survival, social acceptability, and growth (developmental needs) of the child. Her insights here are somewhat flawed by the apparent assumption that these concerns are not seriously altered by (a) the relation to the father, (b) other children or adult parent surrogates, and (c) the responses and options of the child, e.g., whether the child accepts mother's directions in these areas.

8. Marge Piercy's novel (1976) raises all sorts of interesting questions about whether the biological differences between men and women in human reproduction should be totally eliminated in order to permit gender-free childrearing.

9. The history of forms of the Afro-American family differs from these dominant family forms because of the institution of slavery and subsequent attempts by the black family after slavery to cope with the effects of institutionalized racism in the wage labor force. Since the black family has always had a different and more egalitarian internal structure than white family forms, sexism in the Afro-American community needs to be seen as a reflection of dominant white cultural forms (e.g., the sexual division of wage labor, macho images in the media, etc.) rather than as an autonomous structure of the community itself.

10. The theoretical method in use here differs from that followed in Nancy Chodorow's influential work, *The Reproduction of Mothering,* in several respects. First, the claim that mothering in bourgeois nuclear family systems can be seen in terms of a sex/affective triangle between father, mother, and child(ren) places more emphasis on the historically constructed system of parenting and sexual roles than does Chodorow. The nature of the mother-child bond and masculine/feminine gender identities is not simply determined by the fact of primary mother infant care; but by the manner in which the father controls or intervenes, the parents' treatment of sexuality, and the part played by other siblings in the child's interaction with parents. While Chodorow maintains that gender identities are fixed in childhood, she can account neither for the changing conceptions of sexual identities nor for gender identities caused by peer oppositional cultures of the contemporary lesbian/gay and women's movement. In conceptualizing parenting as a historical process that interacts with a historical set of

sexual practices, my approach can take into account race, ethnic, and class differences in motherhood. Its emphasis is more dynamic and agent-centered than Chodorow's, for the aim is to show that women have struggled to redefine motherhood (and consequently gender identities) within the parameters of the sex/affective triangle, given the opportunities afforded by changing economic, political, and cultural variables.

11. The gradual transference of parental authority from fathers to mothers and the intensification of the mother-child relationship would seem to have had contradictory effects for middle-class children. On the one hand, children became economic dependents of the family, as the length of time spent in schooling increased while the practice of apprenticing children decreased. As mothers came to feel children to be their exclusive products, children may have felt at once powerless to escape mothers, yet encouraged to develop some autonomy because of the new permissive childrearing practices coming into fashion. We can thus suppose that certain forbidden sexual practices (masturbation, homosexual play) actually increased among children, in part as a psychological distancing and resistance mechanism. This is quite a different explanation for the increased attention to adolescent sexuality evinced by 18th- and 19th-century writers than that provided by Foucault (1978). According to him, bourgeois sexual discourses (including religious confessional writing, sexual purity writers, and sexologists) created a new bourgeois concern with sexuality not as a response to any changing material conditions, but simply as a spontaneous change of direction in "discourses." My explanation assumes, on the contrary, that a material change in power relations between bourgeois children and parents created new sexual practices, including asexuality among wives and sexuality among children, which then spurred new regulatory discourses.

12. Black women have consistently worked outside the home since the Civil War in proportions that were three to four times higher than for white women. In 1880, for example, about 50 percent of black women were in the labor force, compared to 15 percent of white women. The percentage of married black women working compared to married white women is similarly high. In the 1880s, for example, no more than 10%–15% of white native and immigrant wives worked in wage labor (less in certain immigrant groups, e.g., Jews and Italians). Yet in New Orleans in the 1880s, 30 percent of black wives worked, and in Cambridge, Mass., Nashville, Tenn. and Atlanta in 1886 the figures were from 44 percent to 65 percent. (Degler, 1980, p. 389)

13. Many sources discuss the alienation of contemporary mothers. The classic is Friedan (1963). Others are Wandor (1974) and Bart (1970).

14. Most divorced fathers cop out not only on direct childcare work, but on financial contributions toward child support: 90 percent of divorced women do not receive regular child-support payments from fathers, and those who do do not receive the full payments the legal settlement entitled them to ("Women and Childcare" in *Women's Agenda,* March/April 1976). Welfare mothers are also subject to a male-headed bureaucracy whose interference in personal life and demeaning regulations attempt to reduce women to menial status.

15. This may be why a recent study of black women found that single black mothers had much higher self-esteem than single white mothers, in part because the latter did not compare themselves with married women, but with other single black mothers in assessing social status (Myers, 1980).

Bibliography

Albert, Michael, and Hahnel, Robin. 1978. *UnOrthodox Marxism.* Boston: South End Press.

Allison, Dorothy. 1980. "Weaving the Web of Community." *Quest* 5, no. 1.

Ariès, Philippe. 1965. *Centuries of Childhood: A Social History of Family Life.* Translated by Robert Baldick. New York: Alfred A. Knopf.

Barrett, Michelle. 1981. *Women's Oppression Today.* London: Virago.

Bart, Pauline. 1970. "Mother Portnoy's Complaint." *trans action* 8, nos. 1 and 2.

Benston, Margaret. 1969. "The Political Economy of Women's Liberation." *Monthly Review.* September.

Brown, Carol. 1981. "Mothers, Fathers and Children: From Private to Public Patriarchy." In *Women and Revolution.* Edited by L. Sargent. Boston: South End Press.

Bureau of the Census. 1977. "Marital Status and Living Arrangements: March 1976." *Current Population Reports.* Ser. P-20, no. 306. January.

Campbell, Beatrix. 1980. "A Feminist Sexual Politics," *Feminist Review* 5.

Chodorow, Nancy. 1978. *The Reproduction of Mothering.* Berkeley: University of California.

Contratto, Susan Weisskopf. 1980. "Maternal Sexuality and Asexual Motherhood." *Signs* 6, no. 1.

Degler, Carl. 1980. *At Odds: Women and the Family in America from Revolution to the Present.* Oxford: Oxford University Press.

Delphy, Christine. 1976. "Continuities and Discontinuities in Marriage and Divorce." In *Sexual Divisions and Society: Process and Change.* Edited by D. Leonard-Barker and S. Allen. London: Tavistock.

Demos, John. 1970. *A Little Commonwealth: Family Life in Plymouth Colony.* New York: Oxford University Press.

Donzelot, Jacques. 1979. *The Policing of Families.* New York: Pantheon.

Dworkin, Andrea. 1981. *Pornography: Men Possessing Women.* New York: Perigee/ G. P. Putnam Sons.

Easton, Barbara. 1978. "Feminism and the Contemporary Family." *Socialist Review* 39, vol. 8, no. 3.

Ehrenreich, Barbara, and English, Deirdre. 1975. "The Manufacture of Housework." *Socialist Revolution* 26, vol. 5, no. 4.

———. 1978. *For Her Own Good: 150 Years of the Experts' Advice to Women.* Garden City, NJ: Anchor/Doubleday.

Engels, Friedrich. 1972. *Origin of the Family, Private Property and the State.* Edited by E. Leacock. New York: International Publishers.

Ewen, Stewart. 1976. *Captains of Consciousness.* New York: McGraw Hill.

Faderman, Lillian. 1981. *Surpassing the Love of Men.* London: Junction Books.

Ferguson, Ann. 1979. "Women as a New Revolutionary Class in the U.S." In *Between Labor and Capital.* Edited by P. Walker. Boston: South End Press.

———. 1981a. "The Che-Lumumba School: Creating a Revolutionary Family-Community." *Quest* 5, no. 3: 13–26.

———. 1981b. "Patriarchy, Sexual Identity, and the Sexual Revolution." *Signs* 7, no. 1 (Autumn): 158–72.

Ferguson, Ann, and Folbre, Nancy. 1981. "The Unhappy Marriage of Patriarchy and Capitalism." In *Women and Revolution.* Edited by L. Sargent. Boston: South End Press.

Folbre, Nancy. 1980a. "The Reproduction of Labor Power." Unpublished, Economic Growth Center, Yale University.

———. 1980b. "Of Patriarchy Born: The Political Economy of Fertility Decisions." Discussion Paper #350, Economic Growth Center, Yale University.

Foucault, Michel. 1978. *The History of Sexuality,* vol. 1: *An Introduction.* Translated by R. Hurley. New York: Pantheon.

Friedan, Betty. 1963. *The Feminine Mystique.* New York: Dell.

Gordon, Linda. 1976. *Woman's Body, Woman's Right: A Social History of Birth Control.* New York: Grossman.

Habermas, Jurgen. 1979. "Toward a Reconstruction of Historical Materialism." In *Communication and the Evolution of Society.* Translated by Thomas McCarthy. Boston: Beacon Press.

Hartmann, Heidi. 1979. "Capitalism, Patriarchy and Job Segregation by Sex." In *Capitalist Patriarchy and the Case for Socialist Feminism.* Edited by Z. Eisenstein. New York: Monthly Review Press.

———. 1981. "The Unhappy Marriage of Marxism and Feminism." In *Women and Revolution.* Edited by L. Sargent. Boston: South End Press.

Hartsock, Nancy. 1981. "The Feminist Standpoint." In *Dis-Covering Reality.* Edited by S. Harding and M. Hintikka. Dordrecht: Reidel.

Herman, Judith. 1981. *Father-Daughter Incest.* Cambridge: Harvard University Press.

Hooks, Bell. 1981. *Ain't I a Woman: Black Women and Feminism.* Boston: South End Press.

Jaggar, Alison. 1983. *Feminist Politics and Human Nature.* Totowa, NJ: Rowman & Allanheld.

Marcuse, Herbert. 1964. *One Dimensional Man.* Boston: Beacon Press.

McDonough, Roisin, and Harrison, Rachel. 1978. "Patriarchy and Relations of Production." In *Feminism and Materialism.* Edited by A. Kuhn and A. M. Wolpe. London: Routledge & Kegan Paul.

McIntosh, Mary. 1978. "The State and the Oppression of Women." In *Feminism and Materialism.* Edited by A. Kuhn and A. M. Wolpe. London: Routledge & Kegan Paul.

Mitchell, Juliet. 1973. *Woman's Estate.* New York: Vintage/Random House.

Myers, Lena Wright. 1980. *Black Women: Do They Cope Better?* Englewood Cliffs, NJ: Prentice-Hall.

Person, Ethel Spector. 1980. "Sexuality as the Mainstay of Identity." *Psychoanalytic Perspectives* 5, no. 4 (Summer): 605–30.

Piercy, Marge. 1976. *Woman on the Edge of Time.* New York: Fawcett.

Poster, Mark. 1978. *Critical Theory of the Family.* London: Pluto.

Reich, Wilhelm. 1970. *The Discovery of the Orgone: The Function of the Orgasm.* New York: Noonday/Farrar, Straus and Giroux.

———. 1974. *The Sexual Revolution.* New York: Simon & Schuster.

Rich, Adrienne. 1976. *Of Woman Born.* New York: Bantam Books.

———. 1980. "Compulsory Heterosexuality and Lesbian Existence." *Signs* 5, no. 4 (Summer): 342–67.

Rubin, Gayle. 1975. "The Traffic in Women." In *Toward an Anthropology of Women.* Edited by R. Reiter. New York: Monthly Review Press.

Ruddick, Sara. 1980. "Maternal Thinking." *Feminist Studies* 6, no. 2 (Summer): 342–67.

Ryan, Mary. 1975. *Womanhood in America from Colonial Times to the Present.* New York: Franklin-Watts.

Sahli, Nancy. 1979. "Smashing: Women's Relationships Before the Fall." *Chrysalis* 8. Pages 17–28.

Shorter, Edward. 1977. *The Making of the Modern Family.* New York: Basic Books/Harper.

Simons, Christina. 1979. "Companionate Marriage and the Lesbian Threat." *Frontiers* 4, no. 3 (Fall): 54–59.

Smith, Daniel Scott. 1974. "Family Limitation, Sexual Control and Domestic Feminism." In *Clio's Consciousness Raised.* Edited by M. Hartman and L. W. Banner. New York: Harper & Row.

Smith-Rosenberg, Carroll. 1975. "The Female World of Love and Ritual: Relations Between Women in 19th Century America." *Signs* 1, no. 1 (Autumn): 1–29.

Stewart, Katie. 1981. "The Marriage of Capitalist and Patriarchal Ideologies: Meanings of Male Bonding and Male Ranking in U.S. Culture." In *Women and Revolution*. Edited by L. Sargent. Boston: South End Press.

Wandor, Michelene. 1974. "The Conditions of Illusion." In *Conditions of Illusion: Papers for the Women's Movement*. Edited by S. Allan, L. Sanders, and J. Wallis. Leeds: Feminist Books.

Weeks, Jeffrey. 1979. *Coming Out: A History of Homosexuality from 19th Century to the Present*. Boston: Charles River Books.

———. 1981. *Sex, Politics, and Society*. New York: Longman.

Young, Iris. 1980. "Socialist Feminism and the Limits of Dual Systems Theory." *Socialist Review* 10, no. 50/51 (March/June): 169–88.

Zaretsky, Eli. 1976. *Capitalism, the Family and Personal Life*. New York: Harper & Row.

PART THREE

Concepts of Mothering

11

The Maternal Instinct (1972)

CAROLINE WHITBECK

> Maternal—adj. 1: of, pertaining to, having the qualities of, or befitting
> a mother, *maternal instincts.*
>
> > *The Random House Dictionary of*
> > *the English Language*
> > (unabridged) 1967

The topic I wish to discuss here is the familiar notion of the maternal instinct as applied to human beings. It is, of course, a matter for debate whether what we call maternal instincts are instincts in the sense of innate patterns of activity, but I shall, in any case, retain the expression "maternal instinct."

There are, I am sure, those who would question whether this topic is appropriate for philosophical investigation. Yet we are accustomed to reading philosophical treatises on other affections, dispositions, and traits of character and their causes. That *thumos* (spirit or anger) is given such attention in Plato's *Republic* is, I suggest, a result of his having been a man in a culture which required him to serve in the army. Had he been a woman who bore children, he might have chosen maternal attachment. The fact that it has seemed natural to investigate affections, dispositions, and character traits, such as a warrior's courage, which are particularly significant in the experience of (many) men, but are not similarly significant in the experience of women, while it is thought peculiar to treat matters which are particularly significant in the experience of (many) women, is symptomatic of an important bias in philosophy.

An earlier version of this paper was presented to the regional meeting of the Society for Women in Philosophy which took place at Amherst, Massachusetts, in October 1972. I am indebted to the participants at that meeting and to a large number of women who have subsequently given me useful criticisms of this paper.

This article first appeared in *The Philosophical Forum* 6, nos. 2–3 (Winter–Spring 1974–75). Reprinted by permission of the publisher and the author.

When people talk about maternal instincts, what they seem to be discussing are the inner promptings which induce women to care for their offspring. All this is frequently supposed to be connected with love in some way, and may even be considered to be a particular species of love. What complicates the matter is that whereas we do speak of parental affection, and paternal as well as maternal feelings, there is no talk of *paternal instincts.* (It would be an interesting philosophical task to examine the way in which the notion of instinct itself has evolved in recent years, but it is not one which I will undertake here. I shall simply use the term to mean an innate pattern of activity.)

It would seem, therefore, that while certain feelings may be viewed as characteristic of parents of both sexes, in women this parental affection is viewed as augmented or enhanced in some special way. This view is also implicit in the technical literature on maternal attachment in humans, for although "maternal instinct" is not regarded as determining this attachment—indeed the expression "maternal instinct" is avoided—nonetheless, maternal attachment is viewed as a richer or more complex phenomenon and much more worthy of study than paternal attachment.

I shall argue that factors other than those which are solely the product of socialization influence women, and not men, in their attachment to their children, and that these factors arise from biological differences. According to my analysis, these factors are the *experiences* of pregnancy, labor, childbirth, nursing, and postpartum recovery. As explanatory factors, such conscious experiences contrast with a putative "natural" tendency of women to be either nurturing or masochistic in personal relations, and with simple biological variables such as hormone levels, as well as with the innate patterns of activity that are termed instincts. Thus, these experiences do not readily fall into either the nature category or the nurture category. (Of course, nature and nurture can be seen to influence one another even in the purest of cases.)

Currently a host of arguments about human behavior rely heavily on analogy with animal behavior. Aggression and territoriality have received particular attention, and the maternal instinct has not been neglected. The subject cannot be discussed for long without someone making reference to what Harlow's monkeys do or don't do. Whatever one thinks of arguments from analogy with animals in general, these arguments are useful for us, at least, in fixing a notion of instinctive behavior in animals and its relation to the notion of maternal instinct in humans.

Those who argue for a *difference* between human behavior and that of lower animals have the advantage in citing studies with other primates, because a dissimilarity between findings for monkeys and lower mammals, such as rats, *does* count toward showing that the corresponding data on rats is not to be taken as showing anything about humans. For if a monkey is unlike a rat in a certain respect, we expect a human to be. The arguments for similarity fare less well since even if a monkey is like a rat in certain respects, there may nonetheless be important differences between humans and other primates.

The studies with subhuman primates do, in fact, show an important difference between primates and lower mammals. Both sexual and maternal behavior are demonstrated by lower mammals such as rats and mice, even if these animals have been raised in isolation. The same is not true in the case of monkeys. Rhesus monkeys raised in isolation in general do not mate. The few female isolates who were impregnated by various means behave erratically and often hostilely toward their first-born young, hurling them across their cage as often as they allow them to suck. Some of these unnatural mothers were impregnated a second time and this time for the most part were good or adequate mothers, thus indicating that they had acquired a disposition to maternal behavior from their experience with their first-born. This pattern contrasts with that of normally raised female-monkeys, who tend to be more indulgent with first-born than with subsequent offspring.[1] These results are generally interpreted to show that, in monkeys, sexual and maternal behavior is not instinctive.

If instinct will not serve to explain "maternal instinct," let us consider whether love will fill the bill. Consider the Greek words for love. If any of these terms designate what it is that parents customarily feel for their offspring, we may then ask whether there is any reason to think that women experience this emotion to a greater extent than men. Parental affection has frequently been looked upon as *storge* (as opposed to *philia, eros,* or *agape*). *Storge* is familiar affection, that is, the positive feeling which we have for familiar sights, sounds, smells; thus we feel *storge* for old acquaintances, for our not especially faithful or distinguished dog, and for members of our families. *Storge* requires no particular merit in the object and so serves admirably to tide family members over one another's awkward stages and less endearing moods. Shall we say that the mother's *storge* toward her offspring constitutes the maternal instinct?

This identification has a number of attractions. We could explain the special incidence of *storge* in mothers by their greater familiarity with their infants, which is a product not only of the common view that childcare is woman's work, but also of the necessity of nursing young infants every few hours. But the essential element that is required for *storge,* i.e., familiarity, is lacking. The expression "little stranger" for an infant is certainly well chosen. There may be nothing quite so wonderfully strange as one's own newborn child. However strange, this small bundle generally evokes a curious willingness to protect it with one's life. While such a reaction is not universal, its prevalence is attested to by survival of the human species in those societies and circumstances where the woman was left more to her own resources either during or immediately after delivery.[2] In such circumstances, survival of the newborn child depends upon some sort of inner promptings which tide the mother over the first few weeks when the infant is emphatically not familiar.

In terms of the Greeks' categories of love, I think we do much better by considering *eros.* By *eros,* I do not mean primarily adult genital sexual impulse (although that may be a factor), but rather the feeling we call being in love. I think people do find their offspring fascinating in just that sort of way. A normal, healthy baby is smooth, soft, sweet-smelling, and hairless, in short, beautiful by the standards of many cultures. Regardless of the fact that these standards do not naturally fit women better than they fit men, they are generally considered to be standards of *feminine* beauty. Furthermore, the emotional and mental traits of a baby closely resemble characteristics that many societies, including ours, consider to be feminine, as opposed to masculine, virtues, viz., innocence, receptivity, and emotional sensitivity. Therefore, the attractiveness of babies is a particularly feminine attractiveness, according to the standards of many cultures, and so the beauty of a baby ought to be at least as attractive to men as to women, other things being equal.

In her monograph *The Psychology of Women,* Judith Bardwick tries another approach to maternal instincts. In discussing the effects of body states on the psyche, she expresses the "feeling" that there must be some biological variable which correlates with maternal nurturance, especially of small helpless infants, although none has yet been found. From her work on mood changes and hormone levels in the menstrual cycle, we may gather that hormone level is the sort of biological variable she has in mind. Another favorite variable for correlation with maternal attachment is duration of menstrual flow.[3]

I think such an approach to the maternal attachment is misguided. It represents a holdover from the instinct hypothesis, for again it removes the person, her experience, and the significance of that experience from consideration. We would find that same approach implausible to the point of absurdity in the analogous case of sexual attraction. In subprimates, the female does not experience a sexual drive or desire, except during her fertile period. (In many species, the male also does not produce sperm or mate except at mating season.) The hormone levels provide at least necessary conditions for sexual attraction among lower mammals. We don't, however, expect the same to be true with humans. Women experience sexual desire at infertile periods and then often for a specific male. In a given case we may not know "what it is she sees in him"; but she does "see something in him" and that, rather than her hormone level, attracts her to that individual and not to a host of others.* If hormone level does *not* provide a necessary condition for sexual attraction in women, though it is known to in lower animals, why should we continue to expect it to account for the attachment women feel toward their infants?

Why should we look for some yet-undiscovered biological variable and ignore the question of what a woman sees in her baby? What is it that parents

---

*I mean to allow that what one person "sees in" another may be in large part due to the perceiver's fantasies and projections.

commonly see in their offspring that leads them to care for them? Do men and women differ in this regard?

Things that we see in our children and that give rise to our feelings for them are revealed by considering the answers people give to the following problem:

Suppose you have two children, a four-year-old and a one-year-old. You are out in a boat, several hundred yards from shore, and the boat begins to sink. You realize that you will only be able to save one. Which one would you save?

Two reasons seem to spring to people's minds. Often both reasons occur to the same person, making that person unable to make a choice. The reason for saving the elder is generally that the elder represents a greater investment of oneself (i.e., an investment for a greater period of time). The reason for saving the younger is that one feels a greater responsibility for the younger, more helpless child.

What about these two sources of attachment to one's child? Let us first consider the issue of helplessness. Suppose that in place of the one-year-old, there is an adult offspring who is a quadriplegic. I think that it will be recognized that if anyone is prompted to save the quadriplegic in preference to the four-year-old, it is *not for the same reason* that one is prompted to save the one-year-old in preference to the four-year-old. The helplessness of a baby who claims our care is not simple physical helplessness. An essential aspect of the infant's helplessness is that infants, and to some extent children, cannot reason and make decisions, so we must perform these functions for the infant. Psychologists describe the situation by saying that the mother's ego (or the ego of the "mother substitute," e.g., the father) functions for the infant. The four-year-old's rational functions are more developed than the one-year-old's, and hence the sharing of rational functions does not exist to the same degree.

This sharing of one's rational functions gives use to a special sort of identification with the infant that is a source of strong feeling. Such sharing of ego explains the readiness with which a parent will risk his or her life to protect the child. It is not quite another, but a quasi-self, a self with a whole life before her or him, who must be protected. Here I think we do encounter some differences in the experiences of the two sexes which, other things equal, may be expected to produce differences in the extent to which such an identification is made.

The first obvious difference is that the fetus is carried in the mother's body but not in the father's. I do not wish to make much of this point, since I do not believe that women readily identify the "little stranger" with the familiar fetus. (We may be misled on this point because often during pregnancy a woman looks ahead, anticipating what her child will be like.) The belief that the child is often viewed very differently from the fetus is supported by the finding that there are widespread restrictions on abortion among so-called primitive people. This finding indicates that women are commonly motivated to abort themselves,[4] and thus negatively value pregnancy; women positively value their infants and do not need society's prescriptions in order to care for them.

More significant are the experiences of the last month of pregnancy and of labor. A woman in labor experiences helplessness, and this experience more closely resembles the total helplessness of infants than any other experience a healthy adult is likely to have. Breathing techniques and other so-called "natural childbirth" methods may help the woman in labor to take some distance from its pains, but if the labor is long, as is usual in the case of first births, it is difficult for her to avoid being completely caught up in her bodily experiences. In being entirely caught up in one's bodily experience the woman is like the infant who knows neither future nor past but only present bodily state. At least from the time of the writing of the Book of Genesis, the seemingly pointlessly long and difficult time that women have in normal labor and childbirth has appeared to require explanation. According to this analysis, an arduous labor and delivery can be seen as having adaptive value in preparing the mother to empathize with the infant. (Of course the much greater difficulty that women have as compared with other mammals *arises from* the erect carriage of human beings.)

Helplessness in the form of weakness is also experienced in the postpartum period. This fact is likely to be unknown to those who have not lived through a childbirth experience, either their own or a family member's, and who hear that there is now an emphasis on early ambulation after delivery. In fact, even after discharge from the hospital, women are instructed not to go up and down stairs for two weeks.

Furthermore, in the last month of pregnancy, women not only experience some helplessness due to the disruption of balance brought on by the fetus's considerable weight gain, but also must learn to take thought for their own bodily functions in much the same way that it is necessary to take thought regarding a newborn's. This is necessary because in the last month the enlarged uterus presses on the other organs. The stomach and the bladder, particularly, are constricted and neither can contain very much. Three meals a day are likely to become five or six small feedings. At these times, the expectant mother eats, not the usual things, but those items which she has learned she can digest. Thus, she puts herself on a feeding schedule resembling the one her newborn child will require.

Nursing, which until recently was requisite for infant survival, provides an experience that fosters a different sort of identification with the infant. This identification occurs not because the usual experiences encourage projections of one's ego and feelings of empathy, but because they encourage fantasies of fusion. The let-down reflex, which causes the mother's milk to flow freely, is often triggered by some action of the baby's, such as the baby's cry. Furthermore, the baby's sucking causes the reflexive contractions of the womb. Both of these involuntary responses strengthen the mother's impression that her own body and her newborn baby's function as a unit.

What about the other point brought out by the sinking boat example? We value children in part because they represent an investment of our time and effort. Here the fact that it is the mother who carries the child does become important. For her investment in the newborn child is obviously greater by reason of this nine-month task, other things being equal.

Of course, other things never are equal. Societal demands shape much of our thinking, feeling, and behavior. Furthermore, a child has a special significance peculiar to the family into which she or he is born. However, I am concerned with neither what is peculiar to some family nor with societal demands and social roles. The concern of my investigation has been to discover whether biological differences between men and women are likely to give rise to factors that affect women's, but not men's, attachment to their offspring. I grant that different socialization experiences and individual differences in temperament may more than make up for the sex differences to which I have drawn attention here.[5]

The foregoing argument may be summarized by saying that parental affection or attachment is influenced by experience, and this experience is not confined to socialization experience, but includes, in large measure, bodily experiences that are the same cross-culturally; i.e., all women have special bodily experiences that are likely to enhance those feelings, attitudes, and fantasies which induce people generally to care for their infants. Therefore, I conclude that there is a factual basis for the asymmetry in the expressions we apply to male and female parents. However, the foregoing argument has not turned up anything to which the term "maternal instinct" can be happily applied. We have seen that maternal behavior in humans is not instinctual in the sense of innate. Furthermore, since the bodily experiences we have been discussing enhance rather than augment feelings, etc., which are common in parents of either sex, it would be misleading to say that these experiences *give rise* to a maternal instinct. Finally, the alternative of saying that these peculiarly maternal experiences *constitute* a maternal instinct simply does too much violence to the language to be viable.

That these rather obvious lines of argument have been neglected is substantiated by both continued use of the term "instinct" in the popular literature, and by the almost exclusive attention to biological variables, such as duration of menstrual flow and hormone level, in the technical literature.[6] Whereas the paradigm "labor" for young men in our society—the war experience—is examined, rehearsed, bemoaned, and celebrated in novels and films, the paradigm "labor" for young women, that of bearing children, is neglected. (The soap opera has in recent years provided the only exception to the rule of the disregard of pregnancy and childbirth and, of course, the soap opera is held in low esteem as an art form.) I would venture that the majority of readers have seen at least a half-dozen films about the experiences of men in war, and that this number exceeds the number who have seen even one film about the experiences of women bearing children. Because we, men and women, see representations of male experience, but not female experience, it is not surprising that the causal relations which connect women's experience to other aspects of our lives have remained obscured.

Notes

1. A. M. Schrier, H. F. Harlow, and F. Stollnity, eds., *Behavior of Non-Human Primates,* vol. 2 (New York: Academic Press, 1965), chapter 8.
2. For a comprehensive history of obstetrics, see Harvy Graham, *Eternal Eve,* unabridged ed. (London, 1950).
3. See Julia Sherman's *Psychology of Women* (Springfield, Ill.: Charles C. Thomas, 1971), pp. 217–18, for a review of the literature and comments upon the discrepancy between femininity and maternal ratings in some experiments.
4. See C. S. Ford, *A Comparative Study of Human Reproduction* (New Haven: Yale University Press, 1945).
5. These same bodily experiences might also foster negative feelings, attitudes, and fantasies. Thus, it is plausible to assume that a woman pregnant by rape would be reminded of her attack by her helpless condition in later pregnancy and might even see her infant as a new embodiment of her attacker. I wish to maintain that alternative interpretations of bodily experience are also possible, although some interpretations are likely only in the case of less-common personal histories.
6. An article titled "Maternal Attachment" by Marshall H. Klaus, Richard Jerauld, Nancy C. Kreger, Willie McAlpine, Meredith Steffa, and John H. Kennell *The New England Journal of Medicine,* 2 March 1972, pp. 460–63, reports confirmation of the hypothesis that maternal experiences in the first three days postpartum importantly influence maternal behavior. Although the design of this study does not include attention to those experiences, peculiar to women, to which I have drawn attention, it does represent a welcome shift to an examination of the role of the mother's (bodily) experiences in determining her attachment to her infant.

Afterword to The Maternal Instinct *(1982)*

Precious Creature:

Already I feel you beginning to experiment with adolescent distance. Our mother-child relationship is ending. Soon your intellectual life will become a distinct and increasingly important part of your life. I want to tell you some of what I have learned with you, in part so that you will have alternatives to the masculist interpretative systems that dominate our culture, and even more, so that you will have an awareness of the feminist practice of mindfully speaking out of one's own relations and embodiment, as well as speaking about them.

This practice, with which you are already familiar in the music and lyrics of the women's movement, more than the specific things I have to say, will enable you to do work that is your own.

I want to tell you how living the mother-daughter relationship with you has transformed my thinking and provided a different ground for my philosophical work. "The Maternal Instinct" was the first fruit sprung from that new ground. Reliving the primordial mother-daughter mirroring, this time from the mother's side, has helped to bring me to a new understanding of that self-other distinction, so at variance with much of the larger culture, that lies at the heart of the way in which many women think and live.

When men speak of their experience as disciples of some intellectual or religious teacher, or in psychoanalysis, they describe what sounds like a pale reflection of the mother-daughter relation. It is odd that mothering itself has never been understood as a "way." Is it because men have rarely "mothered," and thus the models and concepts adequate to express this experience have been absent within the masculist culture? Or is it because the idea of learning with and from a "weaker being," such as a child, goes too much against the culture's preoccupation with hierarchy and domination? (In masculist culture it is assumed that profound learning occurs with an "authority" who understands the whole process in advance and is unchanged by it.)

"The Maternal Instinct" was written when you were between two and three months old. Your eyes had just begun to focus on ordinary things and no longer seemed to be looking through all space and time; you smiled. I had not planned to write a paper on mothering. Other work was waiting, but I needed to reflect upon my intense absorptions with you, and to have the critical support of other philsophers in doing so. The first Eastern Division SWIP* meetings were held that October in Amherst. I took you to those meetings and there presented the paper. You were four months old.

I was fortunate to know Angela McBride while I was pregnant with you. She was writing *The Growth and Development of Mothers* and, by and large, encountering only uncomprehending responses from feminist and non-feminist publishers alike. The book finally appeared in 1973. Two years later Adrienne Rich's *Of Woman Born* was published. It may have been Angela's example that encouraged me to go ahead and write "The Maternal Instinct" and so to contravene many unspoken rules that constrain philosophical writing.

The year before you were conceived, I had worked with Carol Christ, your "fairy godmother," as you spontaneously renamed her, on a model affirmative action plan for Yale University, in which we set out some of the positive steps that Yale might take to eliminate sexism. It was my third year of teaching philosophy there, and Carol was just finishing her doctorate in

---

*Society for Women in Philosophy.

religious studies. Marcia Keller, who was completing her doctorate in philosophy, coordinated the cooperation among the clerical workers, students, and faculty, and correctly argued that, as far as possible, everything should emerge from us as a collective. In retrospect, however, I want you to understand the way in which the personal, the political, and the scholarly were woven together in our lives and the way in which we made it possible for one another to rethink our traditions. Among the women of the Yale faculty and Professional Women's Forum I first learned to ask what an academic world that was really open to women might be like.

When I was pregnant with you, Carol, Ginny, Sid, your father, and I were all living together in the house with all the dogwood trees. I remember one evening when Carol pointed out the peculiarity of the philosophical perspective that takes there to be a "problem of other minds." This supposed problem is one of how one might know that other people "have minds." Now, of course, there are many peculiarities about the way in which the problem is usually framed, not the least of which is the assumption that "a mind" is something like an unobservable component or possession, and that what *is* observable is a (mindless) body or, at most, behavior. The more fundamental absurdity, however, which had the two of us hooting and chortling, is what I would now describe as the peculiar conception of the self-other distinction that motivates such a problem. The assumption is that self and other are fundamentally *opposed,* so that the burden of proof is on those who maintain that the self and other are similar in some respect. This masculist construal of self-other distinction as a thorough-going opposition, symbolized (in accord with the experience of a male infant who first differentiates himself in relation to a female nurturer) by an opposition between "the masculine" and "the feminine," runs through the history of western (and eastern) thought from Pythagoras through the Jungians, and explains such peculiar expressions as "the *opposite* sex." (This realization of the peculiar character of the formulations of a number of philosophical problems was my first awareness of what I now identify as the masculist self-other distinction that I began to investigate explicitly in "Theories of Sex Difference.")

During the first year following your birth I was deeply absorbed in a meditative ecstasy of motherhood, in which I recognized in one or the other of us the infant I had been, the person I was then, and the person you were to become, and had to come to terms with each of these persons continuously. I had come to a new realization of the fundamental discrepancy between my experience of you (and therefore of your mirrored experience of me, and mine of my own mother) and the story of the son who strives to displace the father and "possess" the nurturer-mother—the story that structures our culture's models of political and psychic liberation from the 17th century to our own. We emerge into full social personhood in and through a relationship to a nurturer with whom we identify, who is fundamentally like ourselves not only in flesh and bone and bodily origin, but in gender, with all of the social significance of the possibilities of a female body. It was the vividness of the early experience with you that led me to write "The Maternal Instinct" with little recourse to psychiatric or psychoanalytic categories (although at the time I was doing research in the Yale Psychiatry Department, and had for several years conducted a faculty discussion group on psychoanalytic theory).

By the end of your first year I was getting clearer about the masculist character of the received self-other distinction. I first discussed that in "The Feminine," which I presented at the SWIP meetings held at Columbia during your second year, and which was subsequently incorporated in "Theories of Sex Difference." At that time I was making a weekly commute with you to Albany where I had resumed full-time teaching.

Although feminist in content, "Theories of Sex Difference" was more traditional in argument form, and so it was published before "The Maternal Instinct"* Lesson: if you are introducing new content, it is more readily received if you work within accepted forms—the problem is that the forms themselves make it impossible to deal adequately with certain content—content such as the maternal experience. The main argument in "The Maternal Instinct" turns on the consideration of bodily aspects of a woman's personal experience (as oppposed to "the data of sensations"—a fiction that has found extravagant use in the work of some philosophers—or to descriptions of the body). Consideration of the bodily aspects of a woman's personal experience as well as the central topic of maternal attachment make the paper outlandish according to the canons of Anglo-American philosophy. Even in phenomenological circles, in which reasoning from bodily and emotional experience is permissible, technical circumlocutions reassure the reader that the body is still appropriately distanced from the intellects who are the writer and reader. Bodily experience, like human vulnerability and mortality, are subjects that modern philosophy has shunned describing except in the most abstract terms. The fantasy that the philosopher is a "pure" intellect, or even that philosophy is the paradigm activity of "pure intellects," runs through much of the history of western philosophy, and influences both the choice of problems and the mode of discussion and argument. With respect to the topic, this means that if the subject of maternal attachment were to be discussed at all within philosophy, the clear preference would be for an argument that deals solely with "cultural forces" (presumed to act on an abstractly construed subject). More acceptable still would be an account couched exclusively in terms of biological factors, such as hormones, since these influence bodily experience without being a part of it, and which would make the issue the concern of biology, not philosophy.

---

*In *Women and Philosophy,* edited by Carol Gould and Marx Wartofsky (New York: G. Putnam, 1976).

Of course, even for many women arguments such as those that I offer in "The Maternal Instinct" are not easy ones to entertain (and hence critically evaluate and accept or reject). This is not merely because the culture at large is masculist (so that our words and concepts are suited for dealing with men's rather than women's experience), but because the implications of the view are often unwelcome. In particular, it may be disquieting to consider that bodily differences between men and women, together with the social arrangements regarding infant care, may produce quite different conceptual structures, ways of living, and experiences of the human condition for the majority of males and females. For many women it is more comforting to think that an adequate dose of exhortation and encouragement would suffice to bring men to the point of being able to dedicate themelves to parenting and to mutual relationships to the same extent that women do. It may be a hard and somewhat terrifying possibility that a chasm may separate our own thought from that of the masculist culture.

If arguments such as those presented in "The Maternal Instinct" are to be evaluated, then both women's experience and bodily experience and, even more taboo, the bodily aspects of women's experience will have to be considered. (Susan Griffin has written a brilliant account of the origin of this taboo in *Pornography and Silence*.)

The ten years of your life have coincided with the development of the second wave of feminist thought in this country and of a new opportunity to articulate the experience of the mothering relation. Things were quite different for feminist scholars in 1971–72 as I carried and bore you. Then, *Ms.* magazine had largely ignored the mothering experience (despite providing "Stories for Free Children"). The first article to deal with mothering in its physical-emotional-psychological complexity was "In Praise of Breast Feeding" by Sally Wendkos Olds in the April 1973 issue. There were hardly any feminist academic journals. (*Feminist Studies* published a few issues beginning in 1972 and then ceased publication for several years. *Quest* first appeared in 1974, followed by *Signs* in 1975. *Women and Health* began the following winter.)

In the last five or six years there has been increasing attention to mothering in the feminist and psychological literature. In 1976 Dorothy Dinnerstein's *The Mermaid and the Minotaur* was published. In that work she identified many social ills that result when people are "mother-raised." In particular, she discusses how hard it is for the members of our society to recognize female authority as legitimate, or to place reasonable limits upon their demands on women. In *The Reproduction of Mothering,* published in 1978, Nancy Chodorow used psychoanalytic categories to examine the sociology of gender. Like Dinnerstein, Chodorow urges the equal involvement of men in the rearing of young children. By replacing "mother-rearing" with rearing by members of both sexes, Chodorow expects to remedy the present situation in which masculinity is tied to a denial of dependence and a devaluation of women, and the feminine personality is preoccupied with individuation, and both sexes expect women to possess unique self-sacrificing qualities. Both books make valuable contributions, but they set the stage for, rather than contributed to, the development of a feminist ontology and concomitant view of interpersonal relations. Dinnerstein focuses on the negative results of the present situation. Although Chodorow articulates some features of the neglected mother-daughter experience, she relies heavily on psychoanalytic categories that are themselves tied to masculist assumptions and constructs. In terms of that portion of a feminist ontology and account of interpersonal relations that I presently grasp, the most important result of the equal involvement of men in child-rearing is that it would foster in boys the development of a self-other distinction more like that of girls (i.e., one in which the self concept is largely influenced by identification with the nurturer, and according to which the other is presumed to be fundamentally like and related to the self, rather than fundamentally opposed to the self). It seems to me that among men such an understanding of the relation of the self and non-self is often confined to those who are exceptionally saintly, wise, or similarly "exceptional," but that the very survival of humanity may depend upon making such an understanding commonplace.

French feminists like Luce Irigaray, Hélène Cixous, and Catherine Clément (whose thought I have learned largely from Eléanor Kuykendall) are attempting to develop a woman-centered account that is adequate to the experience of a female infant, girl, and woman. Their work is stimulating, but I think it may concede too much to the Freudian account, according to which the infant's attachment to the mother is construed on the model of what is (in our culture at least) a man's sexual attachment to a woman. The Freudian model of infant attachment may not be much of a distortion for the infant boy, especially if he has enough early acquaintance with the father to identify with him from an early age, but I doubt that it fits the mother-daughter attachment very well. Although father-child incest is all too common, mother-child incest is extremely rare. This fact gives me confidence in the generalization that the attachment from the mother's side is not *in the narrow sense* sexual, and insofar as the daughter's attachment mirrors the mother's, the daughter's is not either. Furthermore, as the relationship progresses it loses its dyadic character, and with effort (but without betrayal or abandonment) the relationship comes to involve more and more people. Of course the grand passion of the primordial relation is deeply physical and emotional, and it does prepare the way for all future attachment, sexual and nonsexual.

I will close with some stories that illustrate the present climate of resistance to considerations of women's experience that continues to exist among those who claim to be "educated."

Do you remember when another girl in your kindergarten class brought in bubble bath for show and tell? Your teacher reported that you responded by saying that you couldn't use bubble bath because it would make your vagina sore, and other little girls did not know what "vagina" meant. I fear they had been given no *other* words for their genitals either, although it is unimaginable that a little boy of the same age in this culture would have no words for his. Many little girls are still deprived of social confirmation in the form of language of who and what they are as embodied beings and are, in the cultural sense, castrated.

In 1977 I read a paper, "The Concept of Health," at the APA meetings, in the course of which I argued that the terms "sanitary" and "hygienic" had lost their original connection with health and health promotion. As now used, these words often have nothing to do with disease prevention and mean merely "clean," that is, free of dirt or unwanted matter. I illustrated this evolution in the terms with the example of the use of the expression "sanitary napkin" for a product that, like a table napkin, merely serves to keep clothes clean. The example illustrated my point perfectly, but when I gave it, three delicate individuals rose and walked out—probably to seek "seminal ideas" in the other sessions.

Later that spring I participated in a conference on science and values that included as participants a number of philosophers and figures from science and medicine (three women and about thirty men, a typical ratio). One well-known sociobiologist, or "evolutionary biologist" as he preferred to be called, cited some of his previous research in the course of discussing his methodology. In particular, he mentioned a study he had done to explain "why it is that women do not know when they ovulate." He was quite taken aback when I told him that lots of women know when they ovulate. His only response was that a woman had worked with him on the study.

That our bodies are (an aspect of) ourselves and that human experience is the experience of an embodied being is still often unthinkable for many men and women, and the aspects of bodies and bodily experience that are peculiar to women are still often regarded as unspeakable, even among academics. I would prefer to give you a different world, but the best that I can do is to try to give you some of the truth about the world we do have. You will have to go with that.

Love,
Mommy

12

Parenting and Property

JANET FARRELL SMITH

Introduction

"Having children" and "having a family of one's own" to keep and protect in one's private home sometimes indicates attitudes toward parenting that are analogous to attitudes toward property. As one has a house to rent, use, and decorate as one wishes, one may also have children of one's own to raise, train, and educate as one wishes. These examples indicate how an implicit model of property relations underlies certain views about parenting. It is the task of this essay to analyze the elements of this model, to exhibit its roots in the patriarchal family, and to show how it fails to capture the realities of nurturance in mothering.

"Parenting" is not a monolithic term. In western history parenting has broken down for the most part into a distinctive division of labor between fathering and mothering. The major elements of a property model of human relations, namely, ownership and proprietary control, have had more to do with fathering than with mothering. The realities of mothering, on the other hand, have had more to do with care, nurturance, and day-to-day responsibility. These represent a very different set of moral and political ideals. Yet elements of the property model increasingly pervade both forms of parenting, especially as women take on the full practical and intellectual activities of political participation, and as gender roles break down. The question then arises, which, if any, of the elements of the property model do we want to take over into more egalitarian divisions of tasks in parenting, now and in the future? Which elements of this model are harmless, and which represent ideals that are obsolete or actually harmful to children and families? This essay concludes that the central elements of the father-related property model do not provide adequate moral ideals and that we should look to certain aspects of mothering as a source for a better set of values.[1]

I

A property model can operate in an explicit manner, as for example when legal arguments for parental rights are based on the theoretical premise that parents "have property in their children."[2] It can also incorporate analogies, as when families hired out their children as servants as if they were real property.[3] It operates metaphorically when a parent claims "*My* child can or will do such-and-such," which reflects a possessive or proprietary attitude toward a child. Rituals concerning offspring at their marriage often reflect the assumption of proprietary control and rights. In a traditional Christian marriage ceremony, the father "gives away" the daughter. With the fading of sex differences, the rituals may take on different cultural significance, as in Reform Jewish ceremonies where both mother and father lead son or daughter to the altar. The "giving away" of children, however, still reflects a deep-rooted sense of attachment that is often related to concepts of possession and is sometimes expressed in metaphors of property and control. It is an open question how far these emotions of attachment could be dissipated, and whether they should be.

A critical evaluation of the elements of a property model of parenting will allow us to see which elements are harmless and which elements are based on notions of power and control that are dehumanizing to the parent-child relationship. Some aspects of the model reflect a patriarchal history and fail to capture the realities of care and nurture particularly evident in mothering. These can be seen to operate on a notion of "developmental power," in C. B. MacPherson's term, which promotes a person's "ability to use and develop his own capacities for his own human purposes." On the other hand, it is argued here that the notion of "extractive power" marks off those elements of the property model that treat human relationships on a model of transactions over property and thus do a disservice to both children and their parents. "Extractive power [is the] ability to use other [person's] capacities. [It is] power over others, the ability to extract benefit from others."[4]

The model of property relations, according to this criticism, fails to portray the truly human aspects of concern in parent-child relationships, regardless of whether parenting is carried out by the female or male parent. In part, this defect can be traced historically to the authority and hierarchical power in the patriarchal family. It is exemplified in the ancient custom of primogeniture and in control over sons and daughters by inheritances. This heritage has also left its residue in philosophical concepts, such as possession and control of a proprietary sort as it applies to children.

But what if mothers and fathers cared for children on a completely equal basis,[5] if restrictive roles for women and men regarding parenting disappeared, and if the model were freed of gender bias in its tie to patriarchal power and authority? Would there by any objection to the model then? Would we want to retain aspects of it?

The first consideration concerns rights. The arguments below do not attempt to dislodge aspects of the model that could support legal defenses in the United States of the rights to form a family, to decide whether or not to have children, and to raise those children. Since some of these rights are now established in U.S. constitutional law on a basis of the right to privacy, it would be a strategic mistake to extract that basis from procreative choices. Even so, the rights in question might receive stronger philosophical support from other notions (e.g., individual or familial integrity) without appealing to analogies of property ownership.

Even if freed from its history of patriarchal power and authority over children and over women, the basic model of property relations suffers from the following defects when applied to parent-child relations: (a) it bases the idea of caring for offspring on the concept of possession and interest, rather than upon support and nurture for the free development of the child's capacities. (b) An inequality of power is always implied in possession and proprietary control, even if this is enacted within a struggle of mutual possessiveness. Such a concept of power leads away from, rather than toward, cooperative social relations. (c) The model presupposes an ethic of proprietary control rather than an ethic of nurturance, with the likelihood that extractive power will be used on the former instead of developmental power on the latter. (d) As it incorporates each of the above elements, the model fragments the self as it fragments relationships with others which could otherwise support the full development of human capacities.

II

The term "property" as used here is taken to mean property relations under a system of private ownership within western capitalist economies, in contrast to communal property (as in tribal societies) or state property (as in state socialist societies). The property model as discussed here isolates certain ideals in Anglo-American law and philosophy. It makes no claim to universality nor to represent all aspects of parenting.

To say something is a model is to say that it represents something else in a useful, clarifying, or explanatory way. As in science, where a model like the double-helix chain of DNA clarifies and features aspects of reality that a scientist wishes to explore, a property model may fail to represent all facets of parenting (such as affection, play, and nurture), while still being effective for certain purposes. The model simply does not address these aspects directly, but it could be compatible with them, depending on the circumstances considered.[6]

In applying a property model to parenting, it is important to remember that a parent may not literally assert that a child is a piece of property, but may work on assumptions analogous to those which one makes in connection with property. In other words, the manner in which parents may treat children, or the concepts used to describe such treatment, may be best represented in terms of analogies with property relations. For example, "I have a right to send my children to school wherever I wish" may be analogous to "I have a right to invest my money wherever I wish." Analogies need not be "perfect" to serve a useful theoretical purpose. Nor should analogies be confused with identities. The summary below features those aspects of the property model most relevant to parenting.

RIGHT

The central idea in a model of property relations is the notion of a right. A right can be interpreted as an entitlement to do or have something, to exclude others from doing or having something, or as an enforceable claim. C. B. MacPherson asserts:

> To have property is to have a right in the sense of an enforceable claim to some use or benefit of something, whether it is a right to share in some common resource or an individual right in some particular thing.[7]

The right to claim use or benefit in the case of land might include, for example, the right to till the soil according to one's custom or choice and the right to exclude others from using or benefiting from the land. It would also include the right to buy, sell, or lease the land. The education of one's own children has been discussed in legal cases in terms analogous to the right to exclude others from choices concerning one's land or property.[8] Just as landowners have the right to manage their own land, so parents have the right by law to manage certain aspects of their children's lives by making choices about their lives.

INTEREST

A person has interests as well as rights in property.[9] Central among these interests in a capitalist economy is, of course, profit. A person may have a right to own, buy, and sell a house, but not a right to make a profit on it (though of course one has the right to attempt to make a profit; a person could attempt to make a profit by exercising his rights to manage in a certain way). One could also have an interest in avoiding general loss of profit or wealth. Parents may similarly have definite interests in their children developing in certain ways. They may try to avoid loss of wealth through the child's squandering an inheritance by dissolute behavior, or try to assure their own support in old age by raising their children to flourish economically.

CONTROL

Control may be taken here as a generic term underlying the basic notions of rights and interests, in the kind of ability involved in managing, directing, or disposing of property. It figures into both ownership and possession and may also operate on a metaphorical level in human relationships. The sense of control relevant here implies that the persons who control have the power to exert their will over that which is controlled. The activities of control, in this proprietary sense of control, are enacted through some actual relation of power over the object or person controlled. Hence, proprietary control is a kind of decision-making authority over a thing or person, backed up with the ability to enforce those decisions.

In the case of proprietary control over real estate, control involves the power to manage housing through renting, leasing, selling, and buying. In the case of parenting, the sense of proprietary control is exemplified in the legal definition of a parent as the person who "takes custody and control" of the child by supervising and directing its upbringing.[10]

Not every form of control is proprietary or possessive control. The "control" of a small child's random scurryings into dangerous places by blocking its path or redirecting its way would not necessarily be proprietary control. On the other hand, blocking an adolescent's choice of occupation by threatening to disinherit or refusing to allow certain types of training would be an example of proprietary control on the part of a parent.

OWNERSHIP

Ownership is the concrete form of property rights. It may be defined as a set of rights over possession, use, management, transfer, income, and capital from property, held for an indefinite length of time and exclusive to the owner. Ownership is distinct from possession. I may for a time "possess" a piece of land or occupy a house (suppose I find it vacant in a forest). When challenged, however, I have no right to stay if rights of ownership over it have been secured by others. One person may be the owner of a house, while others may be allowed to possess it temporarily. Ownership must therefore be distinguished from possession by the notion of a right or "claim which will be enforced by society or the state, by custom or convention or law."[11] Ownership in the full sense is the legitimated or sanctioned relation of possession justified by some set of rules or norms (e.g., a legal system).

POSSESSION

Possession may be characterized as the actual set of transactions or management over what is possessed, usually property. When the thing cannot be possessed physically, for example because it is not an object, possession may be metaphorical, as in the direction and supervision of a manufacturing or intellectual process. What is possessed by one person may be contested by another who is the owner. Disputes analogous to those between possession and ownership of real property may be found in parenting. In Bertholt

Brecht's *The Caucasian Chalk Circle,* the peasant woman Grusha rescues and raises an abandoned child, later claimed by his "rightful" biological parent.

PRIVACY

Privacy, as it is connected with a model of property relations, is not only an ability to deny others access to certain aspects of one's life, but also a right or entitlement to exclude others. What property rights secure from interference or intrusion may also be guaranteed by rights to privacy. For example, it is my right to exclude others from watching what goes on inside my house because my house is my property; it is also my right to exclude others from intruding in what goes on within my family, because of my right to privacy. Both rights may result in similar kinds of protection, e.g., from intrusion or surveillance inside the boundaries of my family residence. Yet it appears that, legally, the right to privacy is meant to cover the narrower aspects of a person's personal and intimate life, such as communicative activities and procreative choices, whereas rights to property cover a broader area that includes physical possessions and real property, as well as activities connected with them.[12]

III

Applying the property model to parenting yields three major points of structural correspondence: (a) rights to exclude, (b) analogy between ownership and parenthood, and (c) the notion of proprietary control. Each can be illustrated in U.S. family law, which to some extent sums up traditional mainstream attitudes and values.

First, there is a key correspondence between the right to exclude others from interference with one's property and the right to exclude others from interference with parental choice to raise one's children as one chooses, or even more basically, to raise one's children oneself. The U.S. Supreme Court has defined a "private realm of family life which the state cannot enter," at least not without compelling justification.[13] Under a firmly established series of precedents, parents have the right to raise their "own" children. They also have the right to control the upbringing and education of their children (*Meyer v. Nebraska,* 1923). *Wisconsin v. Yoder* (1972) affirmed the right of parents to educate their children in their religion of choice, the Amish tradition;[14] grounds of religious freedom overrode the state's requirement of public school attendance. Here it is noteworthy that the right to practice the religion of choice was given to the parents, not to the children. The private realm of family life includes the right of parents or other caretakers of children to exclude the state from defining the precise nature of a family. In *Moore v. City of East Cleveland* (1977) the Court supported the right of extended families (in this case a grandmother and grandchildren) to live together without interference by city zoning ordinances.

In these decisions, the U.S. Supreme Court cites tradition and custom: "The history and culture of Western Civilization reflect a strong tradition of parental concern for the nurture and upbringing of their children."[15] It defines the family as the basic societal unit for the nurture and socialization of children, in contrast to other cultural traditions where the entire community raises children (e.g., Plato's ideal society, in which "no parent shall know his own child").

Second, there is a correspondence between rightful owners of property on the property model and rightful parents of children in the context of parenting. Just as there are legal systems of rules for property ownership, such as registration of deeds and titles,[16] there are legal rules for parenthood, as shown in birth certificates. Just as there are legal methods of decision-making to settle disputes over property ownership, there are decision procedures concerning legal parenthood for custody or adoption disputes.[17]

The third and crucial correspondence between parenting and property ownership is the notion of proprietary or possessive control, which provides the critical link in the analogy between property relations and parenting. The root idea of proprietary or possessive control is power over another thing or person by someone who has the ability to direct that thing or person according to his choice or will. In the case of property, proprietary control in U.S. law since the abolition of slavery has mainly been exercised over physical, nonhuman objects or processes. But in the case of parental rights affirmed in cases such as *Meyer,* the right to control is exercised over another person. It is unusual that such a right to control should be strongly grounded in constitutional terms because, unlike other rights of control, it "protects the ability to control another person. Ordinarily constitutional rights do not protect an individual's power to control someone else."[18] In reality, however, proprietary control has not been limited to children since the abolition of slavery—there was also the proprietary control of men as fathers and husbands over a wife and her properties. This tradition, which persisted until a little over a century ago, indicates major historical differences between women and men in parental relations.

IV

The property model as it applies to parenting has its roots in the patriarchal family, where men held power and control over women and children. It should be no surprise, then, if the model concerns the historical role of fathering more than mothering. In fact, while the model captures many of the traditional powers and duties of fathers, it conflicts with many of the responsibilities and feelings of mothers.

Proprietary control over children is obviously no longer gender-specific, since women as well as men can now exercise such control over their children, just as they can now own property. I argue, however, that the property model is gender-related in a historical sense because it originates in the experience and ideas of one gender rather than another. Male heads of families were traditionally the property owners, while women and children were not only excluded from property ownership, but often were part of what was owned. The property model is of course also very much a class phenomenon, since working-class males were excluded from property ownership. Yet even with these class differences, it is still regarded as primarily the father's duty to provide economic support, while the mother's responsibility is to provide infant care.

If gender differences in the property model as it relates to reproduction and child-rearing faded, we could call the model gender-neutral. Even if the practices of fathering and mothering changed, however, the model would still contain a gender bias. Its concepts as well as its practices still retain the notion of power appropriate to a hierarchical structure (the patriarchal family). In this concept of power, some persons have power over others in such a way as to be able to extract benefit from them. The concept of parental rights over children retains a notion of proprietary control. This particular concept of rights corresponds to the historical emphasis on the rights and duties of the father in the patriarchal family, rather than to the care and responsibilities of the mother. This historical residue, however, need not imply deficiencies in all concepts of rights, or the ethical perspectives associated with them. Other more appropriate ones might be developed. Finally, the concepts of the property model also retain an implicit appeal to a gender division of labor. They appeal to the social and psychological experience of fathering rather than mothering. The following examples emphasize this important feature.

Deliberate objections to the gender bias implicit and explicit in a model of property relations can be found in the "Protest" registered publically by Lucy Stone and Henry Blackwell when they married in 1852. They criticized the laws of marriage currently in force which

> refuse to recognize the wife as an independent, rational being, while they confer upon the husband an injurious and unnatural superiority, investing him with legal powers which no honorable man would exercise and which no man should possess. We protest especially the laws which give the husband:
> 1. The custody of the wife's person.
> 2. The exclusive control and guardianship of their children.
> 3. The sole ownership of her personal property, the use of her real estate, unless previously settled upon. . . .
> 4. The absolute right to the product of her industry.[19]

Each element under protest illustrates an element of the property model. The emphasis is on *rights* concerning *ownership* which belong to the husband and father, including ownership of the wife's property and custody of the wife and children. They also mention *proprietary control* over both the children and the wife's labor. This assumes that *interest* in them ought by right to accrue to the husband and father.

In the same period in which Lucy Stone became a women's rights activist and registered her "Marriage Protest," moral and social arguments supported distinct roles for women and men. Some of these ideas still persist today: custody rights are no longer gender-specific to male heads of families, but are extended liberally to women on the "tender years presumption" that a woman who is a mother of a child of tender years is best equipped to care for it.[20] The interest of the father formerly lay in right to custody and right to determine inheritance, which allowed him to exert a kind of proprietary control over his wife and children. The interest of the mother, on the other hand, was and continues to be (as long as women are primary care-takers) more closely identified with that of her growing children.

Responsibility for care of children, given mainly to women in 19th-century England and the United States, crossed class lines. In the working classes, women, whether they worked for wages or not, were primarily responsible for children.[21] In the 19th century the ideology of separate spheres for women and men dominated the middle and upper classes. Historian Nancy Cott quotes women of the early 1800s in New England on the characteristics of the mother's responsibility: "[Her] task is to mold the infant's character." Many women described with awe their great "responsibilities as Mother," contrasting them with the duties of political rulers to "enact laws and compel men to obey them."[22] While no less important than the role of men, the role of women was nevertheless based on a different conception—a specific notion of *responsibility* for the interests of the child and familial unity.

Whereas male roles in parenting emphasized the rights of parenthood, the female role emphasized its responsibilities in the day-to-day care-taking for children. This division of labor may be analogous to that between the owner of property who has rights over it and the manager of property who deals with the mundane daily transactions concerning property. In any case, the father possessed greater economic power, and his role was to exert authority within the family.

The property model is more closely tied to paternal interest in children than to maternal interest. Sara Ruddick has examined maternal practice and identified three primary interests of mothers in children, which contrast with those implicit in the property model: preservation, growth, and acceptability. She considers maternal interest in preservation the "most invariant and primary of the three." It spans the time from pregnancy and childbirth through the adulthood of sons and daughters, as well as grandchildren.[23]

When we contrast the nature of rules governing systems of private property with the rules governing maternal practices, it seems that the former are primarily rules for excluding others, while the latter are primarily rules for including others. This is especially so when we consider that women in most cultures, including our own up to the time of the professionalization of childbirth, have managed the birth process through midwifery and extended kin networks.[24] That is, fathering traditionally has emphasized power over others and proprietary control, while mothering has emphasized growth and preservation. Of course, this does not mean that mothers are not influenced by the property model. In fact, through most of known history they have been controlled by its concepts and practices, partly because they were once daughters. As Jane Addams, speaking of middle-class families, pointed out in 1907, "It is always difficult for the family to regard the daughter otherwise than as a family possession. . . . Her delicacy and polish are but outward symbols of her father's protection and prosperity."[25]

V

Privacy, a central concept in the property model, is at best an equivocal norm. The concept of privacy as exclusion of others from one's individual domain is reversed in maternal practices of inclusion, intimacy, and connection. Yet on the other hand, privacy provides a basis for protecting procreative rights for women's and familial choices, both in U.S. constitutional law and in philosophical argument.

The notion of privacy relates closely to individualism, which in social theory begins with the assumption of separateness. In John Locke's theory each individual has a separate desire to acquire property and preserve himself. Social connection is then construed as the artifice of negotiated contract or rational agreement to limit by political means (government) the unlimited desire of each individual. As Locke says, these limits protect and preserve property in the widest sense of life, liberty, and estates.[26] One's life and oneself are taken as a form of property on this model of social relations; privacy is then a value brought in to protect individual liberties and interests from encroachment by other individuals or the state.

To some extent this value of privacy as a model of social relations reflects the realities of a competitive economy and the dangers of state regulation. But its basic assumptions can be questioned along with the adequacy of the property model in parenting. As a social theory it exhibits only a partial insight into the basis of social relations. If we take seriously the assertion that social relations begin with the mother-child connection, then the beginning or foundation of these relations is connection and intimacy rather than exclusion and separateness. At the least, we can say that this connection exists as one dimension within the complex web of social relations. Why, then, is there any reason to take separateness and individual interest as the basic premise of social theory, rather than connectedness and common interest? If the answer lies in commitment to a general property model of human relations, then the objections raised at the beginning of this paper apply. Let us see what alternatives can be found within reproductive relations rather than competitive productive relations, within the care of mothering rather than the control of the patriarchal family.

The intimate mother-child unit is a prelude to and basis for further connection in social relations. Elizabeth Cady Stanton, leader and theorist of the 19th-century women's rights movement, recognized this both in her practice and her political theories. She was a leader in the Voluntary Motherhood movement, which claimed the right of women to decide when and whether to become mothers. When she traveled, Stanton aided women and families with children. She remarks of one incident: "I know that the care of one child made me thoughtful of all. I never hear a child cry now that I do not feel that I am bound to find out the reason."[27] It is significant that Stanton uses the word "care" here. She implies that the care of a physical, emotional, and social kind for her own biological child extends to a sympathetic care in the sense of concern for all infants and children. This care and concern which Stanton expressed in action illustrate Sara Ruddick's "maternal thinking." In Ruddick's analysis, the nature of maternal thinking lies in connecting thought and action in a self-conscious way. Stanton extended and generalized the care and consciousness she associated with her own mothering to all children. Where is the privacy intrinsic to the property model in all of this?

Here, as in many other community and social contexts, the notion of privacy seems not so much inaccurate as irrelevant. Rather than the individualistic possessiveness and exclusion of others that one finds associated with the property model, we find that knowledge of the interests of individuals and families, combined with a true concern for all, could form the basis of another social order. Individuality, as Stanton recognized, can only be affirmed within a surrounding community of concern and recognition of the interdependence of satisfaction of needs.

Privacy of parental duties, rights, and privileges seems to have more to do with the historical position of the father in the patriarchal family and its relation to ownership of property. In the relatively isolated and disconnected forms of parenting in nuclear families in the United States today, including increasing numbers of female-headed families, privacy may be less of a desirable "right" than it is an unenviable economic and social condition. It is difficult to see how the condition helps or supports mothering, whether in traditional forms or in the dual-career households where women both work for wages and care for their children. In this way "privacy" promotes social isolation rather than encourages social networks of caring and support. Its utility lies in protection of proprietary interests rather than in development of humane forms of parenting for women or for men. Its proprietary origin continues a bias that is helpful to neither women nor men who wish for more integrated forms of community and family. Among urban poor Black families, strategies for survival emphasize cooperation within a closely linked interdependent kin network. The enlarged circle of female and male kin, in addition to mothers and fathers, "contribute positive and valuable resources" to the family.[28] All this points to the aspects of privacy that derive from a particular set of cultural antecedents and reflect its origin within the interests of a particular class position. Given these, the norm of privacy appears not only irrelevant but nonadaptive for many families.

The above observations need not undercut constitutional arguments for the "right to privacy" underlying major decisions affirming procreative choices, such as the right to contraception (*Griswold v. Connecticut,* 1965) or the right to choose abortion (*Roe v. Wade,* 1973). The point is that used in one way, the norm of privacy could reflect its gender- and class-related history and reinforce the elements of the property model that allow for abuses of proprietary control. Used in another way, the norm may shift its meaning, philosophically, from an exclusionary ideal to a notion of the integrity of individual decision-making.[29] If it is taken as the right to self-determination in procreative decision-making, it need not deny the ethic of care and the social realities of interdependence suggested here.

Conclusion

An ethic of care and concern associated with the traditional responsibilies of mothering has several key philosophical advantages over the values associated with the property model.[30] It emphasizes care rather than proprietary control, interdependence rather than exclusion, and recognition of individuality rather than possessive individualism. Its central theme is developmental rather than extractive power. Treating children on the literal premise that they are property, or on the analogy that children are to be controlled as property is controlled, conflicts with the most humane ideals of care for children. If parents are truly concerned with the human development of their children, and if society is truly concerned with reproducing a generation of human beings, they will encourage developmental power within children, rather than exert extractive power over them. They will treat children, not on an analogy with things, but as developing persons.[31]

Such an orientation need not imply that families must discard their rights for autonomy and self-determination, but that any notions of proprietary control should be scrutinized for potential abuses. Parental affection and love alone cannot be corrective balances for, as Mary Wollstonecraft pointed out in 1792, these can "be but a pretext to tyrannize" where power can be exercised with impunity.[32] Love itself can operate on an analogy of investment with return, rather than on a conception of affection freely given.

There is still a need for certain parental rights to protect families from state intrusion that would undermine the alternative ethic suggested here. As long as the present economic and political system remains in force there is a need for their legal guarantee. Yet out of the present customs, traditions, and attitudes, there is a possibility that we may depart from treating children according to elements of the property model, and thence from a tradition in which we learn to treat others and ourselves in this way.[33]

Notes

1. The term "parenting" is used here to include both gender-roles in parenting, that of fathering and mothering in western culture. But this division is not the same in all cultures, nor will it necessarily remain so in the future. For a related treatment of models of parenting, see William Ruddick's contrast between a trustee and a gardener model in "Parents and Life Prospects," in *Having Children: Philosophical and Legal Reflections on Parenthood,* edited by Onora O'Neill and William Ruddick (New York: Oxford University Press, 1979).

2. Ibid., p. 127.

3. Phillipe Ariès, *Centuries of Childhood* (New York: Vintage Books, 1962), pp. 366–67. For general family history I draw on Lawrence Stone, *The Family, Sex and Marriage in England* (New York: Harper & Row, 1977).

4. C. B. MacPherson, *Democratic Theory* (New York: Oxford University Press, 1973), pp. 40–43. MacPherson develops his concepts for productive relations. I extend them to reproductive relations.

5. Virginia Held, "The Obligations of Mothers and Fathers," this volume, pp. 7–20.

6. Mary Hesse, *Forces and Fields* (Totowa: N.J.: Littlefield, Adams, 1965), pp. 21–28; and *Models and Analogies in Science* (London: Sheed and Ward, 1963).

7. C. B. MacPherson's introductory essay to *Property, Mainstream and Critical Positions* (Toronto: University of Toronto Press, 1978), p. 3.

8. In *Meyer v. Nebraska* (1923) and *Pierce v. Society of Sisters* (1925), the U.S. Supreme Court deemed the right of parents to control the upbringing and education of their children "essential."

9. For a distinction between rights vs. interests in property, see Virginia Held, Introduction to *Property, Profits and Economic Justice* (Belmont, Calif.: Wadsworth, 1980), pp. 1–4.

10. *Stanley v. Illinois,* 405 U.S. 645 (1972).

11. MacPherson, *Property,* p. 3.

12. *Griswold v. Connecticut* (1965). See also Judith Thomson, "The Right to Privacy," in *Philosophy and Public Affairs* 4, no. 4 (Summer 1974).

13. *Prince v. Massachusetts,* 321 U.S. 158, 166 (1944). Affirmed in *Moore v. City of East Cleveland,* 431 U.S. 494 (1977). See "The Constitution and the Family," *Harvard Law Review* 93, no. 6 (April 1980): 1166.

14. Cited in W. Wadlington, *Domestic Relations* (New York: Foundation Press, 1978), p. 745.

15. *Wisconsin v. Yoder,* 406 U.S. at 232. Quoted in "The Constitution and the Family," *Harvard Law Review,* p. 1352.

16. See Charles Haar and Lance Liebman, *Property and Law* (Boston: Little, Brown, 1977), pp. 430–36, for a history of rules of property ownership.

17. *Stanley v. Illinois* concerns legal parenthood in a case of illegitimacy. See also *Caban v. Mohammed,* 441 U.S. 380 (1970), in which custody was disputed between (unmarried) mother and father, concerning issues of both adoption and illegitimacy.

18. "The Constitution and the Family," *Harvard Law Review,* p. 1153.

19. Quoted in Barbara Babcock, *Sex Discrimination and the Law* (Boston: Little, Brown, 1975), p. 647.

20. See, for example, *Johnson v. Johnson,* quoted in Wadlington, *Domestic Relations,* p. 789.

21. Mary Lynn MacDougall, "Working Class Women During the Industrial Revolution," in *Becoming Visible: Women in European History,* edited by R. Bridenthal (Boston: Houghton-Miflin, 1977), p. 274. For a recent account of working-class women's lives, see Lillian Rubin, *Worlds of Pain: Life in the Working Class Family* (New York: Harper & Row, 1976). Most historians of the working-class woman and

families recognize that the greater earning power of the husband meant that his wife was usually subordinate to him.

22. Nancy Cott, *The Bonds of Womanhood: "Woman's Sphere" in New England, 1780–1835* (New Haven: Yale University Press, 1977), pp. 47–48, 83.

23. Sara Ruddick, "Maternal Thinking," this volume, pp. 213–230.

24. See Brigitte Jordan, *Birth in Four Cultures* (Montreal: Eden Press, 1978), and "Studying Childbirth," in *Childbirth,* edited by S. Romalis (Austin: University of Texas Press, 1981), p. 182. Jordan remarks: "All cultures have developed rules for managing childbirth."

25. Jane Addams, "Filial Piety," in *Ovenbirds,* edited by G. Parker (New York: Doubleday Anchor, 1972), p. 308.

26. *Second Treatise of Government,* Section 94. Edition edited by Peter Laslett (New York: Cambridge University Press, 1960), p. 373.

27. *Eighty Years and More: Reminiscences, 1815–1897* (Boston: Schocken Books, 1971), p. 122.

28. "Income Support Policies and the Family," in *The Family,* edited by Alice Rossi, J. Kagan, and T. Hareven (New York: W.W. Norton, 1977), p. 154.

29. Disputes over the substantive due process basis in the U.S. Constitution for right to privacy signal judicial and philosophical debate over the legitimacy of the shift. See "The Constitution and the Family," *Harvard Law Review,* pp. 1167–87.

30. See L. Blum, M. Homiak, J. Houseman, and N. Scheman, "Altruism and Women's Oppression," in *Women and Philosophy,* edited by Carol Gould and Marx Wartofsky (New York: G. Putnam, 1976) for critical discussion of an ethic of care as it relates to women's concrete situation. This article discusses the sources of an ethic of care in Butler, Schopenhauer, and Scheler.

31. Carol Gilligan's pioneering work in women's moral development shows that what she calls a "responsibility orientation" tends to show up more frequently in women's moral reasoning. This may have to do with the traditional historical emphasis on responsibility, rather than rights and duties, in women's role. (See the references in Sections IV and V.) See Carol Gilligan, *In a Different Voice* (Cambridge: Harvard University Press, 1981).

32. Wollstonecraft, *Vindication of the Rights of Women* (New York: W.W. Norton, 1963).

33. This essay owes much to the Smith College Mellon Project on Women and Social Change, where I did much of the research as a Research Associate and Fellow (1979–80). I am also indebted to Martha Field of Harvard Law School for helpful discussion, and to my colleagues A. Diller, E. Kuykendall, J. Martin, B. Nelson, and J. Radden for suggestions.

13

Maternal Thinking

SARA RUDDICK

We are familiar with Victorian renditions of Ideal Maternal Love. My own favorite, like so many of these poems, was written by a son.

> There was a young man loved a maid
> Who taunted him, "Are you afraid,"
> She asked, "to bring me today
> Your mother's head upon a tray?"
>
> He went and slew his mother dead,
> Tore from her breast her heart so red,
> Then towards his lady love he raced,
> But tripped and fell in all his haste.
>
> As the heart rolled on the ground
> It gave forth a plaintive sound.
> And it spoke, in accents mild:
> "Did you hurt yourself, my child?"[1]

Though many of the story's wishes and fantasies are familiar, there is an unfamiliar twist to the poem. The maid asked for the mother's head, the son brought her heart. The maid feared and respected thoughts; the son believed only feelings are powerful. Again we are not surprised. The passions of maternity are so sudden, intense, and confusing that we often remain ignorant of the perspective, the *thought* that has developed from mothering. Lacking pride, we have failed to deepen or articulate that thought. This is a paper about the head of the mother.

A longer version of this essay appeared in *Feminist Studies* 6, no. 2 (Summer 1980). © 1980 by Feminist Studies, Inc. Reprinted by permission of the publisher and the author. The present version appeared in *Rethinking the Family,* edited by Barrie Thorne with Marilyn Yalom (N.Y.: Longman, 1982).

I speak about a mother's *thought*—the intellectual capacities she develops, the judgments she makes, the metaphysical attitudes she assumes, the values she affirms. A mother engages in a discipline. That is, she asks certain questions rather than others; she establishes criteria for the truth, adequacy, and relevance of proposed answers; and she cares about the findings she makes and can act on. Like any discipline, hers has *characteristic* errors, temptations, and goals. The discipline of maternal thought consists in establishing criteria for determining failure and success, in setting the priorities, and in identifying the virtues and liabilities the criteria presume. To describe the capacities, judgments, metaphysical attitudes, and values of maternal thought does not presume maternal achievement. It is to describe a *conception* of achievement, the end to which maternal efforts are directed, conceptions and ends that are different from dominant public ones.[2]

In stating my claims about maternal thinking, I use a vocabulary developed in formulating theories about the general nature of thought.[3] According to these theories, *all* thought arises out of social practice. In their practices, people respond to a reality that appears to them as given, as presenting certain *demands*. The response to demands is shaped by *interests* that are generally interests in preserving, reproducing, directing, and understanding individual and group life.

These four interests are general in the sense that they arise out of the conditions of humans-in-nature and characterize us as a species. In addition, particular practices are characterized by specific interests in meeting the demands that some reality imposes on its participants. Religious, scientific, historical, mathematical, or any other thinking constitutes a disciplined response to a reality that appears to be "given." Socially organized thinkers name, elaborate, and test the particular realities to which they respond.

Maternal practice responds to the historical reality of a biological child in a particular social world. The agents of maternal practice, acting in response to the demands of their children, acquire a conceptual scheme—a vocabulary and logic of connections—through which they order and express the facts and values of their practice. In judgments and self-reflection, they refine and concretize this scheme. Intellectual activities are distinguishable but not separable from disciplines of feeling. There is a unity of reflection, judgment, and emotion. This unity I call "maternal thinking." Although I will not digress to argue the point here, it is important that maternal thinking is no more interest-governed, no more emotional, and no more relative to a particular reality (the growing child) than the thinking that arises from scientific, religious, or any other practice.

The demands of children and the interests in meeting those demands are always and only expressed by people in particular cultures and classes of their culture, living in specific geographical, technological, and historical settings. Some features of the mothering experience are invariant and nearly unchangeable; others, though changeable, are nearly universal.[4] It is therefore possible to identify interests that seem to govern maternal practice throughout the species. Yet it is impossible even to begin to specify these interests without importing features specific to the class, ethnic group, and particular sex-gender system in which the interests are realized. In this essay I draw upon my knowledge of the institutions of motherhood in middle-class, white, Protestant, capitalist, patriarchal America, for these have expressed themselves in the heterosexual nuclear family in which I mother and was mothered. Although I have tried to compensate for the limits of my particular social and sexual history, I principally depend on others to correct my interpretations and translate across cultures.[5]

Interests Governing Maternal Practice

Children "demand" their lives be preserved and their growth fostered. Their social group "demands" that growth be shaped in a way acceptable to the next generation. Maternal practice is governed by (at least) three interests in satisfying these demands for preservation, growth, and acceptability. Preservation is the most invariant and primary of the three. Because a caretaking mother typically bears her own children, preservation begins when conception is recognized and accepted. Although the form of preservation depends on widely variant beliefs about the fragility and care of the fetus, women have always had a lore in which they recorded their concerns for the baby they "carried." Once born, a child is physically vulnerable for many years. Even when she lives with the father of her child or other female adults, even when she has money to purchase or finds available supportive health and welfare services, a mother typically considers herself, and is considered by others, to be responsible for the maintenance of the life of her child.

Interest in fostering the physical, emotional, and intellectual growth of her child soon supplements a mother's interest in its preservation. The human child is typically capable of complicated emotional and intellectual development; the human adult is radically different in kind from the child it once was. A woman who mothers may be aided or assaulted by the help and advice of fathers, teachers, doctors, moralists, therapists, and others who have an interest in fostering and shaping the growth of her child. Although rarely given primary credit, a mother typically holds herself, and is held by others, responsible for the *malfunction* of the growth process. From early on, certainly by the middle years of childhood, a mother is governed by a third interest: she must shape natural growth in such a way that her child becomes the sort of adult that she can appreciate and others can accept. Mothers will vary enormously, individually and socially, in the traits and lives they will appreciate in their children. Nevertheless, a mother typically takes as the criterion of her success the production of a young adult acceptable to her group.

The three interests in preservation, growth, and acceptability of the child govern maternal practices in general. Not all mothers are, as individuals, governed by these interests, however. Some mothers are incapable of interested participation in the practices of mothering because of emotional, intellectual, or physical disability. Severe poverty may make interested maternal practice and therefore maternal thinking nearly impossible. Then, of course, mothers engage in practices other than, and often conflicting with, mothering. Some mothers, aware of the derogation and confinement of women in maternal practice, may be disaffected. In short, actual mothers have the same relation to maternal practice as actual scientists have to scientific practice, or actual believers have to religious practices. As mothers, they are governed by the interests of their respective practices. But the style, skill, commitment, and integrity with which they engage in these practices differ widely from individual to individual.

Interests in the preservation, growth, and acceptability of the child are frequently and unavoidably in conflict. A mother who watches a child eagerly push a friend aside as she or he climbs a tree is torn between preserving the child from danger, encouraging the child's physical skills and courage, and shaping a child according to moral restraints, which might, for example, inhibit the child's joy in competitive climbing. Although some mothers deny or are insensitive to the conflict, and others are clear about which interest should take precedence, mothers typically know that they cannot secure each interest, they know that goods conflict, and they know that unqualified success in realizing interests is an illusion. This unavoidable conflict of basic interests is one objective basis for the maternal humility I will shortly describe.

THE INTEREST IN PRESERVING THE LIFE OF THE CHILD

A mother, acting in the interest of preserving and maintaining life, is in a peculiar relation to "nature." As childbearer, she often takes herself, and is taken by others, to be an especially "natural" member of her culture. As child tender, she must respect nature's limits and court its favor with foresightful actions that range from immunizations, to caps on household poisons, to magical imprecation, warnings, and prayers. "Nature" with its unpredictable varieties of dirt and disease is her enemy as much as her ally. Her children are natural creatures, often unable to understand or abet her efforts to protect them. Because they frequently find her necessary direction constraining, a mother can experience her children's own liveliness as another enemy of the life she is preserving.

No wonder, then, that as she engages in preservation, a mother is liable to the temptations of fearfulness and excessive control. If she is alone with and responsible for two or more young children, then control of herself, her children, and her physical environment is her only option, however rigid or excessive she appears to outsiders. Though necessarily controlling their acts, *reflecting* mothers themselves identify rigid or excessive control as the likely defects of the virtues they are required to practice. The identification of liability as such, with its implication of the will to overcome, characterizes this aspect of maternal thought. The epithet "controlling mother" is often unsympathetic, even matriphobic. On the other hand, it may, in line with the insights of maternal thought, remind us of what maternal thinking *counts as* failure.

To a mother, "life" may well seem "terrible, hostile, and quick to pounce on you if you give it a chance."[6] In response, she develops a metaphysical attitude toward "Being as such," an attitude I call "holding," an attitude governed by the priority of keeping over acquiring, of conserving the fragile, of maintaining whatever is at hand and necessary to the child's life. It is an attitude elicited by the work of "world-*protection*, world-*preservation*, world-*repair* . . . the invisible weaving of a frayed and threadbare family life."[7]

The priority of holding over acquiring distinguishes maternal thinking from scientific thinking and from the instrumentalism of technocracy. To be sure, under the pressures of consumerism, holding may become frantic accumulating and storing. More seriously, a parent may feel compelled to preserve her *own* children, whatever befalls other children. The more competitive and hierarchical the society, the more thwarted a mother's individual, autonomous pursuits, the more likely that preservation will become egocentric, frantic, and cruel. Mothers recognize these dangers and fight them.

Holding, preserving mothers have distinctive ways of seeing and being in the world that are worth considering. For example, faced with the fragility of the lives it seeks to preserve, maternal thinking recognizes humility and resilient cheerfulness as virtues of its practice. In so doing it takes issue with popular moralities of assertiveness and much contemporary moral theory.[8]

Humility is a metaphysical attitude one takes toward a world beyond one's control. One might conceive of the world as governed by necessity and change (as I do) or by supernatural forces that cannot be comprehended. In either case, humility implies a profound sense of the limits of one's actions and of the unpredictability of the consequences of one's work. As the philosopher Iris Murdoch puts it: "Every natural thing, including one's own mind, is subject to chance. . . . One might say that chance is a subdivision of death. . . . We cannot dominate the world."[9] Humility that emerges from maternal practices accepts not only the facts of damage and death, but also the facts of the independent and uncontrollable, developing and increasingly separate existences of the lives it seeks to preserve. "Humility is not a peculiar habit of self-effacement, rather like having an inaudible voice, it is selfless respect for reality and one of the most difficult and central of virtues."[10]

If, in the face of danger, disappointment, and unpredictability, mothers are liable to melancholy, they are also aware that a kind, resilient good humor is a virtue. This good humor must not be confused with the cheery denial that is both a liability and, unfortunately, a characteristic of maternal practice. Mothers are tempted to denial simply by the insupportable difficulty of passionately loving a fragile creature in a physically threatening, socially violent, pervasively uncaring and competitive world. Defensive denial is exacerbated as it is officially encouraged, when we must defend against perceptions of our own subordination. Our cheery denials are cruel to our children and demoralizing to ourselves.

Clear-sighted cheerfulness is the virtue of which denial is the degenerative form. It is clear-sighted cheerfulness that Spinoza must have had in mind when he said: "Cheerfulness is always a good thing and never excessive"; it "increases and assists the power of action."[11] Denying cheeriness drains intellectual energy and befuddles the will; the cheerfulness honored in maternal thought increases and assists the power of maternal action.

In a daily way, cheerfulness is a matter-of-fact willingness to continue, to give birth and to accept having given birth, to welcome life despite its conditions. Resilient good humor is a style of mothering "in the deepest sense of 'style' in which to discover the right style is to discover what you are really trying to do."[12]

Because in the dominant society "humility" and "cheerfulness" name virtues of subordinates, and because these virtues have in fact developed in conditions of subordination, it is difficult to credit them and easy to confuse them with the self-effacement and cheery denial that are their degenerative forms. Again and again, in attempting to articulate maternal thought, language is sicklied o'er by the pale cast of sentimentality and thought itself takes on a greeting-card quality. Yet literature shows us many mothers who in their "holding" actions value the humility and resilient good humor I have described. One can meet such mothers, recognize their thought, any day one learns to listen. One can appreciate the effects of their disciplined perserverance in the unnecessarily beautiful artifacts of the culture they created. "I made my quilt to keep my family warm. I made it beautiful so my heart would not break."[13]

THE INTEREST IN FOSTERING THE CHILD'S GROWTH

Mothers must not only preserve fragile life. They must also foster growth and welcome change. If the "being" preserved seems always to be endangered, undone, slipping away, the "being" that changes is always developing, building, purposively moving away. The "holding," preserving mother must, in response to change, be simultaneously a changing mother. Her conceptual scheme in terms of which she makes sense of herself, her child, and their common world will be more the Aristotelian biologist's than the Platonic mathematician's. Innovation takes precedence over permanence, disclosure and responsiveness over clarity and certainty. The idea of "objective reality" itself "undergoes important modification when it is to be understood, not in relation to the world described by science, but in relation to the progressing life of a person."[14]

Women are said to value open over closed structure, to eschew the clear-cut and unambiguous, to refuse a sharp division between inner and outer or self and other. They also are said to depend on and prize the private inner lives of the mind.[15] If these facets of the "female mind" are elicited by maternal practices, they may well be interwoven responses to the changeability of a growing child. A child is itself an "open structure" whose acts are irregular, unpredictable, often mysterious. A mother, in order to understand her child, must assume the existence of a conscious continuing person whose acts make sense in terms of perceptions and responses to a meaning-filled world. She knows that her child's fantasies and thoughts are connected not only to the child's power to act, but often are the only basis for her understanding of the child and for the child's self-understanding.

A mother, in short, is committed to two philosophical positions: she is a mentalist rather than a behaviorist, and she assumes the priority of personhood over action. Moreover, if her "mentalism" is to enable her to understand and love, she must be realistic about the psyche whose growth she fosters. *All* psyches are moved by fear, lust, anger, pride, and defenses against them; by what Simone Weil called "*natural* movements of the soul" and likened to laws of physical gravity.[16] This is not to deny that the soul is also blessed by "grace," "light," and erotic hungering for goodness.[17] Mothers cannot take grace for granted, however, nor can they force or deny the less flattering aggrandizing and consolatory operations of childhood psychic life.

Her realistic appreciation of a person's continuous mental life allows a mother to expect change, to change with change. As psychologist Jean Baker Miller puts it: "In a very immediate and day to day way women *live* for change."[18] Change requires a kind of learning in which what one learns cannot be applied exactly, often not even by analogy, to a new situation. If science agrees to take as real the reliable results of *repeatable* experiments,[19] its learning will be different in kind from maternal learning. Miller is hopeful that if we attend to maternal practices, we can develop new ways of studying learning that are appropriate to the changing natures of all people and communities, for it is not only children who change, grow, and need help in growing; those who care for children must also change in response to changing reality. And we all might grow—as opposed to aging—if we could learn how. For everyone's benefit, "women must now face the task of putting their vast unrecognized experience with change into a new and broader level of operation."[20]

Miller writes of achievement, of women who have learned to change and respond to change. But she admits: "Tragically in our society, women are prevented from fully enjoying these pleasures [of growth] themselves by being made to feel that fostering them in others is the only valid role for all women and by the loneliness, drudgery and isolated non-cooperative household setting in which they work.''[21]

In delineating maternal thought, I do not claim that mothers realize, in themselves, the capacities and virtues we learn to value as we care for others. Rather, mothers develop *conceptions* of abilities and virtues, according to which they measure themselves and interpret their actions. It is no great sorrow that some mothers never acquire humility, resilient good humor, realism, respect for persons, and responsiveness to growth—that all of us fail often in many ways. What is a great sorrow is to find the task itself misdescribed, sentimentalized, and devalued.

THE INTEREST IN SHAPING AN ACCEPTABLE CHILD

The third demand that governs maternal practice is the demand, at once social and personal, that the child's growth be shaped in a manner that makes life acceptable. "Acceptability" is defined in terms of the values of the mother's social group—whatever of its values she has internalized as her own plus values of group members whom she feels she must please or is fearful of displeasing. Society demands that a mother produce an adult acceptable to the next generation. Mothers, roughly half of society, have an interest in meeting that demand. They are also governed by a more stringent form of acceptability. They want the child they produce to be a person whom they themselves, and those closest to them, can appreciate. The demand of appreciability gives an urgency—sometimes exhilarating, sometimes anguishing—to maternal practice.

The task of producing an appreciable child gives a mother a unique opportunity to explore, create, and insist on her own values; to train her children for strength and virtue; and ultimately to develop openness and reciprocity in regard to her child's most threatening differences from her, namely, moral ones. As a mother thinks upon the appreciability of her child, her maternal work becomes a self-conscious, reflective expression of a disciplined conscience.

In response to the demand of acceptability, maternal thinking becomes contradictory—that is, it betrays its own interest in the growth of children. Almost everywhere, the practices of mothering take place in societies in which women of all classes are less powerful than men of their class to determine the conditions under which their children grow. Throughout history, most women have mothered in conditions of military and social violence and often of extreme poverty. They have been governed by men, and increasingly by managers and experts of both sexes, whose policies mothers neither shape nor control. Out of maternal powerlessness, in response to a society whose values it does not determine, maternal thinking has often and largely opted for inauthenticity and the "good" of others.

By "inauthenticity" I designate a double willingness—first, a willingness to *travailler pour l'armée,*[22] to accept the uses to which others put one's children; and second, a willingness to remain blind to the implications of those uses for the actual lives of women and children. Maternal thought embodies inauthenticity by taking on the values of the dominant culture. Like the "holding" of preservation, "inauthenticity" is a mostly nonconscious response to Being as Such. Only this attitude is not a caretaker's response to the natural exigencies of child tending, but a subordinate's reaction to a social reality essentially characterized by the domination and subordination of persons. Inauthenticity constructs and then assumes a world in which one's own values do not count. It is allied to fatalism and to some religious thought—some versions of Christianity, for example. As inauthenticity is lived out in maternal practice, it gives rise to the values of obedience and "being good"; that is, to fulfill the values of the dominant culture is taken as an achievement. Obedience is related to humility in the face of the limits of one's powers. But unlike humility, which respects indifferent nature, the incomprehensible supernatural, and human fallibility, obedience respects the actual control and preferences of dominant people.

Individual mothers, living out maternal thought, take on the values of the subcultures to which they belong and the men with whom they are allied. Because some groups and many men are vibrantly moral, these values are not necessarily inadequate. Nevertheless, even moral groups and men almost always accept the relative subordination of women, whatever other ideals of equality and autonomy they may hold. A "good" mother may well be praised for colluding in her own subordination, with destructive consequences to herself and her children. Moreover, most groups and men impose at least some values that are psychologically and physically damaging to children. Yet, to be "good," a mother may be expected to endorse these inimical values. She is the person principally responsible for training her children in the ways and desires of obedience. This may mean training her daughters for powerlessness, her sons for war, and both for crippling work in dehumanizing factories, businesses, and professions. It may mean training both daughters and sons for defensive or arrogant power over others in sexual, economic, or political life. A mother who trains either for powerlessness or abusive power over others betrays the life she has preserved, whose growth she has fostered. She denies her children even the possibility of being strong and good.

The strain of colluding in one's own powerlessness, coupled with the frequent and much greater strain of betraying the children one has tended, would be insupportable if conscious. A mother under strain may internalize as her own some values that are clearly inimical to her children. She has, after all, usually been rewarded for such protective albeit destructive internalization. In addition, she may blind herself to the implications of her obedience, a blindness excused and exacerbated by the cheeriness of denial. For precariously but deeply protected mothers, feminist accounts of power relations and their cost call into question the worthiness of maternal work and the genuineness of maternal love. It is understandable that such women fight insight as others fight bodily assault, revealing in their struggles a commitment to their own sufferings that may look "neurotic" but is in fact, given their options, realistic.

When I described maternal thought arising out of the interests in growth and preservation, I was not speaking of the actual achievement of mothers, but of a conception of achievement. Similarly, in describing the thought arising out of the interest in acceptability, I am not speaking of actual mothers' adherence to dominant values, but of a conception of their relations to those values in which obedience and "being good" is considered an achievement. Many individual mothers "fail," that is, they insist on their own values and will not remain blind to the implications of dominant values for the lives of their children. Moreover, given the damaging effects of prevailing sexual arrangements and social hierarchies on maternal lives, it is clearly outrageous to blame mothers for their (our) obedience.

Obedience is largely a function of social powerlessness. Maternal work is done according to the Law of the Symbolic Father and under His Watchful Eye, as well as, typically, according to the desires, even whims, of the father's house. "This is my Father's world/Oh let me ne'er forget/that though the wrong be oft so strong,/He is the ruler yet." In these conditions of work, inauthentic obedience to dominant patriarchal values is as plausible a maternal response as respect for the results of experiment is in scientific work.

As I have said, the work of mothering can become a rewarding, disciplined expression of conscience. In order for this opportunity to be realized, either collectively or by individual mothers, maternal thought will have to be transformed by feminist consciousness.

> Coming to have a feminist consciousness is the experience of coming to know the truth about oneself and one's society. . . . They very *meaning* of what the feminist apprehends is illuminated by the light of what ought to be. . . . The feminist apprehends certain features of social reality *as* intolerable, as to be rejected in behalf of a transforming project for the future. . . . Social reality is revealed as deceptive. . . . What is really happening is quite different from what appears to be happening.[23]

Feminist consciousness will first transform inauthentic obedience into wariness, uncertain reflection, and at times, anguished confusion. The feminist becomes "marked by the experience of moral ambiguity" as she learns new ways of living without betraying her women's past, without denying her obligations to others. "She no longer knows what sort of person she ought to be, and therefore, she does not know what she ought to do. One moral paradigm is called into question by the laborious and often obscure emergence of another.''[24]

Out of confusion will arise new voices, recognized not so much by the content of the truths they enunciate as by the honesty and courage of enunciation. They will be at once familiar and original, these voices arising out of maternal practice, affirming its own criteria of acceptability, insisting that the dominant values are unacceptable and need not be accepted.

The Capacity for Attentive Love

Finally, I would like to discuss a capacity—attention—and a virtue—love—that are central to the conception of achievement that maternal thought as a whole articulates. This capacity and virtue, when realized, invigorate preservation and enable growth. Attention and love again and again undermine a mother's inauthentic obedience as she perceives and endorses a child's experience though society finds it intolerable. The identification of the capacity of attention and the virtue of love is at once the foundation and the corrective of maternal thought.

The notion of "attention" is central to the philosophy of Simone Weil and is developed, along with the related notion of "love," by Iris Murdoch, who was profoundly influenced by Weil. Attention and love are fundamental to the construction of "objective reality" understood "in relation to the progressing life of a person," a "reality which is revealed to the patient eye of love.''[25] Attention is an *intellectual* capacity connected even by definition with love, a special "knowledge of the individual.''[26] "The name of this intense, pure, disinterested, gratuitous, generous attention is love.''[27] Weil thinks that the capacity for attention is a "miracle." Murdoch ties it more closely to familiar achievement: "The task of attention goes on all the time and at apparently empty and everyday moments we are 'looking,' making those little peering efforts of imagination which have such important cumulative results.''[28]

For Weil and Murdoch, the enemy of attention is what they call "fantasy," defined not as rich imaginative play, which does have a central role in maternal thinking, but as the "proliferation of blinding self-centered aims and images.''[29] Fantasy, according to their original conception, is intellectual and imaginative activity in the service of consolation, domination, anxiety, and aggrandizement. It is reverie designed to protect the psyche from pain, self-induced blindness designed to protect it from insight. Fantasy, so defined, works in the service of inauthenticity. "The difficulty is to keep the attention fixed on the real situation''[30]—or, as I would say, on the real children. Attention to real children, children seen by the "patient eye of love, . . . teaches us how real things [real children] can be looked at and loved without being seized and used, without being appropriated into the greedy organism of the self.''[31]

Much in maternal practices works against attentive love: intensity of identification, vicarious living through a child, daily wear of maternal work, harassment and indignities of an indifferent social order, and the clamor of children themselves. Although attention is elicited by the very reality it reveals—the reality of a growing person—it is a discipline that requires effort and self-training. The love of children is not only the most intense of attachments, but it is also a detachment, a giving up, a letting grow. To love a child without seizing or using it, to see the child's reality with the patient, loving eye of attention—such loving and attending might well describe the separation of mother and child from the mother's point of view. Of course, many mothers fail much of the time in attentive love and loving attention. Many mothers also train themselves in the looking, self-restraining, and empathy that is loving attention. They can be heard doing so in any playground or coffee klatch.

I am not saying that mothers, individually or collectively, are (or are not) especially wonderful people. My point is that out of maternal practices distinctive ways of conceptualizing, ordering, and valuing arise. We *think* differently about what it *means* and what it takes to be "wonderful," to be a person, to be real.

Murdoch and Weil, neither mothers themselves nor especially concerned with mothers, are clear about the absolute value of attentive love and the reality it reveals. Weil writes:

> In the first legend of the Grail, it is said that the Grail . . . belongs to the first comer who asks the guardian of the vessel, a king three-quarters paralyzed by the most painful wound, "What are you going through?"
>
> The love of our neighbor in all its fullness simply means being able to say to him: "What are you going through?" . . . Only he who is capable of attention can do this.[32]

I do not claim absolute value, but only that attentive love, the training to ask "What are you going through?" is central to maternal practices. If I am right about its place in maternal thought, and if Weil and Murdoch are right about its absolute value, the self-conscious inclusion of maternal thought in the dominant culture will be of general intellectual and moral benefit.

Some Social and Political Implications

I have described a "thought" arising out of maternal practices organized by the interests of preservation, growth, and acceptability. Although in some respects the thought is "contradictory" (i.e., it betrays its own values and must be transformed by feminist consciousness), the thought as a whole, with its fulcrum and correction in attentive love, is worthy of being expressed and respected. This thought has emerged out of maternal practices that are oppressive to women and children. I believe that it has emerged largely in response to the relatively invariable requirements of children and despite oppressive circumstances. As in all women's thought, some worthy aspects of maternal thought may arise out of identification with the powerless and excluded. Nevertheless, oppression is largely responsible for the defects rather than the strengths of maternal thought, as in the obedient goodness to which mothers find themselves "naturally" subscribing. When the oppressiveness of gender arrangements is combined with the oppression of race, poverty, or the multiple injuries of class, it is a miracle that maternal thought can arise at all. On the other hand, that it does indeed arise, miraculously, is clear both from literature (Alice Walker, Tillie Olsen, Maya Angelou, Agnes Smedley, Lucille Clifton, Louisa May Alcott, Audre Lorde, Marilyn French, Grace Paley, and countless others) and from daily experience. Maternal thought *identifies* priorities, attitudes, and virtues; it *conceives* of achievement. The more oppressive the institutions of motherhood, the greater the pain and struggle in living out the worthy and transforming the damaging aspects of thought.

Maternal thinking is only one aspect of "womanly" thinking.[33] In articulating and respecting the maternal, I do not underwrite the still current, false, and pernicious identification of womanhood with biological or adoptive mothering of particular children in families. For me, "maternal" is a social category. Although maternal thinking arises out of actual child-caring practices, biological parenting is neither necessary nor sufficient. Many women and some men express maternal thinking in various kinds of working and caring with others. And some biological mothers, especially in misogynistic societies, take a fearful, defensive distance from their own mothering and the maternal lives of any women.

Maternal thought does, I believe, exist for all women in a radically different way than for men. It is because we are *daughters,* nurtured and trained by women, that we early receive maternal love with special attention to its implications for our bodies, our passions, and our ambitions. We are alert to the values and costs of maternal practices whether we are determined to engage in them or avoid them.

It is now argued that the most revolutionary change we can make in the institution of motherhood is to include men equally in every aspect of childcare. When men and women live together with children, it seems not only fair but deeply moral that they share in every aspect of childcare. To prevent or excuse men from maternal practice is to encourage them to separate public action from private affection, the privilege of parenthood from its cares. Moreover, even when men are absent from the nursery, their dominance in every other public and private room shapes a child's earliest conceptions of power. To familiarize children with "natural" domination at their earliest age in a context of primitive love, assertion, and sexual passion is to prepare them to find equally "natural" and exhaustive the division between exploiter and exploited that pervades the larger world. Although daughter and son alike may internalize "natural" domination, neither typically can live with it easily. Identifying with and imitating exploiters, we are overcome with self-hate; aligning ourselves with the exploited, we are fearful and manipulative. Again and again, family power dramas are repeated in psychic, interpersonal, and professional dramas, while they are institutionalized in economic, political, and international life. Radically recasting the power-gender roles in those dramas just might revolutionize social conscience.[34]

Assimilating men into childcare both inside and outside the home would also be conducive to serious social reform. Responsible, equal childcaring would require men to relinquish power and their own favorable position in the division between intellectual/professional and service labor as that division expresses itself domestically. Loss of preferred status at home might make socially privileged men more suspicious of unnecessary divisions of labor and damaging hierarchies in the public world. Moreover, if men were emotionally and practically committed to childcare, they would reform the work world in parents' interests. Once no one "else" was minding the child, good day-care centers with flexible hours would be established to which parents could trust their children from infancy on. These day-care centers, like the workweek itself, would be managed flexibly in response to human needs as well as to the demands of productivity, with an eye to growth rather than measurable profit. Such moral reforms of economic life would probably begin with professions and managers servicing themselves. Even in nonsocialist countries, however, their benefits could be unpredictably extensive.

I would not argue that the assimilation of men into childcare is the primary social goal for mothers. Rather, we must work to bring a *transformed* maternal thought in the public realm, to make the preservation and growth of *all* children a work of public conscience and legislation. This will not be easy. Mothers are no less corrupted than anyone else by concerns of status and class. Often our misguided efforts on behalf of the success and purity of our children frighten them and everyone else around them. As we increase and enjoy our public effectiveness, we will have less reason to live vicariously through our children. We may then begin to learn to sustain a creative tension between our inevitable and fierce desire to foster our own children and the less compulsive desire that all children grow and flourish.

Nonetheless, it would be foolish to believe that mothers, just because they are mothers, can transcend class interest and implement principles of justice. All feminists must join in articulating a theory of justice shaped by and incorporating maternal thinking. Moreover, the generalization of attentive love to *all* children requires politics. The most enlightened thought is not enough.

Closer to home again, we must refashion our domestic life in the hope that the personal will in fact betoken the political. We must begin by resisting the temptation to construe "home" simplemindedly, as a matter of justice between mothers and fathers. Single parents, lesbian mothers, and coparenting women remind us that many ways to provide children with examples of caring do not incorporate sexual inequalities of power and privilege. Those of us who live with the fathers of our children will eagerly welcome shared parenthood—for overwhelming practical as well as ideological reasons. But in our eagerness, we must not forget that as long as a mother is not effective publicly and self-respecting privately, male presence can be harmful as well as beneficial. It does a woman no good to have the power of the Symbolic Father brought right into the nursery, often despite the deep, affectionate egalitarianism of an individual man. It takes a strong mother and father to resist temptations to domination and subordination for which they have been trained and are socially rewarded. And whatever the hard-won equality and mutual respect an individual couple may achieve, as long as a mother—even if she is no more parent than father—is derogated and subordinate outside the home, children will feel angry, confused, and "wildly unmothered."[35]

Despite these reservations, I look forward to the day when men are willing and able to share equally and actively in transformed maternal practices. When that day comes, will we still identify some thought as maternal rather than merely parental? Might we echo the cry of some feminists—there shall be no more "women"—with our own—there shall be no more "mothers," only people engaging in childcare? To keep matters clear I would put the point differently. On that day there will be no more "fathers," no more people of either sex who have power over their children's lives and moral authority in their children's world, though they do not do the work of attentive love. There will be mothers of both sexes who live out a transformed maternal thought in communities that share parental care—practically, emotionally, economically, and socially. Such communities will have learned from their mothers how to value children's lives.

Notes

I began circulating an early draft of this paper in the fall of 1978. Since then, the constructive criticism and warm response of readers has led me to believe that this draft is truly a collective endeavor. I would like especially to thank Sandra Bartky, Gail Bragg, Bell Chevigny, Nancy Chodorow, Margaret Comstock, Mary Felstiner, Berenice Fisher, Marilyn Frye, Susan Harding, Evelyn Fox Keller, Jane Lilienfeld, Jane Marcus, Adrienne Rich, Amelie Rorty, William Ruddick, Barrie Thorne, Marilyn Blatt Young, readers for *Feminist Studies,* and Rayna Rapp.

1. From J. Echegaray, "Severed Heart," quoted by Jessie Bernard in *The Future of Motherhood* (New York: Dial, 1974), p. 4.
2. Nothing I say about maternal thought suggests that the women who engage in it cannot engage in other intellectual discourse. A maternal thinker may also be an experimental psychologist, a poet, a mathematician, an architect, a physicist. I believe that because most thinkers have been men, most disciplines are partly shaped by "male" concepts, values, styles, and strategies. Unless we have identified "male" and "female" aspects of thought, however, the claim of gender bias is an empty one. I do

not doubt that disciplines are also shaped by transgender interests, values, and concepts, which women, whether or not they engage in maternal practices, may fully share. To the extent that the disciplines are shaped by "male" thought, mothers and other women may feel alienated by the practices and thinking of their own discipline. Correlatively, when thinkers are as apt to be women as men, thought itself may change. On these and related points see Evelyn Keller, "Gender and Science," *Psychoanalysis and Contemporary Thought* 1, no. 3 (1978): 409–53; and idem, "He, She and Id in Scientific Discourse" (unpublished manuscript, 1980).

3. I derive the vocabulary from Jurgen Habermas, *Knowledge and Human Interests* (Boston: Beacon Press, 1971). I have been equally influenced by other philosophical relativists, most notably Peter Winch, Ludwig Wittgenstein, and Suzanne Kessler and Wendy McKenna. See Winch, "Understanding a Primitive Society" and other papers, in *Ethics and Action* (London: Routledge & Kegan Paul, 1972): Wittgenstein, *Philosophical Investigations, Remarks on the Foundations of Mathematics, Zettel,* and *On Certainty* (Oxford: Basil Blackwell, 1953, 1956, 1967, 1969); and Kessler and McKenna, *Gender* (New York: John Wiley & Sons, 1978).

4. Examples of the invariant and *nearly* unchangeable include long gestation inside the mother's body; prolonged infant and childhood dependence; physical fragility of infancy; radical qualitative and quantitative change ("growth") in emotional and intellectual capacities from infancy to adulthood; long development and psychological complexity of human sexual desire, of memory and other cognitive capacities, and of "object relations." Features that are *nearly* universal and certainly changeable include the identification of childbearing and childcaring, the consequent delegation of childcare to biological mothers and other women, and the relative subordination of women in any social class to men of that class.

5. To see the universal in particulars, to assimilate differences and extend kinship, is a legacy of the ecumenical Protestantism in which I was raised. I am well aware that even nonviolent, well-meaning Protestant assimilations can be obtuse and cruel for others. Therefore I am dependent on others, morally as well as intellectually, for the statement of differences, the assessment of their effects on every aspect of maternal lives, and finally for radical correction as well as for expansion of any general theory I would offer. I do not *believe,* however, that the thinking I describe is limited only to "privileged white women," as one reader put it. I first came to the notion of "maternal thinking" and the virtues of maternal practices through personal exchange with Tillie Olsen and then through reading her fiction. Similarly, I believe that "Man Child: A Black Lesbian Feminist's Response" by Audre Lorde, *Conditions* 4 (1979): 30–36, is an excellent example of what I call maternal thinking transformed by feminist consciousness. My "assimilation" of Olsen's and Lorde's work in no way denies differences that separate us nor the biases those differences may introduce into my account. These are only two of many examples of writers in different social circumstances who express what I take to be "maternal thinking."

6. The words are Mrs. Ramsay's in Virginia Woolf's *To the Lighthouse* (New York: Harcourt, Brace and World, 1927), p. 92.

7. Adrienne Rich, "Conditions for Work: The Common World of Women," in *Working It Out,* edited by Sara Ruddick and Pamela Daniels (New York: Pantheon, 1977), p. xvi (italics mine).

8. For the comparison, see Iris Murdoch, *The Sovereignty of Good* (New York: Shocken Books, 1971). Popular moralities as well as contemporary moral theory tend to emphasize decision, assertion, happiness, authenticity, and justification by principle.

9. Ibid., p. 99.

10. Ibid., p. 95.

11. Spinoza, *Ethics,* Book 3, Proposition 42, demonstration. See also Proposition 40, Note, and Proposition 45, both in Book 3.

12. Bernard Williams, *Morality* (New York: Harper Torchbooks, 1972), p. 11.

13. The words are those of a Texas farmwoman who quilted as she huddled with her family in a shelter as, above them, a tornado destroyed their home. The story was told to me by Miriam Schapiro.

14. Murdoch, *Sovereignty of Good,* p. 26.

15. These are differences often attributed to women both by themselves and by psychologists. For a critical review of the literature, see Eleanor Maccoby and Carol Jacklin, *The Psychology of Sex Differences* (Stanford, Calif.: Stanford University Press, 1974). For a plausible account of women's valuing of inner life, see Patricia Meyer Spacks, *The Female Imagination* (New York: Alfred A. Knopf, 1975). Maccoby and Jacklin are critical both of the findings I mentioned and of the adequacy of the psychological experiments they survey for testing or discovering these differences. I make little use of psychology, more of literature, in thinking about the cognitive sex differences I discuss. Psychologists are not, as far as I know, talking about women who have empathically identified with and assimilated maternal practices, either by engaging in them or by identifying with their own or other mothers. It would be hard to identify such a subgroup of women without circularity. But even if one could make the identification, tests would have to be devised that measure not achievement but conception of achievement. Mothers, to take one example, may well prize the inner life, but they have so little time for it or are so self-protectively defended against their own insights that they gradually lose the capacity for inner life. Or again, a mother may not maintain sharp boundaries between herself and her child or between her child's "outer" action and inner life. She *must* maintain some boundaries, however. We value what we are in danger of losing (e.g., inner life); we identify virtues because we recognize temptations to vice (e.g., openness because we are tempted to rigid control); we refuse what we fear giving way to (e.g., either pathological symbiotic identification *or* an unworkable division between our own and our children's interests). It is difficult to imagine tests sophisticated and sensitive enough to measure such conceptions, priorities, and values. I have found psychoanalytic theory the most useful of psychologies and Nancy Chodorow's *The Reproduction of Mothering* (Berkeley: University of California Press, 1978) the most helpful in applying psychoanalytic theory to maternal practices.

16. Simone Weil, "Gravity and Grace," in *Gravity and Grace* (London: Routledge & Kegan Paul, 1952; first French ed., 1947), passim.

17. Ibid, and other essays in *Gravity and Grace.* Both the language and concepts are indebted to Plato.

18. Jean Baker Miller, *Toward a New Psychology for Women* (Boston: Beacon Press, 1973), p. 54.

19. As Habermas argues, *Knowledge and Human Interests.*

20. Miller, *Toward a New Psychology,* p. 56.

21. Ibid., p. 40.

22. I am indebted to Adrienne Rich, *Of Woman Born* (New York: W. W. Norton, 1976), especially chapter 8, both for this phrase and for the working out of the idea of inauthenticity. My debt to this book as a whole is pervasive.

23. Sandra Lee Bartky, "Toward a Phenomenology of Feminist Consciousness," in *Feminism and Philosophy,* edited by Mary Vetterling-Braggin, Frederick A. Elliston, and Jane English (Totowa, N.J.: Littlefield, Adams, 1977), pp. 22–37. Quotes from pp. 33, 25, 28, 29.

24. Ibid., p. 31. On the riskiness of authenticity, the courage it requires of women, see also Miller, *Toward a New Psychology,* chapter 9.

25. Murdoch, *Sovereignty of Good,* p. 40.

26. Ibid., p. 28.

27. Simone Weil, "Human Personality," in *Collected Essays,* chosen and translated by Richard Rees (London: Oxford University Press, 1962). Also *Simone Weil Reader,*

edited by George A. Panichas (New York: McKay, 1977), p. 333.

28. Murdoch, *Sovereignty of Good,* p. 43.

29. Ibid., p. 67.

30. Ibid., p. 91.

31. Ibid., p. 65.

32. Simone Weil, "Reflections of the Right Use of School Studies with a View to the Love of God," in *Waiting for God* (New York: G. Putnam's, 1951), p. 115.

33. Among other possible aspects of women's thought are those that might arise from our sexual lives, from our "homemaking," from the special conflict women feel between allegiance, on the one hand, to women and their world and, on the other hand, to all people of their kin and culture. Any identifiable aspect of women's thought will be interrelated to all the others. Since women almost everywhere are relatively powerless in relation to men of their class, all aspects of women's thought will be affected by powerlessness. Whether we are discussing the thought arising from women's bodily, sexual, maternal, homemaking, linguistic, or any other experience, we are faced with a confluence of powerlessness and the "womanly," whatever that might be.

34. These points have been made by many feminists, most provocatively and thoroughly by Dorothy Dinnerstein, *The Mermaid and the Minotaur* (New York: Harper & Row, 1976).

35. Rich, *Of Woman Born,* p. 225.

14

Preservative Love and Military Destruction: Some Reflections on Mothering and Peace

SARA RUDDICK

In 1979, Dr. Helen Caldicott called women to nonviolent battle.[1]

> A Women's Party for Survival is being organized throughout the US and women all over the world are mobilizing for disarmament. . . . Women have tremendous power. As mothers we must make sure the world is safe for our babies. . . . Look at the changing seasons . . . Look at our growing children. Look at one child, one baby . . . I have three children, and I'm a doctor who treats children . . . I live with dying children. I live with grieving parents. I understand the value of every human life . . . We have only a short time to turn the destructive powers around. A short time. I appeal especially to the women to do this work because we understand the genesis of life. Our bodies are built to nurture life. We have wombs, we have breasts, we have menstrual periods to remind us that we can produce life! We also have a voice in the affairs of the world and are becoming more influential every day. I beg of you: do what you can today.

Three claims are embodied in this call: (a) Women have distinctive interests in and capacities for peacemaking; (b) these interests and capacities are connected with maternity; and (c) although women's peacemaking has hitherto been confined to maternal life, we have "more influence every day" in making the *world* safe for our children.

These claims are plausible and alluring. Men and women alike tend to believe women are peaceful and to notice and reward peacefulness in women and girls. Surveys confirm these beliefs by showing women voters as more anti-militarist than men and predominant among followers of pacifists. Women who organize themselves in peace groups often draw upon images of

---

maternity to explain their commitment and urge it on others. And many men who are dramatically linked with peace reveal a strong identification with their mothers and sometimes themselves come to speak in a recognizably maternal voice. Gandhi, Wilfred Owen, Andre Trocmé, and Randall Jarrell are all examples, in different ways, of maternal men. We can understand why it has been tempting to imagine a world governed by maternal peacefulness. Now that peaceful women are inspirited by feminist assertion, it seems possible for maternal vision to acquire "tremendous power."

Although plausible and alluring, Dr. Caldicott's claims are also dubious and dangerous. Women, perhaps especially mothers, have played their assigned roles in a militarized world. On the sidelines of battle, women have been applauders and suppliers; plunder at the end of the day; home at the end of the war; mourners who let the fighting go on. Mothers have sacrificed their sons to the most vile as well as the most just of causes. When officers deem it appropriate for women to fight—to defend a beseiged city, to take up arms when men have fallen—women fight no less fiercely than men. Women have always been expected to fight defensively in protection of their children and homes. Increasingly, women ask to be in the front lines of combat, "carrying the fight to the enemy" with the fiercest weapons their armies possess.

Women historically have played a dominant role in pacifist movements. Because of their courage and effectiveness as pacifists in a society where women had little voice, these women publicized a pacifism that was self-consciously maternal. But while women pacifists struggled against war and male dominance, other women prepared for war.[2] Both militarists and pacifists have justified their choices in maternal terms. Some mothers wanted their sons freed forever from the threat of war; others wanted them to fight with the best guns and ships their state could produce. "Earlier I buttered bread for him, now I paint grenades and think 'this if for him.'"[3]

Even if we could believe in the peacefulness of mothers, it is not clear that we would want to. If feminism has empowered women, it has often done so by attacking the identification of women with maternity. Conversely, emphasizing the maternity of women has proved an effective strategy of male supremacists. Dr. Caldicott herself, in her celebration of female bodies, slips into a romanticism that is both silly and dangerous. To confine mothers in domestic work and nurturant bodies, and then to praise them for peacefulness, disparages both the woman and the virtue she is said to possess. Mothers rightly resent a sentimentality which obscures the complex power and real, limited abilities of maternal work. Men and women doubt the effectiveness of a virtue acquired in conditions of powerlessness and confined to the home.

Hopes and doubts about traditional female work and virtues are part of a dialog in which feminists are now engaged, a dialog many of us carry on in our heads. As I write in America, in the winter of 1982, the dangers of connecting being female with being a mother seem stark. Once again, women are being forced and are forcing each other into accepting unchosen maternity and into leading powerless, if idealized, maternal lives. Yet at the same time, we are living in a militarized state, armed with insanely destructive and self-destructive weapons, plagued by violences not only against individuals and nations, but against classes and races. "Enemies" abound, self-righteous hatred seems a virtue, murder is legitimate. In these circumstances, any resource of peacefulness should be made politically effective.

Despite the risk and because of the dangers we find ourselves in, I stop the dialog in my head and respond to Dr. Caldicott's call. I believe mothers do have a tradition of peacefulness that can be strengthened and mobilized for the public good. Attending to this female virtue seems justified by the horrors of military and domestic violence. Moreover, on reflection, feminist politics and maternal peacefulness are not at odds. Indeed, I argue later that if domestic pacifism is to become a public good, it must be transformed by feminism. It is true that appeals to womanly maternity have a reactionary sound, if not effect. But finally the dangers of reaction seem outweighed by the possibility that mothers and other women have a distinctive contribution to make to the cause of peace.

Were I a leader and persuader, I would attempt to rally mothers and other women to a mother-identified politics of protest. What I will do here, instead, is to explore some of the connections that justify such a politics: connections between mothers and other women, between maternal thinking and pacifism, between maternal pacifism and feminism. Briefly my claim is this: the conventional and symbolic association between women and peace has a real basis in maternal practice. Out of maternal practice a distinctive kind of thinking arises that is incompatible with military strategy but consonant with pacifist commitment to non-violence. The peacefulness of mothers, however, is not now a reliable source for peace. In order for motherly peacefulness to be publicly significant, maternal practice must respect and extend its pacifism. For this to happen, maternal thinking would have to be transformed by a feminist politics.

The Very Idea of Maternal Thinking

In an earlier paper, I tried to show that distinctive ways of thinking arise out of the work mothers do.[4] In their practices, people respond to a reality they experience as *given,* as presenting certain "demands." Their "interest" in meeting these demands seems equally *given,* a requirement of reason, and therefore a particular kind of psychological motivation.

Maternal practice is governed by "interests" in satisfying "demands" for the preservation, growth, and acceptability of children. In saying that maternal practice is governed by these interests, I am not implying that individual mothers are enthusiastically dedicated to these aims. Actual mothers have the same kind of relation to maternal practices as scientists have to scientific practice, as believers have to religious practice. An individual scientist may hate her work, wish she were writing poetry or swimming in the Caribbean, fabricate her "evidence" (by, for example, painting spots on her laboratory animals), and write up her experiments with half an eye while watching "General Hospital." Nonetheless, in scientific practice the very idea of truth is dependent upon replication by experiment, a logical dependence unaffected by the attitudes of the individual experimenter. To engage in the practice is, *inter alia,* to accept the connection between truth and experimental replication.[5] Similarly, a mother may, on most days, hate her work or even her children. She may ignore or assault them, adore or despair of them. The style, skill, and enthusiasm with which mothers engage in their practice vary enormously. Nonetheless, achievement, in maternal work, is defined by the aims of preserving, fostering, and shaping the growth of a child; insofar as one engages in maternal practice, one accepts these aims as one's own.

Despite differences between mothers, I believe that a distinctive kind of thinking arises when one attempts to understand, control, and communicate the strategies and aims of maternal practice. That is, there is a commonality of childhood life and maternal experience which allows us to speak of the demands of *human* children and of interests in meeting them. But every common feature of childhood development and maternal experience is also subject to social as well as individual variation. The very definition of "childhood," the meaning of "dependence," opportunities for sexual and intellectual development, recognition of complexity, and of course ideas of acceptability are culturally and historically determined. The technological, medical, and material resources available to a woman vary from culture to culture and between classes of a culture. At different times, a child's life is more or less fragile, a child's growth may be a fairly natural process or a struggle to survive. Although the concept of maternal thinking depends upon similarity, to describe that thinking requires recognizing differences that shape every aspect of a mother's day and life.

The particularity, the cultural relativity of maternal thinking is not a defect to be overcome. It is good that we cannot talk meaningfully about *"the* maternal," outside of the technological, historical, geographical, and political contexts in which women mother. We will not, to paraphrase Simone de Beauvoir, be able to float in the universal. Any generalization about maternal thinking must be embodied and exhibited in particular mother-child relations. This requirement has both epistemological and political consequences. For example, fiction, memoirs, and oral history become the primary source material of maternal thought. The silences of mothers can be deafening; no theory, philosophic or statistical, can teach us what mothers would say if they themselves respected and expressed their ordering of our allegedly common world. Moreover, when we look at maternal practice through the lens of shared maternal interest we see the centrality and the devastating effects of poverty or war or racial oppression on mothers' lives. To be a "good enough mother" in a society that does not value your child's life or self-respect transforms the everyday unromantic work of mothering into a heroic task.

Whether one is struck by similarity or differences between people seems partly a matter of temperament and training. The ecumenical Protestantism in which I was raised, and the study of philosophy which followed, taught me to look for a *human* condition underlying social and individual variation. A tendency to universalize, underestimating differences one cannot or will not see, can be personally cruel as well as politically arrogant and dangerous. The very idea of maternal thinking reflects personal and social biases; the application of that notion to a philosophy of conflict accentuates them. It is notorious that definitions of violence and techniques of reconciliation differ markedly in different social groups. I allow that the basis for pacifism I here ascribe to "maternal" thinking may exist only in certain groups with which I am familiar. I necessarily depend upon others of different training and social identity to compensate for the limits of my particular history, to correct my interpretations and expand my vision. Blindness to the differences that truly separate us and to the suffering they cause is, after all, a primary cause of war. It is also true, I believe, that peace in a nuclear age depends upon our learning to understand ourselves as members of a species precariously inhabiting together a particular planet.

My claim that aspects of maternal practice are shared throughout the species should not be confused with a different claim that there are essential ineradicable differences between male and female parents. In a degenderized society, where political and economic power as well as every aspect of childcare are shared between men and women, it is difficult to predict what differences our bodies and distinctive histories would make. We cannot preclude the possibility that some aspects of maternal thinking derive from the infant's, and perhaps from the mother's, biological constitution and experience. In less technologically developed societies the connection between maternal bodies and mothering is made visible in repeated pregnancies and public nursing. Even so, the biological moments of a mother's life make up only a small part of the caretaking her children receive. Almost all grown women menstruate, many bear children, many of these nurse them. I do not believe, however, as Dr. Caldicott seems to, that distinctive peacefulness arises from these ovarian adventures. A love affair with our own bleeding, gestating, birthing, lactating bodies only diverts attention from the daily work women do. I do not deny the intense, if ambivalent, pleasures women get from their own and each others' sexual, nurturing bodies. But these pleasures provide at best an inspiration and metaphor for peacefulness. The real basis of female pacifism lies in the complicated social activity of preservative love.

Mothers and Other Women

Not all women are mothers, nor is maternal thinking the whole of women's thought. Equally important, maternal thinking is not the whole of a *mother's* thought any more than maternity is the whole of a mother's life. Although maternal thinking arises out of the care of actual children, not only mothers are maternal thinkers. Many women express maternal thinking in various kinds of caring for others. Moreover, some men now acquire maternal thinking, and many more could. Nevertheless, in our society, now, their ways of acquisition are necessarily different from ours. It is because we are *daughters* that we early receive maternal love with special attention to its implications for our bodies, passions, and ambitions.

In a society where primary parents are still likely to be mothers and other women, and where so many women eventually become mothers, it is impossible to separate practically or conceptually the maternal from the womanly. Consider, for example, women's alleged greater capacity for empathy arising from a less sharply delineated sense of self, which is a consequence of the special intensity and character of mother-daughter relations.[6] The young girl acquires a capacity for empathy from her mother(s) whom she gradually learns is more or less the same kind of creature she is, an "identity" the mother herself appreciates and conveys. When the young empathic girl becomes a mother, empathy is both elicited and developed in the care of children. (Remember that mothers are typically very young women; their adult psyches are strongly shaped by the maternal practices they engage in.) In the course of maternal caring, empathy becomes a mode of apprehension and caring which I have called "attentive love." The daughter learns this attentiveness from the mother as the mother herself is developing it. Attentiveness is appropriate to maternal care, and (in part) makes possible a maternal competence, which makes possible identification with a mother. Other aspects of maternal thought, such as the cheerfulness, holding, and philosophy of conflict that I will mention later have similar roles. Often, in the literature, attention to the quality and intensity of mother-daughter relations scants their content. When a daughter "identifies" with a mother, the mother does not represent contentless female being, but a distinctive way of caring and knowing. The daughter is a kind of apprentice, learning a work and a way of thinking about it. These "lessons" may shape her intellectual and emotional life even if she comes to hate the work, the thought or, for that matter, the mother.

To put my point generally, female nature both explains and is explained by maternal thinking. Alleged sex differences shape maternal thought. On the other hand, the appropriateness of the sex characteristics to maternal work partly explains their existence and adult development. In the growing feminist literature on sex differences I have found widespread agreement in judgments that are expressed in different disciplinary contexts and languages. Almost always, I have been able to relate these independent findings to maternal thought doubly, both as *explicans* and *explicandum*.

Mothers and Virtue

When I first started writing about motherliness, it was important to me to stress that mothers *think,* that a maternal perspective is not only a matter of feeling or of virtue. I underlined the fact that I was not claiming that mothers are especially wonderful people, nor that maternal practices are noted for their achievements. Rather, I was saying that mothers had a distinctive sense of what it meant to be "wonderful," to be a "person"; that they had distinctive *conceptions* of achievement worth considering. Partly because of my increasing commitment to mothers as a class, a passion which seeped through the lines of my paper, I left unclear the relation of maternal thinking to maternal virtue.

The confusion has important political consequences. If, as some believe, mothers are, just as mothers, especially *good,* then one political strategy is to increase the power of mothers in the interests of the public good. But the story is more complicated. In some cases, maternal thinking does name virtues, that is, it identifies certain strengths appropriate to the work of preservation and growth and acceptability. This is to say not that mothers *have* the virtue, but that they *recognize* it. Moreover, maternal thinkers in recognizing a virtue do not pick out a trait mothers should acquire, but instead identify a struggle they experience. Let me give two examples.

While preserving the physical and psychic life of a child in an indifferent world, a mother identifies a kind of resilient good humor as a virtue, a clear-sighted cheerfulness, which, in Spinoza's words, "increases and assists the power of action." Yet cheerfulness always threatens to break down into cheery denial, its degenerative form. We so wish the world were better for our children—and ourselves—that we deny its true character and power to hurt. If I were to express the moral theory of maternal thinking in simple form, I would say something like this: resilient good humor is necessary to preservation and growth. Yet equally necessary is a realistic perception of the natural and social threats that mothers, and eventually children, must counter. Just because cheerfulness is such a good, the smiles of our children are so comforting, and the natural and social order so indifferent or hostile, cheery denial is always a temptation. We must expect an ongoing struggle, then, to maintain cheerfulness in the face of many reasons for despair, while refusing the dangerous tranquility of cheery denial.

Another example. At the center of maternal thinking is a capacity which, following Simone Weil, I have termed attention, and which is defined interdependently with love.[7] Attention is "a special kind of knowledge of the individual"; it is an ability to ask "what are you going through" and an ability to hear the answer. Continuously, attention calls for a radical kind of self-denial. "The soul empties itself of all its contents in order to receive into itself the being it is looking at, just as he is, in all his truth."[8] But such self-denial, necessary at moments, is not identical with attentive love. On the contrary, attentive love calls for a realistic *self*-preservation on the part of the mother, a mother-self that can be seen and identified by the child who is itself learning attentive love. Again, to put the point very simply, maternal thinking might be construed as saying: attentive love is a mode of apprehension inseparable from care, through which mothers know as they love, and create as they respect, their children. In developing the discipline of attention, however, one must be constantly wary that moments of radical self-denial—which are necessary—do not become the perverted aim of attention rather than its occasional expression. Self-denial is always tempting, especially in societies where adults and children reward mothers for their *failures* in self-preservation. But the attentiveness that aids growth, and which, if children learn it, will enable *them* to love attentively while remaining the assertive creatures whose growth we foster, is an attention that respects both self and other.[9] Pervasive, chronic self-denial leads to a mother's spiritual impoverishment and to her projecting denied needs onto others. It encourages tyranny in the children, especially in the sons who can reject it as a mode of *their* being, and it rewards the misogyny of the world. Maternal thinking identifies attentive love as the fulcrum, the foundation of maternal practice; at the same time it identifies chronic self-denial in its many forms as the characteristic temptation of mothers and the besetting vice of maternal work. In naming the virtue and its degenerative form, it points to a struggle.

I have been discussing virtues and their degenerative forms which maternal thinking has appropriately identified, thereby naming a struggle and imposing a discipline on the practice. I believe that there are also instances in which maternal thinking has *mis*identified virtue, i.e., where the thinking itself is in need of transformation. I have argued that this is the case with much of the thinking arising out of the demand of a social group that children be raised in an *acceptable* way. In response to the demand of acceptability maternal thinking becomes contradictory—that is, betrays its own interests in the preservation and growth of children. It does so by misidentifying inauthenticity as a necessary mode of apprehension and obedience to the good of others as a virtue. Inauthenticity is one of the many forms of maternal self-denial, an inability to take one's self as authority, to trust one's own perceptions of children's needs and capacities.

Finally, in maternal thinking a central tension is created between the fierce desire to foster one's own children and the commitment to the well-being of all children. The more individualistic, hierarchical, and competitive the social system, the more likely that a mother will see the good of her child and her group's children as *opposed* to the good of children of another mother or another "kind". However, I do not foresee that in *any* society mothers will typically and wholeheartedly endorse the common good of children when it conflicts with their own children's interests. Maternal practice assumes a legitimate special concern for the children one has engendered and passionately loves as well as for the families (of various forms) in which they live. Any attempt to deny this special form of self-interest will only lead to hypocritical false consciousness or rigid, totalistic loyalties. Mothers can, I believe, come to realize that the good of their own children is entwined with the good of all children, that in a world divided between exploiter and exploited no children can be both good and strong, that in a world at war all children are endangered. We can as mothers learn to sustain a conflicted but creative tension between personal loyalties and impersonal moral concerns. The conflict between the demands of one's own and the demand of the whole, however, will not disappear. This maternal conflict can bring a sense of realism and moral humility to political struggle; it also suggests real limits to the effectiveness of maternal thinking in political life.

In sum, then, many aspects of maternal thinking embody a metaphysical and moral perspective that anyone might profitably consider. But the relation of maternal thinking to virtue is at best complex. Some aspect of the contradictoriness of maternal thinking will be ameliorated by a feminist consciousness that works against various forms of self-denial. In a less hierarchical society, disciplined imagination and moral reflection could reveal the interconnectedness of children's interests with the causes of peace, ecological sanity, and distributive justice. But mothers know better than to expect perfection of themselves. In the best of nonpatriarchal, socialist worlds, maternal practice will involve conflict; "maternal thinking" will describe a moral activity rather than a virtue achieved.

Maternal Practice and Pacifist Commitment

Maternal virtue cannot translate directly into public good. Nonetheless, there may be goods that mothers have both conceptualized and realized in distinctive ways. One such good is peacefulness. By "peacefulness" I mean a commitment to avoid battle whenever possible, to fight necessary battles nonviolently, and to take, as the aim of battle, reconciliation between opponents and restoration of connection and community. I will call this the "pacifist commitment." Its most prominent controversial feature is the renunciation of violence even in causes whose justice is undisputed. By "violence" I mean strategies or weapons which are intended to *damage* an opponent, or which can reasonbly be expected to do so. By "damage" I mean at least physical or psychological harm for which there is no compensatory benefit to the person damaged and which is, or is likely to be, indefinitely lasting.[10] Military strategy is opposed to pacifist commitment in that it accepts violence to achieve causes deemed good or advantageous and values victory over reconciliation.[11]

In what sense do mothers share with pacifists a rejection of military strategy arising from the renunciation of violence and commitment to reconciliation? Most obviously, maternal preservative love is incompatible with military destruction. Most important, maternal practice gives rise to a theory of conflict similar to that of pacifists, especially to Gandhian *satyagraha*. There is also a war-like cognitive style and an erotics of destruction. I believe that maternal sexuality and cognition contrast with these and are therefore potentially anti-militarist. I will consider in turn each of the four pacifist elements of maternal practice and thinking: preservative love, a philosophy of conflict, cognition, and sexuality.

Preservative Love and Military Strategy

Maternal practice is governed by the primary demand that a child's life and health be preserved. From an early age, a mother trains her children, shapes their growth in a way that is acceptable to adults and, one hopes, good for the child. The child's physical, psychological, and moral well-being are all fragile, are all the object of preservative love. By "preservative love" I do not mean a feeling. Mothers' feelings toward their children vary from hour to hour, year to year. A single day can encompass fury, infatuation, boredom, and simple dislike without being in any way atypical. Preservative love is an *activity* of caring or treasuring creatures whose well-being is at risk.

In response to the demand that she preserve her child in an indifferent and often hostile world, a mother develops an attitude to human and nonhuman nature that I call "holding". This attitude is characterized by the priority given to keeping over aquiring, to reconciling difference, to conserving the fragile, to maintaining the minimal harmony and material conditions necessary to a child's life. Preservative love defines and rewards certain virtues like the clear-sighted cheerfulness I mentioned earlier, just because they enable a mother to hold and maintain the lives of others in an unpredictable world.[12]

It seems obvious, even without resorting to war memoirs and analyses, that military endeavors endanger what a mother seeks to preserve. Quite aside from endangering her children's bodies, military action tends to undermine their capacities for pleasure and work as well as their moral sensibilities. War is terrifying, numbing, morally erosive. Treasuring lives, holding them and the materiel that sustains them, seems directly opposed to the conquest of battlefields, the destruction of wills, bodies, landscapes and artifacts, expected of soldiers.

Nonetheless, good officers are supposed to preserve the lives of their soldiers and to maintain at least the modicum of psychological strength required for fighting. It used to be that soldiers of all ranks were pledged to spare the lives of civilians—though now we no longer expect the pledge, let alone the honoring of it. Officers differ as individuals. Many (I hope) are "maternal" men, determined to avoid "unnecessary" damage to their own—and enemy?—people. Moreover, armies differ nationally and, within a nation, historically, in the kinds and degrees of destructiveness they will encompass.[13]

Soldiers themselves are often said to delight in the destruction battles encourage. Yet many individual soldiers are also said to develop a kind of preservative love suitable for the battlefield. Partly reacting to the destruction around them, they develop a "maternal concern" for themselves, bits of nature, stray animals, fellow fighters, and the wounded enemy. Such concern is the special province of the medic but also necessary for the common soldier. "When soldiers lose this need to preserve and become impersonal killers, they are truly figures of terror."[14] Anyone who doubts that maternal thinking can be expressed on the battlefield and preservative love survive there should read the poetry of Wilfred Owen.

Nonetheless, military strategy, in its very aims, puts at risk not only the bodies but the "hearts and minds" a mother has cared for. And this is to put the point mildly. Twentieth-century technology has only accentuated and made visible what battle reports across the centuries have told us. The "waste" of people by military strategies goes well beyond the requirements of victory. Victory itself is defined in such a way as to be compatible with immense psychological and physical damage to the victorious as well as the defeated. Moreover, war itself undermines whatever responsibility armies or particular officers initially undertake in order to limit their own destructiveness.

> Hatred, bitterness and fear—all of which increase throughout the period of hostility—produce tremendous temptations to set aside the self-denying ordinances (which limit one's own destructiveness) . . . Each war traces a path of moral descent . . . This is a fearful descent. But it can scarcely be described as astonishing in view of its inevitability. For the pressures of war are such that it is as predictable as anything in human life.[15]

On the one side, we have maternal practice whose end is defined by the demand to preserve what is both treasured and at risk. On the other we have military practice which puts at risk those same treasured lives in the name of "victory" or other abstract causes. "Holding," treasuring whatever can maintain or lighten lives, attitudes or preservative love, emerge in an unmysterious way as one meets the demands of childcare. These same attitudes can emerge for soldiers as a reaction against the destruction their work involves. Preservative love is an intelligible response to maternal work; on the battlefield it is truly marvelous.

Preservative love is almost too sharply opposed to military strategy. We are apt to sentimentalize both, sanctifying mothers, demonizing soldiers. I repeat, I am not speaking of good or bad, loving or destroying individuals, but of the practices in which individuals engage. Moreover, the sharp opposition of maternity and militarism raises a question of its own. Why *have* mothers played their parts in military scripts, allowing, even encouraging the sacrifice of their sons? This question may be all the more acute as we appreciate still other, less obvious pacifist tendencies in maternal practice.

Pacifism and Maternal Practice

The pacifist renounces those strategies which the militarist accepts—strategies which, at the very least put at risk, at the worst set out to destroy, the lives which mothers preserve. Pacifist renunciation seems closely linked to preservative love, especially for those religious and (occasionally) secular pacifists who make the "sanctity of life" a basis for their commitment. Preservative love, however, does not play the defining role in pacifist theory that it does in maternal thinking. Pacifism is *defined* by its theory of conflict, with its two components of reconciliation and nonviolent resistance. Explicit beliefs about the preservation of life may, but also may not, underlie the theory. Maternal practice, on the other hand, takes as its defining aim, first, the preservation of life and then maintenance of conditions in which psychological and moral growth take place. Mothers would be happy if conflict were so rare that no theory of conflict were necessary. In fact, conflict is a part of maternal daily life. A mother finds herself embattled with her children, with an outside world at odds with her or their interests, with a man or other adults in her home, with her children's enemies. She is spectator and arbiter of her children's battles with each other and their companions. It is not surprising, then, that maternal thinking has articulated a theory of conflict consonant with the aims of maternal practice. This theory in several ways is congruent with pacifism.

Both in their homes and outside them, mothers typically experience themselves as powerless. They cannot control the vagaries of fate, visited upon them most painfully in the form of accidents and disease that befall their children and people their children depend upon. They are powerless as mothers, unable to determine the wills, friendships, and ambitions of their children. They are usually powerless socially—objects rather than agents of wars, economic plans, and political policies. Most mothers are directly dependent upon the good favor of individual men and publicly effective people—teachers, doctors, welfare workers, dentists, park supervisors, clinic directors, restaurant keepers, movie house owners, selective service administrators, and all those others who decide under what conditions children will be provided with services from the "outside" world.

Like other powerless combatants, mothers often resort to nonviolent strategies because they have no weapons to damage—neither guns, nor legal effectiveness, nor economic clout. Mothers know that officials—teachers, welfare workers, landlords, doctors, and the like—can retaliate against their children as well as against themselves at the hint of maternal violence, perhaps even of anger. Instead of force, then, mothers engage in nonviolent techniques: prayer, persuasion, appeasement, self-suffering, psychological manipulation, negotiation, and bribery. Each of these techniques has its place in public nonviolent coercion.

A striking fact about mothers is that they remain peaceful in situations in which they are powerful, namely in battles with their own and other children. Dorothy Dinnerstein has written eloquently about the power of mothers perceived from the infant-child's point of view.[16] A mother is our first audience, jailor, trainer, protector—a being upon whose favor we depend for our happiness, even survival. The more isolated she is, the greater her power is, since it is shared among other adults and a wider caretaking community. We have learned that at least in our society, we are intensely ambivalent about our early pleasurable and fearful dependency on mothers and other women.

Little has been written about this same maternal power from a mother's point of view. A young, typically powerless woman confronts her children. Hassled if not harassed by the officials of an outside world and, usually, by her own employers, she is nonetheless powerful, the more so precisely the more alone she is. Such a young woman finds herself embattled with weak creatures whose wills are unpredictable and resistant, whose bodies she could quite literally destroy, whose psyches are at her mercy. I can think of no other situation in which someone with the resentments of social powerlessness, under enormous pressures of time and anger, faces a recalcitrant but helpless combatant with so much restraint. It is clear that violence—techniques of struggle that *damage*—is by definition inimical to the interests of maternal work. Indeed, maternal thinking would count as violent just those actions which deliberately or predictably risk the child's life, health, psychological strength, or moral well-being. It is also clear that physical and psychological violence is a temptation of maternal practice and a fairly common occurrence. What is remarkable is that in a daily way mothers make so much peace instead of fighting, and then, when peace fails, conduct so many battles without resorting to violence.

I do not claim that maternal pacifist commitment is a product of deliberation or virtue. There are heavy social penalties for maternal violence, even for the appearance of violence. Moreover, there is a sense in which non-violence comes naturally to many mothers. Young women who have internalized maternal thinking take as their own the demands of preservation, growth, and acceptability from which a commitment to non-violence follows. Renunciation of certain techniques of struggle may come too early, bringing in its wake cheery denial, passivity, inauthenticity, and obedience—forms of *self* renunciation which are the defining vices of maternal practice. I do not want to trumpet a virtue but to point to a fact: that non-violence is a constitutive principle of maternal thinking, and that mothers honor it not in the breach, but in their daily practice, despite objective temptations to violence.

In addition to her own battles a mother must prevent or resolve battles among her children and between her children and their friends. Here too, peace-making is both complex and in a mother's interest. Siblings themselves present a study in relative strength and weakness. A mother working for the growth of each of her children must restrain the powerful, training them in kinds of renunciation, while at the same time preventing the powerless from premature acquiescence or excessive reliance on techniques of manipulation and "self-suffering." Her own favoritism, varieties of inattention, or acceptance of conventional sexual stereotypes often interfere with a mother's task. Again, however, the demands of the practice are clear: a mother must prevent her children from deliberately or predictably using or accepting techniques of struggle that damage.

Battles between her children and their companions present a similar challenge to a mother. Most of her children's "enemies" will be members of her neighborhood and school community, often indeed children of her close friends. Whatever her own intense partisan feelings, a mother will typically be held responsible for the damage her children cause as well as for damage she lets them suffer. Among both siblings and friends peace-making is in a mother's interest. It is also in her interest to let some battles occur so that children may learn to fight back and defend themselves in nondamaging ways. A mother's role as judge, arbiter, and instructor in non-violence (including nonviolent tussling and sparring) gives her an opportunity for reflection, often shared with other mothers and adults she lives with. In moments of reflection she tests and refines a pacifist theory of conflict.

Toward one group of combatants, however, a mother is not reliably non-violent, namely the families and children of her own "enemies." Class, racial, neighborhood, and personal divisions may be played out through children. Indeed, group violence may provide a mother with a rare opportunity for expressing the anger she has abjured. Political or religious allegiance, misguided desire for purity and order, the sheer lust to see one's *children* privileged, all may fuel a violence otherwise too crude to tolerate. The repulsive, contorted faces of white mothers shouting at black children seeking to enter schoolrooms may haunt most women. But they are faces of maternal practice and represent a temptation to which mothers are liable—self-righteous violence against the outsider. Militarists who wish to mobilize mothers in the national interest find this same fearful self-righteousness a resource for violent patriotism.

Maternal theories of conflict are often restricted in scope to those near and alike and are therefore politically weak and morally flawed. I will return later to the imperfections of maternal thinking. Now, however, I would like to compare the pacifist and maternal theories of conflict, each of which, I believe, has something to learn from the other.

Maternal and Pacifist Theories of Conflict

Central to both pacifist theory and maternal thinking is the subordination of ends to means. This subordination is most apparent in the renunciation of violence even if—and where—violence seems the only means to achieve a desired end. This way of putting the point is somewhat misleading. For both pacifism and maternal practice the desirability of a goal is not separable from its being achieved non-violently. However much an outcome may appear identical with an original goal—a child asleep, a sibling left alone—if the methods have physically damaged a child, the "end" is not achieved. One continually redefines and responds to goals in ways that preclude violent means of achieving them. Gandhi made this point when he defined "Truth" interdependently with "God"—and therefore "good"—and then said:

> Without Ahimsa (non-violence) it is not possible to seek and find Truth. Ahimsa and Truth are so intertwined that it is practically impossible to disentangle and separate them. They are like two sides of a coin, or rather of a smooth, unstamped, metallic disc. Who can say which is the obverse, and which is the reverse?[17]

Yet Gandhi continues, "Ahimsa is the means; Truth is the end." Ends are central to a practice, never more than when they are contested. Without ends, participants could neither understand or direct their daily struggles, nor place their limited goals within a larger context. Pacifist theory gives an account of ends, which is tacitly assumed in maternal practice. This account allows ends to be firmly held while at the same time subordinate to means. One of its features is the narrowing of specific, immediate ends to a point where they are quite precise: a particular wage settlement or law repealed; a particular homework lesson finished or household task accomplished. These narrow ends are then subject to negotiation and compromise. (Although legend describes him as an idealistic saint, Gandhi was appropriately criticized in his lifetime because of his willingness to compromise.) The task of parent or pacifist activist is to determine some end which both parties can accept. Acceptance is, to be sure, largely a response to nonviolent coercion. But pride is preserved on both sides in the interests of reconciliation.

Narrowly specified immediate, negotiable ends are related to general goals, such as "home rules," or a "viable, independent adult." These general ends are subject to discussion and redefinition. They can be postponed without being relinquished. One appeals to them to make sense both of the narrower goal and the way it is negotiated. While these discussions about general goals among comrades and mothers are important to clarity and morale, conflict is focused on the specific and negotiable.

Gandhi insisted that both larger and narrower goals be defined in terms of what he called "human needs"—which included for him dignity and autonomy as well as material well-being. The demand to relate ends to needs in fact works as permission to compromise and relativize. One asks of one's opponents, what they, and our common community, need now in order to continue to work for the larger ends we have set ourselves. Mothers, of course, assume a common interest between themselves, other members of their household, and children's well-being. Pacifists must create a common humanity where (often) the clear evil of opponents seems to preclude it. The opposition is not as sharp as it first looks. We are increasingly coming to see that children, parents, and other household members have distinctive, often conflicting needs. Conversely, in a nuclear age, finding common humanity among opponents has become a condition of survival, turning the heroic, creative vision of a King or Gandhi into a required belief.

Even the desire to seek a common humanity depends, as does non-violence itself, upon transforming enemies into opponents for whose well-being one is concerned. Although this transformation is sometimes described as the requirement to "love" one's enemy, words like "respect," "concern," and "consideration" seem more appropriate.

> We should be happy [Jesus] did not say "like your enemies." It is almost impossible to like some people. "Like" is a sentimental and affectionate word. . . . We must develop and maintain the capacity to forgive . . . We must recognize that the evil deed of the enemy-neighbor—the thing that hurts—never quite expresses all he is . . . We must not seek to defeat or humiliate the enemy.[18]

> to act on the assumption that all men's lives are of value, that there is something about any man to be loved, whether one can feel love for him or not.[19]

The reasons pacifists give for "loving" the enemy are various, combining practical with moral, selfish with altruistic, considerations. They *must* give reasons. Mothers, by contrast, though they do not like their children all of the time, are expected to love them. They needn't justify their refusal to harm the beings whose growth is in their care. Pacifist commitment is a conscious and surprising choice; maternal non-violence is a presupposition of maternal practice and often unquestioned. Despite differences in origin and justification there are striking similarities between pacifist and maternal conceptions of the "enemy."

Both mothers and pacifists, for example, believe that forcing opponents to change their "evil" ways is an act of love, because it is good for the opponents. Mothers believe this most obviously about their own children, but also about many of their children's enemies. Both tend to believe that hatred "scars the soul,"[20] injuring both hater and hated. Both believe that it is wrong to accept injustice or aggression passively, wrong for the sufferer and harmful to the aggressor. "Personal defense" is a part of pacifist as well as maternal practice; finding nonviolent means of proud resistance is an urgent task of both maternal and pacifist strategists. And again, both mothers and pacifists believe that non-violence *works* not only to preserve community but also to change the opponent.

> It is precisely solicitude for his person in combination with a stubborn interference with his actions that can give us a very special degree of control . . . We put upon him two pressures—the pressure of our defiance of him and the pressure of our respect for his life—and it happens that in combination these two pressures are effective.[21]

We expect a mother to control a child by non-violence; we are skeptical that the pacifist even tries to do so. Nonetheless, Deming's description of pacifist action could serve to describe a mother's action as well. Moreover, when mothers are locked in combat with adolescents or young adults whose actions frighten, disappoint, or enrage them, even maternal love for the "enemy" can seem astounding. Yet mothers take risks, accepting their children's words and claims, trusting in their futures when no objective observer would, hoping when despair seems the saner council, displaying their belief in the permanent possibility of reconciliation. I am not saying that this always happens, that many mothers don't go through long nights of rejecting, hating, giving up on their children. But the risking, trusting, and hoping so central to a pacifist's relation to an enemy seems predictable in maternal practice.

I hope I have made the case for similarities between pacifist theory and maternal thinking. I believe that both pacifist and maternal thinkers could learn from their differences, especially if they were conscious of their kinship. A clear instance of similarity and beneficial difference emerges if we consider "self-suffering," a central feature of both Gandhian Satyagraha and maternal practice. Both mothers and pacifists use their own suffering to force their opponents to change. Self-sufferers appeal to the conscience of their opponents and, where conscience is unavailable, to reputation in the eyes of others. An opponent may feel guilty, ashamed, or simply inconvenienced by the long-suffering, innocent endurance of an adversary. However, neither mothers nor Satyagrahi are morally easy or politically confident about the moral emotions they induce. Mothers, I believe, have a clearer sense of the temptations and limits of self-suffering. This is largely because of the different circumstances in which their non-violent acts are called for. Whereas pacifists turn what might rightly be seen as a holy war into a conflict between humans, mothers must never allow what is only human conflict to become unduly moralized.

The limits of self-suffering illustrate the general limitation of moralism in maternal practice. Conscientiousness is a slowly developing, unpredictable capacity. Children must not see themselves as "bad," since shame and guilt can lead to anger, indifference, or uncontrollable inhibition. Although a mother will resort to techniques of self-suffering in order to affect her child's behavior, she (usually) knows that a child will not be, and cannot afford to be, too long or deeply affected by maternal tears. Nor can she restrain bigger, stronger children by a moralism that turns conscience against its possessor; nor can she allow younger, smaller children to rely excessively on the power of their suffering to influence age mates or adults.

Mothers themselves would suffer from the use of moralism. Violence is a temptation and frequent occurrence of maternal practice. Mothers do, for example, see their children, and let them see themselves, as "bad"; mothers hate and they hit; they moralize and despair. Hence, if they are committed to non-violence they must learn to blame themselves without self-hate and to forgive themselves compassionately. Maternal thinking recognizes the inevitability of "failure" and identifies moral humility as a virtue. Yet guilty self-hate (on bad days, or years) and competitive self-righteousness (in the good times) are liabilities. Both stem from an inability to acknowledge the strains and complexities of maternal life.

Violence and non-violence take many forms. What can be expected to damage, what actually damages, varies from family to family, from culture to culture. Mothers know this and avoid rigid definitions of violence or quick, judgmental identifications of the violent. Nor are they likely to escalate requirements for non-violence, to include thoughts and feelings as well as action, or to count as violent an action which only hurts or offends. Gandhi's exhortations to his satyagrahi would sound strange to maternal ears.

> Not to hurt any living thing is no doubt a part of ahimsa [non-violence]. But it is its least expression. The principle of ahimsa is hurt by every evil thought, by undue haste, by lying, by hatred, by wishing ill to anybody.
> Ahimsa really means that you may not offend anybody, you may not harbor an uncharitable thought even in connection with one who may consider himself to be your enemy.[22]

Mothers who adopted the Gandhian ideal would be in for sleepless nights. In contrast to Gandhi, they ask just which hurts, hastes, and lyings are truly damaging. They want to distinguish between the hating thought and the hateful action, since they must accept themselves as well as the complicated, unpretty psychic lives of their children.

In short, when pacifism and maternal thinking are joined, mothers can bring to the meeting realism, distrust of moralism, a sense of the limitations of self-suffering, and an awareness of the dangers of masochism and moral heroism. Rather than sharp division, the meeting could produce a shift in emphasis: from what one is willing to suffer, to what one is determined to enjoy and preserve. Though I will not argue the case here, I believe such a shift is necessary if pacifism is to become practical, widely accepted, and truly loving.

It is equally true that mothers have much to learn from the meeting. Knowledge of pacifist history and theories would make mothers aware of the pacifist bases of practices they take for granted. This would, perhaps, increase mothers' self-respect. Aware of their own kind of pacifism, mothers could extend their philosophy of conflict to enemies of their "kind," neighborhood, class or nation. Nevertheless, the natural pacifism of maternity, natural because it arises from the demands of work, feels unnatural, like vulnerable weakness in the larger world. Even humanist mothers of goodwill toward all people would have to *learn* the political significance of domestic pacifism. I maintain, first, that a basis for this lesson already exists in the maternal philosophy of conflict and, second, that mothers will be not only pupils, but teachers as well.

Thinking Warfully

I am convinced that a certain style of thinking—a tendency and ability to abstract—is connected to warfare. "Abstraction" refers to a cluster of interrelated dispositions to simplify, dissociate, generalize, and sharply define. Its opposite, which I will call "concreteness," respects complexity, connection, particularity, and ambiguity. Neither abstraction nor concreteness is good or bad in itself. Most intellectual activities require ability to abstract and in some, mathematics for example, ability and pleasure in abstraction are central. Nonetheless, I believe an inclination to think abstractly helps to explain why so many of us undertake or support violent enterprises.

There is no a priori reason why men should think more abstractly than women. I hope that in time women will take as much pleasure in their mathematical powers as men. There are, however, fairly well substantiated claims that in our society women have a cognitive style distinctly less abstract than men's.[23] I would like provisionally to accept this claim of gender difference in order to make three separate points about the possible connections between maternity, abstraction, and war.

First, if we assume that women do have a concrete cognitive style, this characteristic can be partly explained as an intelligible response to maternal work. Concreteness can be seen as a mix of interwoven responses to a growing, changing child. Neither a child nor a mother responding to her can sharply distinguish reality from fantasy, body from mind, or the child herself from the people she lives among. A mother attends to a particular child and understands her as best she can on a given day, tolerating both the ambiguity of the child's actions and the tentativeness of her own interpretations. She will eschew generalization, not only because children are very particular beings to whom she attends, but also because they confound prediction. A mother will express her knowledge in a personal voice, respecting the complexity of the children she studies and the human, social situation in which they learn.[24] In short, her thinking will be "holistic," "field-dependent," "open-ended," not because of any innate sex differences, but because that is the kind of thinking her work calls for.

Second, abstraction and concreteness have consequences for morality and therefore yield differences in men's and women's moral lives. Separating moral and human significance from other aspects of a plan or action is an aspect of abstraction. It is often said that men are more apt to engage in this sort of moral dissociation than women. Certainly, it is impossible to separate sharply moral from other aspects of maternal work or, usually, of child behavior. Along with pervasiveness of morality goes a distinctive female moral voice.[25] Women are said to be less concerned with claiming rights, more with sharing responsibilities. They do not value independence and autonomy over connection and the restraints of caring, but rather assume that the conflict between rightful self-assertion and responsible interdependence is at the heart of moral life. "Aware of the danger of an ethics abstracted from life," the development of women's moral judgment "appears to proceed from an initial concern with survival (first of herself, then of her own) to a focus on goodness, and finally to a principled understanding of non-violence as the most adequate guide to the just resolution of moral conficts."[26]

Concreteness and its moral consequences seem an unmysterious development in mothers and daughters (or sons), who learn from them a cognitive style, but evidence about the distribution of abstraction or concreteness between men and women is inconclusive. What seems to me much clearer is that abstraction and the morality to which it is conducive are warlike. Willing warriors are loyal to abstract causes and abstract states. They are encouraged to develop an "abstract hatred for the enemy" that will allow them to kill.[27] They invent weapons and pray for victories whose victims most of them would not be willing to imagine. The Physicians for Social Responsibility, who tell us what we would suffer in a nuclear holocaust, are in a long tradition of pacifist poets and writers.[28] Now, however, abstraction seems to have gripped the imagination itself. People cannot see the battles they contemplate fighting nor speak in any detail of the causes which drive them to arm themselves.

We may be able to fight only if war remains an abstract idea; we may forgive ourselves for fighting only because we can resort to the idea of a "just war" to legitimize our violence. In distinguishing between permitted and forbidden acts of war, just-war theories actually give us the conceptual tools to justify any war. They do so partly by inventing a language that encourages us to turn away from the details of suffering, to see instead the just causes and conventional rules of war. Good is distinguished from evil, soldier from civilian, war from peace. States are real entities with clear boundaries in which one's pride is invested. Autonomy, a distinct way of life, collective ownerships and identities, take precedence over the particularities of individual and community well-being. Although a civilizing presence when compared to amoral militarism, just-war theory is an exercise in abstraction.[29]

Abstract hatred and loyalties play their part in maternal militarism, too. A woman is apt to acquire men's loyalties and hate with vehemence the enemies they fight. Just as it is easier for many warriors to kill from a distance, so also it is easier to hate from well behind the lines. Often a woman finds the loss of "her" men and boys so painful that she must brutalize an image of the killer to explain his act. Moreover, her inability to separate morality from politics, combined with her long tradition of non-violence, may lead a woman to assume that a great evil is required to match the violence her "good" men perpetrate. Yet women often declare themselves disloyal to states and other abstract entities and causes. ("As a woman I have no country. As a woman I want no country. My country is the whole world.")[30] Even now, women seem especially susceptible to an imaginative grasp of the pain and hope of all fighters, and of the dailiness of the lives fighting destroys.[31] When women no longer take refuge in supportive, mourning activities, or when we no longer fight vicariously but assume responsibility for the fighting done in our name, then the "female imagination" elicited by maternal practice may apprehend the horrors of violence in all their specificity.

For warriors and for mothers, for all people, fear has a complicated significance in war and the preparation for war. Fear of our enemies gives us reason for arming, later for firing. But effective fear both creates and depends upon an abstract idea of "enemy." When we see that we are shooting at conscripts, who are young, often poor, boys, when we look at the homes where the bombs fall, pity and realism tend to crowd out fear. On the other hand, in a nuclear age, if we look closely at the destruction we contemplate, we become truly terrified. In this instance, abstraction blankets fear; close attention may terrify us into disarmament.

Fear is, then, a force for war when it creates and can depend upon abstraction; but it is also a force for peace when it is an emotional response to the apprehension of weapons' horror. Mothers are often said to be fearful creatures, which is not surprising since their children are fragile, willful beings. Fearful people feel the need of arms, and mothers are no exception. But if fear is informed by maternal concreteness, it will give way to compassion in war and to terror at its prospect. In either case, a maternal cognitive style becomes an instrument of peace.

Concreteness seems a condition of nonviolent battle. Nonviolent combatants are more apt to consider their opponents, to understand the pain their coercion causes, and of course the suffering which they themselves choose to bear. Some weapons and some opponents may be abstract—for example, an economic boycott at a distance. But if the struggle is committed to avoiding psychological as well as physical damage, the fighters or their leaders must retain some grasp of the lives they are affecting.[32] Although pacifists—like all of us—will *tend* to conceive opponents in the abstract in terms of their hated or feared group characteristics, nonviolent "love" for the "enemy" is a built-in corrective for the abstract moralism to which all fighters are liable.

Even pacifism is not immune from abstraction. In particular, the renunciation of violence may itself become abstract. If pacifists demand (as our draft boards require) that a person abjure violence in every place, at every time, or that s/he take as opponents those who choose differently, then pacifism too is asking for abstract commitment. This may show that abstraction has its place in peace as in war; I myself think it shows that pacifists should learn from maternal practice to attend to the battle at hand. But the question is a difficult one. Many peoole refuse to rule out in advance the violence that might be necessary to protect oneself or one's loved ones from immediate danger. But except in the case of a single, instantaneous response to physical attack, violence requires of good people denial and abstraction for the sake of conscience. Abstraction, once induced, then works in the interests of further violence, violence having a tendency to escalate (or so Gandhi and others thought when they demanded a general and simple renunciation of violence). When mothers become self-conscious pacifists, it will be interesting to see whether pacifism itself will change.

Eros and Destruction

Popular legend has it that the lust for battle and sexual desire are closely akin. Gandhi was sufficiently convinced of the connection between sex and violence that he urged celibacy on his followers except for rare procreative acts. On the other hand, many believe that sex and destruction are enemies, that if we would only make love we would not make war. Maternal sexuality figures ambiguously in these popular beliefs. Some pacifists and militarists who connect sex with violence believe mothers are the friends of peace, partly because they are (wrongly thought to be) asexual; nonmaternal women, by contrast, whether as adorers of the soldier-hero or submissive objects of his love, fuel the pleasure of destroyers. But to those who urge love as an alternative to war, asexual "puritanical" maternity is an obstacle to the deployment of eros in the service of peace. Each of these beliefs catches a part of the complex connections between maternity, sex, and violence. I myself believe that there is a kind of opposition between military and maternal sexuality, one that pacifists could but have not exploited. On the other hand, given the present institutions of motherhood and sexuality in America, maternal sexuality tends to be a force for war rather than peace. These hunches (they are not yet more than that) I will explore briefly.

Battlefield love and sexual fantasies arise in a misogynistic military society that exploits rigid, dichotomous definitions of "male" and "female". Indeed, it seems that soldiers are deliberately trained in a masculinist ideology that endorses blatant contempt for women. Many marching chants include degrading references to anything feminine. Sexist terms for women and their bodily parts (the two often taken to be the same) are common in military discipline as well as in play. Given the prevailing gender ideology, it is not surprising that the sexuality ascribed to soldiers on the battlefield is not only distinctly male but also narcissistic, assaultive (if not actually rapist) and predatory, indifferent to women if not actually violent toward them. Whatever destructive and abusive tendencies men may have controlled in civilian life are not only permitted but encouraged in war.

Moreover, not only is sexuality misogynistic and destructive, but worse, destruction is eroticized. Many battlefield accounts report the obvious sexual pleasure some men take in killing and in various other abusive acts—to women certainly, but also to men, especially racially different men, and even children. Officers often encourage this lust, for no abstraction or moral conviction can insure the battle spirit that will ensure easy killing.[33]

Destruction, heterosexual fantasy, and heterosexual acts take place within a military society that, at least in our society, is officially and blatantly homophobic. The all-male military experience would seem to provide considerable opportunity for exploring homoerotic pleasures unavailable in civilian life. Certainly the ecstatic bonding between men responsible for many acts of courage or outrageous cruelty has its strong erotic components. And surely some homosexual love flourishes in the battlefield. But explicit homophobia and masculinism preclude for many the homosexual experiences that could recall the pleasures of connection, could make the body adored and treasured. Friendship between men has been called the "true enemy of battle," for it encourages a love of self—one's own and one's friend's—which destroys the destroyer's pleasure.[34] Were such love sexualized, battle might stop. On the other hand, Plato felt that an army of homosexual lovers would be invincible. They would fight for love and for honor in each others' eyes, and their courage would know no moderation. Certainly, our own ecstatic male bonders seem akin to Plato's ideal soldiers.[35]

I myself am not sure of anything about soldiers' sexual lives let alone sexual fantasies. Often the individual soldier seems anything but excitedly battle-like. Cold, frightened, exhausted, numb, confused, and eager to get home, he seems neither sexually excited nor sexually (as opposed to maternally) desirable. I believe that many soldiers sometimes take an orgasmic pleasure in acts of destruction and cruelty, that many more routinely abuse women as a matter of battle right. How many? And how central are these erotic destroyers and destructive lovers to the military enterprise? I don't know.

Some soldiers, of course, have romantic attachments to their sweethearts at home or those they meet behind the lines and love passionately, poignantly, and tenderly in the midst of danger. Moreover, soldiers engage in one kind of love that is attributed to women (at least it is specifically feared and punished in women): love between a woman and a soldier she considers her enemy. Who is this woman? Who is the sweetheart? How does female sexuality fit into the military picture?

There is some reason to believe that women are less apt than men to eroticize combat, more apt to eroticize reconciliation. "Sleeping with the enemy" arises, I suppose, as often from poverty and fear as from any passion. Yet men may be correct to suspect in women a sexuality that is in the service of connection rather than separation, a "making-up" rather than an undoing. When women do eroticize combat, they may be more apt to eroticize submission than conquest. If women do tend to eroticize reconciliation and, in combat, submission, then female libidinal energy will not inspire in women the lust for battle. The sweetheart, however, may reward, or at least condone, that lust in men. Her purer love is able to redeem the soldier from the destructive sexuality and eroticized destruction which he undergoes, as it were, carried "outside of himself." Were the women at home to find a fighting soldier disgusting, his pleasure in fighting might be significantly diminished.

I have been talking about possible *female* sexual fantasies and sexual roles. Female sexuality includes, for some women who are mothers or are otherwise intensely involved in maternal work, a maternal sexuality that is a quieter, less obviously sexual aspect of the whole erotic life. Maternal sexuality is not, of course, separable from the entire adult sexual life in which it is embedded. Although some mothers insist on separating maternal from sexual love, even those women bring to their relation with children their own variant of "female" sexual fantasies, whatever these may be. I cannot explore here the fascinating connections between adult sexuality and maternal love. Rather, I want to focus on a narrower maternal sexuality with interesting connections to military gender ideology and the erotics of destruction.

By *maternal sexuality* I mean the diffuse eroticism that arises from and is shaped by caring for children. This sexuality has at least two aspects, one deriving from the infant-mother, then child-mother, relation, the other deriving from the independent eroticism of the maturing child. Much has been written about maternal sexuality from the child's point of view. Dorothy Dinnerstein has evocatively described our longing for the pleasure of mother love with its diffuse sensuality, guiltless materiality, and total merging.[36] We know that we resentfully abandon our first mother-loves and both long for and fear a return to them. Nonetheless, little has been written about this phenomenon from the point of view of a mother who is herself a grown-up infant with the ambivalent longings that Dinnerstein describes.

Mothers witness, to some extent direct, and are frequently an object of the infant-child's primitive, pan-erotic desires. Mothers enjoy, control, or deny their own erotic responses to their children. Later a mother watches with mixed feelings as a child develops a sexuality nearly independent of her. Contrary to legend, many mothers recognize that their children's independent sexuality is a condition of their autonomous, pleasurable adulthood. Yet this same sexuality is an important phase in a mother's "losing" her children to adulthood and in her recalling her own unresolved earlier sexual conflicts. Moreover, in our society, especially for girls, sexuality is frequently a source of folly, pain, and danger to her children which a mother is helpless to control. This watching, separating, fearing, and vicariously enjoying is part of a mother's life in a society which most often denies and exploits her own sexuality, leaves her little control over her own sexual-reproductive life, and little power except over small children. It is not surprising that explicable tendencies to fearfulness and suppression are magnified. Even now, many mothers take the adolescence of their children as an occasion to reflect upon and reaffirm the good of sexual pleasure and autonomy.

It may be true, however, that in our society maternal sexuality is as conducive to battle as to peace. The sexual morality explicitly urged on mothers is one of denial and repression. Unrecognized desires can enhance the lure of the soldier, find vicarious expression in battlefield lust, or be transmogrified by projection into the body of an enemy attacker. Moreover, denial and repression can take on a life of their own, psychically impoverishing the mother and estranging the child. I believe, however, that a mother freed from excesses of denial and repression could encourage an eroticism inimical to the military in at least two ways. She could welcome the surprisingly various erotic pleasures and fluid gender identities she witnesses and experiences with her children. Second, and at the same time, she could control in herself and in her children battlelike sexual impulses.

Mothers have a special opportunity to welcome infant-child erotic life. This involves protecting, even cherishing, disordered, sensual, bodily being; it requires tolerating surprising, intense desires in one's self and one's child; it means playing with new and expansive gender identities rather than fearfully controlling them. Welcoming and acknowledging eroticism where it begins is a first step in what Dorothy Dinnerstein has called the "mobilization of eros." A mother at ease with the complexities of eroticism could welcome in young adults genuine diversity in sexual expression and choices. Sexual freedom and the pleasure it allows are at odds with a rigid, dichotomous gender ideology, with monolithic military control of sexual variety and with the simple, predatory sexuality of battle.

On the other hand, a kind of sexual permissiveness dear to libertarians (and to me) will remain at odds with maternal practices in the freest societies. The vulnerability of an infant, the necessity of adolescent independence, the inappropriateness of genital or other explicit sexual acts with children all make maternal self-control necessary, not just some puritan fantasy. Recognizing the complexities of eroticism, mothers can also respect its power. A mother will insist upon "moralizing" sexual-aggressive life. Many sexual impulses, if acted upon, could only exploit or hurt her children. For example, the alluring helplessness of a child who is also stubborn and disobedient could be a powerful stimulus to sadistic excitement both for a mother and an older sibling. But sadism, however understandable, is not permitted. Children are not "consenting adults." For good reasons, a mother must often control in herself and discourage in her children the sexualization of conquest, cruelty, destruction, and domination, the very same impulses that are encouraged and sexualized in battle. In general, the simultaneous acceptance of disorderly, pleasureful eroticism, combined with the moralization of specific sexual-aggressive impulses, could put maternal sexuality distinctly at odds with military mores.

Military Mothers and Feminist Politics—A Concluding Note

I hope I have shown that there is some basis for the claim that mothers have distinctive interests in and capacities for reconciliation and nonviolent battle. Maternal preservative love is at odds with military destruction but requires a philosophy of conflict with many similarities to pacifism. The cognitive style that arises from maternal practice and articulates its thinking is opposed to war-like abstraction. If there is a female sexuality, it may well be opposed to the sexuality encouraged in battle. Ideal maternal sexuality encourages a self-respecting, disorderly eroticism inimical to military control. Moreover, mothers control in themselves and their children the very impulses that militarists exploit.

Yet, as we know, mothers are militarists. Some mothers, those we (pacifists) like to remember first, fight in defense of their homeland or in civil revolutionary struggles to bring justice to their children. Self-defense and armed revolutionary justice can seem a direct expression of preservative love, as long as we allow the use of violence in any cause. Thus, these cases, although crucial for developing a realistic, humane commitment to non-violence, do not seriously undermine the case for a pacifist basis of maternal practice. But self-defense and revolutionary struggle often acquire erotic destructiveness, abstract hatreds, and chimerical victories so characteristic of war. Moreover, women in increasing numbers are insisting on the right to fight—to bomb, spray nerve gas, release torpedoes—and their reasons for fighting seem no more moral, no less moralized, rationalized, and abstract, than men's. Or, more accurately, since I know little about these women, even if female warriorhood is now less easily violent than men's, there is no reason to believe that such a difference would survive military training, changed social relations, and a new conception of female strength.

Pacifism certainly does not flow from women's nature. Even if it arises understandably from maternal practice, it will have to be articulated and honored if it is to become a basis for organizing women in the interests of peace. But, for this to occur, maternal pacifism would have to become publicly pacifist. I do not believe that the militancy of mothers is incompatible with the maternal pacifism I have described. But if maternal peacefulness is to become a force for peace, maternal practice itself must be transformed.

The principal agent of transformation is, I believe, feminist politics. By "feminist politics" I mean the commitment to eliminate all restrictions of power, pleasure, and mastery arising from biological sex or social constructions of gender, so that women will have as much (and as little) control as men over their individual and collective lives. This is both a restrictive and inclusive definition of feminism. It is inclusive because it allows people to be feminists who are statists or anarchists, capitalists or socialists, men or women. It focuses on a single intellectual and emotional source of feminism, a sense of injustice to women and a determination to rectify it. It is restrictive because it ignores the many other social ideals feminists hold. Most feminists, (and I too) believe that a commitment to justice for all women entails a commitment to economic and racial justice for all people. Many feminists (and I too) believe that feminism leads to anti-militarism both on economic and moral grounds. For the purposes of this paper, however, I leave the wider implications of feminism to one side. Feminists, in my sense, committed to women's equality with men, can be (and unfortunately have been) racist, exploitative, hierarchical, and militarist. Nonetheless, I believe this restricted feminism will be a transformative agent in rendering maternal peacefulness publically effective. Maternal militarism arises in part from womens' confinement and powerlessness.[37] It also arises from human, broadly social, and maternal conditions. Feminism is not the only force for maternal peacefulness, nor is it a sufficient one. But by undermining a number of interdependent motives for militarism, it can free women to articulate for themselves a publicly effective pacifism. Let me give some examples.

For women confined in domestic life, war offers real education, new training and job experience, economic power, travel, and a sense of communal life. It is no wonder then that they welcome its occurrence. "Consciously she desire(s) our splendid empire; unconsciously she desire(s) our war".[38] Freedom and effectiveness would do much to reduce this desire. Mothers' need for order, frustrated by the unpredictability of the world, finds a relief in military discipline. When women and men share both the burdens of parenthood and the pleasures of mastery, mothers will have new opportunities and energies for satisfying their need for control and order. In war, unacknowledged violent impulses find a legitimate expression, vicariously safe. Feminism breaks down the split between male and female, attributing to both sexes capacities for rage as well as gentleness. It insists on human—not sexual—responsibility for public actions. It grants to women the authority of conscience, with all its discomforts. Mothers beginning to see the world through feminist eyes would find it difficult to enjoy *vicarious* battle pleasures and angers, and impossible to maintain a split-off innocence.

Even women who are now true peace lovers, who dread war's horrors and value the texture of the lives it destroys, can come to endorse the war policies of their government. Women, a powerless group, may be especially fearful of alleged aggression. In the face of real or imagined threats, weapons can be wonderful, especially if carried by others, while to let one's "own men" remain unarmed can seem the epitome of vulnerability. And perhaps most important, even peace-loving women, especially if undereducated and economically dependent, allow men, both the leaders and those at home, to judge for them the reality of a danger and the best method of meeting it. "The mother of her race, with all her fine emotions of sheltering care, comes through dependence to the opinions of the fighting male.³⁹

Feminism, by increasing women's power, independence, and authority, undermines all these sources of militarism. Perhaps its effect would be most profound in changing maternal sexuality into a moral, welcoming eroticism opposed to the military. Even the most restricted feminism takes as one of its central aims understanding and overcoming homophobia. For only women undaunted by charges of lesbianism and unafraid of their own homoerotic desires will be able to sustain an identity with women and rid themselves of female self-hatred. Mothers aware and unafraid of their homosexual as well as heterosexual desires should be better able to tolerate the surprising complexity of their own and their children's eroticism. Feminist analysis of sexuality breaks down the distinction between socially constructed and biologically compelling desire, between "normal" and "deviant" sexual practices. It reveals the power politics of sexuality and asks everyone to be responsible for the choices and character of their sexual lives. Some women will still be liable to the psychosexual desire to serve and adore an armed endangered male. But any sexual desire is less compelling and more subject to reflection, if most sexual desires can seem normally natural and socially variable.

No amount of feminist change is sufficient to eliminate tendencies toward or trust in violence. Parents of both sexes will always have to deal with the mess and chanciness of mortal life, varieties of desire that make sex destructive or destruction erotic, unmanageable fears of those who hate, of the hateful who are armed. Nor is feminist politics always the surest way to combat motherly militarism. At this time in America, for example, I believe that the full employment of young people in minimally dignified work would do more to undermine maternal support for the All Volunteer Forces than any feminist reform. But feminism, I believe, undermines most deeply and lastingly a variety of interdependent motives mothers have for trusting in violence and in the states which organize and perpetrate it.

No one cay say what, if anything, will enable our species to renounce weapons that damage and to learn nonviolent methods of getting what we need and protecting what we love. Our nightmare fears and moral visions reveal the same truth: we must learn to live together nonviolently or perish as a species, as peoples, as the individuals we are and care for. I know that "peace" is not a single condition but means very different things to oppressor and oppressed, to privileged and impoverished. Yet pacifist renunciation seems to be a necessity—eventually for everyone, right now for any people whose armies possess nuclear or even highly destructive conventional weapons.

In my hopeful moments, it seems to me that women who insist simultaneously on newly defined independent female strength and on traditional feminine nurturance comprise an original peace brigade—erotic, courageous, protective, and sane. The orgins of war and peacefulness are obscure. Yet it is certain that some of the roots of violence are embedded in our sexuality and gender arrangements, while important roots of protectiveness and connection are embedded in our memories and visions of maternal care. It seems, then, not unreasonable to expect new possibilities of peace when a feminist transformation of gender and sexuality is joined with an ancient preservative love.

Notes

I am grateful to Carol Ascher, Evelyn Keller, William Ruddick, and Marilyn Young for careful, critical readings of an earlier draft of this paper.

1. Dr. Helen Caldicott, quoted in the War Resisters League Calendar, 1981.
2. See especially Barbara J. Steinson, " 'The Mother Half of Humanity': American Women in the Peace and Preparedness Movements in World War I," in *Women, War and Revolution,* edited by Carol R. Berkin and Clara M. Lovett (New York: Holmes & Meier, 1980); and Jean Bethke Elshtain, "Women as Mirror and Other: Towards a Theory of Women, War and Feminism" (unpublished manuscript).
3. A Nazi mother cited in Leila J. Rupp, *Mobilizing Women for War* (Princeton: Princeton University Press, 1978).
4. "Maternal Thinking," this volume, pp. 213-230.
5. See Jurgen Habermas, *Knowledge and Human Interests* (Boston: Beacon Press, 1971).
6. See especially Nancy Chodorow, *The Reproduction of Mothering* (Berkeley: University of California Press, 1978); and Carol Gilligan *In a Different Voice: Psychological Theory and Women's Development* (Cambridge, Mass.: Harvard University Press, 1982).
7. Ruddick, "Maternal Thinking," this volume, pp. 213-230.
8. Iris Murdoch, *The Sovereignty of Good* (New York: Schocken, 1971), pp. 28, 65, 91, passim. Simone Weil, "Reflections on the Right Use of School Studies with an Eye Toward the Love of God," and "Human Personality," in *Simone Weil Reader,* edited by George A. Panichas (New York: McKay, 1977), pp. 51 and passim, and pp. 313-39, respectively.
9. See especially Nancy Chodorow, "Feminism and Difference: Gender, Relation and Difference in Psychoanalytic Perspective," *Socialist Review,* July–August 1979; Carol Gilligan, "In a Different Voice"; and especially Jean Baker Miller, *Toward a New Psychology of Women* (Boston: Beacon Press, 1976).
10. Throughout, I will present the basic concepts of pacifism oversimply. Although I myself am increasingly pacifist and certainly believe that non-violence is required of any nuclear power, I am not, in this essay, attempting to convince the reader or assuming

her agreement. Nor am I doing justice to the intricacies and complexity of pacifist theory, which would require a paper in itself.

11. Whether or not there is a military strategy which all warring nations and groups fall into as violence escalates is a controversial question. I am inclined to think that, despite variation, there is a "law of violence" to which the best intended fighters fall prey. But I do not argue this point—which is one that divides pacifists and just-war theorists—here.

12. The phrase "preservative love" comes from Harriet Stanton Blatch, *A Woman's Point of View: Some Roads to Peace* (New York: The Woman's Press, 1920). By "preservative love" I mean the activity of caring for children, governed by the three interests in preservation, growth, and acceptability. For more on this activity and the thinking that arises from it, see my "Maternal Thinking," this volume.

13. I have drawn my very limited knowledge of the military from several battle memoirs and, more important, from analyses of battle and just-war theory. I recommend particularly John Kegan, *The Face of Battle* (New York: Viking, 1976); Arthur Danto, "On Moral Codes and Modern War," *Social Research,* Spring 1978; H. J. N. Horsburgh, *Non-Violence and Aggression* (London: Oxford University Press, 1978); Michael Walzer, *Just and Unjust Wars* (New York: Basic Books, 1977); Paul Fussell, *The Great War and Modern Memory* (New York and London: Oxford University Press, 1975); and Kenneth Kaunda, *The Riddle of Violence* (New York: Harper & Row, 1980). By far the most useful book on war has been J. Glenn Gray, *The Warriors* (New York: Harper Torchbook, 1959, 1967, 1970). I have cited nothing from Gray that was not corroborated in at least two other analyses or memoirs.

14. Gray, *The Warriors,* p. 86.

15. Horsburgh, *Non-Violence and Aggression.*

16. Dorothy Dinnerstein, *The Mermaid and the Minotaur* (New York: Harper & Row, 1976).

17. M. K. Gandhi, *Non-Violent Resistance* (New York: Schocken Books, 1961), p. 43. Also quoted in Joan V. Bondurant, *Conquest of Violence: The Gandhian Philosophy of Conflict* (Berkeley: University of California Press, 1971).

18. Martin Luther King, "Loving Your Enemies," a speech delivered Christmas, 1957, at Montgomery, Alabama.

19. Barbara Deming, *Revolution and Equilibrium* (New York: A. J. Muste Memorial Institute Essay Series, 1981).

20. King, "Loving Your Enemies."

21. Deming, *Revolution and Equilibrium.*

22. Bondurant, *Conquest of Violence,* pp. 24, 25. Many of the points I make here are similar to those made by Erik Erikson, *Gandhi's Truth* (New York: W.W. Norton, 1969).

23. For a critical review of the literature, see Eleanor Maccoby and Carol Jacklin, *The Psychology of Sex Differences* (Stanford: Stanford University Press, 1974). Maccoby and Jacklin are critical of the beliefs I report here. For a discussion of my use of "evidence" see my "Maternal Thinking." See also the evidence summarized in Helen Block Lewis, *Shame and Guilt in Neurosis* (New York: International Universities Press, 1971); and Patricia Meyers Spack, *The Female Imagination* (New York: Alfred A. Knopf, 1972). See also the research reported by Phyllis Rose on the work of psychologist David McClelland, in *Woman of Letters: A Biography of Virginia Woolf* (London: Oxford University Press, 1978), p. 101. The preliminary reports of Mary Belenky, Blythe Clinchy, Nancy Goldberger and Jill Tarule on their project "Education for Women's Development" seem to me strongly to support these claims (may be obtained from Nancy Goldberger, Simon's Rock of Bard College, Great Barrington, MA 02130). Belief in women's relative concreteness is widespread; it is supported by the work of numerous women writers of fiction and (especially feminist) art critics and

literary critics of women's work. Chodorow and Gilligan make theoretical sense of the difference, if it exists, as does Evelyn Fox Keller in her various writings on women and science. For Keller, see especially "Gender and Science," in *Psychoanalysis and Contemporary Thought* (1978); and *He, She, and Id in Scientific Discourse* (New York: Longman, forthcoming). Jean Baker Miller, in *Toward a New Psychology of Women* (Boston: Beacon Press, 1973), has undertaken to describe and honor women's special interests and capacities while insisting on the possibility and necessity of change. I consider her work to be the clearest predecessor of my own.

24. Belenky, et al., Newsletter #2, available from Nancy Goldberger.

25. Carol Gilligan, "In a Different Voice."

26. Ibid., p. 515.

27. J. Glenn Gray, *The Warriors,* passim; Horsburgh, *Non-Violence and Aggression,* especially chapter 1.

28. For example, Mark Twain's "War Prayer" and several poems of Wilfred Owen. It is now becoming commonplace to speak of the abstraction required of those who plan for or contemplate nuclear war. Nonetheless, I continue to find truly shocking the way in which men and women deny and distort the activities in which they are engaged, concealing the human significance of those activities in clichés suitable, if at all, for former conventional wars in which some died and some survived, or, more often, concealing the true nature of their projects in the language of high-tech weapons research. My (few) personal conversations with Pentagon officials and military advisors entirely support the now-common claim that planners do not think of lives—of the bodies or psyches they are putting at risk—but of numbers, "victories," "enemies" and the like. One short illustration of the inclination to abstract by one who formerly engaged in it is by Henry T. Nash, "The Bureaucratization of Homicide," in *Protest and Survive,* edited by E. P. Thompson (New York and London: Monthly Review Press, 1981).

29. Walzer, *Just and Unjust Wars,* is the best (and an excellent) presentation of just-war theory. Kaunda, *The Riddle of Violence,* both attacks the theory and expresses a moving and coherent version of it. Danto, "On Moral Codes," defends the theory but gives a provocative rendition of it that seems to require non-violence of any country possessing and therefore likely to use (see Horsburgh and Walzer) high-tech conventional, let alone nuclear, weapons.

30. Virginia Woolf, *Three Guineas* (New York: Harcourt, Brace and World, 1936). Her words—and this particular statement—have obviously appealed to countless women who now make use of them. Other feminist writing also expresses anti-state sentiments of feminists.

31. For a wonderful example of the struggle between concreteness and ferocious abstraction as a young girl tries to understand war and its killing, see Ella Leffland, *Rumours of Peace* (New York: Popular Library, 1980).

32. In discussing nonviolent action it is important to distinguish damage—serious and indefinitely lasting, often irreparable harm—from temporary psychological or physical pain, which may be a necessary adjunct to change, and/or which has compensatory benefits.

33. See Gray, *The Warriors;* Tim O'Brien, *If I Die in a Combat Zone* (New York: Dell, 1979); and David Marlowe, "The Manning of the Force and the Structure of Battle: AVF, Draft, Men, Women," in *Conscripts and Volunteers: Military Requirements, Social Justice, and the All-Volunteer Force,* edited by Robert K. Fullinwider (Totowa, NJ: Rowman & Allanheld, 1983), for three quite different accounts of misogyny, masculinism, and sexuality in the military. My remarks here do not seem controversial (although they sound as if they should be). On the other hand, many believe that military misogyny and predatory sexuality are not *necessarily* adjuncts of war, and even that certain armies (e.g., the army of Israel) may now be free of them.

34. Gray, *The Warriors.*

35. Plato, *The Symposium.*
36. Dinnerstein, *The Mermaid and the Minotaur.*
37. Restrictive feminism is nonetheless radical. To confront, analyze, and work against the subordination of women requires rethinking and changing our sexual, domestic, intellectual—and eventually even fantasy—lives. I use this restrictive definition of feminism for three reasons. First, by being inclusive, it allows feminists of quite different persuasions to talk (and listen?) to each other. Second, it acknowledges the dangers many feminists (and I too) feel when women begin to celebrate the maternal. A restrictive definition of feminism at least allows and supplies words for the plausible charge that projects like mine are *anti*-feminist. I want to maintain tension and keep the dialogues going, including those within our ranks and within our own heads. Finally, I believe that this restrictive feminism leads quickly to a focus on the very issues of authority, cheery denial, inauthenticity, homophobia, and repressive sexuality that are central both to the failures of maternal thinking and the militarism of mothers.
38. Woolf, *Three Guineas,* p. 39.
39. Blatch, *A Woman's Point of View,* p. 169.

15

Toward an Ethic of Nurturance: Luce Irigaray on Mothering and Power

ELÉANOR H. KUYKENDALL

Nurturance, or the providing of material and emotional support to a dependent or vulnerable being, such as a child, has traditionally fallen to women, and especially to mothers. Sometimes nurturance has been seen as a culturally imposed task, and so as an aspect of women's oppression in which women become merely mothers. But sometimes the capacity to nurture, as in mothering, has been seen instead as a gift, or rather as a special power at once corporeal and psychic. In French feminist theory there has recently appeared *écriture féminine* (feminine writing), writing that evokes women's power as women's bodily experience, as of giving birth and nursing. Some of these works have become available in English. They are fascinating for the reader but demand explanation and evaluation.

Two works by Luce Irigaray, a French psychoanalyst trained as a philosopher, are psychological and mythic descriptions of mothering that imply a feminist ethic of nurturance. The first, "And the One Doesn't Stir without the Other,"[1] was published in English as a poetic article evoking the ambivalence of the mother-daughter relationship and seeking a resolution of that ambivalence. The second *Le corps à corps avec la mère*, is a speech and two interviews explaining the first and other works in ordinary French.[2]

I will begin by presenting Irigaray's "And the One Doesn't Stir without the Other" as a feminist interpretation of transformative power and mutuality through the mother-daughter relationship. In Part II I will suggest that the ethic of nurturance implicit in Irigaray's proposals for a matriarchy lacks a supporting political analysis.

I

Two principles, at least, are necessary to the development of a feminist ethic of nurturance. The first is that the power exercised by the nurturer toward the nurtured (as by mother toward child) be not merely dominant or controlling, but primarily healing, creative, and transformative. The second principle, which complements the first, is that the relationship between the nurturer and the nurtured be not merely symmetrical, but at least potentially mutual and reciprocal. To offer an example, if I am your biological sister and you are my biological sister, the relationship between us is so far merely symmetrical; but if we engage in a further relationship that transforms both of us, then the relationship becomes mutual and reciprocal in the feminist sense of "sister."

These conceptions of power and mutuality can, of course, be characterized in other ways. For example Mohandas K. Gandhi's conception of *satyagraha,* or truth-force, is also of a healing, transformative, nonviolent creative power, used morally to oppose the British Empire. And Immanuel Kant's vision of a Kingdom of Ends (in which each person would treat every other person as an end, or ultimate value, rather than as merely a means) is a utopia in which mutual and reciprocal relationships would prevail. Both of these are essentially spiritual conceptions of power and mutuality. But developed conceptions of transformative power and mutuality are to be found especially in the writings of feminists of varying persuasions, e.g., Mary Daly, Audrey Lorde, Tillie Olsen, Adrienne Rich, and Simone de Beauvoir. Yet Beauvoir has consistently held that the received description of much of women's bodily experience, which is culturally bound, is not to be replaced by a feminist description of it as a manifestation of a natural power.

Among these various approaches we find general agreement that there is something revolutionary about that power characterized as healing and transformative, especially if it can also be characterized as women's power. As Simone de Beauvoir said in 1978 in response to an interviewer who asked whether more women should stand for election to offices in which, of course, power would be enacted classically as dominance: "It is a delicate problem because if women want to take power in the manner of men, it's not worth it. What we really want to change is all these notions and values."[3] There is general agreement, as well, that feminist conceptions of mutual and reciprocal relationships carry with them a conception of mutual recognition by each person of the other, involving transformative contact. For example, in interviews with Sartre recorded in 1974 and published later by Simone de Beauvoir, she reproaches him for his unwillingness to ask directions in strange cities by observing, "To ask someone the name of a street or to ask a small favor of someone is to place oneself within a schema of reciprocity; it is to recognize the other person in sum as your equal, as just anyone, like you; it is not then to go to beg like a beggar."[4] Recent feminist arguments emphasize recognition rather than equality as a mark of mutuality, and some, like Luce Irigaray's, verge on a conception of mutuality as identity, as in the identity of mother with daughter.

For Irigaray as well, a feminist enactment of mutuality between mother and daughter amounts to mutual empowerment:

> It will be necessary for us somehow to mourn an all-powerful maternal presence (the last refuge) and to establish with our mothers a relationship of reciprocity woman to woman, where they could also eventually feel themselves to be our daughters. In sum, to liberate ourselves with our mothers. That is an indispensable condition for our emancipation from the authority of our fathers. The mother/daughter, daughter/mother relation constitutes an extremely explosive core in our societies. To think it, to change it, leads to shaking up the patriarchal order.[5]

It is clear from this passage that Irigaray does not think that there is now a psychological or political climate of mother/daughter reciprocity in the cultures we know.

"And the One Doesn't Stir without the Other" is as much about the psychic struggle to attain reciprocity as it is about empowerment. It concerns the mother's ambivalence toward the daughter and the daughter's toward the mother, the mother's resentment of sacrifice and the daughter's resentment of control. This work, although written personally and anecdotally, can be seen as both developmental and historical. The conception of nurturance presented by Irigaray through the example of mothering is also dialectical in the historical sense that previous stages of biological and moral development appear to contradict the present one.

Since people develop and change over time, to propose transformative power as as fundamental principle of nurturance is not to deny that there may also be an element of control, since little children have to be controlled and since through their own dependencies they control those upon whom they are dependent. There may also be an element of asymmetry in a nurturing relationship, as in the mother's relationship with the newborn who is entirely dependent and who cannot at first offer her nurturer even a smile. But to propose transformative power and reciprocity as principles of nurturance is to carry with this proposal a further commitment: in any relationship that persists through time, as in the relationship between daughters and mothers, the relationship is ethical to the degree that the participants are able to develop it as primarily mutual and reciprocal, and as supportive and transformative of both.

Luce Irigaray's psychological evaluation in "And the One Doesn't Stir" is that too often this does not happen between mother and daughter. Rather, the two become locked in ambivalence, as Simone de Beauvoir had already suggested in *The Second Sex,* and reconciliation with the mother is painful, as Beauvoir had already suggested in *A Very Easy Death,* which concerns the death of her own mother. The physical processes of pregnancy and birth, as well as nursing, require the mother to accept constantly shifting definitions of her body and to accept her growing infant as Other in much the same way as Beauvoir claims in *The Second Sex* that men view women as Other. The Otherness of the infant is wounding to both, according to Irigaray, who writes that our irreparable wound is the cutting of the umbilical cord and not, as Freud had fantasized, castration.[6] When the infant separated from the mother is a daughter, Irigaray argues on the basis of her practice as a psychoanalyst, both the mother's and the daughter's definitions of themselves become confused. Of course, established psychoanalytic theory (Freud, as interpreted in France by Jacques Lacan) concerns itself primarily with the problems of the male infant who must separate himself from his mother.[7] These patriarchal conceptions of the mother-infant relationship, Irigaray proposes, overlook the daughter's psychic need to identify with her mother; they also overlook the mother's psychic need to identify with her daughter as a being not only of the same sex but also of the same sort of sexuality, which she experiences in a way that differs from traditional psychoanalytic definitions of that need for identification.

Consequently, mother and daughter become caught in a classic double bind in which they cannot act, because each depends on the other in a way that neither can define. In this double bind, the mother's approach to the daughter or the daughter's to the mother becomes misunderstood, and neither mother nor daughter can resolve the situation. "And the One Doesn't Stir" is written from the point of view of the daughter (or, perhaps, of the daughter's therapist) and is intended to evoke in us, rather than to lead us cognitively to comprehend, the double bind between mother and daughter that Irigaray believes damages both, and which she takes as her task, both as therapist and as theorist, to help mother and daughter break.

Irigaray characterizes this double bind by use of bodily imagery, and indeed the nurturing that any mother must offer her child is primarily of a physical nature at first. But Irigaray has the daughter open the essay with a chilling image of the psychic paralysis into which she has thereby fallen in receiving this nurturance:

> With your milk, Mother, I swallowed ice. And here I am now, my insides frozen. And I walk with even more difficulty than you do, and I move even less. You flowed into me, and that hot liquid became poison, paralyzing me. My blood no longer circulates to my feet or my hands, or as far as my head. . . . And I can no longer race toward what I love.[8]

The daughter here speaks of a paralysis psychically transmitted to her by a mother who herself was paralyzed by a like process:

> You look at yourself in the mirror. And already you see your own mother there. And soon your daughter, a mother. Between the two, what are you? What space is yours alone? In what frame must you contain yourself? And how to let your face show through, beyond all the masks?[9]

Here it will be helpful to explain that underlying Irigaray's attempt here to evoke the sense of powerlessness which, she believes, mothers transmit to their daughters, is a method that might be thought of as historical or, better yet, as genealogical, in at least three ways. First, it locates the source of what Irigaray believes is a psychic paralysis common to women in the transmission of that paralysis from generation to generation, by way of the mother. Second, in tracing the genealogy or origins of both life-affirming and life-negating emotions, Irigaray is treating them not in an isolated fashion as psychic phenomena, but rather as represented symbolically in the body, itself a hierarchy of forces whose organization indicates health or disease. Thus, the values of reciprocity and of healing power in mother-daughter relationships or in any other relationships are values that must be arrived at rather as a diagnostic of the organization of a symbolic system—the body or language—than as given in advance. All that is given in advance is that an ethical mode of action must be life-affirming and that in our bodies or in our speech we manifest these life-affirming values, or we do not. Third, Irigaray is clearly proposing that relationships between mother and daughter be recreated as supportive of life-affirming emotions, and that when this done, the revolutionary result will be psychological empowerment of women.[10]

From these three points we can see that an ethic which Irigaray can develop from her perception of women as experiencing ourselves as paralyzed, unable to act, must begin by healing what she believes is a life-destroying breach between mother and daughter. But how can this healing happen when, according to the assumptions of a patriarchal ethic such as Freud's, it is the obligation of both mother and daughter to separate from one another, even as the daughter's existence assures the mother's descendence, but at the same time destroys her: "With your milk, Mother, you fed me ice. And if I leave, you lose the reflection of life, of your life. And if I remain, am I not the guarantor of your death? Each of us lacks her own image; her own face, the animation of her own body is missing."[11] The ethical imperative that Irigaray would draw in "And the One Doesn't Stir" is to cease to pursue the psychic separation between mother and daughter required by patriarchy. For she writes at the end, "What I wanted from you, Mother, was this: that in giving me life, you still remain alive."[12]

Suppose, then, that we consider the possibility of a matriarchal ethic to replace that patriarchal imperative to separate mother from daughter. I have already said that an ethic of nurturance, to which I believe a matriarchal ethic might contribute, must affirm reciprocity and transformative power as animating principles in human relationships. But how can we develop these notions from the essentially poetic, noncognitive analysis of mother-daughter paralysis and separation found in "And the One Doesn't Stir without the Other"? In her Montreal interviews Irigaray provides further explanations (in ordinary French this time), which I will now translate into English to try to make some progress in answering this question.

First, when asked to comment on the last line of "And the One Doesn't Stir," which is, "What I wanted from you, Mother, was this: that in giving me life, you still remain alive," Irigaray said in the interview, "That means, 'Don't be only a mother,' and, as Hegel said, 'Don't let the child that I am kill the mother that you are, but be something other than the simple maternal function.' " When asked to elaborate, Irigaray added as a further interpretation of this passage:

> Don't reduce yourself to a maternal function and don't reduce me to the function of a child. That would mean: it's a mortal conflict, the mother that you were and the mother that I will become. . . . If I become something other than your production, you will continue to exist. If you are a woman and I am a woman, we don't reduce ourselves to a simple maternal function prescribed by society.[13]

These views would be accepted by any feminist and by many others as well. But to them Irigaray adds a far more controversial point, which presents a view common to all of her writings. It is that we must seek the life-affirming values of reciprocity and healing power in discovering the positive characteristics of feminine sexuality. By this she explicitly means characteristics other than those of the biological or psychic processes of mothering, other than those a woman discovers with a man, but rather what women can come to discover through identification with their mothers and through their mothers, with other women. For Irigaray thinks of the mother-daughter relationship as erotic and as a model for other possible relationships among women.

Irigaray's proposal for healing or transformative power as a principle of action is tied to this notion of identification with our mothers, and so too is her conception of reciprocity. The resulting ethic is a matter of giving up the conception of power with which men operate and which, Irigaray says, men have imposed on women in confining us to the maternal function. For example, in *The Critique of Dialectical Reason* Sartre wrote of an ethical relationship of brotherhood which, he proposed there, originated in the bonding of men who perceived themselves as oppressed, "We are brothers in that *we are our own sons,* our common creation."[14] If the reverse were true it might read, in accordance with Irigaray's proposal for mother-daughter reciprocity, "We are sisters in that *we are our own daughters,* our common creation," a rewriting of the myth of male creation that Sartre perpetuates.

But Irigaray has specifically warned that she is not advocating a simple reversal of male power relationships within the same system. Nor can a conception of matriarchy as sisterhood adopt a simple reversal of the roles into which male dominance casts women. Sartre's image, though he was no Freudian, suggests that revolutionary transformation is accomplished by killing an oppressor seen as a father. But we cannot now expect Irigaray to defend a conception of revolutionary transformation that requires us to see the oppressor as our mother. Nor yet does Irigaray think of the establishment of matriarchy-sisterhood as a matter, either, of killing or injuring either father or brother.[15] Thus, a simple reversal of the male myth of patriarchy-brotherhood, Freudian or non-Freudian, in which the male dominates by violence, leaves us once again with life-denying violence. Matriarchy-sisterhood cannot be about violence. But it is not clear, either, what more general interpretation can be offered to support a psychological interpretation of that relationship as conducive of fusion, rather than separation, with the ensuing mutuality and empowerment. Nonetheless, Irigaray's exploration of myths of the births of gods in *Amante Marine* answers this question by establishing the spiritual sources of empowerment as feminine.[16]

II

Such a vision of regenerative, transformative contact nevertheless remains, in its abstraction, mythic. The mythic reinterpretation of feminine sexuality as empowering and mutual does offer the image of an ethic. But no ethic, and certainly no ethic of nurturance, can be realized without a supporting politic. The criticisms I must now offer of Irigaray's proposals recognize the positive power of her images of mutuality as extending far beyond the maternal function. But in these criticisms I must now ask, as well, how these images of mutuality and power might be practiced, given present cultural conditions for maternity. Irigaray herself has said that in her dismantling of patriarchy she seeks neither to build a rival system nor to collect disciples. Yet she has also shown herself sensitive to and receptive to Marxist criticisms of the existing systems. The import of my criticisms is that in this receptivity she has not gone far enough.

Since Irigaray's proposals are not political in a practical, material sense, it is not surprising that they are not so presented. Instead, as we have seen, they are offered as highly experimental avant-garde writing, full of metaphor and allusions to unnamed major figures in philosophy and psychoanalysis. This style offers, first, major obstacles to the ordinary reader. Second, Irigaray's proposals offer psychoanalytic explanations of the mother-daughter relationship that overlook the social influences now conceded even by Freudians. Third, Irigaray's vision of an alternative matriarchy is utopian, mythic, and to some, escapist. Fourth and finally, Irigaray hardly begins the material and economic analysis of mother-daughter oppression that many critics would take to be essential. In ending this essay I will examine each of these criticisms in turn.

The first question for a political analysis of Irigaray's psychologic and mythic proposals for matriarchy is whether it is elitist, hence in its very form an undercutting of a feminist politic, separating women from one another by class. The form of Irigaray's proposals that I question here is of course literary, but by her own description classifiable neither as fiction nor as theory.[17] This *écriture féminine* attempts to raise women's consciousness by using the text as metaphor for women's bodily experiences. But one may ask whether this kind of writing is the most appropriate way to raise consciousness. Simone de Beauvoir, for example, who names none of its authors, has suggested that *écriture féminine* is an inappropriate way to do feminist political work, which would be more effectively accomplished by using everyone's language, ordinary language.[18] Experience confirms this impression. In conversation with nonacademic French feminists I found many who had read isolated essays of Irigaray's, including, in the original of course, "And the One Doesn't Stir without the Other," and found them extraordinary. But I found no one, up until a year after its publication, who had been able to read *Amante Marine,* with its complex literary allusions; and indeed a French academic advised me to start with its second part, which presents cognitive linear arguments, in order to understand the experimentally written first and third parts. What, then, is the political force of a writing style inaccessible to all but those highly trained academically?

In response to this first criticism Irigaray has replied that to evoke the primary experiences of women—surely a legitimate political goal—requires new forms of expression. Creating new forms of expression, as in feminist therapy or as in feminine writing, is itself a political effort, although of course an intellectual one. Thus, in her literary experiments Irigaray shares the plight of all intellectuals, who have to reconcile the separation of the contemplative life, which writing demands, with the collective needs of the group, whose political goals committed writers seek to advance. But experience also confirms that, at least some of the time, experimental writing does advance political goals. Talking with American undergraduates whose background was hardly upper class or sophisticated, I found that everyone who had read carefully the essays by Irigaray so far available in English, including not only "And the One Doesn't Stir without the Other," but also "When Our Lips Speak Together,"[19] a radical and innovative celebration of feminine sexuality as feminine power, understood very well what she was saying. In response to some of its critics I can therefore suggest that an experimental literary style such as *écriture féminine* is not necessarily inaccessible, although at times it may be. If it is, its author can also offer other, more popular works. This Irigaray did, of course, in her informal interviews, which even in translation display a far more ordinary speaking style than the writing style of her literary experiments.

The second criticism of Irigaray's work that I have to consider is that her psychoanalytic account of the separation of mother from daughter, although highly critical of Freud and of Freud's interpreter, Lacan, is nevertheless tied to them in overlooking the social origins of the roles played out by mothers and daughters in separating from one another. In *The Second Sex* Beauvoir had already offered criticisms of Freud's notions of the castration complex and of penis envy as a displaced justification of a socially sanctioned conception of male dominance. Such arguments are by now very familiar to an American audience. Since Lacan introduced into France a theoretical interpretation of the power to speak as male sexual power or potency, American critics might contend that subsequent feminist writings such as Irigaray's, which are tied to empowering women disenfranchised from language by a Lacanian Freud, emphasize rather too much the metaphysical or symbolic interpretation of language imposed by the Freudian Lacan in France. By contrast, the same critics might continue, Irigaray's writings attend too little to the facts, as documented even by Nancy Chodorow, who remains in many respects sympathetic to Freud.[20] Mother-daughter ambivalence is a complex product of the nuclear family Freud was describing, and although a feminist political analysis of that ambivalence cannot continue to support the nuclear family as a social structure, neither can it overlook its present effect.

Irigaray might, of course, respond to this second criticism that empirical sociology is hardly her project, that she writes rather from her own experience as a therapist, in which women's problems are treated and healed individually and intuitively. What she does offer is not an empirical sociological analysis but rather a utopian conception of matriarchy—an idealization of a social structure not yet realized. In other words, another myth. Marge Piercy, who wrote the utopian feminist novel *Woman on the Edge of Time,* has proposed to me in conversation that one might argue in support of such a project that it is important to explore myths of matriarchy[21] to find out how women have gone wrong in the past and to build a political structure that will work in the future.

But in response to this proposal one might contend critically, in the third place, that the very notion of a matriarchy as a utopia is at issue here. In the same interview in which she suggested that *écriture féminine* was elitist, Simone de Beauvoir said also, again without naming any of its authors:

> I am mistrustful of all of these tales of matriarchy. But I studied the question not a little for *The Second Sex:* there have been societies where the woman certainly had much more power, was much more highly valued, and had a much more important place, but concerning matriarchy, strictly speaking, I do not think that there has ever been one. Having said that, I have no further interest in the question. What is interesting is what we will become and not what we were yesterday, and we can't find indicators of our future in what we could have been mythically.[22]

Whether the creation of matriarchal utopias or of matriarchal writing styles is appropriate to feminism is evidently a deeper political question that I can resolve here. In any case, utopian conceptions are far removed from the social and from the material questions which, in the opinion of others who might also criticize Irigaray's writings, have been largely overlooked in them.

In the fourth place, Irigaray's writings fall vulnerable to the sort of criticism to which the writings of various American proponents of feminist spirituality also fall vulnerable. For example, a materialist might point out that mothering, presently a trap, is not so much felt as a spiritual failure as it is lived as a scarcity of economic resource. Of course, Irigaray is not by any means insensible to the material question. In "When the Goods Get Together,"[23] she addresses the question of women's being used as material goods to exchange as tokens of men's dominance. But she does this by outlining, again, a utopia with the men absent, in which women would deal directly and mutually with one another. In her Montreal interviews Irigaray uses the Hegelian and Marxist terminology of alienation as well as the psychoanalytic terminology of separation and ambivalence to characterize women's oppression as women's separation, one from the other. But the difficulty with Irigaray's excursions into materialist analysis is that they are few and limited, and that in their utopian visions these idealizations overlook practical experience. As Beauvoir recently reaffirmed, it is a mother's practical experience that presents mothering as a trap for women:

> Either the woman is a single woman and she carries everything on her back, or she lives with a man, married to him or not, and then, even if the father helps her, that very word indicates that he doesn't really take responsibility. As long as everything thus falls to women, it is extremely difficult, if not dangerous, to be a mother, a woman who works, who does something and who engages in feminist struggle.[24]

But as still another critic might stubbornly rejoin—both to Beauvoir's argument and to Irigaray's idealizations of the psychic experience of mothering—the problem of the mother as drained nurturer might rather be resolved by rearranging the political structure so that men would have no economic control of the circumstances in which children are reared, so that women could get on with the job without interference. That change would empower women in a material sense of taking control of the economic conditions of labor. It would also empower women in a matriarchal sense which I have already attributed to Irigaray—by promoting structures to ensure and recognize the primacy of women's spiritual contact between generations, through the mother. Such contact now happens, Irigaray has observed, in women's spaces.[25] What if all nurturing of children were done in women's spaces? That arrangement, finally, might approach a matriarchy.

We can see from these four criticisms of Irigaray's works that there is not yet a developed feminist ethic of nurturance to be drawn from them, nor a developed account of matriarchy. There is a spiritual vision of mothering as it is lived. But there is lacking still a transition between Irigaray's often-eloquent celebrations of the maternal and erotic potentiality of women's bodily experience as the source of a spiritual matriarchy, and a developed proposal for a body politic. That project awaits our undertaking.[26]

Notes

1. "And the One Doesn't Stir without the Other," translated by Hélène Vivienne Wenzel, *Signs* 7 (Autumn 1981): 60–67.

2. "Le corps à corps avec la mère" (Montreal: Les éditions de la pleine lune, 1981). My translations will follow.

3. "Si les femmes veulent prendre le pouvoir à la manière des hommes, ce n'est pas la peine, c'est ce que nous voudrions changer justement, toutes ce notions et ces valuers." "Entretien avec Simone de Beauvoir," in *Les écrits de Simone de Beauvoir,* edited by Claude Francis ad Fernande Gontier (Paris: Gallimard, 1979), p. 589.

4. Simone de Beauvoir, *La cérémonie des adieux, suivi de entretiens avec Jean-Paul Sartre* (Paris: Gallimard, 1981), p. 365. My translation: "Demander le nom d'une rue à quelqu'un ou demander un tout petit service à quelqu'un, c'est se mettre sur un plan de réciprocité; c'est le reconnaître en somme comme votre égal, comme n'importe qui, comme vous, ce n'est donc pas aller mendier comme un mendiant."

5. "Le Corps," p. 86: "Il nous faudra en quelque sorte faire le deuil d'une toute-puissance maternelle (le dernier refuge) et établir avec nos mères un rapport de réciprocité de femme à femme, où elles pourraient aussi éventuellement se sentir nos filles. En somme, nous libérer avec nos mères. C'est une condition indispensable à notre émancipation de l'autorité des pères. La relation mère/fille, fille/mère constitue un noyau extrêmement explosif dans nos sociétés. La penser, la changer, reveient à ébranler l'ordre patriarcal."

6. Irigaray, "Le Corps," p. 23.

7. For example, see Freud's introduction of the famous "fort . . . da" example in his *Beyond the Pleasure Principle* (London: Hogarth Press and Institute of Psychoanalysis, 1951), *Standard Edition* (1955), Vol. 18, chapter 2. See also, for a summary in English of Lacan's views, Anika Lemaire, *Jacques Lacan,* translated by David Macey (London: Routledge & Kegan Paul, 1977), pp. 51–52. See also Jacques Derrida, *La Carte Postale* (Paris: Aubier-Flammarion, 1980), and Luce Irigaray, "La Croyance, Même," in *Les fins de l' homme: A partir du travail de Jacques Derrida* (Paris: Galilée, 1981).

8. Irigaray, "And the One Doesn't Stir," p. 60.

9. Ibid., p. 63.

10. This approach is essentially Nietzschean. See Sarah Kofman, *Nietzsche et la métaphore* (Paris: Payot, 1972), p. 178.

11. "And the One Doesn't Stir," p. 66.

12. Ibid., p. 67.

13. "Le corps," pp. 65–66: "Ça veut dire: ne sois pas seulement mère et comme le dit Hegel: que l'enfant que je suis ne tue pas la mère que tu es, mais que tu sois quelque chose d'autre que la pure et simple fonction maternelle . . . Que tu ne te réduises pas à une fonction maternelle et que tu ne me réduises pas à une fonction d'enfant. Ça voudrait dire: c'est un conflit mortel, la mère que tu as été et la mère que je vais devenir. . . . Si je deviens autre chose que ta production, tu continueras à exister. Si tu es femme et que je suis femme, nous ne nous réduisons pas à une simple fonction maternelle prescrite par la société."

14. Jean-Paul Sartre, *The Critique of Dialectical Reason,* translated by Alan Sheridan-Smith (London: NLB, 1976), p. 437 (his italics).

15. "Le corps," p. 64.

16. Luce Irigaray, *Amante Marine* (Paris: Minuit, 1980).

17. "Le corps," p. 47.

18. "Sur quelques problèmes actuels du féminisme: entretien avec Simone de Beauvoir," *La revue d'en face* 9–10 (1st trimester 1981): 10–11.

19. Luce Irigaray, "When Our Lips Speak Together," translated by Carolyn Burke, *Signs* 6 (Autumn 1980): 69–79.

20. Nancy Chodorow, *The Reproduction of Mothering* (Berkeley: University of Calif. Press, 1978). See also Marianne Hirsh, "A Mother's Discourse: Incorporation and Repetition in *La Princesse de Clèves,*" Yale French Studies, No. 62 (1981), pp. 68–73.

21. For example, J. J. Bachofen, *Myth, Religion, and Mother Right,* Bollingen Series 84 (Princeton: Princeton University Press, 1967).

22. de Beauvoir, "Sur quelques problèmes actuels," p. 10: "Je suis très méfiante par rapport à toutes ces histoires de matriarcat. J'ai quand même pas mal étudié la question pour le "Deuxième Sexe": il y a eu des sociétés où la femme avait certainement beaucoups plus de poussance, était beaucoup plus valorisée, et avait une place beaucoup plus grande, mais de matriarcat proprement dit, je ne crois pas qu'il y en ait jamais eu. Ceci dit, personnellement, je m'en moque. Ce qui est intéressant, c'est ce que nous allons devenir et non ce que nous avons été hier, et il n'y a pas à chercher les gages de notre avenir dans ce que nous avons pu être mythiquement."

23. Irigaray, "When the Goods Get Together," in *New French Feminisms,* edited by Elaine Marks and Isabelle de Courtivron, translated by Claudia Reeder (Amherst: University of Massachusetts Press, 1980), pp. 107–10.

24. de Beauvoir, "Sur quelques problèmes actuels," p. 12: "Ou bien la femme est mère célibataire et elle porte tout sur son dos, ou elle vit avec un homme, mariée ou pas, et alors, même si le père aide, ce mot même indique bien qu'il n'y a pas pris en charge réelle de sa part. Tant que tout repose ainsi sur les femmes, il est extremement difficile, sinon dangereux d'être une mère, une femme qui travaille, qui fait quelque chose et que lutte dans le féminisme."

25. "Le corps," p. 49.

26. Earlier versions of this paper were presented at Eastern SWIP, Union College, Schenectady, New York, 14 November 1981; at The College of Our Lady of the Elms, Chicopee, Mass.; and at a Conference on Women and Power, SUNY, New Paltz, 24 April 1982. Thanks to those audiences and to Danielle Gualda, Lucie Lopez, Janet Farrell Smith, Mary Vetterling-Braggin, and Caroline Whitbeck for discussion. Parts of this argument are influenced by correspondence conducted during 1979 and 1980 by a group of members of Eastern SWIP discussing the ethics of roles, and by a paper by Caroline Whitbeck, "The New Erotics," delivered at Eastern SWIP, SUNY, Stony Brook, 29 April 1979. The argument is also influenced by Kathryn Pyne (Parsons) Addelson, "Nietzsche and Moral Change," in *Nietzsche* edited by Robert C. Solomon (Garden City, N.Y.: Anchor Books, 1973), pp. 169–93. But none of these people is responsible for the application of concepts of nurturance, the erotic, or moral change to Irigaray's work that I have attempted here.

16

The Answer Is Matriarchy

BARBARA LOVE and ELIZABETH SHANKLIN

Just as we have been conditioned to feel negatively toward ourselves as women, as lesbians, and as mothers, we have been very effectively conditioned to feel negatively about matriarchy. When we hear the word "matriarchy," we are conditioned to a number of responses: that matriarchy refers to the past and that matriarchies have never existed; that matriarchy is a hopeless fantasy of female domination, of mothers dominating children, of women being cruel to men; or that matriarchists are reactionaries escaping from capitalist society into a romantic dream of goddesses and tribal life.

Conditioning us negatively to matriarchy is, of course, in the interests of patriarchs. We are made to feel that patriarchy is natural; we are less likely to question it, and less likely to direct our energies to ending it.

The struggle toward matriarchy has nevertheless been waged in the past century.[1] There is now a vital and conscious movement toward matriarchy.[2] We intend this article to be a theoretical contribution to that movement, and we are going to limit our discussion here to defining the word. What do we mean by *matriarchy*?

Toward a Definition of Matriarchy

By "matriarchy" we mean a nonalienated society: a society in which women, those who produce the next generation, define motherhood, determine the conditions of motherhood, and determine the environment in which the next generation is reared.[3]

This essay first appeared in *Our Right to Love,* edited by Ginny Vida (Englewood Cliffs, N.J.: Prentice-Hall, 1978). Reprinted by permission of the authors.

We now live in a patriarchy. We mean by *patriarchy* a society ruled by fathers. Rule by father implies the expropriation of the child and the exploitation of women as mothers. Mothers bear children for nine months within their bodies, and labor—even at the risk of their lives—to give birth to their children. In patriarchy the child at birth becomes the property of the father. This expropriation of the child is carried out in historic patriarchies through a set of institutions.

Patriarchy, then, refers not only to male domination, but to a specific set of institutions that ensures the alienation of the child from the mother. While some aspects of these institutions change, the basic relationship between the father, the mother, and her child is fundamental to patriarchy.

The expropriation of the child from the mother was more easily recognized in the past. In the United States in the 19th century, for example, the law made the father the sole guardian of the mother's child. The father might apprentice the child, determine how and whether it was educated, and make all decisions relative to its well-being and health—in opposition to the preferences of the mother and the child. The father could will that at his death a total stranger to the mother become the guardian of her child.

Today, the alienation of the child from the mother persists. But now the alienation occurs less through the power of individual fathers and more through impersonal institutions. The mother is now permitted to be the legal guardian of her child, but that function no longer carries the decision-making power it used to have. The patriarchal state now decides when, where, and how her child will be employed. Institutions now dictate how her child will be socialized. Each child is conditioned daily through the public schools, the economic structures, the media, and religion so that her/his behavior and attitudes are regulated to serve the interests of the dominant patriarchs.

The mother must, for example, yield up her child at age five to "educational" institutions designed by fathers. She must by law send her child to be socialized in a competitive system that will stratify her child according to the interests of those in power. She must prepare her child to function in a warrior economy.[4] She must resort to the idea of the father as the sole creator if she wishes her child to belong to any established religion; she must permit her child to be conditioned by corporate interests through television if she wishes her child to share a frame of reference with other children; to have a child "legitimately," she must marry the father. She is then bound to give sexual and domestic service. She must also give the child the father's name as token of his proprietary interest. Typically, if her daughter decides to repeat this pattern, the father will be acknowledged as her owner and will give her away to the next possessor.

Therefore, through the institutions of patriarchy, the child is alienated from the mother. The child becomes the property of the father and institutions designed by him. These institutions have usurped the maternal function, and then defined for women what a mother's role is to be. Patriarchal institutions make the mother the servant of patriarchy. Like any servant, the mother is directed in the tasks that she is to perform vis-à-vis the property of the owner. She is made the custodian of his child and told that her job is to help her child function in institutions designed by men. If she should permit any activity threatening to patriarchs, she can at any time be declared an unfit mother—for example, if she should allow her child to have a lesbian relationship or if she should allow her child to withdraw from public school.

Understanding our society as a patriarchy explains the special oppression of lesbian mothers. The lesbian commitment to women rather than to men is an act of independence improper for the mother's role as servant to patriarchy. While a single mother's child is considered "illegitimate," the single heterosexual mother does not threaten the continuation of patriarchy to the degree that a lesbian mother does. For the lesbian relationship implies commitment to denial of male authority over the mother's own and her child's life. Therefore, the lesbian mother constitutes a threat to the continuation of patriarchal society.

It's a myth that lesbians aren't mothers. It's a myth that lesbians don't want to be mothers. What is frequently true is that lesbians don't want to pay the price to be mothers in patriarchy: to be reduced to the custodian of one's own child; to be a wife; to be isolated, financially dependent, and stigmatized. What is true is that lesbians don't want to be mothers as men have institutionalized motherhood, usurping the mother's power and rights. Sometimes, lesbians simply don't like being around children, but under different conditions, who knows?

It is in the interests of patriarchy to direct lesbians—a critical revolutionary force—away from bearing and rearing children. It is patriarchal manipulation to say that lesbians should not influence children—even their own children—and thus leave them vulnerable to be indoctrinated by fathers and their institutions into patriarchal ways.

Are we implying that every lesbian should be a mother to be a revolutionary? No. What we are saying is that our liberation as women and as lesbians will never be acccomplished until we are liberated to be mothers. Until we have the power to define the conditions under which we exercise our biological potential, until we define for ourselves the role of motherhood to include the power to determine the conditions of motherhood and to determine the environment in which our children are reared, we have no real choice. And until we have choices, we are not free.

To say that we must end the expropriation of children by fathers implies the first real revolution known to history. For male "revolutions" have actually meant only a change in the class of men in power, leaving intact the fundamental exploitation of patriarchy—the alienation of the mother from her child. For regardless of which class has been in power in patriarchy—the aristocracy, the middle or working class—the alienation between the mother and the child has persisted. The child has been expropriated by feudal lords, capitalist institutions, and the socialist state.

By "matriarchy" we mean a society in which the mode of childrearing is nurturant—that is, strengthens the unique will of each individual to form open, trusting, creative bonds with others.

The mode of childrearing in patriarchy is to control and dominate the child's will. In capitalism the child's will is directed toward serving the interests of corporations; in socialism it is directed toward serving the state. In patriarchy to nurture oneself is actually a revolutionary act.

Therefore, although women are told that they are the nurturers of the world, women in patriarchy do not have the power to nurture—if by nurturance we mean supporting the unique will of the child to grow into its full potential as a self-regulating individual. Capitalism and socialism, institutions of patriarchy which control the mother and child, both conflict with nurturance.

Under capitalism, mothers are faced with a dilemma. They can force their children to conform to a competitive economy, to a competitive educational system, to competitive games, to bourgeois codes of behavior, dress, and lovemaking. But if they do all this, they crush their children's desire to live openly, creatively, trustfully, and safely with others. On the other hand, mothers can choose to nurture their children's wills to form open, trusting bonds with others. But if they do this, they are permitting their children to risk exploitation, poverty, stigma, and isolation. Most of us are some amalgam of these two, always in conflict, struggling to find ourselves, to be able to maintain deep and steady contact with others of our choice.

Under socialism, a mother who attempted to nurture the unique will of her child would most likely be denounced or arrested. However, she has the compensation that the socialist patriarchs (at least under Mao) socialized her child to relate to others (and others to her child) in a supportive, noncompetitive way. But this support does not stem from strengthening of the unique being of each individual. Children are not socialized to think for themselves, and are therefore doomed to be prey to political manipulation. Since children have been dominated and indoctrinated instead of nurtured into positive relations with others, they will be dependent on the benevolence of dictators.

The matriarchal mode of childrearing in which each individual is nurtured rather than dominated from birth provides the rational basis for a genuinely healthy society, a society of self-regulating, positive individuals.[5] Matriarchy, as we define it, then implies the elimination of every institution of patriarchy—its economic, political, sexual, social, and educational institutions. Each of these institutions defines how the next generation is to be reared.

Each of these institutions structures the mother's role, reducing motherhood to simple custodianship of what one has biologically produced. Just as the power of mothers to determine the socialization of their children is increased, in matriarchy the identification of who is a mother would also expand. With the breakdown of the nuclear patriarchal family, collective living arrangements have been emerging in which both women and men without children share the children of other members of the collective. The lesbian community has been developing an expanded sense of motherhood; for example, lovers frequently share children, and movement conferences show a consciousness of the need for sharing responsibility for all children. One need not be a biological mother in order to mother.

By "matriarchy" we mean a society in which all relationships are modeled on the nurturant relationship between a mother and her child.

As a consequence of our alienation from our mothers that is institutionalized in our patriarchal society, each of us has been denied to some degree the fundamental source of security. We have been denied that interaction between a nurturant person and ourselves throughout our early years. We have been denied that interaction that could have strengthened our capacity to be secure, to be open, to trust, to be ourselves, to realize our sensory, emotional, intellectual, energetic potential.

We become estranged from our real feelings. We learn to suppress, to deny; we project, we fragment. We squander our life's energies in anxieties and angers. We are alienated from ourselves. Being alienated and fragmented, we lead defensive or programmed lives. We lose the capacity to live deeply in contact with ourselves, others, and nature. We lose the capacity to govern ourselves, to be self-regulated. Our alienation from our mothers has left us to some degree crippled for life.

We must go to psychiatrists to learn what it is to nurture ourselves. We spend years learning how to form a nurturant relationship with another person. For, being to some degree alienated from ourselves, and confronting other alienated people, we form alienated relationships.

We have been taught to base our personal relationships on the warrior mode of competition—beating and conquering our friends and associates in games, in business, and in politics. Our relationships throughout society—our work relationships, movement relationships, love relationships—can really be understood only in terms of how in those situations we deal with our alienation. Genuine contact that persists, genuine openness and trust that is steady, is very rare, and is constantly threatened by patriarchal habits of competition.

In matriarchy this basic alienation (as well as the alienation of labor) is eliminated. Institutions do not usurp the mother's right to determine that the environment, both social and natural, be nurturant to her child. The conditions of motherhood, having been defined by women, support the mother and her interest in the child's growth into a self-regulating, trusting individual. The conditions of socialization—the economic, educational, and governmental institutions—reinforce and support the bonds of nurturance.

In matriarchy no institutions conflict with the nurturance of each individual to form open, trusting bonds with others; in addition, each individual is nurtured deeply in a secure relationship with her/his mother. The consequences of deep nurturance and nurturant social structures are that individuals would be capable of relating to others in open, trusting, and supportive ways. In addition, the energies generated and released under these conditions promise creativity and productivity unimaginable within patriarchy. This is what we mean when we say that in matriarchy all relationships would be modeled on the nurturant relation of the mother and the child: each of us would learn how to be nurturant to ourselves and to others.

Matriarchy, then, provides the only reasonable basis for a genuinely harmonious society, a society of self-regulating, positive individuals.

By indicating that women, as the bearers of the next generation, should have the power to nurture, we are obviously expanding popular concepts of the scope of nurturance. Nurturing includes not only feeding and clothing and cleaning a child, but strengthening the child's unique will. Inasmuch as the child is not reared in a vacuum, the bearers of the next generation in order to be nurturant must have the power to determine that the economic, political, educational, and social environment in which the next generation is socialized is nurturant. We are therefore saying that in order to be nurturant, women must determine the social structures of society.

By "matriarchy" we mean a society in which the maternal principle, the nurturance of life, informs all social structures; this implies the elimination of all patriarchal institutions: economic, political, sexual, and educational.

Each institution of patriarchy has an exploitative function. The elimination of every exploitative structure would be necessary in order to create social structures that support the nurturance of the unique will of each individual to trusting, open relationships with others.

Matriarchy, in fact, provides, through the liberation of the maternal function from subservience to warrior institutions, the basis for the elimination of the patriarchal state. Only through the nurturance of each individual to self-regulation can one expect to eliminate the need for a dominating government or state.

We mean by "matriarchy" a society in which production serves the interests of reproduction; that is, the production of goods is regulated to support the nurturance of life.

In both capitalist and socialist states, the production of things that produce wealth and military power dominates and determines the quality of life in the society. The way in which the next generation is conceived, born, and reared—that is, the mode of reproduction—is dictated by the interests of production.

We mean by matriarchy a society in which the production of things is not to accumulate wealth, to defend or wage war, but to strengthen each individual's capacity to live openly in trust with others. It is not rational to expect a person to live in trust with another so long as one can survive only through the destruction of the other or the exploitation of the other. Therefore, matriarchy implies a worldwide socialist economic base, but a liberation of reproduction from subordination to the socialist state.

Matriarchy, as we have defined it, is the solution to a number of problems that concern many of us deeply. Men have questioned how to eliminate exploitation, war, racism, classism, sexism, and they have devised innumerable answers to these problems. These answers have proven inadequate. They have been inadequate because men have refused to eliminate patriarchy. The question is how to create a nurturant society. The answer is matriarchy.

If the creation of matriarchy seems an impossible dream, it is because we are among the first to overcome the myth of the inevitability of patriarchy and to realize the possibility of matriarchy. If the vision of uniting nurturance with economic transactions and political organizations appears a hopeless fantasy, it is because it requires our gaining power that men tell us we have never had. If we are torn in facing up to the need for matriarchy, it is because we are paid by patriarchs to support them. If linking motherhood to economic and political power seems to be vain imagining, it is because patriarchs have conditioned us to link motherhood with powerlessness and to think of mothering as trivial. If matriarchy seems irrelevant to lesbian liberation, it is because every institution in this society so controls us that we are directed away from examining the total system.

The task of ending patriarchy and creating matriarchy is not so awesome as it might first appear. We will be summoning up energies that are suppressed now; we will be releasing our creative energies, our own buried needs and desires. And we will be aligned with the struggle for life that strongly asserts itself in each new generation as it battles with patriarchal institutions that seek to dominate and subjugate it. We will be aligned with the struggle for life in each oppressed person, and the oppressed are many.

Innumerable men, women, and children have not yet become political, but are dissatisfied with the current system. Many of these people have not become political because they have realized that the patriarchal political movements that promised a classless society, for example, provided no hope of producing people who were capable of a classless society. Matriarchy will.

We believe that the matriarchal movement will find support among people of both sexes and of all classes, races, and ages. The cry for a more nurturant society has manifested itself in the black movement, the labor movement, the Native American movement, the Third World movement, the environmental movement, the consumer movement, the radical education movement, the radical medicine and psychology movements, and the children's liberation movement, as well as the mother's movement, the gay movement, the lesbian movement, and the women's movement.

Every movement for liberation is, we think, an unconscious movement toward matriarchy. Therefore, we have potential allies who are now struggling, unawakened to the fact that patriarchy is the problem—that under patriarchy we can never create a nurturant society. These various movements have often felt some common denominator with one another. That common denominator is the need for matriarchy.

Whereas women's liberation and lesbian liberation have been largely founded around the concepts of freeing ourselves from domination, matriarchal theory provides the rational basis for women to restructure and guide the institutions in society. As the bearers of life, it is our right and responsibility to determine that life is nurtured.

Notes

1. We need herstories of the matriarchal movement. To date none has been published. Some indication of the movement in the 19th century can be found in Elizabeth Shanklin's paper, "Elizabeth Cady Stanton, Our Revolutionary Mother," presented at CUNY Women's Conference, 1976. Stanton proposed matriarchy as the ultimate goal of women's liberation. Drawing upon Bachofen and Morgan, who did not advocate matriarchy but who lifted the curtain on the past, Stanton drew her own conclusions. Engels has been a major contributor to the movement. Such a herstory would surely include the contributions of Helen Diner and Robert Briffault. The reception given Briffault's *The Mothers,* a three-volume work explicitly delineating the need for matriarchy, and the way in which his work is ignored today or discredited by "scholars," would be stimulating material for herstorical analysis.

2. Indications include: the publication of "scholarly" articles by anthropologists and historians stridently "proving" that there never was a matriarchy because they don't admit or have the evidence that there was; the publication of *The Inevitability of Patriarchy;* communities across the country which identify themselves as matriarchal; conferences across the country devoted to matriarchy or containing workshops on matriarchy; courses in the politics of motherhood; the day-care movement demanding that mothers control their own centers; the interest in matriarchal ritual and matriarchies of the past; but publication of Adrienne Rich's *Of Woman Born.*

3. Our set of assumptions includes the following:

   a. That whether or not there has ever been a matriarchy like the one we need will not determine whether there will or will not be one in the future.

   b. That human nature is malleable in the following ways: if people are surrounded by nurturant institutions, i.e., institutions that are nurturant to people and that reward people for being nurturant, then people will tend to become nurturant; if people are surrounded by institutions that are exploitative, i.e., if people are exploited and rewarded for exploiting others, then people will tend to become exploitative.

   c. That a woman who chooses to bear a child is interested in its growing to its full potential into a self-regulating, whole person, and that any distortion of that nurturant bond between a mother and her child will have been caused by the environment in which they have lived and/or continue to live.

   d. As long as the design of a society is based on exploitative structures, the genuine liberation of lesbians—or any other group—cannot be achieved.

4. We use the term "warrior economy" to refer to the economies of patriarchy. We use the term as Veblen used it in *The Theory of the Leisure Class*. Marx has many descriptions of the warrior character of presocialist economies. The warrior aspect of socialist society, we assert, resides not in its economic base, but persists in its mode of reproduction, i.e., the taking of the child from the person who produced it. A simple definition of a warrior might be a person who survives by taking what others have or have produced.

5. The ability to nurture oneself and to nurture others is developed through the experience of having been nurtured. The discipline of psychology clearly indicates that our early childhood years are the most influential in establishing character.

PART FOUR

Pronatalism and Resistance

17

Feminism, Pronatalism, and Motherhood

MARTHA E. GIMENEZ

Introduction

Motherhood, if conceived as a taken-for-granted dimension of women's normal adult role, becomes one of the key sources of women's oppression. The notion that *all* women *should* be and *desire* to be mothers has always been used to keep women in a subordinate position while paying lip service to the social importance of their role. In this essay, I propose to explore the credibility and theoretical relevance of an unusual criticism directed at the mainstream of the U.S. women's liberation movement:[1] the notion that its unqualified support of motherhood as one of the most important women's rights is insufficiently critical of its oppressive dimensions.[2] It is very important to investigate this matter because, to the extent that the current prescriptive nature of motherhood is not theoretically and politically challenged, the struggle for genuine alternatives for women could be self-defeating.

The argument that feminism has not fundamentally challenged the compulsory nature of motherhood has been persuasively developed by sociologist Judith Blake in her research paper "Coercive Pronatalism and American Population Policy," prepared for the Commission on Population Growth and the American Future.[3] As a sociologist, Blake is highly critical of the voluntaristic assumptions underlying the ideas of both family-planning advocates and those who fear that policies aimed at curbing population growth may elicit coercive measures curtailing individuals' reproductive freedom. In her view, neither family planners who emphasize parents' right to choose their family

This article first appeared in *International Journal of Women's Studies* 3, no. 3, 1980. Copyright © International Journal of Women's Studies. Reprinted by permission of the publisher and the author.

size, nor those who assume that smaller families could be attained only by coercion, are correct in taking for granted the existence of reproductive freedom. On the contrary:

> Neither takes into account that at present, reproductive behavior is under stringent institutional control and that this control constitutes . . . a coercive pronatalist policy. Hence, an effective anti-natalist policy will not necessarily involve an increase in coercion or a reduction in the "voluntary" element in reproduction, because individuals are under pronatalist constraints right now. *People make their "voluntary" reproductive choices in an institutional context that severely constrains them not to choose non-marriage, not to choose childlessness, not to choose only one child, and even not to limit themselves solely to two children.*[4]

American society, like all societies, is pronatalist because parenthood is universally prescribed. There are no legitimate or socially rewarded alternatives to the performance of parental roles. Instead, parenthood is a *precondition* for women's and men's adult roles; i.e., the primary basis for achieving full social participation.[5] Deviations from the established role expectations (e.g., homosexuality, childlessness, single status, etc.) are punished by a variety of social, economic, and psychological sanctions.

The essence of Blake's criticism is the following: feminists have overlooked the compulsory nature of parenthood and its relevance for the full understanding of the structural and ideological foundations of women's secondary status. Present-day feminists are uncritically supportive of motherhood as a right, and this is reflected in their advocacy of the "do both" syndrome; i.e., motherhood and careers not as alternative and equally legitimate choices for women, but as a combination to which all women have a right. The women's liberation movement is implicitly supportive of pronatalism because it has aimed its struggles to the goal of eliminating the social, economic, legal, educational, and psychological barriers standing in the way of women's ability to "do both," thus stressing women's right not to have to make a choice.[6] Focusing her analysis on the social constraints that further compulsory parenthood for both sexes, Blake makes a theoretical suggestion that opens the way for developing a deeper understanding of the structural basis of sexism. She argues that the barriers women encounter in their efforts to change the existing conditions cannot be exclusively understood as consequences or effects of male dominance; they should also be considered as consequences of "the intense societal supports for the *family roles* of father and mother."[7] It would follow, therefore, that male supremacy and female oppression could be viewed as structural effects of social constraints designed to place women *and* men in parental roles.

Blake criticizes feminist politics (they have unanticipated pronatalist implications) and suggests an interesting and important direction for theoretical inquiry: the investigation of the relationship between pronatalism and sexism.

My immediate reaction to these criticisms was one of rejection and incredulity. I also found outrageous her argument that the claim for women's right to have a career and a family was tantamount to declaring that women should have the equal right to neglect, like men, their family obligations.[8] Believing that feminists had subjected every dimension of the female condition to the most trenchant critical analysis, I reread feminist literature, confident that the issue of pronatalism and its theoretical and political implications could not have been entirely overlooked. I was, however, disappointed. I had to conclude, for reasons that I will state later, that Blake was basically correct. Furthermore, as I examined more carefully her arguments and their relevance for women, I realized that she had identified an important issue leading to questions that feminists could not afford either to ignore or to consider as already answered:

Why should everyone, regardless of sex, be expected to have children, even though their primary commitments and concerns might lay elsewhere?

Why should nominal parenthood, for both women and men, be required as a symbol of respectability, normality, or conformity?

What are the social consequences of family formation by persons marginally committed to childbearing?

What is the relationship between social constraints that force people into parental roles and male dominance?

It is obvious that a critical assessment of the politics of the women's movement in the light of Blake's criticisms and the exploration of the relationship between pronatalism and sexism are crucial for feminist theory and politics. It follows, from her discussion, that *women's liberation from male dominance is inextricably linked to women's and men's liberation from compulsory parenthood*. To the extent the movement does not subject the dominant pattern of universally prescribed parenthood to thorough analysis and criticism, it unwittingly contributes to consolidation of one of the structural foundations of the situation it aims to change. It is my purpose in this essay to begin that critical and analytical task. I will first present an assessment of the validity of Blake's criticisms through the examination of feminist literature. Next I will develop further the theoretical analysis of these issues through the investigation of the capitalist supports of pronatalism and sexism. As I have argued elsewhere, Marxist theory is a source of extremely valuable theoretical and methodological guidelines for feminists.[9] From a Marxist theoretical standpoint, the issues raised by Blake cannot be fully understood if subject only to demographic and functional analysis; they must be examined in their historical dimensions through the investigation of the relationship between capitalism, pronatalism, and sexism.

I should add that I have hesitated a great deal before writing this essay. To appear in any way critical of motherhood may be threatening to women who already have or plan to bear children. It might also seem misguided because feminist writings have been so outspokenly critical of the family and sex roles. But criticism of present sex roles and family arrangements is not necessarily criticism of their pronatalist dimensions, if by *pronatalism* is meant *the existence of structural and ideological pressures resulting in socially prescribed parenthood as a precondition for all adult roles.*

Pronatalism and Feminism

I proceeded to examine feminist literature under the assumption that it reflects the major concerns of the women's liberation movement. In searching it for theoretical arguments, conceptualization of problems, articulation of policy objectives, etc., I was particularly concerned with the analysis of motherhood and its past, present, and future relevance in determining the status of women. More specifically, I was interested in the definition of reproductive freedom. An analysis of reproduction that takes into consideration the universally prescribed nature of the mother role and its effect upon the oppression of women would have to define reproductive self-determination as the right of women to choose (a) *how many* children to have; (b) *when* to have them; and (c) *whether* to have them. On the other hand, an analysis of reproduction that did not question the prescriptive nature of motherhood would stress only the first two dimensions of reproductive self-determination: women's right to control their family size and the timing of births. I was also concerned with the place given to the "do both" syndrome in the articulation of feminist demands and goals. I wanted to find out whether motherhood was presented as the main option, or as one alternative among others *equally* and *clearly* defined. My examination of the literature, which was only exploratory, yielded unexpected and disappointing results. The "do both" syndrome was the rule, rather than the exception. Reproductive self-determination was defined around the question of number and timing of births; *the right of women not to have any children was not clearly and specifically incorporated in the feminist analysis and critique of reproduction.* I had to conclude, therefore, that Blake had been basically correct in her appraisal of present-day feminism.

Before presenting the "evidence" supporting my conclusions, I will briefly explain the reasoning that led me to them. In contemporary society, pronatalism is structurally and ideologically dominant at the societal and the personality structure levels of analysis. In this context, statements which do not *explicitly* challenge pronatalism become *implicitly* supportive of it, because of the objective conditions that not only determine their emergence but also their socially accepted meaning. For example, statements proclaiming women's right to control their bodies or their reproductive behavior *without* including in the content of that right the possibility of opting out of motherhood altogether are, *by omission,* supportive of prescriptive motherhood, because they are bound to be interpreted in the context of the dominant ideology surrounding motherhood. There are no neutral statements in the context of ideological and political struggle. Unclear, ambiguous, or unspecified concepts support the dominant social arrangements by default, because the social arrangements tend to rule out interpretations of the concepts that might radically challenge the status quo. The logic underlying my analysis and conclusions is open to two kinds of criticism: (a) that what really matters are the motives of feminist writers and, given their commitment to women's liberation, it would be unfair to suggest that their writings might uphold oppressive structures and ideologies; and (b) that many statements that I believe to support pronatalism could be otherwise interpreted. It should be clear, however, that I am not concerned with the motivations of feminist writers but with the social implications of their writings. The fact that they are open to opposite interpretations only proves that they are essentially ambiguous and, as such, supportive of the status quo. My contention rests upon an assessment of their socially accepted meaning which, as it emerges from the analysis of feminist literature, does not question pronatalist assumptions about motherhood. If that were not the case, childlessness as a legitimate option for women would have appeared in the literature just as frequently as the "do both" syndrome, and this essay would not have been written.

STATEMENTS AND MANIFESTOS

The women's liberation movement is heterogeneous; each sector defines "the woman question" somewhat differently and offers different explanations and solutions.[10] In an examination of manifestos and statements of principles included in anthologies, I identified the following themes related to reproduction:[11]

1. A critique of current sex role definitions and expectations. Some writings glorify female attributes at the expense of male traits, although the most frequent vision is that of future androgyny.

2. A critique of marriage and the nuclear family, followed by the proposal of alternatives (e.g., communes, female-headed households, etc.) which assume the presence of children. This involves the striving for equalitarian and/or androgynous relations within households where, it is suggested, all members, regardless of sex, should assume responsibility for housework and childcare.

3. An analysis of the exploitation of women not only sexually and psychologically but also as housewives, mothers, consumers, and members of the working force reduced to the jobs with the lowest status and pay.

4. Concern with attaining control of reproduction. With only two excep-

tions, this meant demand for sex education, inexpensive and safe contraception, and abortion rights.

5. A demand for nurseries and childcare services for working women. As most women work out of economic necessity, this demand is crucial for their economic survival.

Only two manifestos added a call for women's right to choose whether to bear children.[12] In the overwhelming majority of the writings, nothing was said, specifically or unequivocally, about the possibility of a childfree status as a legitimate option for women: motherhood was taken for granted throughout.[13] Women's right to control their reproduction was consistently and narrowly defined in relationship to the means to attaining that control—i.e., legal and safe means of controlling fertility through contraception and abortion. Such a limited notion of reproductive control does not present a radical challenge to the pronatalist institutions in which it remains embedded.

ARTICLES

A review of articles that established the theoretical and ideological basis for developing a scientific and political understanding of women's status in modern society led me to similar conclusions because of their main general concerns:[14]

1. The desirability of androgyny.
2. An awareness of the compulsory nature of motherhood taken as the basis for the formulation of alternative ways of coping with childcare and housework, and qualitatively different sex roles.
3. A strong faith in the power of contraceptive technology to determine women's control over reproduction.

To acknowledge, no matter how strongly, the oppressive nature of motherhood (e.g., "in a woman, not having children is seen as an incapacity somewhat akin to impotence in a man";[15] "I think we can defer dropping children on cultural command . . . I am not making a call for eternal celibacy, but for intelligent birth control and a rethinking of the compulsion to have children"),[16] is not equivalent to conducting a thorough analysis of the consequences of motherhood as a taken-for-granted aspect of women's lives. These writings do not fully and comprehensively question the assumption that most women will eventually be mothers; they question the social arrangements surrounding the practice of motherhood, which interfere with women's ability to participate in the educational and occupational structure. This is reflected in the emphasis given to the discussion of alternative household arrangements, childcare services, androgyny, and qualitative sex role changes. The possibility that the latter might also include childlessness is never brought up in the analysis, with only one exception that I will discuss later. I found only one instance of total rejection of motherhood, in the advocacy of "the right to artificial reproduction, which is the key to real control of our own bodies and autonomy to determine our lives."[17] It seems unquestionable that the hold of the dominant ideology of motherhood over people's minds limits their ability to perceive alternatives. These limits push people into either total acceptance of motherhood or total negation, thus precluding the emergence of a standpoint which, transcending both, could provide an effective challenge to the status quo.

Lucinda Cisler's analysis is the only one that suggests, albeit ambiguously, the possibility that the decision whether or not to bear children might enter in the definition of reproductive control. In her view, the lack of reproductive control is at the root of the dominant societal definition of women as childbearers. In this light, advances in birth control technology become threatening to (a) the maintenance of social control over women's reproductive capacities, and (b) the relationship between the sexes based upon that control.

Her analysis gives too much weight to the potential impact of birth control technology and overlooks the strength of existing pronatalist patterns. She argues that the technology of birth control is "value free . . . *people* impute meaning to it; *people* determine the uses to which it will be put and the consequences of those uses."[18] Whether birth control leads to the sexual enslavement of women or to their liberation will ultimately depend on women "actively . . . defining the values that surround birth control technology."[19] Unlike most feminists, she is critical of the fact that among the rationales for allowing women to control their reproduction, "a woman's own simple wish not to bear any more (*or even any*) children is conspicuously absent."[20] As she points out, the dominant ideology is such that only "deserving" women (i.e., those who already have had too many children, or would face death or serious disability if they had a child) are generally considered suitable recipients of birth control information and technology. On the other hand, "An undeserving woman . . . is one who is concerned with her own self-interest and actively seeks to preserve it by deciding she does not want to bear *a* child."[21] Her argument, in the absence of further elaboration on the issues of women's right not to have *any* children if they so desire (as Cisler had intimated earlier), is not strong enough to constitute a clear-cut indictment of pronatalism. Her views, which could have served as the starting point for the development of a revolutionary concept of reproductive control, were not taken up by other feminists.

An interesting reversal in the analysis of motherhood can be found in the work of Alice Rossi, whose early articles were so important to the movement. Initially, she was highly critical of the social definition of motherhood as the major source of women's fulfillment. She condemned American society for having institutionalized motherhood as a full-time occupation for women to the detriment of their participation in the social, economic, and political structure. She was also outspokenly critical of the crucial role played by the social sciences in legitimating the hegemony of that image of women.[22] Her criticisms were exclusively aimed at the full-time pattern of motherhood and, as a solution, she advocated the legitimation of part-time mothering and the development of androgynous sex roles. She was never critical of the prescriptive nature of motherhood as such, which might account for her acceptance of the sociobiological claims about the biological roots of social organization. She now proposes the existence of a *maternal instinct*, a product of human evolution and, as such, impossible to change through deliberate political action.[23] Her analysis, whose scientific shortcomings and conservative political implications have been effectively singled out and criticized,[24] is perhaps the most blatant and dangerous pronatalist statement to date. Its reliance on biology lends it, in the eyes of the uninformed, an unquestionable legitimacy that is likely to be used effectively by the anti-feminist/pronatalist forces currently struggling against abortion rights and the Equal Rights Amendment.

I should end this section by pointing out that, in her insightful article "What Does 'Control Over Our Bodies' Really Mean" Elizabeth Moen expands the meaning of the feminist slogan beyond its usual connotations: i.e., women's right to safe and available contraception and abortion to enable them to choose the number and timing of births.[25] She unequivocally includes women's right to bear or not to bear children and convincingly argues that to be effectively in control of reproduction women should also have economic independence and political control over the society itself.[26] Her critical analysis of the meaning of "control over our bodies" is not aimed at highlighting its shortcomings in dealing with the taken-for-granted nature of motherhood as a component of the expected female adult role. Instead, she is concerned with the social, economic, and political consequences of aggregate fertility and their implications for women's ability to control reproduction. It is important to notice, however, that her explicit consideration of motherhood as an option for women is exceptional in the literature.

MAJOR FEMINIST WRITINGS

I will now discuss some major theoretical contributions that not only shed light upon the scope and limitations of the feminist analysis of reproduction, but also strengthen my conclusions about the adequacy of Blake's criticisms.

One of the first important theoretical attempts to deal with the oppression of women was Juliet Mitchell's article "Women: The Longest Revolution."[27] Mitchell argues that women's role in the family, which appears to be based upon the biological universal of motherhood, is actually determined by the historically specific combination of three structures (reproduction, sexuality, and socialization) into a monolithic unit: the family or mode of reproduction. In her view, as long as birth control technology was unreliable, the mode of reproduction remained essentially unchanged; heretofore, reproduction has been defined by "its uncontrollable, natural character and to this extent has been an unmodified biological fact. [Modern contraception means that] today there are the technical possibilities for the transformation and 'humanization' of the most *natural* part of human culture. This is what a change in the mode of reproduction could mean."[28] She further develops this point as follows:

> As long as reproduction remained a *natural* phenomenon . . . women were effectively doomed to social exploitation . . . They had no choice as to whether or how often they gave birth to children (apart from precarious methods of contraception or repeated abortions); their existence was essentially subject to biological processes outside their control.[29]

Given those premises, contraception is logically hailed as the key for changes in the mode of reproduction:

> what it means is that at last the mode of reproduction *potentially* could be transformed. Once childbearing becomes totally voluntary [it] need no longer be the sole or ultimate vocation of woman: it becomes an option among others.[30]

Mitchell's argument rests upon a questionable assumption: that until the advent of modern contraception, reproduction was a natural fact over which women had little or no control. Granting the greater efficacy of modern birth control methods, social scientists concerned with the study of fertility would disagree with her assumption, because no society has abstained from surrounding reproduction with the most elaborate social patterns. Mitchell overlooks both the existence of pronatalist pressures and the existence of ways to regulate fertility that have always been present in all societies. The evidence from the social sciences suggests that women in precapitalist societies had greater control over reproduction than feminists generally seem to admit, and that modern women have far less autonomy in reproductive matters than feminists would like to believe.[31] In my view, the availability of contraception has indeed the potential to modify the mode of reproduction, but is not sufficient to trigger drastic changes in reproductive patterns. In order for childbearing to become totally voluntary and one option among others, radical changes in the capitalist modes of production and reproduction would have to occur; i.e., changes in the relations of production and in the relations of reproduction.[32] Although Mitchell is critical of Shulamith Firestone's biological determinism,[33] she seems to share it to the extent that she overestimates the power of contraceptive technology to give women control over their reproductive lives and underestimates the power of pronatalist social and psychological structures that contain and modify its potentially revolutionary effects. Her analysis is, however, unusual in its straightforward advocacy of childbearing as an option among others.

Another consequence of the availability of contraception is the separation of sexuality from reproduction. Feminists, for reasons that deserve careful investigation, seem to have given greater theoretical consideration to the analysis of sexual exploitation. This standpoint is conducive to a relative theoretical neglect of reproduction, which is thus unwittingly or deliberately relegated to the realm of nature, to biology. Consequently, the complex pronatalist patterns conditioning reproduction are not scrutinized thoroughly, and the notion of women's control over their reproductive lives remains bound to the dominant pronatalist alternatives. Sheila Rowbotham, for example, greatly stresses the impact of contraception on sexuality: "contraception lays the basis for a great explosion in the possibility of female pleasure."[34] The grounds contraception establishes for "a great explosion" in alternatives with respect to childbearing remain unexplored in her discussion of women's control over reproduction.

Linda Gordon's work is unique in its grasp of pronatalist structures. It would be impossible to dwell on all the valuable insights she offers in *Woman's Body, Woman's Right;* my remarks will be based, primarily, on the last chapter, "Sexuality, Feminism, and Birth Control Today," which summarizes her main points and is most relevant to this essay.

In Gordon's view, reproductive freedom is a dimension of human freedom and is thus affected by all the institutions that in one way or another curtail that freedom. For example, class structure affects the reproductive pattern of all classes, which thus seek in family formation goals as varied as the maintenance of political and economic power, meaning, and satisfaction to compensate for the consequences of alienated labor, economic and social security, etc. Unlike most feminists, Gordon correctly acknowledges the existence of pronatalist pressures affecting all adults which:

> make children potentially the victim of adults' unsatisfactory lives. These pressures systematically push reproduction decisions *beyond* the reach of technological solutions. Only the liberation of children from the burdens of being useful to adults can make childbearing a free choice, emanating from the desire to perpetuate human life, not oneself.[35]

She points out that, although men and women are subject to those pressures, reproduction creates more difficulties for women who, whether they are employed outside the home or not, have sole responsibility for childcare.

Feminists have consistently denounced the negative psychological, social, and economic consequences of socialization patterns that stress motherhood as women's major social role. Gordon expands that critique to include the analysis of the pronatalist dimensions of the motherhood mystique. Socialization creates a female personality structure for which motherhood becomes a need not easily rejected. To be childless becomes synonymous with failure, and those feelings are reinforced by cultural and social pressures which condemn childlessness. The equation of motherhood with self-realization, in conjunction with the lack of desirable alternatives and the enhanced opportunities for sexual exploitation resulting from a "sexual revolution" in the midst of sexual inequality, make women's attainment of reproductive freedom structurally impossible: "Self-determination cannot exist if none of the options is attractive. Reproductive options cannot be separated from economic, vocational, and social choices."[36] Under these conditions, Gordon argues, women "fall into motherhood" for, in spite of its problematic aspects, it is not only more creative and rewarding than most alternatives, but is also a source of meaning and comfort that compensates for the alienating features of the work to which most women are relegated.

Gordon's critique of motherhood is important because she does not share the optimistic view on the liberating power of contraceptive technology that characterizes most feminist analyses of reproduction. On the contrary, she outlines the variety of pronatalist pressures, which, operating at the social and psychological levels, "push reproduction beyond the reach of technological solutions."[37]

Her concept of reproductive freedom remains ambiguous: it *does not* mean population control, birth rate reduction, or family planning.[38] What *does* it mean? It would seem, deducing from the text, that it means voluntary childbearing:

> Involuntary childbearing has burdened all women . . . poor women most, and the sexual inequality that resulted has helped perpetuate all other forms of inequality and weakened struggles against them. Reproductive self-determination is a basic condition for sexual equality and for women to assume full membership in all other human groups.[39]

The concept of voluntary childbearing is simply the negation of the present situation in which childbearing is determined by pronatalist constraints. It is not concretely defined, specifying the choices women would have if they were to attain reproductive self-determination. It remains, therefore, an empty, abstract statement of freedom.

At this point, Gordon's argument takes a surprisingly voluntaristic and idealistic turn that contrasts with her previous research and understanding not only of the pronatalist pressures underlying reproductive behavior today, but also of the *social nature of reproduction* whatever its historical context. For example, she suggests that women could resist current population policies by using contraceptive knowledge "to help make *their own decisions* about childbearing."[40] Given that individual decisions *always* have a social content, because of the dominant social arrangements that rule out childlessness as a desirable option, such "voluntary" decisions would most likely be limited to establishing the timing and frequency of childbearing. This lack of specificity blunts the potential effect of this work to increase women's awareness of the full dimensions of pronatalism.

The only feminist work which not only recognizes pronatalism as a barrier to women's liberation but also advocates nonprocreative lifestyles is Shulamith Firestone's *The Dialectic of Sex.* Hers is a biological determinist analysis of women's oppression that considers sexual inequality as the first "class" antagonism arising from the biological fact of reproduction. Her main argument is that "sex class" is directly determined by biological imperatives: (a) the subordination of women to their biology prior to the development of birth control technology; (b) the special mother/child relationship created by the long time required by humans to grow up; and (c) the biological difference between the sexes that gives rise to the first division of labor. This biological family is a constant that underlies, in her view, all institutional variations which, in the best bourgeois tradition, she dismisses as mere proofs of the "flexibility" of "human nature."[41] Having established a biological premise for her argument that relegates reproduction, again, to the realm of nature, she proceeds to argue—predictably—that the "natural" (i.e., biological reproduction) is not a "human" value.[42] Technology is again endowed with the power to "humanize" nature; women must seize control over reproduction, and the final goal would be the elimination of sex as a social category. Technology would break the tyranny of the biological family and

> The reproduction of the species by one sex for the benefit of both would be replaced by (at least the option of) artificial reproduction: children would be born to both sexes equally, or independent of either, however one chooses to look at it; the dependence of the child on the mother (and vice versa) would give way to a greatly shortened dependence on a small group of others in general.[43]

On the issue of reproduction Firestone's analysis is challenging, although faulty in its exclusive and utopian reliance on technology. She succeeds, however, in raising the issue of motherhood as a possible option rather than as a prescriptive role and part of the value of her analysis lies precisely in that recognition of the need to free women from compulsory motherhood. As she indicates, the myth of motherhood as some kind of inherent attribute of all women is so powerful that women who dare to challenge it are likely to be punished:

> Artificial reproduction is not inherently dehumanizing. At the very least, development of an option should make possible an honest examination of the ancient value of motherhood. At the present time, for a woman to come out openly against motherhood on principle is physically dangerous. She can get away with it only if she adds that she is neurotic, abnormal,

childhating, . . . "unfit" . . . This is hardly a free atmosphere of inquiry. Until the taboo is lifted, until the decision not to have children or not to have them "naturally" is at least as legitimate as traditional childbearing, women are as good as forced into their female roles.[44]

Firestone not only unerringly identifies the compulsory nature of motherhood and the current "deviant" status of non-motherhood, but also questions the existence of a parenthood instinct affecting women and men. She argues that it is difficult to establish whether the fact that most people want children at the present time stems from "an authentic liking for children" or "a displacement of other needs."[45] To avoid the suffering that ensues when children are used as a means to fulfill their parents' needs, she suggests a number of alternatives predicated upon the social recognition of reproduction as a real option for women and men: single, couple, and group living arrangements with or without children, through which adults and children could freely move at a pace imposed by their own developmental needs.

Her overall analysis of the oppression of women rests upon biological and technological determinism and, as such, it is inherently conservative in its theoretical assumptions and political implications. Her work is uniquely important, however, because of its outspoken and radical critique of reproduction and the taken-for-granted nature of parental roles. The fact that her work attracted more theoretical criticisms with respect to her theoretical foundations than attention and praise for some of her insights about the nature of reproduction and parenthood is in itself a manifestation of the ideological hegemony of pronatalism in American society.

This admittedly incomplete review of the literature lends support to Blake's criticism. The idea of optional motherhood is presented either casually, as if it were an already agreed upon objective; as a matter of political expediency; or as a drastic rejection of biological reproduction calling for at least the option of artificial reproduction. Needless to say, such approaches are not likely to have major theoretical or political impact. The rejection of biological motherhood calls forth visions of test-tube babies and the horrors of conditioning as depicted in *Brave New World* and similar utopias:[46] the genuine concern for freedom and self-realization inherent in those suggestions becomes necessarily lost in the technological nightmare they evoke. On the other hand, abstract statements about the desirability of reproductive freedom are no substitute for well-developed theoretical and political arguments.

Pronatalism, Sexism, and Feminism

The possibility of developing an effective challenge to pronatalism rests upon the political and theoretical starting points provided by the gains of the women's movement and by feminist theory. On the other hand, the fact that feminist writings do not deal critically and specifically with pronatalism, do not examine its relationship to sexism, and do not clearly posit a childfree status as real and legitimate option for women *tacitly* and unwittingly supports the dominant pronatalist ideologies and practices that take motherhood for granted.[47] This theoretical shortcoming reflects the experience and needs of the movement's constituency: women raised in a pronatalist context who, in their overwhelming majority, are or expect to be mothers. Their concerns are reflected in the primacy given to the in-depth analysis of sexual and psychological oppression while the oppressive aspects of reproduction are viewed at a different level, as if it were possible to overcome them through practical measures: abortion, contraception, childcare. The conscious form in which women's oppression has been experienced and acted upon has been, ultimately, one in which women (and their children) gather together to support each other in their struggle against male supremacy inside and outside households. The fact that the fastest growing type of U.S. household is the female-headed household may have helped highlight the problems confronting women as working mothers, thus overshadowing other aspects of reproductive oppression.[48] Concern with economic discrimination and the conditions supporting it, and concern with the exploitation of women as "sex objects" have obscured the exploitation of women as "reproductive objects." Women's oppression was analyzed primarily from the general vantage point of women and, more specifically, from the vantage point of present and future mothers. As motherhood was taken for granted, the main issue became one of finding ways to combine it with an active working life. The issue of parenthood was considered in the context of role sharing and developing ideologies about the benefits and desirability of androgyny. Ideologically, reproduction was conceptualized as a female issue; structurally, sexual inequality led to the identification of men as the main source of oppression. Given those ideological and structural boundaries that determine the historically specific form in which women's oppression under advanced capitalism is experienced, the issue of pronatalism, which questions not just compulsory motherhood but compulsory parenthood and considers reproduction as a process affecting both women and men, could not possibly emerge as a paramount issue. On the other hand, *the lack of specific theoretical and political concern with pronatalism among women at this time does not invalidate its existence and its negative impact on all women.* Given the present material conditions, working mothers (whatever their socioeconomic status) face a series of social, economic, and psychological obstacles. The situation is worsened for women who are the sole support of themselves and their children. Many of those women might not have become mothers and today would have considerably better opportunities if pronatalism had not impelled them into motherhood. In a sense, pronatalism compels women to handicap themselves, sometimes very early in their lives, and a similar argument could be made with respect to men. As Blake pointed out, pronatalist reward structures impel women and men marginally committed to parenthood to form families because that is the price to be paid for normality, respectability, credibility, and fulfillment of adult sex role expectations. The high incidence of child abuse and battered wives, the high divorce and remarriage rates, the high increases in illegitimacy and teenage pregnancy, and the growth of female-headed households are phenomena which should highlight the importance of investigating the negative consequences of prescriptive parenthood. I am *not* arguing that pronatalism is their only cause or even their major cause; I am suggesting that it is likely to be a strong contributing factor because it pressures women and men, sometimes at very early ages, to enter into relationships for which they might not be entirely suited and under conditions that turn those relationships into mere means to accomplish personal goals. A drastic change in the social organization of reproduction is not likely to do away with those processes entirely, but it is very likely to drastically reduce their incidence. What follows is an attempt to examine theoretically the relationship among capitalism, sexism, and pronatalism in an effort to clarify some of the issues raised in the preceding discussion.

Capitalism, Pronatalism, and Sexism

Demographically, precapitalist societies were characterized by high death and birth rates, high infant mortality rates, and short life expectancy. Under these conditions, social mechanisms ensured—through complex networks of rewards and punishments—that most adults engaged in reproduction to ensure societal survival. This is a functional argument advanced to explain the demographic origins of pronatalism: the answer to high mortality conditions is universally prescribed parenthood. From the standpoint of Marxist theory, a demographic functional explanation is adequate only to account for pronatalism abstractly and in isolation from any historical determinations: i.e., as a universal feature of all societies. A purely functional explanation, however, is in itself insufficient to account for the origins and variations of the pronatalist institutions operating in concrete social formations at a given time. Such institutions (e.g., values, sex roles, norms about family size, etc.) must be linked, structurally and historically, to the mode of production dominant in a given social formation at a given time. Given the world dominance of the capitalist mode of production, to develop a Marxist theoretical analysis of pronatalism it is necessary to identify its capitalist origins and the capitalist structures and processes that support it. *I am not arguing that pronatalism originated with capitalism.* Following Marx's methodological principles,[49] I am arguing that a functional explanation (i.e., the need to ensure societal survival) cannot explain the historically specific form taken by pronatalism under capitalism nor the specifically capitalist institutions that support it.

Capitalism emerged in a social context where high birth and death rates were dominant and so it inherited a variety of pronatalist institutions. Research would show that the features pronatalism acquired in the capitalist mode of production are likely to be qualitatively different from those characteristic of precapitalist social formations. A thorough comparative analysis is beyond the scope of this essay, for it would require hypotheses about the origins and determinants of pronatalism, its relationship to sexism, and its relationship to the organization of production within capitalist and pre-capitalist modes of production. Such frameworks are yet to be developed. I have limited my contribution to developing a general theoretical argument outlining my understanding, at this point, of the relationship between sexism, pronatalism, and capitalism. For reasons of space my analysis will examine the impact of pronatalism only on the working class.

The impact of the process of capitalist development upon the family that resulted in the division between private and public spheres of production and social life has been amply documented.[50] This is the material basis for women's oppression under capitalism.[51] Women are segregated in the home as reproducers of the present and future generation of workers. Their participation in the public sphere is subordinate to their household role and they, and their children, are economically dependent on men. Although increasing numbers of women have been drawn into the labor force, women have not been successful in their struggle for equal jobs with equal pay. The material constraints to women's labor force participation result from the contradictions of the capitalist mode of production and the changing strategies with which the capitalist classes attempt to resolve those contradictions. Such strategies determine fluctuations in real wages as well as fluctuations in the quantity and quality of the demand for labor, which in turn determine the size and composition of the reserve army of labor. These material constraints have been justified in a variety of ways. While feminists have identified sexism as one of the most powerful justifications, Blake suggests that the maintenance of family roles may be just as important:

> The difficulties women experienced who wished to challenge the identity of sexual and parental roles have not been simply "male dominance" or "male power," but rather the intense societal supports for the *family roles* of mother and father. The opposition to women working thus stemmed fully as much from the obligatory nature of family formation (and the sex differentiation of parents) as from fear for the diminuation of male authority generally.[52]

This is an important theoretical insight, suggesting that sexism could be productively analyzed as a result of pronatalist structures and ideologies aimed at placing men and women in family roles. Blake's argument rests upon an analysis of the social processes through which men and women are recruited into family roles. She points out that, contrary to the dominant feminist assumptions, family formation entails direct costs and opportunity costs not only for women but also for men: "men's chances for social and personal mobility, for education, for promotion, etc., may be impaired by parenthood."[53] Male supremacy is the main social inducement that pressures men into domesticity. The social and economic advantages it provides them compensate for the opportunities they may forego, and for the problems, humiliations, and setbacks experienced in the labor market and in their jobs. In turn, women are pushed into family roles not only by institutionalized sexism, but also by the social and psychological rewards attached to those roles.

Her analysis discloses a complex interrelationship between sexism and pronatalism. Pronatalism places women and men into family roles through structures and ideologies that reward the latter while punishing the former: sexism. This inherently unstable situation is stabilized by pronatalist ideologies about motherhood that reward women's compliance with pronatalist and sexist sex role expectations. Sexism obscures the costs of parenthood for men, while the motherhood mystique obscures the costs of parenthood for women; both reflect pronatalist social constraints that support family roles as a taken-for-granted component of adult roles.

To establish the relevance of Blake's insights for the understanding of sexism under capitalist conditions, it is necessary to investigate the relationship between pronatalism and the capitalist material basis of sexism. If sexism is structurally supported by the specifically capitalist division of production into a public and a private sphere, where does pronatalism fit? The answer to that question might be found in the relationship between alienated labor and reproduction depicted by Marx in his early writings on alienation.[54] Capitalist production rests upon the exploitation of labor. All labor is, thus, alienated labor; i.e., instead of furthering self-realization, labor becomes a process of self-degradation and conversely, everything else becomes a means of self-realization.[55] In Marx's graphic terms,

> man (the worker) feels himself to be freely active only in his animal functions—eating, drinking, and procreating, or at most in his personal adornment—while in his human function he is reduced to an animal.[56]

Marx has vividly portrayed the dichotomy permeating social life under capitalism that has enshrined "personal life" while destroying the possibilities for fruitful and creative public life. The full meaning of alienated labor involves the alienation of the workers from themselves, from their work, from the product of their work, and from their fellow workers. Women and men are compelled to seek meaning, under such conditions, in a variety of individual pursuits—some constructive (among which family roles are the most important) and some self-destructive. Social scientists investigating the determinants of fertility patterns have documented the significance of family roles as the major source of individuals' satisfaction in contemporary society, as well as the relationship between high fertility and feelings of alienation, powerlessness, isolation, and failure to achieve occupational success.[57] It would appear that, in the context of advanced capitalism, family formation patterns as well as fertility patterns reflect pronatalist constraints supported by the alienating and exploitative nature of the economic and social organization.

The specific features characterizing pronatalism and sexism under capitalist conditions are the result of capitalist structures, processes, and contradictions. I have outlined my argument in Figure 1 and I will now explain the meaning of the relationships I have postulated.

The strategies for capital accumulation followed by the capitalist classes at any given time are the product of the contradiction between capital and labor, and the contradiction between the forces and the relations of production.[58] One important consequence of the accumulation process, at the level of the overall organization of production, has been the division of production into a domestic and a public sector; this is the key underpinning of sexism under capitalist conditions. At a different level of analysis—the relations of production within each sector—the most prominent phenomenon is the exploitation and alienation of labor; this is the key underpinning of pronatalism under capitalist conditions. Alienation and exploitation of labor, and the separation between household and public production, are two aspects of the same process. It is important to differentiate them analytically in order to establish their different modes of affecting sexism, pronatalism, the nuclear family and family relations and, most important, the status of women in capitalist society.

Sexism and pronatalism are two qualitatively different sets of oppressive structures and ideologies, both of which are supported by the overall capitalist organization of production and by the nature of the relations of production. They are reproduced by the process of capitalist accumulation, which constantly reproduces their structural underpinnings, and by the pertinent ideologies that contribute to their reproduction at the level of the personality structure of women and men living under capitalism.

Sexism and pronatalism are mutually interrelated and support each other by providing compensatory ideologies and practices that relieve the tensions and contradictions they create in the relationships between the sexes and between generations. For example, the exploitation of male workers is made more bearable by male supremacy and its attendant social, economic, and domestic privileges. Because of their secondary status in production, women are exploited in the labor and sexual markets while they experience economic and reproductive oppression at home. On the other hand, pronatalist ideologies about family roles, the nature of motherhood, the meaning of children, etc., compensate for a great deal of the oppression women experience inside and outside their homes. The alienation women and men experience in their lives is resolved in the idealization of the family, which is structurally supported by the contradictions inherent in capitalist relations operating directly, through the organization and relations of production, and indirectly, through pronatalist and sexist constraint. As feminists have pointed out, the ideological

PRONATALISM, SEXISM
AND CAPITALISM

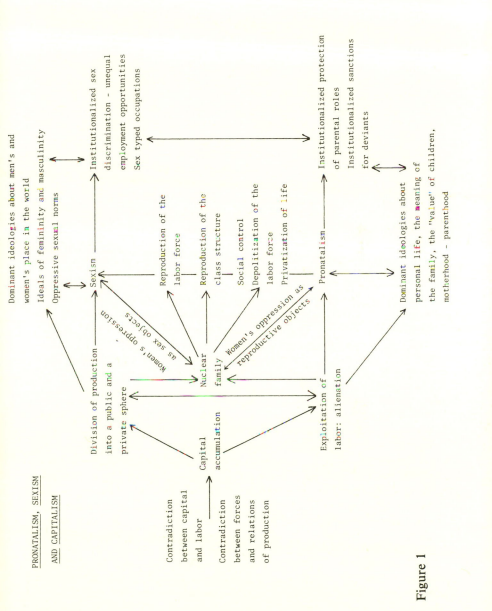

Figure 1

construction of the family as a place of total peace and refuge constantly breaks down, for it reproduces the contradictions of the mode of production in ways that are ultimately destructive to its members.[59] Nevertheless, although the problematic nature of family relations in contemporary society has been widely acknowledged, families continue to be formed. Why? Not only because they fulfill important structural and ideological functions for the capitalist mode of production but also, and this is where Blake's contribution sheds light, because parental roles are a taken-for-granted aspect of adult roles. Structurally and psychologically, family formation is not a choice for either women or men.

The development of the productive forces has brought about a decline in the death rate which has rendered obsolete not only the high fertility previously required for societal survival but also the pronatalist constraints that went with it. Advanced capitalism has created the material conditions necessary to undermine prescriptive parenthood in the context of advanced capitalist societies, and allow for the emergence of a qualitatively different form of institutionalized pronatalism that would make optional motherhood possible. On the other hand, advanced capitalism continues to reproduce the material conditions that make prescriptive parenthood (as well as sexism) an important tool for maintaining social control and the exploitation of labor. The contradiction between the demographic consequences of the development of the productive forces and the pronatalist and sexist implications of the capitalist organization and relations of production is reflected in the mutually reinforcing and, at the same time, contradictory relationship between pronatalism and sexism. For example, capitalism tends to undermine sexism by allowing greater economic and educational opportunities for women, but at the same time it supports sexism through pronatalist ideologies that compel women to subordinate their social and economic self-reliance and advancement to family roles. Capitalist processes undermine pronatalism by creating the material conditions for a qualitatively different form of reproductive freedom, while at the same time supporting it by (a) denying real, desirable options to women, so that family roles remain more appealing whatever gains women may experience in labor force participation; and (b) strengthening sexist relations between women and men that interfere with women's ability to use contraception effectively and consistently.

Bringing pronatalism into the theoretical analysis of sexism is helpful not only for understanding the structural underpinnings of sexism, but also for devising effective measures against it. Sexism is not likely to disappear as a result of changes in the mode of production unless such changes also lead to the demise of pronatalism as currently structured. While pronatalist constraints ensuring population replacement are a given in all modes of production, the analysis so far developed in this essay has led to the following general theoretical insights:

1) In modes of production based on class and the private appropriation of the surplus, pronatalist constraints are linked to the oppression of women and class exploitation in ways that are yet to be investigated.

2) In transitional socialist societies, characterized by heightened class struggles aimed at abolishing the old institutions and creating the material and subjective conditions for a classless society, pronatalism and sexism are likely to persist to the extent that changes in the material conditions and "socialist accumulation" are emphasized to the detriment of changes in the subjective conditions and in the quality of life. The persistence of sexism in transitional socialist societies today might be partially explained by the fact that reproduction is held subordinate to production requirements,[60] and alienating labor conditions have not yet been superseded.[61]

3) In classless modes of production based upon the collective ownership of the means of production and the collective appropriation and enjoyment of the surplus, pronatalist constraints will change their theoretical and empirical location in the mode of production. From being part of the structural constraints determining the behavior of individuals independent of their will, they will become part of the conscious effort of the collectivity to achieve mastery over its own processes of production and reproduction, both in terms of the production of goods and services and in terms of generational reproduction. The collective will be able to choose its replacement rate in accordance with a rational assessment of its material constraints and possibilities while giving maximum freedom of choice to its individual members.

In this section I have explored the relationship between capitalism, pronatalism, and sexism and I have briefly touched upon the changing nature of pronatalism and sexism under different modes of production. In the light of the experiences of the woman's movement since the 1960s and the resurgence of right-wing anti-feminist forces in the late 1970s, pronatalism and sexism emerge as tools of class domination which capitalist processes tend to undermine in times of economic prosperity and reinforce in times of economic downturns, when women's increased pressure for full socioeconomic participation contributes to exacerbate the contradictions of the system.[62]

I have discussed these issues at the highest level of analysis, the mode of production. The empirical manifestations of the relationships postulated in Figure 1 will vary from one social formation to another according to their historically specific characteristics.[63] I have not intended to present a theory of pronatalism under capitalist conditions but simply to suggest a framework useful for future investigation.

Conclusion

Present pronatalist structures and ideologies that rule out a childfree status as a legitimate and desirable option for women as well as for men have undesirable social and demographic effects; more important, they play a key role in supporting sexism. In arguing that feminists should take pronatalism seriously, I am *not* suggesting that they should take an "anti-child" stance. I am, however, suggesting that reproduction be considered *one among other options* rather than the main option. This implies giving to the loosely defined "right to control one's body" a concrete content: women's right to determine not only *how many* children they want and *when* they want them, but also *whether* they want *any* children at all.

The reader should be aware of the limitations of this expanded concept of reproductive freedom. Present capitalist constraints determine the emergence and dominance of an abstract notion of reproductive freedom as the pure negation of constraint. I have argued in this essay that the apparently radical advocacy of reproductive freedom in the abstract, without specifying a content including the option to remain childfree, remains trapped in the dominant pronatalist problematic and unwittingly lends support to it. On the other hand, while positing a more concrete and effective challenge to pronatalist and sexist institutions, this expanded notion of reproductive freedom is itself conditioned in its scope and relevance by the nature of the present social arrangements. It is formulated as a woman's right and, as such, it remains caught in the individualistic approach to rights that characterizes the capitalist legal and political traditions, and in the dominant approach to reproduction that views it as a purely female concern. As Blake pointed out, pronatalism also has oppressive consequences for men. Furthermore, from a Marxist theoretical standpoint, reproduction is more than the reproduction of the human species; reproduction is a class strategy for survival, and the study of changing reproductive patterns cannot adequately proceed in the absence of an analysis of their roots in class relations and class struggles.[64] This involves, in turn, the analysis of the specific ways in which sexism and pronatalism operate in the context of different classes and sectors of classes. I have not pursued these lines of inquiry because these issues would have taken me beyond the purposes of this essay, which are to determine the adequacy of Blake's criticisms and to explore the theoretical and political importance of pronatalism for the feminist struggle. This concept of reproductive freedom which presents a childfree status as a legitimate option for women is in itself an important advancement that needs further consideration and elaboration by feminists and should be incorporated as a specific goal of the present struggle for reproductive self-determination.

Both the early feminist standpoint, according to which women should choose between spinsterhood and careers *or* motherhood, and the modern feminist support of women's right "to do both" are uncritically built around motherhood as an ascriptive status, as a taken-for-granted aspect of women's lives. Awareness of pronatalism and its relationship to sexism would lead to critical questioning of prescriptive motherhood and the oppression of women as "reproductive objects" in as deep and systematic a way as feminists have questioned women's oppression as "sex objects." Unless a critical examination of parenthood is accomplished and clear alternatives to it are outlined, lip service to women's right to control their reproductive lives will not suffice to free women from present pronatalist constraints. *Theoretically,* the task is to develop a thorough analysis of the relationship between capitalism, pronatalism, and sexism. The different ways in which pronatalism affects the sexes, classes, sectors of classes, and ethnic groups should be empirically established to provide a sound basis for political action. *Ideologically,* the advocacy of clearly defined alternatives for women that go beyond the "do both" syndrome to include, among others, a childfree status as well as full-time motherhood as legitimate options, would contemplate not only the needs of all women at this time, but would also present younger women with options that challenge the pronatalist orientation of the society.

Marx argued that, in the process of studying social transformations,

> it is necessary to distinguish between the material transformation of the economic conditions of production, which can be determined with the precision of natural science, and the legal, political, religious, artistic, or philosophic—in short, ideological forms in which men become conscious of this conflict and fight it out. Just as one does not judge an individual by what he thinks of himself, so one cannot judge such a period of transformation by its consciousness but, on the contrary, this consciousness must be explained from the contradictions of material life.[65]

Current contradictions in the material conditions of production and reproduction have made possible the rise of feminist and anti-feminist political forces as well as the theoretical analysis of sexism and pronatalism from a variety of standpoints. Blake approached these issues as a demographer concerned not only with the excess population generated by pronatalist patterns but also with their individual and social costs. Like her article, mine is also a product of the times and could not have been written without her valuable insights, and without the groundwork prepared by feminist theory and feminist struggles. However, it must be acknowledged that most feminist analyses depict the ideological forms in which women have become aware of these contradictions and have fought them. The present mainstream consciousness of the movement is a product of the dominant contradictions affecting women for whom the most pressing problem is that of combining home and work. The ideological hegemony of pronatalism makes it difficult to perceive its contribution to the existence of the problems affecting women; as Blake pointed out, social pressures ensuring the performance of parental roles are generally perceived as men's efforts to keep women in their place. The reality of male supremacy overshadows the reality of pronatalism as well as the connections between the two.

It might be argued that it would be unrealistic and perhaps counterproductive to criticize pronatalism, on the grounds that, at the present time, most women are or plan to be mothers. That argument would be as self-defeating as the suggestion that one should not combat sexism because, after all, we have all been socialized in a sexist society and everyone is sexist in one way or another. Without denying the legitimacy, validity, and timeliness of the dominant concerns of the present generations, it must be acknowledged that *theory cannot be entirely subordinate to practical concerns without becoming a mere reflection of dominant interests rather than a scientific effort to disclose the nature of social reality.* Lenin's often-quoted statement, "without revolutionary theory there can be no revolutionary movement,"[66] is pertinent. A revolutionary theory of the oppression of women, i.e., one that uncovers all the manifold determinations of sexism in the capitalist mode of production in order to effectively struggle against it, is one that goes beyond the immediate forms in which sex and class struggles are perceived and fought. Awareness of pronatalism and research on its relationship to sexism is an important step in that direction.

Notes

I am greatly indebted to the helpful suggestions and criticisms of Renate Bridenthal, Carmen Diana Deere, and Terry Fee.

1. The terms "women's liberation movement," "women's movement," and "the movement" are used in a purely descriptive sense to refer to the heterogeneous organizational and ideological mobilization of women that emerged in the United States in the late 1960s.

2. Judith Blake. "Coerceive Pronatalism and American Population Policy," in *Pronatalism: The Myth of Mom and Apple Pie,* edited by Ellen Peck and J. Senderowitz (New York: Thomas Y. Crowell, 1974), pp. 44–50. Judith Blake is a demographer who has written extensively on the relationship between social structure and fertility. To my knowledge, her systematic analysis of pronatalism and its significance for the status of women is unique in the literature.

3. Ibid., pp. 29–67.

4. Ibid., p. 30 (emphasis mine).

5. Ibid., p. 33 (emphasis in the text).

6. Ibid., p. 45.

7. Ibid., p. 36 (emphasis in the text).

8. Ibid., p. 47.

9. Martha E. Gimenez, "Marxism and Feminism," *Frontiers, A Journal of Women's Studies* 1, no. 1 (1975): 61–80; "Structuralist Marxism on the Woman Question," *Science and Society* 42, no. 3 (1978): 301–23.

10. See Barbara Deckard, *The Women's Movement* (New York: Harper & Row, 1975), for an excellent overview.

11. See Judy MacLean, "N.O.W.," *Socialist Revolution* 29 (1976): 39–50; *Sisterhood Is Powerful,* edited by Robin Morgan (New York: Vintage Books, 1970), pp. 512–31, which contains a series of "Manifestos"; Brigid Brophy, "Women Are Prisoners of Their Sex," in *The New Feminism in Twentieth-Century America,* edited

by June Sochen (Lexington, Mass.: D. C. Heath & Co., 1971), pp. 73–79; Roxanne Dunbar, "Female Liberation as the Basis for Social Revolution," in Sochen, *The New Feminism,* pp. 172–92; Kathy McAfee and Myrna Wook, "Bread and Roses," in *From Feminism to Liberation,* edited by Edith Hoshino Alback (Cambridge, Mass.: Schenckman Publishing Co., 1971), pp. 21–38; "Southern Female Rights Union Program for Female Liberation," in *Voices from Women's Liberation,* edited by Leslie B. Tanner (New York: Signet Books, 1970), pp. 112–15; "Congress to Unite Women—What Women Want," in Tanner, *Voices,* pp. 124–26; "Women Unite for Revolution," in Tanner, *Voices,* pp. 129–32.

12. "Congress to Unite Women," and "Women Unite for Revolution," in Tanner, *Voices from Women's Liberation,* pp. 124–26 and 129–32.

13. The term "childfree," which denotes choice rather than the deprivation implied by the term "childless," is used by Peck and Senderowitz in the introduction to *Pronatalism.* A childfree status, as a legitimate choice, is advocated by N.O.N., National Organization for Non-Parents.

14. Alice Rossi, "Sex Equality: The Beginning of Ideology" in *Masculine/Feminine: Readings in Sexual Mythology and the Liberation of Women,* edited by Betty Roszak and Theodore Roszak (New York: Harper & Row, 1969), pp. 173–86; "Equality Between the Sexes: An Immodest Proposal," in Sochen, *The New Feminism,* pp. 87–112; Jo Freeman, "The Revolution Is Happening in Our Minds," in Sochen, *New Feminism,* pp. 149–60; "The Women's Liberation Movement: Its Origins, Structures, and Ideas," in *Family, Marriage and the Struggle of the Sexes,* edited by Hans Peter Dreitzel (New York: Macmillan, 1972), pp. 201–16; Marlene Dixon, "The Rise of Women's Liberation," in Roszak and Roszak, *Masculine/Feminine,* pp. 186–201; "Why Women's Liberation—2?" in *Female Liberation,* edited by Roberta Salper (New York: Alfred A. Knopf, 1972), pp. 184–200; "Women's Liberation: Opening Chapter 2," in *Canadian Dimension* 10, no. 8 (June 1975): pp. 56–58; Margaret Benston, "The Political Economy of Women's Liberation," *Monthly Review* 21, no. 4 (1969): p. 13–25; Linda Gordon, "Functions of the Family," in Tanner, *Voices from Women's Liberation,* pp. 193–99; Lucinda Cisler, "Unfinished Business: Birth Control and Women's Liberation," in Morgan, *Sisterhood Is Powerful,* pp. 245–88; Roberta Salper, "The Development of the American Women's Liberation Movement," in Salper, *Female Liberation,* pp. 169–84; Judith Benninger Brown, "Female Liberation First and Now," in Roszak and Roszak, *Masculine/Feminine,* pp. 222–29.

15. Dixon, "Why Women's Liberation—2?" p. 189.

16. Brown, "Female Liberation First and Now," p. 226.

17. Salper, "The Development of the American Women's Liberation Movement," p. 184.

18. Cisler, "Unfinished Business," p. 288 (emphasis in the text).

19. Ibid.

20. Ibid., p. 248 (emphasis mine).

21. Ibid., (emphasis mine).

22. Rossi, "Equality Between the Sexes," pp. 92–93.

23. Alice Rossi, "A Biosocial Perspective on Parenting," *Daedalus—A Special Issue on the Family* 106, no. 2 (1977): 1–31.

24. The reader is referred to the following excellent critiques of Rossi's arguments: Margaret Cerullo, Judith Stacey, and Wini Breines, "Alice Rossi's Sociobiology and Anti-Feminist Backlash," and Nancy Chodorow, "Considerations on a Biosocial Perspective on Parenting," both in *Berkeley Journal of Sociology* 22 (1977–78): 167–77 and 179–97.

25. Elizabeth W. Moen, "What Does 'Control Over Our Bodies' Really Mean?" *International Journal of Women's Studies* 2, no. 2 (1979): 129–43.

26. Ibid., p. 136.

27. Juliet Mitchell, "Women: The Longest Revolution," *New Left Review* 40 (1969): pp. 19–26; expanded and reprinted in *Woman's Estate* (New York: Pantheon Books, 1971).

28. Mitchell, *Woman's Estate,* pp. 107, 108 (emphasis mine).

29. Ibid., p. 107.

30. Ibid., p. 108 (emphasis mine).

31. See, for example, Kingsley Davis and Judith Blake, "Social Structure and Fertility: An Analytical Framework," *Economic Development and Cultural Change* 4 (1956): 211–35.

32. For an understanding of the concept "mode of production," see, for example, Louis Althusser and E. Balibar, *Reading Capital* (New York: Pantheon Books, 1979).

33. Mitchell, *Woman's Estate,* p. 90.

34. Sheila Rowbotham, *Woman's Consciousness, Man's World* (London: Penguin Books, 1974), p. 114.

35. Linda Gordon, *Woman's Body, Woman's Right* (New York: Grossman Publishers, 1976), p. 405 (emphasis mine).

36. Ibid., p. 408.

37. Ibid., p. 405.

38. Ibid., p. 414.

39. Ibid., p. 417.

40. Ibid., p. 418 (emphasis mine).

41. Shulamith Firestone, *The Dialectic of Sex* (New York: Bantam Books, 1971), pp. 8–9.

42. Ibid., p. 10.

43. Ibid., p. 11.

44. Ibid., pp. 199–200.

45. Ibid., p. 299.

46. Aldous Huxley, *Brave New World* (New York: Harper & Row, 1969).

47. It is true that to overlook pronatalism is not the same as to actively support it. On the other hand, neutrality is impossible in situations of power inequality. In the arena of ideological struggles, to have low consciousness about crucial issues that challenge the status quo has the unintended effect of lending support, albeit unwittingly so, to the dominant views sustaining the status quo.

48. The reader can find a thorough study of this trend in Heather L. Ross and Isabel V. Sawhill, *Time of Transition: The Growth of Families Headed by Women* (Washington, DC: The Urban Institute, 1975).

49. See Marx's important methodological considerations in Karl Marx, *A Contribution to the Critique of Political Economy* (New York: International Publishers, 1970), pp. 188–214; also Maurice Godelier, "System, Structure, and Contradiction in *Das Kaptial,*" in *Introduction to Structuralism* (New York: Basic Books, 1970), pp. 340–58.

50. See, for example, Eli Zaretsky, "Capitalism, the Family, and Personal Life," *Socialist Revolution* 13–14 (January–April, 1973): 69–125; Wally Secombe, "The Housewife and Her Labor Under Capitalism," *New Left Review* 83 (1974): 3–24; and Mary P. Ryan, *Womanhood in America* (New York: New Viewpoints, 1976).

51. I am making a theoretical point similar to that previously developed about pronatalism. *I am not arguing that sexism originated with capitalism.* From a Marxist standpoint, knowledge of the "origins" of sexism—in chronological terms—is not very helpful for understanding how it operates today, its institutional supports, and how to fight effectively against it (and this principle is relevant for the study of any other issue). In order to understand how sexism operates under capitalist conditions it is necessary to identify its capitalist "origins" and functions; i.e., the specifically capitalist processes

that incorporated sexism into the fabric of capitalist structures and ideologies, and the uses of sexism in the interest of the capitalist class. For a detailed development of this argument, see Gimenez, "Marxism and Feminism" and "Structuralist Marxism" (note 9); for methodological sources, see note 49.

52. Blake, "Coercive Pronatalism," p. 36 (emphasis in the original).

53. Ibid., p. 49.

54. Karl Marx, "Alienated Labor," in *Karl Marx: Early Writings,* edited by T. B. Bottomore (New York: McGraw-Hill, 1964), pp. 120-34. I have begun the development of this argument in my article "Befolkningsproblemet—Marx kontra Malthus," *Den Ny Verden* 8 Argang/ no. 3 (1973): 74-88; see also the section on "Fertility" in my article "Population and Capitalism," *Latin American Perspectives* 4, no. 4 (1977): 5-40.

55. See, for example, Special Task Force to the Secretary of Health, Education and Welfare, *Work in America* (Cambridge: M.I.T. Press, 1973); Harry Braverman, *Labor and Monopoly Capital: The Degradation of Work in the Twentieth Century* (New York: Monthly Review Press, 1974).

56. Marx, "Alienated Labor," pp. 124-25.

57. See, for example, H. Theodore Groat and Arthur G. Neal, "A Social Psychological Approach to Family Formation," in *Population Studies: Selected Essays and Research,* edited by Kenneth C. W. Kammeyer (Chicago: Rand McNally, 1975), pp. 46-59; "Social Class and Alienation Correlates of Protestant Fertility," *Journal of Marriage and the Family* 35 (1973): 83-88; Judith Blake, "Demographic Science and the Redirection of Population Policy," *Journal of Chronic Diseases* 18 (1965): 1811-1200; "Are Babies Consumer Durables?" *Population Studies* 22 (1968): 5-25; Peter M. Blau and O. C. Duncan, *The American Occupational Structure* (New York: John Wiley, 1975), pp. 427-28.

58. For a clear explanation of these concepts see Gören Therborn, *Science, Class and Society* (London: NLB, 1976), pp. 353-86.

59. Mitchell, *Woman's Estate,* chap. 8, offers an excellent analysis of this topic.

60. In the Soviet Union, for example, concern with declining birth rates and future labor shortages overrides considerations about women's rights to control their reproductive lives. In an effort to encourage women to bear more children, the state is attempting to discourage premarital sex (separate from reproduction) and extols the joys of marital sex and childbearing. Blatant pronatalist arguments are used for that purpose; it is suggested, for example, that the birth of the first child is the best cure for female frigidity ("Russia Battles Birth Rate with Sex Education," *Intercom* 4, no. 2 [1976]: 14). Also, pronatalist rewards and penalties have been instituted to foster childbearing: "Women still receive medals for having more than ten children, and a couple pays a penalty tax of 6 percent of their salaries until they have their first child" ("Liberated Women in Russia? Nyet", *Intercom* 4, no. 9 [1976]: 14).

61. See, for example, Ernest Mandel, "Progressive Disalienation Through the Building of Socialist Society or the Inevitable Alienation in Industrial Society," in Mandel, ed. *The Formation of the Economic Thought of Karl Marx* (New York: Monthly Review Press, 1971), pp. 187-210.

62. For a comprehensive account of the processes aiming to undermine abortion rights, see Kristin Booth Glen, "Abortion in the Courts: A Laywoman's Historical Guide to the New Disaster Area," *Feminist Studies* 4, no. 1 (1978): 1-26. For an excellent theoretical and empirical analysis of the relationship between the capitalist economic cycle and the politics of feminist repression, see Peggy Powell Dobbins, "Towards a Theory of the Women's Liberation Movement and Women's Wage-Labor," *The Insurgent Sociologist* 7, no. 3 (1977): 53-68.

63. While the capitalist structural supports of pronatalism and sexism are the same in all social formations where the capitalist mode of production is dominant, their em-

pirical manifestations will be modified in historically specific ways that vary with the characteristics of each social formation (e.g., the kinds of precapitalist modes of production with which capitalism is combined, the ethnic composition of the population, the kinds of economic opportunities determined by the natural environment, etc.), their legal, political, and ideological structures, and their dominant or subordinate place in the world capitalist system. For a theoretical discussion of these issues, see, for example, Louis Althusser, *For Marx* (New York: Vintage Books, 1970), p. 80–128 and 162–218.

64. For further elaboration of this point, see, for example, Martha E. Gimenez, "Population and Capitalism," *Latin American Perspective* 4, no. 4 (1977): 5–40; "Theories of Reproductive Behavior: A Marxist Critique," *The Review of Radical Political Economics* 11, no. 2 (1979): 17–24; and Eric R. Weiss-Altaner, "The Influence of Socio-Economic Conditions on the Fertility of Women in the Third World," paper presented at the session on Household Model of Economic-Demographic Decision Making, International Population Conference, Mexico City, 1977.

65. Marx, *Critique of Political Economy,* p. 21.

66. V. I. Lenin, "What Is to Be Done?" in *Collected Works,* vol. 5 (Moscow: Progress Publishers, 1975), p. 369.

18

Motherhood: The Annihilation of Women

JEFFNER ALLEN

I would like to affirm the rejection of motherhood on the grounds that motherhood is dangerous to women. If woman, in patriarchy, is she who exists as the womb and wife of man, every woman is by definition a mother: she who produces for the sake of men. A mother is she whose body is used as a resource to reproduce men and the world of men, understood both as the biological children of patriarchy and as the ideas and material goods of patriarchal culture. Motherhood is dangerous to women because it continues the structure within which females must be women and mothers and, conversely, because it denies to females the creation of a subjectivity and world that is open and free.

An active rejection of motherhood entails the development and enactment of a *philosophy of evacuation.*[1] Identification and analysis of the multiple aspects of motherhood not only show what is wrong with motherhood, but also point to a way out. A philosophy of evacuation proposes women's collective removal of ourselves from all forms of motherhood. Freedom is never achieved by the mere inversion of an oppressive construct, that is, by seeing motherhood in a "new" light. Freedom is achieved when an oppressive construct, motherhood, is vacated by its members and thereby rendered null and void.

A small and articulate group of radical feminist and radical lesbian feminist authors agree that motherhood is oppressive to women. Simone de Beauvoir's position in *The Second Sex,* that woman's "misfortune is to have been biologically destined for the repetition of life,"[2] is reaffirmed in her recent interviews: "I think a woman must not fall into the trap of children and marriage. Even if a woman wants to have children, she must think very hard about the conditions in which she will have to bring them up, because child-bearing, at the moment, is real slavery."[3] Shulamith Firestone, following de Beauvoir, finds that, "the heart of woman's oppression is her childbearing and childrearing roles."[4] That woman's "reproductive function . . . is the critical distinction upon which all inequities toward women are grounded" is also asserted by Ti-Grace Atkinson at the beginning of the second wave of the women's liberation movement.[5] Monique Wittig writes that a female becomes a woman and a mother when she is defined first, and above all else, in terms of "the capacity to give birth (biology)."[6]

The claim that a direct connection exists between woman's oppression and her role as breeder within patriarchy also entails the recognition that men impose a type of sexuality on women through the institution of motherhood. De Beauvoir agrees that "frigidity seems . . ., in the present state of malaise created by the power relationship between men and women, a reaction at least more prudent and more reasonable [than woman's being trapped in sexuality] because it reflects this malaise and makes women less dependent on men."[7] Atkinson answers affirmatively the more specific question "Do you still feel that sexual instincts would disappear if 'sexual intercourse' no longer served the function of reproduction?"[8] Wittig holds that, "Sexuality is for us (lesbian feminists) an inevitable battleground insofar as we want to get outside of genitality and of the sexual economy imposed on us by the dominant heterosexuality."[9] Andrea Dworkin states clearly and without equivocation, "There is a continuum of phallic control. In the male system, reproductive and nonreproductive sex are both phallic sex."[10] I engage in a philosophy of evacuation as a radical lesbian feminist who questions, analyzes, and describes how motherhood is dangerous to women.

Speaking of motherhood as the annihilation of women does not disclaim either women's past or present as mothers. Women as mothers make the best of motherhood. Women are mothers because within patriarchy women have no choice except motherhood. Without the institution of motherhood women could and would live otherwise. Just as no single woman, or particular mother, is free in patriarchy, no group of token women, mothers in general, are free in patriarchy. Until patriarchy no longer exists, all females, as historical beings, must resist, rebel against, and avoid producing for the sake of men. Motherhood is not a matter of woman's psychological or moral character. As an ideology by which men mark females as women, motherhood has nothing to do with a woman's selfishness or sacrifice, nurturance or nonviolence. Motherhood has everything to do with a history in which women remain powerless by reproducing the world of men and with a present in which women are expected to do the same. The central publication of the Soviet Women's Committee, for instance, writes, "Considering motherhood to be a woman's most important social function . . ."[11]

I am endangered by motherhood. In evacuation from motherhood, I claim my life, body, world, as an end in itself.

Where Do Children Come From?

The question "Where do babies come from?" is frequently dismissed with a laugh, or cut short by recourse to scientific authority. In present-day discourse, both God's prescience and the stork are generally thought to be inadequate responses. A satisfactory and "progressive" explanation is found in a scientific account of the union of egg and sperm. The appeal to science is misleading, however, for it ignores and conceals the social intercourse which first brings men and women together either indirectly, through the use of medical technology, or directly, by means of physical copulation.[12] The question "Where do babies come from?" might be approached more appropriately through the social and historical circumstances in which conception takes place: *Children come from patriarchal (male) sexuality's use of woman's body as a resource to reproduce men and the world of men.* Similarly, *motherhood* is men's appropriation of women's bodies as a resource to reproduce patriarchy.

The scientific explanation of where children come from avoids placing conception within the continuum of social power relationships that constitute motherhood: heterosexual intercourse, pregnancy, and childraising. Compulsion marks every aspect of the motherhood continuum: the mandatory heterosexuality imposed on women by men is thought "natural"; pregnancy is viewed as a biological fact; obligatory childraising by women is so "normal" that in the United States 39 percent of black families and 12 percent of white families are headed by women.[13]

Seduction and pregnancy, for instance, are remarkably similar: both eroticize women's subordination by acting out and deepening women's lack of power.[14]

> Male instinct can't help ITself; women need IT either because of their sexiness or their maternal instinct. IT, the penis, is big; IT, the child, is large. Woman's body is made for IT. Women's bodies have the right fit, or proportions. Women ask for IT, want IT. IT's a maturing experience in her becoming a woman. She takes IT. No real harm is done.

In seduction and pregnancy the power imbalance between men and women assumes the appearance of sexual difference, regardless of whether such activities are "affectionate" or "brutal."

> If women didn't want IT, IT wouldn't happen. Therefore, women must choose IT. Since many choose IT, IT must be part of their nature.[15]

I am defenseless within the motherhood continuum.

IT, "male instinct," passes through heterosexual intercourse to become the IT of motherhood. In motherhood, IT, male sexuality as a man-made social power construct, marks females with ITself. IT compels women to ITself: to male sexuality and its consequences, namely, birthing and raising men and the world of men. Children come from IT, from male-defined, male-dominated social intercourse. It names ITself as "virility": belonging to, characteristic of a man; the power of procreation, especially for sexual intercourse; the masculine member, the generative organs; force, energy, drive considered typically masculine; to pursue, to hunt.[16] Virility comes from *vir*, which in Latin means "man." Women's "misfortune is to have been biologically destined for the repetition of life"[17] precisely because ITs power, force, energy, drive appropriates women's biological possibility in order to produce ITself. IT pursues ITs own continuation, silencing my questions: is IT needed? Is IT desired? IT pursues ITs own evolution, constituting motherhood as a given, as compulsory for women, a danger to women.

The Representation

The question remains: "Where do children come from?" Or, more precisely, if children are produced by IT, by male sexuality as a man-made social power construct, how does male sexuality appropriate women's biological possibility in order to reproduce ITself? How do men constitute the motherhood continuum of heterosexual intercourse, pregnancy, and childraising as compulsory for women?

Analysis from a radical lesbian feminist perspective suggests that motherhood is constituted by male sexuality's use of woman's body to represent ITself to ITself. As such, motherhood is a paradigmatic instance of men's creation of representational thinking and of men's appropriation of the "world" by means of representational thought.

Representational thinking does not mean the production of a picture, copy, or imitation *of* the world. Representational thinking means, rather, to conceive and grasp the world *as* picture.[18] In representational thinking, man manipulates, pursues, and entraps the world in order to secure it as picture. Man brings into play his unlimited power for the calculating, planning, and molding of all things; by conceiving and grasping the world as picture, he gives the measure and draws up the guidelines for everything that is.[19] As such, he creates and determines what is real, and what is not. Not only is the man who has made the picture already in the picture, he is that which he pictures to himself. Yet, to acknowledge himself as the picture would be to destroy himself as he who conceives and grasps the world as picture. Only by maintaining a privileged stand outside the picture can he claim to be the creator, and not the object, of the activity of representation. Withdrawn from representation as the representer, however, he enters into the picture as "the incalculable," "the gigantic."[20]

The object of representational thought, in turn, is allowed to be only insofar as it can be overpowered—manipulated, pursued, entrapped—by representational thought. Once conceived and grasped as picture, the object is said to call forth, to provoke, the particular way in which it is pictured and the activity of picturing as such.[21] The object can, indeed, must repeat itself exactly as it has been thought. It must even claim to establish, maintain, and justify its objectification. Its sole "activity" is reproductive: the reiteration and reinforcement of itself as picture.

Reproductive thinking thereby generates, unavoidably and of necessity, an ideology that is reproductive: motherhood. Athena is born from the head of Zeus alone; children are born from the head of man alone.[22] Athena springs fully armed from the head of Zeus; a child springs form the head of its father, fully adorned with the markings of patriarchy. Zeus sees his world in his full-grown offspring; man pictures his world in his children who soon will be adults. Even if the child is female, man incorporates the female into his world as picture. The man with the child in his head, with the child as image in his head, represents himself to himself in the child that he has made. In contrast, Athena's mother, Metis, cannot be manipulated, pursued, trapped. She cannot be bound, secured, by man's representational thought. Athena's mother, children's mothers, are not.

In representational thought, woman is made pregnable (from *prehendere,* Latin for "to take"), understood in its literal sense as vulnerable to capture, taken. She is compelled to have man's child, to reproduce throughout her world of experience men's thoughts, words, actions. She must reproduce the life of the species, that is, man and his immortality. Captured by representational thinking, woman can never be genuinely pregnant (*pregnas,* akin to *gignere,* to produce): she cannot provide her own life and world. Woman is what-in-men's-eyes-she-seems-to-be[23] is invisible, except insofar as her body is used by man to reproduce himself and his world. Woman as what-I-am-in-my-own-eyes is not. Motherhood passes through the mind of a man, of a man who does not see woman's body as her body. The man with the child in his head does not see the woman with the child in her body. Throughout the motherhood continuum of heterosexual intercourse, pregnancy, and compulsory childraising, motherhood exists as a dialogue between men about an invisible woman.

Key to the specific mode of representation that defines motherhood, including the articulation of women's sexuality within the confines of motherhood, is male sexuality's setting of the bounds within which life and death are to be recognized. Man, the representer, assumes a greater-than-human power over life and death. Man, the representer, fixates on life and death as the central defining moments of one's life and as the two parts, or pieces, which comprise one's life. Within the framework of man's representation of life and death, woman's body is reduced to a lifeless instrument, even when her body is a carrier of life and death. The very manner in which man represents to himself his own life and death precludes, moreover, an experience of what is always already given: the continuity and discontinuity of an individual life, the strength and power of its ongoing action in the world, the authentic subjectivity of the woman who is *as* she is.

While man is giving birth to himself, woman dies. I, bound to the representation of woman as mother, leave that representation behind: evacuation to another way of thinking, to a productive empowering of the female who has been both woman and mother.

The Mark

The question "Where do children come from?" may be answered by a radical lesbian feminist phenomenology of consciousness, in terms of the representation. The representation is that form of consciousness by which patriarchal (male) sexuality constitutes a world in which woman's body is used as a resource to reproduce men and the world of men. "Where do children come from?" may also be answered by a similarly radical phenomenology of existence, through reference to the mark.[24] The mark is the form of specific difference imposed on women's bodies when appropriated by men as a resource to reproduce patriarchy. An idealist interpretation of the representation and a materialist analysis of the mark converge so as to portray, when taken together, the social intercourse that is motherhood. A philosophy of evacuation from motherhood proposes, accordingly, that from which women must collectively remove ourselves: patriarchal thinking, the representation, and patriarchal existence, the mark.

One may object that even within patriarchy some types of motherhood are free of the representation and the mark, that some individual women do not occupy woman's traditional position as she who is marked. Such women, when truly exceptional, successfully assume man's traditional position as the representer of motherhood. A distinction must be made, however, between the hope that it expressed by such an objection, i.e., that women might live more freely, and the fact that is ignored by the objection, i.e., how women actually live. Such an objection involves a non-appropriation of the female body, as if motherhood could miraculously pass through woman's mind and not through her body.[25] In fact, a female cannot escape being a mother unless she no longer produces for men, unless she is no longer compelled to reproduce the biological children, material goods, and ideas of patriarchy. Identification with the patterns traced on woman's body by the representation and the mark of motherhood is a necessity for the survival of all women. Indeed, identification with any single aspect of the motherhood continuum is an identification with every aspect of the motherhood continuum, for no single aspect exists as separable from the whole of its context. Women's identification with all women as mothers is a positive endeavor which points to what can be done, to actionary possibilities for the creation of a subjectivity that is genuinely free and open. I am no longer within patriarchy when I and all females have rendered null and void the ideology and institution of motherhood.

A radical lesbian feminist perspective suggests that the mark imposed by patriarchy on the bodies of all women compels all women to exist as mothers. The mark of motherhood inscribes the domination of men into woman's body, making motherhood appear as a natural phenomenon. Yet, motherhood is not a natural phenomenon, and mothers do not exist as a natural group. On the contrary, female biological possibilities are first "naturalized" by men as women's specific difference and then claimed as the reason for the existence of motherhood.[26] Through this "naturalization," or marking, the female's biological possibility to give birth is made to appear as the intrinsic cause of women's place in motherhood and as the origin of women's social, economic, and political place in the world. The female's biological possibility to bear a child thereby becomes the defining characteristic of all women.

The closer a mark is to the body, the more indelibly it is associated with the body and the more the individual as a whole is pursued, hunted, trapped.[27] In the case of woman, the mark has absolute permanence, for woman's entire body, and the body of her world, is marked: MOTHER. The permanence of the mark is the sign of the permanence of the male domination that marks all women as mothers.

Marking operates by focusing on isolated fragments of the female body.[28] Such fragments, vagina, breasts, etc., are marked with a significance that is presumed to be intrinsic, eternal, and to characterize the whole of the female body. Forms of activity and character traits termed "natural" to women are then deduced from the marking imposed on the body fragments.

The institution of motherhood is unique among those created by marking in that there is no other institution in which so many persons can be destroyed by the mark, and yet, a sufficient supply of persons to be marked remains. In all other forms of war, attrition eventually threatens the supply of persons who can be marked and thereby usually limits the activity of marking, at least for a time. The mark of motherhood is distinctive in that one of its by-products is the regeneration of more females to be marked as women and mothers.

The object marked, woman as mother, experiences the mark as pain. The inscription of the mark of motherhood on women's bodies is never without pain—the pain of not "owning" our bodies, the pain of physical injury, the pain of being compelled to never produce a life or world of our own. Pain (from Greek *poiné*, punishment, penalty, payment) is the punishment, the penalty we must pay, for being marked by men as woman and mother. Pain has nothing to do with what we do, that is, our success or failure at being good, well-informed, or willing mothers. Pain is a sign that we, as women, are put in danger by men who mark us. *If and when* the pain of the mark is not successfully "naturalized" by men, that is, is not or does not remain imprinted on females as belonging to our nature either physiologically or psychologically, we attempt to evade pain. Our pain breaks through the force of the mark. We do not endure the pain. We do not put up with the mark. We avoid, resist, the mark. We neither need nor desire the mark. We will get out of the mark. The immense amount of pain that marking entails is both an experience that always accompanies the mark of motherhood and an experience that can lead to the end of the mark of motherhood.

Outside the social power relationship within which marking occurs, the mark does not exist.[29] Outside patriarchy, the mark of motherhood cannot even be imagined.

Stamped, firmly imprinted on women's bodies, is the emblem that our bodies have been opened to the world of men: the shape of the pregnant woman's stomach. From conception to abortion, acts which are biologically different and yet symbolically the same, our stomachs are marked: MOTHER.

In present-day patriarchal society, the marking impressed on woman's stomach is man's proof of his virility, that he can reproduce himself. When the mark remains on women's stomachs from conception to the birth of an infant, male virility not only can, but does, reproduce itself. In contrast, when the mark remains imprinted on our stomachs from conception to the abortion of a fetus, male virility can, but does not—yet—reproduce itself. Either the time is judged as not right—yet, or the right time has passed by—already. When abortion is permitted, either officially or unofficially, there need not be an immediate and direct link between conception and the birth of an infant. There must, however, be an indirect link between male virility which can reproduce itself and male virility which does reproduce itself. The right time must eventually be found such that man both can and does reproduce himself, either by means of biological children or through the material goods and ideas of patriarchy. Indeed, within patriarchy the fact that abortion may sometimes be permitted does not make abortion a genuinely free choice, for women have no alternative but abortion if we are already impregnated and do not want to reproduce. Nor does the right to abortion make motherhood voluntary, for a woman in patriarchy cannot abort, or do away with, the mark of motherhood itself. The right to abortion in patriarchy cannot, in principle, recognize that women may choose abortion because we will not reproduce men and the world of men, because we will not be mothers.

The woman who does not remove the mark from her stomach, who does not have an abortion, may be killed: on the West Bank one such Arab woman a week is found "poisoned or burned to death and the murder is made to look accidental."[30] Women who survive an initial decision to not remove the mark from our stomachs, to not have an abortion, in defiance of the traditions of male virility, may be persecuted as non-virgins and unmarried mothers.[31] Yet, the women who do remove the mark from our stomachs, who abort, may also die. Five thousand women a year are estimated to die in Spain and Portugal alone as a result of complications arising from illegal abortions.[32] In Latin America, abortion causes 20 percent to 50 percent of all maternal deaths.[33] Complications from illegal abortions account for 4 percent to 70 percent of maternal deaths in the hospitals of developing countries.[34] "A woman undergoing a properly performed abortion has six times less risk of death from complications than a woman having a child."[35] In childbirth our bodies as a whole are stamped with the mark of pain, terror, and possible death.

To speak of birth without violence is to ignore the violence of childbirth. The most frequent cause of death of women is childbirth:[36]

> In a number of developing countries . . . maternal mortality rates in excess of 500 per 100,000 live births are by no means exceptions. Rates of over 1000 per 100,000 have been reported in parts of Africa.
>
> In the areas with the highest maternal mortality, i.e., most of Africa, West, South, and East Asia, about half a million women die from maternal causes every year.
>
> Age-specific death rates for women rise sharply at ages 20–30 in many countries, where women often have less chance than men of surviving from 15 to 45 years of age.[37]

Already, as female children, women as a whole are marked—"undesirable." College students in the United States, for instance, favor what amounts to a decrease in female births, with the overall ratio of girls to boys desired being 100:116. Also, "from 66 to 92 percent of men have been found to want an only child to be a boy . . ., and from 62 to 80 percent prefer a first child to be a boy,"[38] a chilling thought as the United States, like Western Europe, moves toward zero growth.

As female foetuses, women as a whole are stamped "to be aborted." A recent Chinese report, for example, shows that when sex determination tests were performed on 100 foetuses with the sole purpose being the determination of the foetus's gender, there were 30 planned abortions. Of those 30 aborted foetuses, 29 were female.[39]

As female infants, women as a whole are marked "dead." Men, rather than regulate men and men's use of women, claim that because there is not enough food, resources, etc., "female fertility" must be controlled by the elimination of women.[40] From the Athens of antiquity to the present, infanticide has been, largely and for the most part, femicide.[41]

Women as mothers are marked: Dead.

Man the marker continues with himself, his sons, his mark.

The Society of Mothers

Man remains with his representation and his mark. Women need not remain. The representation and the mark, and not existing females *per se,* are integral to motherhood. Indeed, if and when the representation and the mark of motherhood can be affixed to something other than the female body, women may not be at all.

The society of mothers, comprised of all women within motherhood, is dangerous to all its members.[42] The society of mothers continues, by definition, the ideology and institution of motherhood as oppressive to women. The motherhood lived out by the society of mothers is also the annihilation of women. When motherhood involves men's reproduction and marking of females as women and mothers, (a) motherhood may entail our physical death and our non-existence as mothers and as female infants, and (b) motherhood always entails the death of a world in which women are free. In the contemporary ideology and institution of motherhood, women's annihilation is also involved in that (a) men's representation and marking of females as women and mothers may continue and, at the same time, (b) men may represent and mark objects (from the domain of the sciences and technology of reproduction) and persons other than females (from among those men held to be "lesser" in power and merit) to reproduce men and the world of men, such that (c) the class, women as mothers, has no further use function, and thus need no longer be reproduced. Both forms of annihilation are dangerous to women. The specifically contemporary manifestation of motherhood, however, shows clearly that women are not necessary to motherhood. Patriarchal men must represent and mark something as MOTHER, but that which is so designated need not be women.

The society of mothers exhibits, in multiple forms, the dangerous situation of woman, the womb and wife of man, and mother, she who produces for men. In modern times, the collectivity of females who are compelled to live within motherhood is composed of those who must reproduce the biological children of patriarchy and those who must reproduce the material goods and ideas of patriarchal culture. Women who reproduce the biological children of patriarchy do so in widely differing manners.[43] All such women, however, are represented and marked by motherhood. In fact, so determinate is men's regulation of women's reproduction of children that the world population growth is projected as coming to a halt in 130 years, at which time, "nearly nine-tenths of this projected 10.5 billion people will be living in developing countries. The poorest regions of the world—Africa and South Asia—will account for more than 60 percent of the world's people . . . the industrialized world's share of the world population will see a drop of today's 24 percent to about 13 percent.[44]

Members of the society of mothers who reproduce the material goods and ideas of patriarchal culture may manifest the ideology and institution of motherhood in differing ways. Despite such differences, the women remain mothers. The limitation of the society of mothers to those who reproduce only the biological children of men is to ignore that men use women's bodies in a multitude of ways to reproduce patriarchal life. Women who do not give birth to biological children are still involved in the "regeneration" of men,[45] in virtue of our work, unpaid and paid, to continue the products, both ideal and material, of motherhood. Even when men can produce biological children by use of the sciences and technology of reproduction, women may be kept in existence as those who perform various services for men, or women may be bred out of existence. Within a patriarchal context, even the production of females by parthenogenesis need not alter the social and historical circumstances of the society of mothers into which they are born.[46] Men may or may not continue to impose patriarchal (male) sexuality on women. Men may or may not relate in explicitly sexual modes to women, and women may still be kept in our service function as the society of mothers.

The representation and mark of motherhood claim not just the surface, but the whole of women, such that the society of mothers not only reproduces, but often defends, the patriarchal world of men: "Confined to their cities the mothers were no longer separate, free, complete individuals and they fused into an anonymous collective consciousness."[47]

In the production of the son for the father, in the production of goods for the father, for the benefit of the son, we are not our bodies, we are not ourselves. A means to men's ends, never an end in ourselves, we are selfless, worldless, annihilated. The experience of our servitude takes seriously our danger and holds, firmly and strongly, to the conviction that together we must get out of motherhood.

Priorities and Alternatives

To show how motherhood, in its many forms, is dangerous to women is also to suggest how women may get out of motherhood. Further questions such as "Why do men impose motherhood on women by means of the representation and the mark?" and "Why do women form a society of mothers?" can lead to idle speculation, unless the questioner's focus centers on how motherhood exists in actuality and how women's actions may form a horizon of possibility in light of which all women may succeed in breaking free of the ideology and institution of motherhood.

Central to a philosophy of evacuation from motherhood is the primacy of women's daily lives and the power of our possible, and sometimes actual, collective action. In breaking free from motherhood, I no longer focus on birth and death as the two most important moments of my life. I give priority, rather, to that which is always already given, my life and my world in their actual presence to me. The moment of birth and the moment of death have, in themselves, no special value. They need not determine who I am or who I may become. I—my activities, body, sexuality—am articulated by my actions and choices which, apart from patriarchy, may be made in the openness of freedom. Similarly, I no longer give a primacy to that which I have reproduced. I claim as primary my life and world as I create and experience them. New modes of thinking and existing emerge as the evacuation from motherhood empowers the female who has been both woman and mother. In that evacuation I, as an individual female, and we, as the community of all females, lay claim, with firmness and strength, to the presence of our own freely chosen subjectivities, to the priorities and alternatives we produce as our own.

Because the evacuation from motherhood does not simply seek to alter motherhood as it exists currently, its focus is not specifically on the development of alternative means of intercourse, pregnancy, or childraising.[48] Women who use artificial insemination and whose children have no known father, as well as women who live as lesbian mothers, clearly challenge, but need not break with, the ideology and institution of motherhood. Each of these alternatives is significant for women's survival within patriarchy, but none is sufficient for women's effective survival, that is, for the creation of a female's self-chosen, nonpatriarchal, existence.

A precondition for women's effective survival may be established, instead, by the female's power to not have children. A decision not to have children may be made, not because a female's biological possibility causes the ideology of motherhood, but because,

1. To not have children opens a time-space for the priority of claiming my life and world as my own and for the creative development of radically new alternatives.

2. The biology from which a child is born does not determine or control the course of that child's life. Females and males, younger and older, create the shapes of our lives through our individual choices.

3. Women who wish to be with younger females or males can do so collectively, with others of similar interests, or individually, through adoption.

4. Currently, there is no question of women's absolute biological extinction.

At present, and for several thousands of years past, women have conceived, borne, and raised multitudes of children without any change in the conditions of our lives as women. In the case that all females were to decide not to have children for the next twenty years, the possibilities for developing new modes of thought and existence would be almost unimaginable.

The necessary condition for women's evacuation from motherhood is, even more significantly, the claiming of our bodies as a source. Our bodies are not resources to be used by men to reproduce men and the world of men while, at the same time, giving death to ourselves. If necessary, women must bear arms, but not children, to protect our bodies from invasion by men.[49] For our effective survival, women's repetitive reproduction of patriarchy must be replaced by the genuine, creative, production of ourselves. In particular, the areas of food, literacy, and energy sources and supplies for women must be reexamined as crucial to the claiming of our bodies as a source.

Women's hunger is one of the specific conditions affecting the possibility for men's continuing success in representing and marking women as mothers. Within the current patriarchal economy, women do not have access to sufficient crops to feed ourselves:

> In many countries where malnutrition is prevalent, up to half the cultivated acreage is growing crops for export to those who can afford them, rather than food stuffs for those who need them. . . . The cash crops are generally cultivated by men while food crops are grown by women. Practically all the agricultural land in developing countries is owned by men. Men always eat first and most of the food: Women and children go hungry and are the vast majority of malnourished everywhere, especially in Asia and Africa.[50]

Nor do women have access to the money necessary to purchase food: in 1979, women living in poverty constituted 12 percent of the total, worldwide, female population and 75 percent of all people living in poverty.[51]

Women's literacy is the second specific condition that enhances the possibility for men's continuing success in maintaining the ideology and institution of women as mothers. Women have insufficient access to the basics of literacy, that is, reading, writing, and simple arithmetic. In fact, from a global perspective, women are two-thirds of the illiterates of the world.[52] In almost all countries, "girls already begin school in fewer numbers than boys; on the average, the difference even at the start of school is 10–20 percent. By the time higher education is reached, the ratio between boys and girls is at least 2:1, but in many cases more."[53] In many African countries, less than 10 percent of the women read and write. The education gap between men and women is growing all over the developing world.[54] Yet, even in industrialized societies, women have no access to determining what constitutes an education, which areas of research are the most pressing, and what comprises the development of more liberating forms of thinking and speaking.

Energy sources and supplies for women are a third area which undermines women's endeavors to break free of motherhood. In African villages, women work about three hours per day more than men because it is the women who must gather the food, water, and fuel necessary for survival.[55] Generally speaking, technological information on alternative means of energy is not made available to such women, any more than it is to most women in industrialized countries. In all societies, women's non-control of energy sources and supplies necessary to our survival keeps us in subordination to men.

Women's non-access to food, education, and energy sources greatly facilitates men's representation and marking of women as mothers and, as such, forms one of the central foundations of the ideology and institution of motherhood. Women's sexual and material oppression by men go hand in hand, as is evidenced by the multiple forms of violence by which men rigidly enforce women's non-access to ourselves. To claim our bodies as a source, to get out of the reproduction of motherhood, females of all ages must work together to establish female-defined alternatives that express and fulfill our current needs and desires for food, education, and energy. The goal of such an endeavor is neither to save the world nor to become "healthy" mothers who reproduce "healthy" children. Female-defined access to food, education, and energy forms a necessary condition for women's collective evacuation from motherhood in that such access claims as a source the whole of our bodies and world. As females who engage in evacuation from motherhood, we shape the whole of ourselves and our world in the present of our own lifetimes.

Notes

1. I am indebted to Julie Murphy for suggesting the phrase "a philosophy of evacuation."
2. Simone de Beauvoir, *The Second Sex,* translated by H. M. Parshley (New York: Vintage Books, 1974), p. 72.
3. De Beauvoir, "Talking to de Beauvoir," *Spare Rib* (March 1977): 2.
4. Shulamith Firestone, *The Dialectic of Sex* (New York: Bantam Books, 1971), p. 72.
5. Ti-Grace Atkinson, *Amazon Odyssey* (New York: Links Books, 1974), p. 1.
6. Monique Wittig and Sande Zeig, *Brouillon pour un dictionnaire des amantes* (Paris: Grasset, 1976), p. 94; and Wittig, "One Is Not Born a Woman," *Feminist Issues* 1, no. 2 (Winter 1981): 1.
7. De Beauvoir, "Talking to de Beauvoir," p. 2.
8. Atkinson, "Interview with Ti-Grace Atkinson," *Off Our Backs* 9, no. 11 (December 1973): 3.
9. Wittig, "Paradigm," in *Homosexualities and French Literature,* edited by George Stambolian and Elaine Marks (Ithaca: Cornell University Press, 1979), pp. 118-19.
10. Andrea Dworkin, *Pornography: Men Possessing Women* (New York: Perigree, 1981), p. 222.
11. *WIN News* 7, no. 4 (1981): 68. Citation from the "Soviet Women's Committee" booklet.
12. A more "sophisticated" appeal to science is misleading for similar reasons. Feminist biologists are currently questioning accounts of egg and sperm production, for instance, in an attempt to dislodge sexist assumptions with respect to their production and union.
13. *WIN News* 6, no. 2 (1980): 76. U.S. Department of Labor, "Facts About Women Heads of Households and Heads of Families."
14. Catherine MacKinnon, *Sexual Harassment of Working Women* (New Haven: Yale University Press, 1979), p. 221.
15. Iona Wieder, "Accouche!" *Questions Féministes* 5 (February 1979): 53-72.
16. *The Oxford English Dictionary*
17. De Beauvoir, *The Second Sex,* p. 72.
18. Martin Heidegger, "The Age of the World Picture," in *The Question of Technology,* translated by William Lovitt (New York: Harper & Row, 1977), pp. 129-30.

19. Ibid., pp. 134-35.

20. Ibid., p. 135.

21. Dworkin, *Pornography,* pp. 108, 109.

22. Jane Harrison, *Prolegomena to the Study of Greek Religion,* 3d. ed. (Cambridge: Cambridge University Press, 1922), pp. 302, 303.

23. De Beauvoir, *The Second Sex,* p. 155.

24. Collette Guillaumin, "Race et Nature: Systeme des marques. Idée de groupe naturel et rapports sociaux," *Pluriel* 11 (1977): 39-55. Giullaumin develops the concept of the mark to analyze racial oppression. She does not apply it to women or to motherhood.

25. See Jeffner Allen, "The Naming of Difference" (unpublished manuscript).

26. Guillaumin, "Race et Nature," pp. 48, 54, 55.

27. Ibid., p. 45.

28. Ibid., p. 49.

29. Ibid., p. 55.

30. *WIN News,* vol. 7, no. 2 (1981): 52. From *Journal Americain* (3 January 1981).

31. *International Tribunal on Crimes Against Women,* edited by Diana Russel and Nicole Van de Ven (California: Les Femmes, 1976), pp. 31-33.

32. *WIN News,* vol. 7, no. 3 (1981): 22. From AGENOR, "Abortion: The Facts/European Survey."

33. *WIN News,* vol. 7, no. 4 (1981): 17. From World Health Organization, "Towards a Better Future: Maternal and Child Health."

34. *WIN News,* vol. 6, no. 4 (1980): 37. From "Population Reports" (Series F/Number 7/July 1980).

35. *WIN News,* vol. 7, no. 3 (1981): 22.

36. *WIN News,* vol. 7, no. 4 (1981): 24. From The Population Institute, *International Dateline.*

37. *WIN News,* vol. 7, no. 3 (1981): 16. From World Health Organization, "Sixth Report on the World Health Situation."

38. Jalna Hanmer, "Sex Predetermination, Artificial Insemination and the Maintenance of Male-Dominated Culture," in *Women, Health and Reproduction,* edited by Helen Roberts (London: Routledge & Kegan Paul, 1981), pp. 167, 168.

39. Ibid., p. 176.

40. Jalna Hanmer and Pat Allen, "La Science de la reproduction—solution finale?" *Questions Féministes* 5 (February 1979): 39.

41. Elizabeth Fisher, *Women's Creation* (New York: Doubleday, 1980), p. 335.

42. Monique Wittig and Sande Zeig, *Lesbian Peoples: Material for a Dictionary* (New York: Avon, 1979), p. 83.

43. *WIN News,* vol. 7, no. 3 (1981): 21. From U.S. Agency for International Development, "Illustrative Statistics on Women in Selected Developing Countries." See also, The Environmental Fund, "World Population Estimates: 1981."

44. *WIN News,* vol. 7, no. 4 (1981): 23. From The Population Institute, *International Dateline.*

45. Ulrike Prokop, "Production and the Context of Women's Daily Life," *New German Critique* 13 (Winter 1978): 26.

46. Hanmer and Allen, "La Science de la reproduction," p. 39.

47. Wittig and Zeig, *Lesbian Peoples,* p. 76.

48. *WIN News,* vol. 7, no. 4 (1981): 19. *The American Journal of Obstetrics and Gynecology* (July 1981) shows that the mortality rate in the United States for babies aided by midwife-assistance deliveries is 9 percent per 1000 births, in comparison with 16.9 percent per 1000 births among physician-aided deliveries. Such alternative means have positive implications for women as mothers.

49. Julie Murphy, personal communication, December 1981.

50. *WIN News,* vol. 7, no. 4 (1981): 23, 24.

51. *WIN News,* vol. 7, no. 4 (1981): 73. From the National Commission on Working Mothers, "Women at Work: News about the 80 percent."

52. Fran Hosken, "Editorial," *WIN News,* vol. 7, no. 2 (1981): 1.

53. *WIN News,* vol. 7, no. 1 (1981): 21. From World Bank Headquarters, "Education: A World Bank Sector Policy Paper."

54. Fran Hosken, "Editorial," *WIN News,* vol. 6, no. 3 (1980): 1.

55. *WIN News,* vol. 7, no. 4 (1981): 6. From U.N. Conference on New and Renewable Sources of Energy, "Conference Report."

About the Contributors

AZIZAH AL-HIBRI: I was born and educated in Beirut, Lebanon. I came to the United States in 1966 to pursue my education and since then have earned a Ph.D. in philosophy from the University of Pennsylvania and taught at Texas A&M University and Washington University in St. Louis. In the fall of 1982 I returned to the University of Pennsylvania to study law. My original research interests were in the areas of logic, ethics, and political theory. Since then I have expanded my interests to include philosophy of technology, feminism, Third World philosophies, and Islamic religion and tradition. I have published several works, including a book in logic and a coedited anthology entitled *Technology and Human Affairs*. I also guest-edited the journal issue "Women and Islam" for *Women's Studies International Forum*. My most recent article is entitled "Reproductive Technology and the Future of Women." I am an active member of the Society for Women in Philosophy and the National Women's Studies Association, as well as editor of *Hypatia: A Journal of Feminist Philosophy*.

JEFFNER ALLEN: I am a feminist philosopher at the Center for Research on Women, Stanford University. Recently, I have completed a book of essays in feminist philosophy. I have also published extensively in phenomenology, including papers on Husserl, Heidegger, Merleau-Ponty, and phenomenological psychology.

PAULINE B. BART: I am Professor of Sociology in the Department of Psychiatry at the University of Illinois Medical Center, Chicago, and the Department of Sociology, Chicago Circle Campus, University of Illinois. I am a casualty of the fifties, when I left the University of California, Los Angeles, after my master's degree to live in a tract house in Culver City, California, and spent the decade being a permissive mother and a sloppy housekeeper. For me the American dream was the American nightmare. In 1961 I returned to

UCLA and wrote my dissertation on depression in middle-aged women (better known as "Portnoy's Mother's Complaint"). After receiving my doctorate, I held three jobs in four years because of discrimination. As someone said at the elite institution where I was a lecturer, "It was a question of image. We couldn't have our first woman be a Jewish mother." I taught the first course on women there in the spring of 1969 and have been teaching such courses ever since. I have been writing on the intersection between gender roles and health, both physical and mental. I am currently finishing a book with Pat O'Brien, comparing women who were attacked and raped with those who were attacked and avoided or stopped their rapes, in which we disprove the myths about how a woman should behave when attacked. The book will be published under the title *Stopping Rape: Women Who Did*. I belong to the Earth Mother wing of the feminist movement and am very proud that after nursing my granddaughter twice my milk came back in.

DIANE EHRENSAFT: I am a developmental and clinical psychologist, recently very active in a movement to bridge psychoanalysis and social action. I received my Ph.D. from the University of Michigan in 1974. As so much of our work is autobiographical, my experience as a feminist, as a psychologist, and as a mother has brought me to my present interest in shared parenting between women and men. I am a faculty member of the Wright Institute in Berkeley and also work as a psychotherapist in the Bay Area. I am currently doing research on a book about shared parenting and child development, investigating social, psychological, and political ramifications of the phenomenon.

ANN FERGUSON: I am a lesbian socialist-feminist mother of a twelve-year-old interracial daughter, Kathy, and I live in a cooperative household with two women housemates and their (and my) daughter Sarah (age nine). I also have two grown stepsons and a foster son. I teach philosophy and women's studies at the University of Massachusetts at Amherst, where I have been teaching for 18 years. I am working on a book on motherhood and sexuality, doing sporadic political work around left and feminist issues, playing music at demonstrations, maintaining my house and garden, and feeding many cats and a dog.

MARTHA E. GIMENEZ: I am Associate Professor of Sociology at the University of Colorado, Boulder, where I teach courses in theory, population studies, family, and social stratification at the undergraduate and graduate levels. I have published several articles on feminist theory and on population theory. I studied law and sociology at the Universidad Nacional de Cordoba, Argentina, and received my M.A. (1969) and Ph.D. (1973) from the University of California, Los Angeles.

VIRGINIA HELD: My daughter was born in 1957 while I was working for *The Reporter* magazine. Strengthened by the feelings of impending motherhood, I dared to write my first major article. My son was born in 1962, after I had decided to give up journalism and go back to graduate school in philosophy. The years when my children were small were years of great strain, when I had no money, no sleep, and no encouragement for my professional hopes. I received a Ph.D. from Columbia in 1968. With the women's movement and my steady progress in teaching and writing, the 1970s were for me a time of growing personal satisfaction. My most recent books are *Property, Profits, and Economic Justice* (1980) and *Women's Realities, Women's Choices* (forthcoming, 1983), written with seven colleagues. I am a professor of philosophy at Hunter College/CUNY. My daughter is a biologist, my son a windsurfing instructor; both are joys and wonders.

EVA FEDER KITTAY: I am an assistant professor of philosophy at SUNY, Stony Brook. I received my B.A. from Sarah Lawrence College and my Ph.D. in philosophy from the Graduate School of the City University of New York. I have published articles in the areas of philosophy of language and metaphor, and on feminist and ethical issues. I am currently engaged in writing a book on metaphor and am venturing into the social and ethical issues regarding mental retardation. I am also the mother of two exceptional children, a highly gifted seven-year-old boy and a profoundly retarded twelve-year-old girl. My children, with their special gifts and handicaps, have significantly shaped the direction of all but my most abstract philosophical inquiries, as my experience with them has contributed to the essay in this volume.

ELÉANOR H. KUYKENDALL: I was born and brought up in Ohio and northern Ontario, earned a Ph.D. in philosophy from Columbia University, and became Associate Professor of Philosophy at SUNY, New Paltz, to which I have returned after a five-year absence. I spent the time away in Cambridge, Massachusetts, studying linguistics; in Paris, France, directing an undergraduate exchange program with the Sorbonne; and again in Cambridge, in a women's collective. My published work explores the connections between linguistics, feminism, and French semiology. I am close to my sister, Nancy Brown, who delivered her second child during the writing of this paper and helped me to connect the practice of mothering with some of the theory.

BARBARA LOVE: While my primary identity is as a gay activist and feminist, I earn my living as a magazine editor. I also have an interest in psychology (master's degree), and was a cofounder of Identity House in New York, a counseling center for gay people and their families, now ten years old. I am coauthor with Sidney Abbott of *Sappho Was a Right-On Woman: A Liberated View of Lesbianism* (1973). I have also been on the National Gay

Task Force board of directors for nine years. Through Elizabeth Shanklin's work, I began to see a new worldview in matriarchy, which brought order to all the liberation movements and their objectives. It is very important that ideas on matriarchy be published in an effort to bring about a more nurturant society.

SUSAN RAE PETERSON: I am a philosopher doing adjunct teaching at Adelphi University and New York Institute of Technology–Old Westbury, both on Long Island. Originally from Milwaukee, I studied at the University of Wisconsin–Madison and received my B.A. in Humanities from the New School in New York City. I have a master's degree in philosophy from San Francisco State University (1971), and am currently finishing my doctoral dissertation on professional rights at the City University of New York Graduate Center. My field is ethics, and during graduate studies at the University of Toronto, I also studied criminology and cofounded the Toronto Rape Crisis Centre (in 1974). I was Director of the Nassau County (L. I.) Rape Crisis Center (1978–79) and provided counseling services for crime victims. For two years I served as Executive Secretary of the Eastern Division of the Society for Women in Philosophy (SWIP). I enjoy dancing of all kinds and have season tickets to the New York City Ballet. I run, swim, and lift weights regularly, have season tickets to the New York Islanders and Knicks, and avidly follow the Yankees and Jets. I am currently teaching "Philosophy of Sports" and have found a new interest in the feminist analysis of athletics.

M. RIVKA POLATNICK: I grew up in New York and became an enthusiastic participant in the Women's Liberation Movement there in the fall of 1968. Since 1970 I've lived in Berkeley, California, where I've continued my involvement in women's liberation and other left causes. Recently I've begun facilitating workshops and speakouts on "What Next for Women's Liberation?" I'm completing my dissertation in sociology at the University of California, Berkeley, on the political theory and strategy of the late sixties radical feminists, and will shortly join the faculty of Friends World College in Huntington, New York. My given name honors my great-grandmother Rivka, a Czechoslovakian Jew who was known as a wisewoman and lived until the Nazis came. I remain optimistic about the struggle for a just, humane social order, here and everywhere.

SARA RUDDICK: I teach at the Seminar College, a small program within the New School for Social Research. This intensely intellectual but caring program has allowed me to combine "independent intellect" with a "maternally caring" style of teaching. With Pamela Daniels, I edited *Working It Out,* a collection of essays in which women artists and intellectuals reflect personally and openly upon the meaning of "chosen" work in their lives. I am now writing a book on mothering, feminism, and peace, describing the values and perspectives elicited by the work of mothering. I wish to honor maternal thinking, and mothers as a class, while at the same time insisting that the thinking be transformed by a feminist consciousness. Also, along with Carol Ascher and Louise DeSalvo I am editing *Between Women: Women Write about Their Relation to the Women They Study,* to be published in 1984. In this collection of personal essays, women who have written on other women reflect upon their relation to these "foremothers," on the needs they bring and the strengths they acquire from their research. Now that my children are grown (18, 16) I realize that motherhood never ends. I am increasingly interested in the parenting of adolescents and the chance for moral reflection this later phase of mothering allows. I have much more free time, and have become a mother-watcher and mother-listener, both in my reading and in wandering around as many supermarkets, playgrounds, and living rooms as I can find. I would love to hear from other mothers and from people who do "maternal work" or are mother-watchers themselves.

ELIZABETH SHANKLIN: Having experienced burn-out, I am now happily married to a community organizer and await the inspiration to know what to do next to further matriarchy.

JANET FARRELL SMITH: After growing up in a large family in a small New England town, I was educated at Wellesley College and Columbia University in New York, where I received a doctorate in philosophy. I am especially committed to the education of women of all racial and class backgrounds, and have been involved in multidisciplinary feminist scholarship at Smith College and the University of Massachusetts at Boston, where I now teach philosophy. My own mother has been a strong influence through the vigorous and friendly late-night discussions we have had for many a year since my childhood. I am now working on a theory of reproductive rights.

JOYCE TREBILCOT: I grew up in California with my nose in a book (according to my mother) and a deep need to control my own life. After college at Berkeley in the fifties, I escaped to Mexico and later to Europe; six years later I could no longer support myself abroad and returned to the United States, where I enrolled as a graduate student in philosophy at the University of California at Santa Barbara. I wrote a dissertation on the concept of emotion, and worked as a teacher, first at Santa Barbara, then at Bryn Mawr, and briefly at the University of Wisconsin–Milwaukee, after which I joined the tenure track at Washington University in St. Louis. During those years, feminism became increasingly central in my life and work. Today, I earn my living at Washington University as coordinator of women's studies and associate professor of philosophy. I am given hope by the fact that so many women have committed their lives to one another and to the cause of our freedom.

LUCIA VALESKA: Lucia Valeska was a feminist activist in Albuquerque, New Mexico, from 1967 to 1979, and was one of the founders of women's studies at the University of New Mexico. She was selected by *Ms.* magazine as one of its "Women to Watch in the 80's" and has been executive director of the National Gay Task Force.

CAROLINE WHITBECK: I did my doctoral work in the philosophy of physics at M.I.T., during which time I became actively involved in peace work. My first full-time teaching job was in the philosophy department at Yale in 1968, the year before Yale began coeducation. That experience made me a feminist activist; I became deeply involved in the women's movement. I survived in that situation for three years and then did two years of research in the psychiatry department at Yale. During this time I bore my daughter, Evelyn, who is a great joy in my life. Since then I have taught at SUNY/Albany, had a post-doc at the Hastings Center, and am now associate professor at the Institute for the Medical Humanities at the University of Texas Medical Branch, Galveston. Being a feminist and being a Friend (Quaker) are the key (highly compatible) sources of my understanding of my life. I am happy.

IRIS MARION YOUNG: I am a socialist-feminist activist living in Northampton, Massachusetts. There I have engaged in various feminist activities, including writing and editing for a local feminist newspaper, the *Valley Women's Voice.* I teach philosophy at Worcester Polytechnic Institute. My writings on socialist-feminist theory and practice have appeared in *Women: A Journal of Liberation, Socialist Review,* and *The Guardian.* My writings on theory of justice have appeared in several philosophy publications.